Outsourcing Rulemaking Powers

OXFORD COMPARATIVE CONSTITUTIONALISM

Series Editors

Richard Albert, William Stamps Farish Professor of Law,
The University of Texas at Austin School of Law

Robert Schütze, Professor of European and Global Law,
Durham University and College of Europe

Comparative constitutional law has a long and distinguished history in intellectual thought and in the construction of public law. As political actors and the people who create or modify their constitutional orders, they often wish to learn from the experience and learning of others. This cross-fertilization and mutual interaction has only accelerated with the onset of globalization, which has transformed the world into an interconnected web that facilitates dialogue and linkages across international and regional structures. Oxford Comparative Constitutionalism seeks to publish scholarship of the highest quality in constitutional law that deepens our knowledge of local, national, regional, and global phenomena through the lens of comparative public law.

Outsourcing Rulemaking Powers

Constitutional Limits and National Safeguards

CEDRIC JENART

Magistrate Belgian Council of State (Auditeur)
Visiting Professor University of Antwerp

OXFORD
UNIVERSITY PRESS

OXFORD
UNIVERSITY PRESS

Great Clarendon Street, Oxford, OX2 6DP,
United Kingdom

Oxford University Press is a department of the University of Oxford.
It furthers the University's objective of excellence in research, scholarship,
and education by publishing worldwide. Oxford is a registered trade mark of
Oxford University Press in the UK and in certain other countries

First Edition published in 2022

Impression: 1

Published in the United States of America by Oxford University Press
198 Madison Avenue, New York, NY 10016, United States of America

British Library Cataloguing in Publication Data

Data available

Library of Congress Control Number: 2021946681

ISBN 978–0–19–289783–1

DOI: 10.1093/oso/9780192897831.001.0001

Printed and bound by
CPI Group (UK) Ltd, Croydon, CR0 4YY

Foreword

This book and the PhD thesis on which it has been based, earning Cedric Jenart the title of Doctor of Laws, will undoubtedly attract the attention of all those interested in one of the major developments in the methods of legislation in our time.

Traditionally, rulemaking power has been exercised by the legislature, which may delegate it to a certain extent and under certain conditions, often specified in the constitution, to the executive. However, in our increasingly complex society, the legislator is often faced with the task of regulating highly technical and often also highly specific issues, which require an understanding, knowledge and expertise often lacking among traditional rulemakers. Hence the tendency to outsource rulemaking power to independent public agencies and even to private actors, who can be deemed to have the required insights but who are not politically accountable to the people or to the people's representatives. Although the phenomenon is spreading, its constitutional embedding often leaves much to be desired.

It is to Cedric Jenart's great credit that he has clearly mapped out the various techniques of outsourcing—delegation, referral and reception—and that he has then succeeded, on the basis of an in-depth analysis of the case law of mainly the European Court of Human Rights and the Court of Justice of the European Union and of the legislation, case law and jurisprudence of five national legal systems (Belgium, France, Germany, the United Kingdom and the United States), to distil a number of common constitutional principles, both on the limits to the possibility of outsourcing rulemaking powers and on the minimum standards with which these actors have to comply in exercising these powers.

Cedric Jenart has, I believe, succeeded admirably in outlining a constitutional framework that makes the outsourcing technique reconcilable with the principles of democracy and the rule of law. His book will therefore be a beacon for constitutional and legislative drafters, policymakers, legal practitioners and of course academia on the status and development of outsourced legislation in western democracies.

With his research, Cedric Jenart has fully lived up to the high expectations we in the Faculty of Law at the University of Antwerp, had placed on him. Cedric Jenart has been an excellent student. He achieved highest distinction in both his Bachelor's and his Master's studies. From the very outset, he showed an interest in academic work. Cedric not only studied in Antwerp; he has also ventured beyond the walls of our law faculty, at seven very prestigious law faculties abroad. After having attended summer courses at Cambridge University, the Sorbonne, the University of Leiden in cooperation with Columbia Law School and the University of Heidelberg, he spent a semester at the Free University of Berlin within the framework of the Erasmus student exchange programme. Last but not least, he was given the opportunity, as a Fulbright Boas and BAEF Scholar, to study at Harvard Law School, where he graduated in 2014 with an additional LL.M., Master of Laws. We were very happy that Cedric returned to Antwerp afterwards. He became a research and teaching assistant in Constitutional law in 2014 and has been a Fellow of the Research Foundation Flanders (FWO) from 2015 to 2019. In that capacity, he wrote his PhD which took him as a visiting researcher to the University of Oxford, to the Max Planck Institute in Heidelberg and to the Université de Lille.

However Cedric Jenart is not only an excellent academic, he has always been very eager to practice law as well. As part of his Master's thesis, he held an internship at the Belgian Constitutional Court. Every year, during the summer vacation he interned at a renowned law firm in Brussels. He also passed the New York State Bar Exam. In 2019—after placing first in the entrance exam—he has been appointed a magistrate (auditor) in the Belgian Council of State, Legislative Section, where his outstanding constitutional skills, especially in the legislative process, can fully bear fruit.

It is therefore as a proud promoter of Cedric Jenart's original PhD thesis, that I recommend this excellent piece of scientific scholarship to the reader and that I wish him all the best in his future career.

Jan Velaers
Full Professor Constitutional Law,
University of Antwerp
Assessor in the Belgian Council of State
Member of the Venice Commission
(European Commission for Democracy through Law)

Advance Praise

On this major issue of contemporary law that is constituted by the more and more frequent outsourcing of rulemaking powers, Cedric Jenart delivers a veritable treatise. His book is particularly remarkable in its systematic reflection on the beneficiaries of outsourcing—executive, autonomous bodies of a public, private or hybrid nature—as well as on its mechanisms—delegation, referral, reception-, equally on the principles that should govern outsourcing practices -transparency, hierarchy of rules, judicial review, effectivity, representativeness-. Another very stimulating aspect of the book is the analysis of the limits that certain international fundamental rights protection norms place on outsourcing. Let us add that, to his erudition, the author adds something which does not spoil anything on the contrary: the rigorous demonstration of a judge.

Jean-Bernard Auby,
Emeritus Public Law Professor of Sciences Po Paris, France

Complex and fragmented societies are faced with an overwhelming demand for the regulation of economic, social, environmental, and other problems. Rules, however, are set not only by parliament(s), but by a wide range of public and private standard setters. In his excellent piece of scholarship, Cedric Jenart covers the constitutional ground for this decentralised system of rulemaking across a number of jurisdictions. The book is a most welcome in-depth contribution to a Pan-European discussion about the function and the responsibilities of Parliaments in relation to other governance-capacities within modern societies.

Florian Becker,
Public Law Professor,
Christian-Albrechts University, Germany

Outsourcing rulemaking power is common in many polities. It raises complex issues of constitutional principle and legal doctrine. Cedric Jenart's book is a valuable addition to the literature in this area. It examines in depth and from a comparative perspective the twin features that shape this area: the constitutional limits to outsourcing by the legislature and/or the executive; and the standards that must be complied with by actors outside the traditional governmental structure if outsourcing is allowed.

Paul Craig,
Emeritus Professor of English Law,
St John's College, Oxford, UK

Building on the rulemaking practices of the executive, Cedric Jenart argues for incorporating the regulatory activities of independent public agencies and private or semi-private institutions into modern public law. With a wealth of legal material and case studies, plus a fascinating look at the World Anti-Doping Agency, Jenart argues that such delegation can be justified in a democracy but should take different forms depending their expected value: insulation from politics, the need for expertise, or stakeholder involvement.

Susan Rose-Ackerman,
Henry R. Luce Professor Emeritus of Law and Political Science and
Professorial Lecturer in Law, Yale University, USA

Governments around the world increasingly delegate or "outsource" the power to make rules imposing obligations upon citizens, to public-private partnerships, purely private organizations, and NGOs, or absorb those organization's rules into public law. In this valuable contribution to comparative constitutional and comparative administrative law, Cedric Jenart gives us a comprehensive study of the limits principles of democracy and legality—as embodied in international and domestic law—place on outsourcing, delegation, and absorption reveals a surprisingly wide range of legal limits on an equally surprisingly range of practices. The concluding study of anti-doping regulations in sport provides an illuminating concrete example of why the question is important.

Mark Tushnet,
William Nelson Cromwell Professor of Law emeritus,
Harvard Law School, USA

Preface

Aims

Imagine a rule that confers powers on an independent regulator to decide on technicalities related to electricity and gas. Imagine a rule that incorporates articles of a code against doping in sports developed by a privately notarized Swiss organization (World Anti-Doping Agency). Imagine, finally, a rule that was made by private persons that would bind third parties even without legislative ratification. Would these outsourced rules not undermine our image of a Legislature's or Executive's primary responsibilities? In reality, we do not have to imagine these rules, as they already exist to various degrees in the national law of numerous states.

The overarching issue investigated in this book is: how may rulemaking powers be outsourced? This overarching question can be separated into two more precise research hypotheses. This first research hypothesis concerns the limits to a Legislature or Executive outsourcing rulemaking power. Constitutional provisions or—mainly—constitutional principles may allow for some powers to be transferred to other actors or institutions, while obliging the Legislature and/or the Executive to exercise other powers themselves. The second research hypothesis concerns the standards and guarantees that rules made by actors outside the three traditional branches must heed in order to comply with the principles of good rulemaking in a similar manner to traditional rulemakers. Here, the book aims to lay bare the principles of good rulemaking, normally protected by the Legislature or the Executive.

Readership

This book will be of interest to civil servants, public and private lawyers, judges, and legal scholars and their students, who will be able to arm their national law against the challenges of a modernized, technological, and globalized world by upholding these principles, possibly by moulding them in the form of constitutional, statutory, or even executive framework provisions.

The overarching focus of this monograph should interest the readership of a number of diverse edited volumes, such as: Sabino Cassese (ed.) (2006), *Research Handbook on Global Administrative Law*, Edward Elgar; Nicholas Bamforth and Peter Leyland (eds) (2013), *Accountability in the Contemporary Constitution*, Oxford University Press; Susan Rose-Ackerman, Stefanie Egidy, and James Fowkes (eds) (2014), *Due Process of Lawmaking*, Cambridge University Press; and Petra

Dobner and Martin Loughlin (eds) (2010), *The Twilight of Constitutionalism*, Oxford University Press.

Although the methodology remains a pure exercise of comparative constitutionalism, the monograph offers a bridge between traditional constitutional law, on the one hand, and a global community of comparative constitutionalism, global administrative law, and transnational private law, on the other, due to its original topic. At the same time, it also offers a link between legal practitioners and the scholars who identify with these legal schools and theories.

Dealing with the transfer of arguably the most significant power—rulemaking power—this book therefore targets a readership that spans traditional constitutional law scholars, administrative law scholars, and more transversal and comparative constitutional scholars (including their students). Moreover, the book will be of interest to legal practitioners who may outsource and/or receive outsourced rulemaking powers. Finally, the book is a roadmap for every lawyer seeking an overarching perspective on outsourcing rulemaking powers in comparative public law.

Coverage and place in the literature

As mentioned, by providing a framework on the outsourcing of rulemaking powers, this book offers a unique bridge between traditional comparative constitutional law, on the one hand, and transnational private regulation and global administrative law, on the other. This no man's land has attracted the attention of competitive scholarship, which underlines the strong and increasing relevance of a standard work on outsourcing rulemaking powers. However, the approach and the scope of these works have always essentially differed from this book.

First, this book is strongly grounded in doctrinal, comparative legal research. This contrasts, for example, with philosophical (legal), economic policy or political science monographs such as Pauline Westerman (2018), *Outsourcing the Law*, Edward Elgar; Paul Tucker (2018), *Unelected Power*, Princeton University Press; and Dietmar Braun and Fabrizio Gilardi (2006), *Delegation in Contemporary Democracies*, Routledge, respectively.

Second, the comparative research in this book is specifically focused on comparative 'domestic' constitutional law, as opposed to, for example, EU institutional law, EU economic law, or domestic private law, found in Marta Simoncini (2018), *Administrative Regulation Beyond the Non-Delegation Doctrine*, Hart; Mislav Mataija (2016), *Private Regulation and the Internal Market: Sports, Legal Services, and Standard Setting in EU Economic Law*, Oxford University Press; and Paul Verbruggen (2014), *Enforcing Transnational Private Regulation*, Edward Elgar, respectively.

Third, even when the constitutional approach to the transfer of rulemaking power has been investigated, it has focused on the three traditional branches and has not included private, hybrid, and autonomous public bodies as a whole, which are engaged through three outsourcing techniques (delegation, referral, and reception).

To date, legal scholarship has focused on:

- the three traditional branches, for example Bogdan Iancu (2012), *Legislative Delegation: The Erosion of Normative Limits in Modern Constitutionalism*, Springer; or Christoph Möllers (2013), *The Three Branches*, Oxford University Press;
- autonomous public bodies, for example Stéphanie De Somer (2017), *Autonomous Public Bodies and the Law*, Edward Elgar;
- private parties, for example Catherine Donnelly (2007), *Delegation of Governmental Power to Private Parties*, Oxford University Press;
- one outsourcing technique, such as referral, for example US scholarship by Emily Bremer;
- international or transnational bodies, for example Harm Schepel (2005), *The Constitution of Private Governance: Product Standards in the Regulation of Integrating Markets*, Hart; or Colin Scott, Fabrizio Cafaggi, and Linda Senden (eds) (2011), *The Challenge of Transnational Private Regulation. The Conceptual and Constitutional Debates*, Wiley.

Special features

The front cover of the book symbolizes its title and content: 'Outsourcing' (streams of water) 'Rulemaking' (a dam as linear and manmade construction) 'Power' (generating electricity as type of power).

Being proficient in five languages, I was able to acknowledge monographs written on the transfer of rulemaking powers (in a broad sense) in Dutch (e.g. Popelier, Neerhof), French (Tusseau, Perroud), Portuguese (Cardona), and German (e.g. Marburger, Karpen, Hartlieb, Becker).

Ultimately, I have a particular affinity with both the academic and the professional worlds through my academic experience as a doctoral researcher and lecturer and my professional experience as a magistrate in Belgium's highest administrative court. The latter not only aided in the selection of cases, but also gave me first-hand knowledge of the precise problems administrations and lawyers face in their daily practice.

Cedric Jenart

Antwerp, Belgium
11 June 2021

Acknowledgements

January 2014: Temperatures hit –10°C in snowy Cambridge, Massachusetts. From my residence at Hastings Hall, at the heart of Harvard Law School, I receive a call: 'Why not write a PhD?' With the liberty to choose a topic from the countless legal issues out there, my thoughts go to this increasing phenomenon of 'outsourcing rulemaking powers'.

Thus, an idea turned into a research project, which turned into a PhD, which eventually turned into this monograph.

The time has come to thank the institutions and people without whom this monograph would not have come into being.

At the institutional level, I thank the University of Antwerp and Research Foundation Flanders (FWO) for giving me a chance as a teaching assistant and research fellow and, Linguapolis, for its assistance. I also express gratitude to Oxford University, the Max Planck Institute for Comparative Public and International Law in Heidelberg, and the Université de Lille 2 Droit et Santé for receiving me as a visiting researcher. Moreover, I am grateful to the Belgian Council of State for its support, since I was nominated as a magistrate in March 2019 which is when I started to fundamentally develop and rework the PhD into a monograph. Ultimately, I wish to thank Oxford University Press for publishing the research that has become so dear to me.

On a personal level, I would like to thank Professor Jan Velaers for not only being there at the beginning of my research trajectory, as my PhD supervisor, but also every step of the way, with perceptive commentary, sharp evaluations, and helpful advice. My gratitude also goes to the members of my individual doctoral committee. Professor Patricia Popelier is not only an excellent scholar but she always manages to ask the right questions. Professor Ingrid Opdebeek has developed a sixth sense for structuring legal texts, usually accompanied by a generous smile. I would equally like to show appreciation to the other members of my PhD jury. Throughout my years of research, I often relied on the scholarship of Professor Florian Becker, Professor Paul Craig, and Professor Guillaume Tusseau—three absolute authorities on outsourcing rulemaking powers in respectively Germany, the UK, and France. In the same vein, I acknowledge the dean of the faculty, Professor Frederik Swennen, for his continuous encouragement. Subsequently, many thanks go to Professors Robert Schütze and Richard Albert, Oxford Comparative Constitutionalism Series Editors, for believing in me. Finally, I wish to acknowledge the three anonymous reviewers for their helpful comments and suggestions and the OUP commissioning editors (Jamie, Brianne, Alex, and Charlotte) for their clear communication and helpfulness.

To my family, particularly my brother, and parents. Thank you for challenging me, for your support, and for all the love, dedication, and affection. Everything we achieve is because of each other. To my friends for their patience and inspiration.

To my wife, Ana. We continue to motivate each other to realize our dreams. If ever there were a testament to love, this is it. To my infant son, Gabriel, who taught me what it really means to 'outsource' any type of control. Thank you, from the bottom of my heart, for everything.

Summary Contents

Detailed Contents

List of Abbreviations

AAI	autorité administrative indépendante
AFLD	Agence Française de la Lutte contre le Dopage
AG	Advocate General/Attorney General
AJDA	American Journal of Drug and Alcohol Abuse
AöR	Archiv des Öffentlichen Rechts
APB	autonomous public body
API	autorité publique indépendante
APT	Administration publique—Trimestriel
CAS	Court of Arbitration for Sport
CLA	collective labour agreement
CRISP	Centre de recherche et d'information socio-politiques
DVBl	Deutsches Verwaltungsblatt
ECHR	European Convention on Human Rights
ECJ	European Court of Justice
ECtHR	European Court of Human Rights
EHRLR	European Human Rights Law Review
FCC	German Federal Constitutional Court (Bundesverfassungsgericht)
HFR	Humboldt Forum Recht
HRC	Human Rights Committee
IACHR	Inter-American Convention on Human Rights
IACtHR	Inter-American Court of Human Rights
ICANN	Internet Corporation for Assigned Names and Numbers
ICCPR	International Covenant on Civil and Political Rights
ICLQ	International and Comparative Law Quarterly
ICON	International Journal of Constitutional Law
IOC	International Olympic Committee
ISO	International Standardization Organization
JLEO	Journal of Law, Economics, & Organization
JT	Journal des Tribunaux
JZ	Juristenzeitung
LIEI	Legal Issues of Economic Integration
MJ	Maastricht Journal of European and Comparative Law
NADA	Die Stiftung Nationale Anti-Doping Agentur Deutschland
NADO	national anti-doping organization
NGO	non-governmental organization
NJB	Nederlands Juristenblad
NJW	Neue Juristische Wochenschrift
NQHR	Netherlands Quarterly of Human Rights
OJLS	Oxford Journal of Legal Studies

RCJB	Revue critique de jurisprudence belge
RDP	Revue du droit public et de la science politique en France et à l'étranger
RDSS	Revue de droit sanitaire et social
RFDA	Revenue française de droit administratif
RIA	regulatory impact assessment
RW	Rechtskundig Weekblad
SGB	sports governing bodies
TBP	Tijdschrift voor Bestuurswetenschappen en Publiekrecht
TEU	Treaty on European Union
TFEU	Treaty on the Functioning of the European Union
TORB	Tijdschrift Onderwijsrecht en Onderwijsbeleid
UKAD	UK Anti-Doping
USADA	United States Anti-Doping Agency
VVDStRL	Veröffentlichungen der Vereinigung der Deutschen Staatsrechtslehrer
WADA	World Anti-Doping Agency
ZaöR/ZaöRV	Zeitschrift für ausländisches öffentliches Recht und Völkerrecht
ZöR	Zeitschrift für öffentliches Recht

1
Introduction

1.1 Problem formulation

Parliaments have always been regarded as playing a pivotal role in the creation of rules within democratic states.[1] According to Jean-Jacques Rousseau's unwavering axiom, Parliament represents the will of the people.[2] Assuming that members of a parliament are elected and records of their debates are readily accessible, the Parliament is taken to represent the opinions and interests of the society which it serves through the legislative process.

However, what if Parliament is dead?[3] In an increasingly globalized world, nation-states are confronted with issues that require international cooperation, expert knowledge, and flexibility to resolve. The shockwaves sent by the Covid-19 pandemic have made this increasingly clear. Rather than taking the lead, Parliaments are now settling for a managerial position;[4] they are outsourcing their rulemaking powers (and other constitutional responsibilities) rather than exercising those powers themselves. Much has already been written on the delegation of such powers to governments and their ministers, which is one type of

[1] This monograph is a thoroughly revised, concretized, and updated version of the successfully defended PhD thesis by the same author: 'Constitutional principles on outsourcing rulemaking powers to non-politically accountable actors in European states', University of Antwerp (June 2019) 602 with jury members: Paul Craig, Patricia Popelier, Guillaume Tusseau, Florian Becker, Ingrid Opdebeek, Frederik Swennen (Dean), Jan Velaers (Supervisor). For wider information and references, the reader is referred to this thesis. All opinions expressed in this book are personal to the author and do not bind his institutions.

[2] Jean Jacques Rousseau, *Du contrat social* (Mourer et Pinparé 1797) 84. However, in some states it represents the will of the nation.

[3] Inspired by 'God is dead', Friedrich Nietzsche, *Thus Spoke Zarathustra* (Algora Publishing 2003) 67.

[4] Willem Witteveen, 'Het politieke primaat als regie van de wetgever' in Willem Witteveen, H. R. B. M. Kummeling, and F. A. M. Stroink, *Het primaat van de politiek. Staatsrechtsconferentie 1999* (Tjeenk Willink 2000) 1–23.

Outsourcing Rulemaking Powers. Cedric Jenart, Oxford University Press. © Cedric Jenart 2022.
DOI: 10.1093/oso/9780192897831.003.0001

outsourcing that has become established practice. By contrast, much less attention has been given to outsourcing rulemaking powers to autonomous public, hybrid, or private actors that, unlike governments and their ministers, are neither elected by the people nor directly controlled by Parliament.

For the purpose of this research, I therefore focus on the exercise of rulemaking powers by autonomous public, hybrid, or private actors. Outsourcing rulemaking powers to such actors was not unknown in previous centuries; however, such action would either be harshly condemned or accepted as a 'necessary' exception to the general rule, especially in the case of collective labour agreements or deontology codes. Today, outsourcing has received a remarkable boost in both quantitative and qualitative respects.[5]

At least five reasons have been suggested to explain why a Legislature or Executive would outsource rulemaking powers.

First, there is the *feasibility* argument where it is considered that only experts are able to fully grasp the subject matter.[6] Early delegation of rulemaking powers was often linked to technical matters related to banking and insurance. Health care is also considered a playground for such experts. Liberalization and neo-liberalization have opened up even more domains for potential delegation to expert regulators.[7]

Second, because of their generally limited constitutional entrenchment, autonomous public, private, and hybrid actors enjoy more *flexibility* to regulate a matter using a wide array of techniques. These techniques include rules but also extend to elements such as advisory opinions, reports, and sanctions.[8] The delegation of rulemaking powers is often accompanied by the potential for using such alternative techniques. It is also possible that these techniques are more transparent and counteract the hidden and insular decision-making processes found in traditional chains of delegation.[9]

Third, outsourcing rulemaking power through delegation might appear to increase the *legitimacy* of highly sensitive and controversial decisions.[10] Here, an

[5] Fabrizio Cafaggi, 'The Many Features of Transnational Private Rule-Making: Unexplored Relationships Between Custom, *Jura Mercatorum* and Global Private Regulation' [2015] *U. Penn. J. Int'l L.* 876–938; Dominique Custos, 'The Rulemaking Power of Independent Regulatory Agencies' [2006] *Am. J. Comp. L.* 615–40.

[6] John Alder, *General Principles of Constitutional and Administrative Law* (Palgrave 2002) 140; Xavier Delgrange, Luc Detroux, and Hugues Dumont, 'La régulation en droit public' in Benoît Jadot and François Ost (eds), *La loi aujourd'hui, mission impossible?* (Publications FUSL 1999) 82.

[7] Robert Andersen, 'Les autorités administratives indépendantes en droit belge' [2008] *Annuaire Européen d'Administration Publique* 27.

[8] Catherine Teitgen-Colly, 'Les instances de régulation et la Constitution' [1990] *RDP* 155. Pierre Nihoul, 'Les autorités administratives indépendantes en Belgique' [2013] *RFDA* 898, § 8.

[9] Gül Sosay, 'Consequences of Legitimizing Independent Regulatory Agencies in Contemporary Democracies: Theoretical Scenarios' in Dietmar Braun and Fabrizio Gilardi (eds), *Delegation in Contemporary Democracies* (Routledge 2006) 182.

[10] Hermann Pünder, 'Democratic Legitimation of Delegated Legislation—A Comparative View on the American, British and German Law' [2009] *ICLQ* 353, 374; Gül Sosay, 'Consequences of Legitimizing Independent Regulatory Agencies in Contemporary Democracies: Theoretical Scenarios'

autonomous public, private, or hybrid actor relieves the state from having to intervene directly in a sector which, for example, is sensitive with respect to civil liberties.[11] The British Human Fertilisation and Embryology Authority, for example, takes the form of a body corporate that does not act on behalf of the Crown (despite its main officials being appointed by the Executive).[12] The Authority has several functions, among which is regulating the storage of sperm, eggs, and embryos. A cynical approach to this delegation of powers is that it is used by politicians who want to hide behind experts on moral issues which will not hinder their electoral success.[13]

A fourth reason concerning *political strategy* is even more prosaic. The constitutional status quo often does not correlate with the ideal of a state because it coincides with one stage in the process of political negotiations. Empirical research has shown that governing parties tend to develop different strategies on the outsourcing of rulemaking powers depending on the current and expected future strength of their opposition.[14] Legal research has pointed to similar reasoning behind ruling majorities creating constitutional courts.[15] Even though delegating rulemaking power is not generally entrenched in a constitution, it is a thorny issue to scrap a politically independent regulator. Outsourcing rulemaking power thus possibly serves to further the political agenda of a ruling majority party. This fourth reason may apply domestically and also internationally. For example, the US famously funded the first research project that would eventually lead to the development of the internet.[16] Initially, the US maintained primary control over several key regulatory features of the World Wide Web. After the worldwide spread of the internet, however, several international organizations, such as the International Telecommunications Union (ITU), began to question the US monopoly on internet regulation. In response, the Clinton administration outsourced considerable regulating powers to a private non-profit organization, the Internet

in Dietmar Braun and Fabrizio Gilardi (eds), *Delegation in Contemporary Democracies* (Routledge 2006) 176.

[11] Xavier Taton, 'Les recours juridictionnels contre les décisions des autorités de régulation' in Hugues Dumont, Pierre Jadoul, and Sébastien Van Drooghenbroeck (eds), *La protection juridictionnelle du citoyen face à l'administration* (La Charte 2007) 219; Catherine Teitgen-Colly, 'Les instances de régulation et la Constitution' [1990] *RDP* 153, 155.

[12] Tony Prosser, 'The Powers and Accountability of Agencies and Regulators' in David Feldman (ed.), *Oxford Principles of English Law. English Public Law* (Oxford University Press 2009) 278. Dissenting Opinion Antonin Scalia *Mistretta v. United States*, 422 US 361 (1989).

[13] Tony Prosser, 'The Powers and Accountability of Agencies and Regulators' in David Feldman (ed.), *Oxford Principles of English Law. English Public Law* (Oxford University Press 2009) 279.

[14] Craig Volden, 'Delegating Power to Bureaucracies. Evidence from the States' [2002] *JLEO* 187, 192–3.

[15] Ran Hirschl, *Towards Juristocracy: The Origins and Consequences of the New Constitutionalism* (Harvard University Press 2007) 11.

[16] Byung-Keun Kim, *Internationalizing the Internet: The Co-evolution of Influence and Technology* (Edward Elgar 2005) 2.

Corporation for Assigned Names and Numbers (ICANN).[17] The existence of such a private actor over which the US would still have greater practical control, was preferred to a multilateral international organization. A clear political strategy lies behind the creation and support of this entity.

The fifth present-day reason for the delegation of rulemaking powers, at least within the EU Member States, is the international influence of the EU.[18] Generally speaking, the EU has created a tidal wave that has made Member States accustomed to a lengthy chain of delegation through framework and ordinary directives. More specifically, independent regulators in sectors such as energy and telecommunications have stirred up the public law of Member States with directives in these areas precluding a hierarchical connection between the regulator and the government and requiring independence.[19]

Commentators have highlighted the need for a constitutional framework for regulation that emanates from private actors and from public institutions that do not have direct political responsibilities.[20] By providing such a framework, this research responds to a scholarly outcry that has echoed for years. It transcends existing scholarship through its focus on both constitutional principles and on autonomous public, private, and hybrid actors. In addition, it is the first comprehensive research to compare the stance of the US, the UK, Germany, France, Belgium, and other nations on this issue.

1.2 Scope

The title of this monograph, *Outsourcing Rulemaking Powers: Constitutional Limits and National Safeguards*, contains several weighty legal notions that deserve some initial consideration.

The book hinges on the three concepts that are expressed or implied in the title. First, 'rulemaking powers' are defined in Section 1.2.1, with the decision to use this phrase enabling us to focus specifically on the 'lawmaking function' in various legal documents. Second, the meaning of 'outsourcing' is explained in Section 1.2.2. Third, the research is limited to autonomous public, private, and hybrid actors. In Section 1.2.3, I explain why I chose these actors that fall outside the scope of the three branches of government.

[17] Kal Raustiala, 'Governing the Internet', UCLA Research Paper No. 16-33 (2016) 4 and 13.

[18] Pierre Nihoul, 'Les autorités administratives indépendantes en Belgique' [2013] *RFDA* 898, § 8.

[19] Recital 13 of Directive 2009/140/EC and article 3a Directive 2002/21/EC; recital 34 of Directive 2009/72/EC; recital 30 of Directive 2009/73/EC; Koen Muylle, 'Het grondwettelijk delegatieverbod en het Unierecht' in André Alen and Jan Theunis (eds), *Leuvense Staatsrechtelijke Standpunten 3* (die Keure 2012) 339.

[20] Paul Tucker, *Unelected Power* (Princeton University Press 2018) 558; Patricia Popelier and Jeroen Van Nieuwenhove, 'Decentralisering en privatisering van wetgeving' in Jef De Mot (ed.), *Vrank en vrij: liber amicorum Boudewijn Bouckaert* (Die Keure 2012) 284–6.

1.2.1 Rulemaking powers

There are many types of power that might be executed or outsourced: administrative, individual decision-making, management, rulemaking, incentivizing, indicative, consultative, and even punitive.[21] In fact, considerable research on privatization relates to 'executive' power, which is then described as the authority to unilaterally determine an individual citizen's legal rights and obligations.[22] This research, however, focuses on the most archetypical power that the Legislature and the Executive share: rulemaking powers.

Because the definitions of 'lawmaking', 'legislative', 'statutory', 'normative', 'regulatory', or even 'normative powers' differ in the various jurisdictions,[23] I opted for a research-specific category of 'rulemaking' powers. Rulemaking powers—as applied in this research—are powers: *to enact, accept, or establish abstract, general, and obligatory norms that have the purpose and effect of altering legal rights, duties, and relations between persons*.[24]

This definition deserves additional clarification. A rule should be *abstract*. An act is abstract when it does not exhaust its validity after the first use and when it can be applied in the future in any number of cases.[25] An act is *general* when it is capable of regulating an undetermined number of situations, even if in practice the act is only applied once.[26] In other words, the act does not have to be applied to everyone but does at least have to be applied to people who did not create the act.[27] Finally, an act is *obligatory* if it is intended to be binding and if it entails the means to enforce obedience.[28] Mere acts of consultation, coordination, and flexible benchmarking will not amount to rulemaking acts. However, 'agreements'

[21] Michel Pâques, 'Décentralisation, régulation et contrôle démocratique: l'arrêt 130/2010 en question' in David D'Hooghe, Kurt Deketelaere, and Anne Mie Draye (eds), *Liber amicorum Marc Boes* (die Keure 2011) 411, 418 and 423.

[22] e.g. Mathias Rose Svendsen, 'Constitutional Limitations on the Competence to Entrust the Exercise of Authority to Private Entities' (2017) 13 *Eur. Const. L. Rev.* 705.

[23] Hermann Pünder, 'Democratic Legitimation of Delegated Legislation—A Comparative View on the American, British and German Law' [2009] *ICLQ* 353, 354.

[24] This definition is based, among others, on Dumon's definition of 'law' in his 1978 opening address of the legal year and on Chief Justice Burger's majority opinion of the US Supreme Court in *INS v. Chadha*: F. Dumon, 'De motivering van de vonnissen en arresten en de bewijskracht van de akten' [1978–9] *Arr. Cass.* 1, 23; *INS v. Chadha* 462 US 952 (1983). See also Arnaud Haquet, 'Le pouvoir réglementaire des autorités administratives indépendantes. Réflexions sur son objet et sa légitimité' [2008] *RDP* 395.

[25] Belgian Council of State Administrative Litigation Section, no. 222.828, 12 March 2013, *Stichting Maharisihi Global Financing Research c. La commune de Walhain*, 4. In the terminology of the US Administrative Procedure Act, I principally only study the 'rules' not the 'orders' (Administrative Procedure Act, § 551(4) and (6)).

[26] Belgian Council of State Administrative Litigation Section, no. 104.634, 13 March 2002, *Rousseau c. La commune de Sambreville*, 5.

[27] Johannes Köndgen, 'Privatisierung des Rechts. *Private governance* zwischen Deregulierung und Rekonstitutionalisierung' [2006] *Archiv für die civilistische Praxis* 477, 499.

[28] Belgian Council of State Administrative Litigation Section, no. 229.606, 18 December 2014, *l'asbl Ligue des Droits de l'Homme c. L'état belge*, 5.

imposed by professional organizations with a monopoly of power, which the members of those professional organizations cannot escape, could establish abstract, general, and obligatory norms that influence the legal rights, duties, and relations of those members.[29]

Using the notion of 'rulemaking powers', it is perfectly possible to compare powers in line with their objective function, rather than their institutional background. In fact, in the US 'rulemaking' powers are indeed a vital object of study since the adoption of the Administrative Procedure Act in 1946 which distinguished between rulemaking and adjudication.[30]

While every exercise of adjudicatory powers can at some level be considered an exercise of rulemaking powers,[31] I have omitted the adjudicating function from the core of this research and its research hypotheses. Without doubt, in common law countries the adjudicatory function sometimes seems to garner more attention than the rulemaking function. Duxbury concludes from a relatable metaphor that rulemaking is generally underappreciated, as opposed to adjudication.[32] Law schools—even in continental Europe—tend to allow the use of rulemaking texts when taking exams. Only on occasion do they allow printed case law. However, this does not imply that rulemaking powers are inferior to adjudicatory powers. If calculators are permitted in mathematical or engineering exams, that does not mean that calculus is not important for mathematics, but rather that is *so* crucial that it seems wasteful to allow the students to build on shaky foundations. The same applies to the crucial function of rules in law. Rules ultimately determine and guide the behaviour of the regulated.[33]

1.2.2 Outsourcing

'Outsourcing' is the operative word in the title and subject of this monograph. The need to outsource governmental powers evolved in the *context* of the welfare state. As a result of this, the notion of 'outsourcing' received a substantial *content*.

1.2.2.1 Context of outsourcing

In the first stage of modern legal theory, Parliament was generally seen as the prime body responsible for enacting rules in the form of statutes. Alexis de Tocqueville

[29] They can be applied an infinite amount of times (*abstract*), they apply to people who ordinarily did not create the act (*general*), and they are binding (*obligatory*).

[30] Administrative Procedure Act 1946; David L. Shapiro, 'The Choice of Rulemaking or Adjudication in the Development of Administrative Policy' [1965] *Harv. L. Rev.* 921–1 and more recentlyKathryn A. Watts, 'Rulemaking as Legislating' (2015) 103 *Geo. LJ* 1003–60.

[31] Laurence Claus, 'Montesquieu's Mistakes and the True Meaning of Separation' [2005] *OJLS* 437–8.

[32] Neil Duxbury, *Elements of Legislation* (Cambridge University Press 2012) 63, fn. 30.

[33] David L. Shapiro, 'The Choice of Rulemaking or Adjudication in the Development of Administrative Policy' [1965] *Harv. L. Rev.* 932–3.

allegorized Parliament as a man navigating a sailing boat in the middle of the ocean: he can steer the ship but cannot influence its structure nor can he create wind or stop the currents.[34] I wish to expand on this allegory. Within the constraints of the ship (the constitution) and of the powers of nature (the democratic flow), the captain (Parliament) decides in which direction to head. Soon, however, it will become apparent that the captain requires sailors (the Executive) to execute his orders and sometimes the sailors will have to make decisions that go beyond the pure execution of orders (rulemaking powers of the Executive). Initially, the boat is able to steer clear of uncharted waters, however a combination of sea currents and the ambition of the captain later lead the boat into more treacherous waters.[35] In order to avoid danger and stay afloat, the captain has to appeal to local experts (actors outside the *Trias Politica* or autonomous public, private, and hybrid actors). The US Supreme Court put it as follows in *Mistretta*: 'In our increasingly complex society, replete with ever-changing and more technical problems, Congress simply cannot do its job absent an ability to delegate power under broad general directives.'[36] Outsourcing is thus a strategy to deal with governmental responsibilities.[37]

1.2.2.2 Content of outsourcing

When rulemaking power is transferred, political scientists and many legal scholars tend to call this 'delegation'.[38] This term fits within a general philosophy of public law. Public authority derives directly from a successive chain of delegation.[39] There is always a principal who grants well-defined powers to his or her agent to realize the former's objectives.[40] The theory owes a great deal to Rousseau's idea of the social contract. In the first stage, the people delegate their power to politicians who will contribute to the people's goals by making laws. Whether it be the 'Legislature',[41] 'législateur', 'Gesetzgeber', or 'wetgever', the law is 'brought' or

[34] As cited in Marc Uyttendaele, *Trente leçons de droit constitutionnel* (Bruylant 2011) 347. Witteveen used another metaphor, namely a lead actor (Parliament) that—over time—settled for a directorial position. Willem Witteveen, 'Het politieke primaat als regie van de wetgever' in W. J. Witteveen, H. R. B. M. Kummeling, and F. A. M Stroink (eds), *Het primaat van de politiek. Staatsrechtsconferentie 1999* (Tjeenk Willink 2000) 9–13.

[35] Catherine Donnelly, *Delegation of Governmental Power to Private Parties. A Comparative Perspective* (Oxford University Press 2007) 89.

[36] *Mistretta v. United States*, 488 US 372 (1989); Hermann Pünder, 'Democratic Legitimation of Delegated Legislation—A Comparative View on the American, British and German Law' [2009] *ICLQ* 353, 355; Rob van Gestel, 'The Deparliamentarisation of Legislation: Framework Laws and the Primacy of the Legislature' (2013) 9 *Utrecht L. Rev.* 109

[37] Olaf Kwast, 'Uitbesteding van wetgeving: strategie en dienstverlening' in Nederlandse Vereniging voor Wetgeving, *Uitbesteding van wetgeving* (Wolf Legal Publishers 2017) 39.

[38] Gunther Teubner, 'The King's Many Bodies: The Self Destruction of Law's Hierarchy' [1997] *L. & S. Rev.* 763, 768.

[39] Dietmar Braun and Fabrizio Gilardi, 'Introduction' in Dietmar Braun and Fabrizio Gilardi (eds), *Delegation in Contemporary Democracies* (Routledge 2006) 12.

[40] Ibid., 1; Kaare Strøm, Wolfgang C. Müller, and Torbjörn Bergman, 'The Moral Hazards of Parliamentary Democracy' in ibid., 29.

[41] '*Lature*' or '*lateur*' is derived from the Latin '*latus*' which is the past participle of '*ferre*'; to bring.

'given' back to the people. The people's authority is subsequently passed on by the Legislature to the government, to ministers, to the administrations of ministers, and—eventually—even to autonomous public, private, or hybrid actors.

I deploy the notion of 'outsourcing'[42] rather than 'delegation' because the scope of this research is broader than merely the outward transfer of rulemaking powers by the Legislature and a government or its ministers. Moreover, less intrusive means of transferring rulemaking powers than delegations, such as referrals and the reception technique, will also be analysed.

1.2.2.3 Degrees and techniques of outsourcing

As a whole, one can describe the outsourcing of rulemaking power in terms of a sliding scale of governmental influence. There are three degrees of leeway granted to non-state actors in the lawmaking process.

First, their influence may be informal, by means of lobbying, advice, or preparatory drafting skills.[43] This type of outsourcing is excluded from the central scope of the monograph. An official and institutionalized role of an autonomous public or private actor in the rulemaking process is required. The decision to exclude mere consultations with professional experts from the scope of the research is mirrored in comparable legal scholarship.[44] It also finds support in the national approaches of the research countries and beyond. For example, Belgian Members of Parliament asked no questions in 1999 on the adoption of legislation which Price Waterhouse Cooper (PwC) had strongly influenced through an external audit on meat chain inspections.[45] Sometimes this phenomenon is still scrutinized. A Luxembourgish Member of Parliament recently inquired into the role of 'law firms and consultancy agencies' in the preparation of Luxembourgish financial legislation.[46] In the Netherlands, ING Bank—which had purportedly predesigned beneficial legislation for banks—found itself in the eye of a media storm.[47] In addition, questions have been raised in France and Germany on the role of expert organizations and law firms (respectively LexisNexis and Linklaters) in the preparation of rules. In the UK, the issue was discussed whether judges who were heard by Parliament in

[42] 'Outsourcing' also fits the description better than alternatives such as 'privatization', as suggested by Gillian E. Metzger, 'Privatization as Delegation' (2003) 103 *Colum. L. Rev.* 1367–502; or 'collaboration'; or see Akritas Kaidatzis, 'A Typology of the Constitutional Limitations on Privatization' [2009] *Hellenic Rev. Eur. L.* 79–96.

[43] Pauline Westerman, *Outsourcing the Law* (Edward Elgar 2018) 48.

[44] See for similar considerations in similar research: ibid., 5.

[45] Statutory proposal *houdende oprichting van het Federaal Agentschap voor de Veiligheid van de Voedselketen* (Parliamentary Documents Chamber of Representatives no. 50/232-4, 1999–2000) 22–4.

[46] Parliamentary question David Wagner, Question no. 3197 regarding procedure in financial legislation, 2 August 2017. See also the appeasing answer of the Luxembourgish Minister of Finances, denying any legal problems with this standard practice (31 August 2017, Q-2016-O-E-3197-02).

[47] F. J. Van Ommeren, 'Referaat—Uitbesteding van wetgeving: op zoek naar waarborgen' in Nederlandse Vereniging voor Wetgeving (ed.), *Uitbesteding van wetgeving* (Wolf Legal Publishers 2017) 111.

order to improve legislation violated constitutional principles such as the separation of powers.

However, these central constitutional qualms can be rebutted because the ordinary rulemaking processes of the Legislature and the Executive remain intact.[48] Receiving advisory opinions from judges, lawyers, consultants, lobbyists, etc. may become problematic in the light of specific basic rights such as equal protection and should be supervised, but that does not raise concerns with regard to how constitutional principles limit the transfer of rulemaking powers. Members of Parliaments are inherently influenced by their environments. This is why institutionalized constitutional safeguards (such as majority requirements, two houses of a Parliament, or even a constitutional court) have been put in place. These safeguards still operate for rulemaking that is subject to external influence. The purpose of this research has been to analyse how such limits and safeguards materialize when autonomous public or private actors *formally* wield (an aspect of the) rulemaking powers.

Second, private enactments may resemble governmental acts very closely through their de facto impact, but may fall short of being instruments that have direct binding and executive force as the exercise of governmental powers. In the first instance, private actors, especially private corporations, may make international agreements with governments in order to prompt investment.[49] In the second instance, non-state actors may give more substance to a legal 'open rule'. Often legal acts and codes use phrases such as 'due care', 'common technical rules', or 'safe'.[50] It is difficult for a judge to assess this without the necessary expertise. Furthermore, the legislative preparatory work often does not provide much more professional insight. Privately drafted documents can make elements concrete that were still abstract for the original rulemaker. A telling example is the executive decree of the Flemish government recognizing the quality standard for martial arts. The Flemish government recognizes this privately developed standard that aims to improve safety within the practice of martial arts,[51] although it does not consider the standard to be binding: 'These standards *can be a useful tool* to comply with the legislative obligations resting on martial arts organizations.'[52] Sometimes

[48] Most notably Fritz Ossenbühl, 'Outsourcing von Gesetzesentwürfen. Ein Scheinproblem' in Matthias Ruffert (ed.), *Dynamik und Nachhaltigkeit des Öffentlichen Rechts—Festschrift für Professor Dr. Meinhard Schröder zum 70. Geburtstag* (Humblot & Duncker 2012) 359 and 396; W. Konijnenbelt, 'Vreemdelingen in het vooronder: een nabetrachting' in Nederlandse Vereniging voor Wetgeving (ed.), *Uitbesteding van wetgeving* (Wolf Legal Publishers 2017) 99; F. J. Van Ommeren, 'Referaat—Uitbesteding van wetgeving: op zoek naar waarborgen' in ibid., 112–13 and 120.

[49] Julian Arato, 'Corporations as Lawmakers' [2015] *Harv. Int'l LJ* 229 95.

[50] Belgian Council of State Legislative Section, Advisory opinion no. 38.642/4 of 13 July 2005, section 3. Catherine Donnely, *Delegation of Governmental Power to Private Parties* (Oxford University Press 2007) 59.

[51] Article 1 Executive Decree 28 October 2016, no. 2016/36590, *Besluit van de Vlaamse Regering tot erkenning van de kwaliteitsstandaard voor het organiseren van risicogevechtssporten*.

[52] Legislative preparation Flemish statute 20 December 2013 (Flemish Parliament 2013–14, no. 2280) 19 (emphasis added).

the law can even attach a rebuttable presumption to a privately made standard, ensuring that it complies with the required care, technical rules, or acts in good faith.[53] The acts of this second degree of outsourcing are not yet constitutive but remain declarative.

Third, the autonomous public, private, or hybrid actor may have an institutionalized rulemaking function. This monograph is firmly focused on this function. In what follows, I elucidate the three main techniques that traditional rulemakers use when they outsource rulemaking powers. The first technique implies the genuine delegation of rulemaking powers. The second technique occurs when the traditional rulemakers refer to a standard document. The third technique requires the reception, and possible extension by the Legislature or the Executive, of rules made by professional organizations.

1.2.2.3.1 Delegation: the newest despotism?

The delegation of rulemaking powers is arguably the most far-reaching technique. In this case, the delegator (i.e. the Legislature or Executive) mandates the autonomous public, private, or hybrid actors to exercise well-defined rulemaking competences in its place. Potentially, the delegator thus relinquishes its final word on the rule.

This research is able to build on a framework that already exists for delegating rulemaking powers in every country: the delegation of rulemaking powers from the Legislature to the Executive is one of the most debated issues in the history of (comparative) constitutional law.[54] As a practical matter, the transfer of rulemaking powers has only increased over time. In a 1929 seminal contribution to the scholarship on delegation in the UK, Lord Hewart objected to the—at that time—recent manifestation of rulemaking delegation to the Executive. He compared the phenomenon to the despotism of, for example, the English kings before the Glorious Revolution. He argued that while the despotism of the kings, which was defeated, presented Parliament with a challenge, despotism through the delegation of rulemaking powers offered parliament an anaesthetic. The strategy differed, but the goal was the same.[55] Lord Hewart framed the Executive as lulling the naïve Parliament to sleep and running off with its powers; in particular, he

[53] Johannes Köndgen, 'Privatisierung des Rechts. Private governance zwischen Deregulierung und Rekonstitutionalisierung' [2006] *Archiv für die civilistische Praxis* 477, 490.

[54] The way in which the Executive relates to the Legislature in the context of delegated legislation has been compared to the bond between a child and its parent. A growing child is expected to eventually alleviate the burden of its parents. Cecil Carr, *Delegated Legislation: Three Lectures* (Cambridge University Press 1921) 2. This debate is also considerably more developed than delegation to e.g. private actors: Kimberly N. Brown, 'Public Laws and Private Lawmakers' (2016) 93 *Wash. U. L. Rev.* 615, 637. See also Eric Posner and Adrian Vermeule, 'Interring the Nondelegation Doctrine' [2002] *U. Chi. L. Rev.* 1721.

[55] Lord Hewart of Bury, *The New Despotism* (Ernest Benn 1929) 17. *Contra*: Carl Schmitt, 'Vergleichender überblick über die neueste Entwicklung des Problems der gesetzgeberischen Ermächtigungen (Legislative Delegationen)' [1936] *ZaöRV* 252, 252–3.

feared the unfettered and supreme power of the Executive should the delegation of rulemaking powers be accompanied by an ouster clause limiting judicial review of the transferred power.

While Lord Hewart famously named his contribution on the delegation of rulemaking powers to the Executive, *The New Despotism*, the title of this section questions the 'newest despotism' of the delegation of rulemaking powers to autonomous public, private, or hybrid actors.

In favour of the latter assertion, the Executive at least has a constitutional function as one of the branches of government; however, there is generally no mention of other actors in national constitutions. Moreover, the people still directly control the Executive via the Legislature. This is not the case for autonomous public, private, or hybrid actors. Finally, delegation to autonomous public, private, or hybrid actors frequently serves to avoid the democratic process and, in a European context, is often instigated by the EU—which has rarely been praised for its democratic features.

Against the assertion of despotism in the case of these 'newer' rulemakers, the traditional rulemaking branches, the Legislature and the Executive, simply cannot continue to 'steer the ship alone'. Parliament does not have the resources to understand the most complicated and technical matters that need regulation.[56] Moreover, the flexible techniques that are often used by autonomous public, private, or hybrid actors may allow for more transparency and input legitimacy than the traditional lawmaking processes. Finally, it is also argued that the Executive can avoid congestion by offloading some of its responsibilities.[57]

1.2.2.3.2 Referral

A second technique of outsourcing rulemaking powers occurs when a Legislature or Executive does not want to go as far as to delegate its power to an autonomous public, private, or hybrid actor, but instead, the Legislature or the Executive refers in its own rulemaking to an external document that was produced by such an actor. Referral is a technique that is used in various legal contexts, such as contract law, private international law, federalism, and the implementation of international law. This research focuses on the intricacies of rulemaking referral to external documents or standards produced by standardization organizations.

There are two types of referral: static referral and dynamic referral. 'Static referral' implies that the rule is connected to the external document *as it is*. 'Dynamic referral' means that the rule is linked to the external document *as it is and as it will be*. Static referral prevents rulemakers from finding themselves cast adrift when

[56] J. E. Kersell, *Parliamentary Supervision of Delegated Legislation* (Stevens & Sons 1960) 2. Yseult Marique, 'The Rule-Making Powers of Independent Administrative Agencies ("QUANGOs"). Comparative Analysis in Fifteen Countries' (December 2007) 11.3 *Electronic J. Comp. L.* 4.

[57] Yves Lejeune, *Droit constitutionnel belge* (Larcier 2014) 121.

changes to the external document occur, by limiting the applicability of the external document to a certain date. The downside of static referral then lies in the fact that the referring document will have to be amended multiple times in order to keep up with any evolutions in the external document referred to. Dynamic referral is volatile because if the external document referred to changes, the referring rule changes as well. An obvious risk in this technique is that the original rulemaker cannot control subsequent changes to the external document.

The external documents that are referred to in this book are produced by autonomous public, private, or hybrid actors. If such an actor alters the referred-to document, in the case of dynamic referral the legal rules will also be amended automatically. Circuitously, that actor can thus 'make' the rule.[58] This equally applies for *mandatory* certification, because when the certification authority changes its standards, it will be necessary to comply with the new standard in order to be able to undertake the activity. In the context of standardization, dynamic referrals are thus sometimes called direct undated referrals.[59]

I mainly focus on referral to documents produced by autonomous public, private, or hybrid actors that were not set up as treaty bodies; in particular, the core of this book will not be concerned with autonomous public, private, or hybrid actors directly founded by the EU. As EU standardization inherently implies non-binding referrals—at least de jure—it can thus only allow occasional comparison.[60] Again, this does not imply that EU law cannot exert influence on constitutional principles which govern referral to documents of standardization organizations.

Examples of autonomous public, private, or hybrid actors that will be discussed are: general standardization institutions such as the Belgisch Instituut voor Normalisatie, the Deutsches Institut für Normung, the Association Française de Normalisation, and the British Standards Institution; and specific standardizations institutions such as the Verein Deutscher Ingenieure; and *sui generis* NGOs or non-profit foundations such as the International Standardization Organization (ISO) and the World Anti-Doping Agency (WADA). WADA, for example, prides itself on being a non-profit foundation constituted under the Swiss Civil Code.[61] The

[58] See Mirjam Elferink, 'Verwijzingen in wetgeving. Over de publiekrechtelijke en auteursrechtelijke status van normalisatienormen', Doctoral thesis, Leiden University (1998) 263.

[59] ISO and IEC, 'Using and referencing ISO and IEC standards to support public policy' (2015) 26; European Commission, 'Methods of referencing standards in legislation with an emphasis on European legislation' (2002 update 2014) 7.

[60] e.g. Dagmar Schiek, 'Private Rule-Making and European Governance—Issues of Legitimacy' [August 2007] *E. L. Rev.* 443, 455;Henri Culot and Dries Van Eeckhoutte, 'La normalisation et ses écueils potentiels en droit privé et en droit public' in Jérémie van Meerbeeck, *Droit public/droit privé* (Anthemis 2019) § 19; Pieter-Jan Van De Weyer, 'Geharmoniseerde Europese normen: de New Approach van de Europese Unie en de zoektocht naar legitimiteit' [2014] *TBP* 333, 338. Johannes Köndgen, 'Privatisierung des Rechts. *Private governance* zwischen Deregulierung und Rekonstitutionalisierung' [2006] *Archiv für die civilistische Praxis* 477, 486.

[61] PricewaterhouseCoopers, 'World Anti Doping Agency Lausanne. Report of the statutory auditor to the foundation board on the financial statements 2013', 8.

most famous creation of WADA is its World Anti-Doping Code. In Chapters 4 and 6, I explain how especially the Belgian Legislature and Executive refer to WADA-made standards.

The ISO itself has confirmed the global use and impact of the referral method by listing examples from Brazil, Canada, China, South Africa, and the US.[62]. For a long time this technique remained under the radar in the US, but recent scholarship has refocused on it. Direct referrals are commonplace in the US, with approximately 9,500 incorporations by reference in the US Code of Federal Regulations.[63] In federal aviation administration, for example, airworthiness directives are 'legally enforceable rules that apply to ... aircraft, aircraft engines, propellers and appliances' through referral by the Federal Aviation Administration.[64]

It is not always clear where the allegiance of an autonomous public, private, or hybrid actor lies. It could be with the government, which entrusts it with a role in the lawmaking process. It could also be with the businesses from which it draws its expertise and technical knowledge.[65] Moreover, the question of whether a dynamic referral should give way to at least a static referral also arises. These questions will be further addressed later when engaging with both research hypotheses and the case study.

1.2.2.3.3 Reception

Sometimes the Executive and the Legislature do not wish to delegate specific power to autonomous public, private, or hybrid actors, most of which are self-created, nor do they want to refer to one of their enactments. Rather, they aim to 'receive' the rulemaking initiatives of grassroots professional organizations. 'Reception' seems the most appropriate term to describe such action because it recognizes the creative work and autonomy of the autonomous public, private, or hybrid actor.[66] Sometimes the professionally produced documents are extended so that they bind more people to them or so that the binding force is increased for the original parties. The Legislature perceives self-regulating layers of society and creates the framework for the reception of their rulemaking. The most well-known examples

[62] ISO, 'National Examples Using and referencing ISO and IEC standards to support public policy' <https://www.iso.org/publication/PUB100358.html> (last accessed May 2021).

[63] Emily S. Bremer, 'Incorporation by Reference in an Open-Government Age' (2013) 36 *Harv. J. L. & Pub. Pol'y* 135.

[64] 14 US Code of Federal Regulations, § 39.3 (2012). Emily S. Bremer, 'Incorporation by Reference in an Open-Government Age' (2013) 36 *Harv. J. L. & Pub. Pol'y* 146.

[65] Colin Scott, 'Standard-Setting in Regulatory Regimes' in Robert Baldwin, Martin Cave, and Martin Lodge (eds), *The Oxford Handbook of Regulation* (Oxford University Press 2010) 114.

[66] Nikitas Aliprantis, *La place de la convention collective dans la hierarchie des normes* (Librairie générale de droit et jurisprudence 1980) 38.

of this technique are: (1) collective labour agreements; and (2) codes of professional organizations.[67]

(1) In a political system of consultation and dialogue, it should not come as a surprise that methods such as collective labour agreements arise.[68] Collective labour agreements (*die Tarifverträge* in German; *les conventions collectives* in French; and *de collectieve arbeidsovereenkomst* in Dutch) obviously have different contents in the various countries researched. Nevertheless, I discern two potentially problematic levels of their use in general: their applicability to non-unionized sector members, on the one hand,[69] and the government declaration of general applicability (*allgemeinverbindlicherklä rung*[70] in German; *déclaration d'obligation générale*[71] in French; *algemeen verbindendverklaring*[72] in Dutch), on the other hand. Both levels risk questionable representativeness and procedural shortcomings in rulemaking. With this reception technique, the Legislature and the Executive keep the decision-making process under close scrutiny. Often, their rules need to be ratified by the Executive or Parliament before they become binding.[73]

(2) Deontology codes may constitute binding rules for practitioners of free professions (and indirectly also their customers) without their consent. Thus, they are in a sense enforced members. In Germany, these organizations are often recognized as self-regulating public corporations (*Selbstverwaltungsk örperschaften des öffentlichen Rechts*). Moreover, there are also other professional organizations, such as sports organizations, in which the submission of members—in this case, athletes—to privately developed codes is enforced because their livelihood depends on it. Under certain circumstances, the internal codes of professional sports organizations may thus actually equate to rules and fall under the reception technique.

Thus, why is reception potentially more problematic for a country than using pressure groups as advisors before making the state laws itself? At this point, it suffices to cite two arguments.

[67] In Belgium, e.g., Article 15 § 1 of 10 November 1967 Royal Decree no. 79 (*Koninklijk besluit nr. 79 betreffende de Orde der artsen)*; Article 15 § 1 of 10 November 1967 Royal Decree no. 80 (*Koninklijk besluit nr. 80 betreffende de Orde der apothekers*).

[68] Patricia Popelier, *Democratisch regelgeven* (Intersentia 2001) 138.

[69] e.g. in Belgium, Article 26 of the statute of 5 December 1968 on the collective labour agreements (*Wet betreffende de collectieve arbeidsovereenkomsten en de paritaire comités*).

[70] § 5 of Tarifvertraggesetz.

[71] Article L. 164-8 of the Code du Travail.

[72] Article 28-34 of the statute of 5 December 1968 on collective labour agreements (*Wet betreffende de collectieve arbeidsovereenkomsten en de paritaire comités*).

[73] e.g. Julie Castiaux and Juan Alardin, *Le droit disciplinaire dans la jurisprudence. Une analyse des arrêts de la Cour de Strasbourg, de la Cour constitutionnelle et de la Cour de Cassation* (Larcier 2014) 82; Imre Kovalovszky 'À propos du pouvoir réglementaire' [1995–6] *Administration publique trimestriel* 301, 304.

First, the state organs could lose their right of initiative; if not de jure at least de facto.[74] In some situations, the representatives would merely become 'the notaries of the social partners'.[75]

Second, professional organizations can equally encroach upon the human rights of their members. A number of national courts and authors have maintained that controlled self-regulation (such as collective labour agreements, orders of free professions, or even sports governing bodies) cannot be regulated because these organizations exercise their fundamental freedom of assembly and of association and even their collective right to work.[76] States would then have a duty to respect those rights by recognizing the exercise of 'rulemaking' power and—if needed—extend their binding powers. It has been argued that practitioners of free professions, employers or employees, and professional athletes waive or limit their rights to property or privacy by being part of these professional organizations. Through similar reasoning, the state should accept this waiver of rights.

However, the state can and should set limits on waivers of fundamental rights—and thus also on the reception technique—by exercising its duty to fulfil and protect human rights. The case law of two worldwide influential courts, namely the European Court of Human Rights and the US Supreme Court, can clarify these limits.

In a first instance, in the case of *D. H. v. Czech Republic*, the European Court of Human Rights (ECtHR) had to rule on whether Czech parents of Roma origin had consented to their children being put into 'special schools'.[77] It could be suggested that the parents had waived their children's right to equal treatment. However, the ECtHR stated that: 'under the Court's case-law, the waiver of a right guaranteed by the Convention—in so far as such a waiver is permissible—must be established in an unequivocal manner, and be given in full knowledge of the facts, that is to say on the basis of informed consent and without constraint'.[78] For example, article 6 of the European Convention on Human Rights (ECHR) cannot be waived if a layperson is asked whether he or she consents to being tried by an unlawfully

[74] Patricia Popelier, *Democratisch regelgeven* (Intersentia 2001) 297; Jan Velaers, *De Grondwet en de Raad van State Afdeling Wetgeving* (Maklu 1999) 383.

[75] Quote of Hendrik Vuye by Zico Saerens, 'N-VA: "Niet verkozen als notaris van de sociale partners"', 18 October 2015 <http://deredactie.be/cm/vrtnieuws/politiek/1.2471707> (last accessed May 2021).

[76] Article 6 § 2 of the revised European Social Charter. European Committee of Social Rights no. 118/2015, 7 July 2018, *Confédération Générale du Travail Force Ouvrière (FO) v. France*, § 60. 'The Committee recalls that the objective of Article 6 § 2 is to promote collective bargaining, both free and voluntary, involving parties representing free and duly informed organisations. According to the Committee's interpretation, in accepting the terms of this provision, the State Parties undertake not only to recognise, in their legislation, that employers and workers may settle their mutual relations by means of collective agreements, but also actively to promote the conclusion of such agreements if their spontaneous development is not satisfactory and, in particular, to ensure that each side is prepared to bargain collectively with the other.'

[77] *D. H. and others v. Czech Republic* no. 57325/00 (ECtHR, 13 November 2007).

[78] Ibid., § 202.

constituted court (*voluntarily and with full knowledge*) or under threat of immediate and heavy sanctions (*no constraint*).[79] Moreover, the waiver must occur in an 'unequivocal manner, must not run counter to any important public interest and must be attended by minimum safeguards commensurate with its importance'.[80] Ultimately, as was shown by the 2018 *Mutu and Pechstein* judgment of the ECtHR with regard to the questioned 'choice' of an athlete to be subjected to Court of Arbitration for Spor (CAS) arbitration in doping disputes, 'one cannot assert that the [athlete] has accepted the clause in a free and non-equivocal fashion'.[81] If the athlete has no choice but to accept a clause in a professional agreement in order to guarantee his or her livelihood, there is no waiver of constitutional rights.

In a second instance, in 1972 the US Supreme Court in *Fuentes v. Shevin* was called upon to rule on state laws that allowed for the seizure of a person's property without notice and without the opportunity to be heard. The US Supreme Court decided that:

> There was no bargaining over contractual terms between the parties who, in any event, were far from equal in bargaining power. The purported waiver provision was a printed part of a form sales contract and a necessary condition of the sale. The appellees made no showing whatever that the appellants were actually aware or made aware of the significance of the fine print now relied upon as a waiver of constitutional rights.[82]

Later, in *Town of Newton v. Rumery*, a businessman had waived his right to claim damages from the state for libel.[83] Subsequently, he backtracked and wished to claim damages. Here, the US Supreme Court confirmed that Rumery had waived his right because he had been well informed, had had time to reconsider, and was supported by an experienced lawyer.[84]

Most of these cases concerned the waiving of fundamental rights to the state. However, the doctrine of the horizontal effect of human rights in the Council of Europe, and *Fuentes v. Shevin* in the US, imply that these conditions on waiving human rights also apply to private parties. Therefore, the 'rules' of professional organizations can become problematic.

In summary, the reception technique is distinguished from delegation by the fact that rulemaking power is not actually ceded to the autonomous public, private, or hybrid actor. An existing professional contract is, rather, elevated to rulemaking status because of governmental intervention. While doing this, the Legislature and

[79] *Simeonovi v. Bulgaria* no. 12/05/2017 (ECtHR, 12 May 2017) § 115; *Pfeifer and Plankl v. Austria* no. 10802/84 (ECtHR, 25 February 1992) §§ 37–8; and *Deweer v. Belgium* no. 6903/75 (ECtHR, 27 February 1980) § 51.

[80] *Correia de Matos v. Portugal* no. 56402/12 (ECtHR, 4 April 2018) § 128.

[81] *Mutu and Pechstein v. Switzerland* nos 40575/10 and 67474/10 (ECtHR, 2 October 2018) § 115.

[82] US Supreme Court, *Fuentes v. Shevin*, 407 US 94–6 (1972).

[83] US Supreme Court, *Town of Newton v. Rumery*, 480 US 386 (1987).

[84] Ibid., 397–8.

the Executive cannot alter the content of the rule.[85] The reception technique is also different from referrals because here traditional rulemakers do not draft an incomplete rule while incorporating an external document of an autonomous public, private, or hybrid actor. Rather, they take note of the socially structuring activities of the grassroots organizations and choose to broaden their applicability to a wider section of the constituency. As a whole, the reception technique represents a paradigm shift compared to the two previous techniques. Instead of focusing on the traditional rulemakers who somehow outsource their rulemaking power to 'newer' rulemakers, I scrutinize how mostly private actors see their agreements broadened to generally binding rules. In other words, the act of outsourcing rulemaking powers becomes, in fact, more declaratory than constitutive.[86] The perspective therefore flips from top-down to bottom-up, with a focus on functional self-regulation.

1.2.3 To whom?

First, the scope of this research is limited to rulemaking powers that are outsourced to autonomous public, private, or hybrid actors. These actors can be presumed to have a lower degree of political accountability. Political accountability should be distinguished from other types of accountability such as judicial or legal accountability.[87]

1.2.3.1 Definition of autonomous public, private, or hybrid actors

Autonomous public, private, or hybrid actors within a nation-state are actors that are not held directly responsible by the citizens through democratic elections.[88]

Regardless of the governmental system (parliamentary, presidential, or semi-presidential), the Legislature and the Executive do not qualify as autonomous public, private, or hybrid actors. Citizens choose their parliamentary representatives within a systematic time frame. The Executive is either directly democratically elected or controlled by Parliament and, thus, by the people. To a similar extent, individual ministers acting on behalf of the government are also subject to the political scrutiny of the government.[89] Even the complete apparatus of civil servants falls under the hierarchical authority of the government, which is why no

[85] Thorsten Anderl, *Gesetzgebung und kooperatives Regierungshandeln* (Berliner Wissenschafts-Verlag 2006) 203.

[86] Thomas Clemens, 'Die Verweisung von einer Rechtsnorm auf andere Vorschriften' [1986] *AöR* 114.

[87] Paul Craig and Adam Tomkins, 'Introduction' in Paul Craig and Adam Tomkins (eds), *The Executive and Public Law* (Oxford University Press 2010) 4.

[88] Kimberly N. Brown, 'Public Laws and Private Lawmakers' (2016) 93 *Wash. U. L. Rev.* 615, 650; Jonathan Weinberg, 'ICANN and the Problem of Legitimacy' (2000) 50 *Duke LJ* 187, 191. On the comparability of these actors, see Mathias Rose Svendsen, 'Constitutional Limitations on the Competence to Entrust the Exercise of Authority to Private Entities' (2017) 13 *Eur. Const. L. Rev.* 719.

[89] Imre Kovalovszky, 'À propos du pouvoir réglementaire' [1995–6] *Administration publique trimestriel* 301, 306.

division of any central administration is considered to be an autonomous public, private, or hybrid actor as defined in this research.[90] This does not imply that the outsourcing of rulemaking powers to actors such as the government and ministers will not be considered at all; to the contrary, the manner in which these latter actors receive rulemaking powers provides a template for other actors as recipients of rulemaking powers.

Rather than focusing on the status of rulemakers, this study concentrates on their political accountability, which is considered more important with respect to the question of their eligibility to receive rulemaking powers. It is easy to establish the absence of political accountability within private bodies, such as social partners as authors of collective labour agreements. However, only a limited number of public bodies lack scrutiny from the people—these are autonomous public bodies (APBs). Independent regulators, in particular, are required by the EU to have a guaranteed buffer against political influence. Consider, for example, the national electronic communications and energy regulators. These phenomena of APBs[91] and private lawmakers[92] have both been the subject of recent interest in legal scholarship. Their comprehensive combination is unique to this research. It is important to reiterate that this research does not focus on rulemakers that fall under the umbrella of the EU or the Council of Europe, but rather on national and transnational autonomous public, private, or hybrid actors.[93]

In theory, the Judiciary is also an autonomous actor that is not held politically accountable in Europe or US federal courts and that could receive rulemaking powers. In the US, for example, in the *Mistretta* case, the Supreme Court addressed the Sentencing Reform Act of 1984.[94] This Act established the US Sentencing Commission which had the goal of setting *mandatory* federal guidelines for criminal sentencing. In doing so, Congress battled the inconsistency in criminal sentencing. The Commission was construed as an 'independent commission in the judicial branch' and consisted of seven voting members appointed by the President with the consent of the Senate. The Supreme Court ultimately validated the delegation of rulemaking powers to the judicial sentencing commission. In doing so, it

[90] Belgian Council of State Legislative Section, Advisory opinion no. 42.986/4 of 2 May 2007, section 1.2.

[91] e.g. Stéphanie De Somer, *Autonomous Public Bodies and the Law. A European Perspective* (Edward Elgar 2017) 384; Guy Scoffoni, 'Les "agences réglementaires indépendantes" dans le système fédéral américain' in Robert Andersen (ed.), *En hommage à Francis Delpérée. Itinéraires d'un constitutionnaliste* (Bruylant 2007) 1420.

[92] Catherine Donnelly, *Delegation of Governmental Power to Private Parties. A Comparative Perspective* (Oxford University Press 2007) 457.

[93] For more on these types of autonomous public, private, and hybrid actors, see Bardo Schettini Gherardini, 'Harmonised European Standards and the EU Court of Justice: Beware Not to Open Pandora's Box', European Law Blog (27 May 2016); Walter Van Gerven and Steven Lierman, *Beginselen van Belgisch Privaatrecht—Algemeen Deel Veertig jaar later—Privaat- en Publiekrecht in een Meergelaagd Kader van Regelgeving, Rechtsvorming en Regeltoepassing* (Kluwer 2010) 334.

[94] *Mistretta v. United States*, 488 US 361 (1989).

confirmed its case law of *Wayman v. Southard*.[95] Outsourcing rulemaking powers to the Judiciary is rare in the five researched countries considered here. Moreover, it has to be approached whilst paying special attention to the guarantees that constitutional democracies provide for the Judiciary. Finally, I wish to steer clear of the highly debated issue of whether rule creation is inherent in judicial interpretation of the law.[96]

Therefore, in summary, this monograph limits itself to actors falling outside the three traditional branches of government, with the common feature that they are not directly politically responsible to citizens through democratic elections.

1.2.3.2 Added value of studying a residuary category of rulemakers

Not all authors agree that private and independent public actors might amount to a single category. In fact, private and autonomous public actors are not generally considered one group but are more commonly seen as two or more irreconcilable clusters. How, after all, would it be possible to compare the rules of private professional groups with those of public regulators?

Dorfman and Harel, for example, cling to the distinction:

> In contrast to public officials, private actors possess a valid claim-right against state interference insofar as they act within the designated arena of permissibility. ... Agents of apolitical public institutions, by contrast, ... have no valid claim of their own against state intervention whenever the polity determines that the judgments of these agents disserve the public interest.[97]

Whereas an independent public actor relies on *a mandate from* the polity, a private actor holds a *right against* the polity.[98] However, if the *right* of the private actor can only be invoked 'insofar as they act within the designated arena of permissibility', then outsourcing rulemaking powers also gives a *mandate* to the private actor which in that instance takes precedence. Since this research also analyses the permissibility and conditions of granting such a mandate to hybrid actors, the traditional public/private divide is to little avail. Thus, a new and residuary categorization will prove to be advantageous.

There is a logical and constitutional connection between the rulemaking competences of autonomous public bodies and private rulemaking. The Legislative Section of the Belgian Council of State and the Belgian Constitutional Court

[95] 23 US (10 Wheat.) 1 (1825).

[96] See for this debate among others, Mauro Cappelletti, *The Judge, Lawmaker or Interpreter* (Law Foundation of New South Wales 1980) 41; Walter Van Gerven, *Het beleid van de rechter* (Standaard Wetenschappelijke Uitgeverij and W. E. J. Tjeenk Willink 1976) 163.

[97] Avihay Dorfman and Alon Harel, 'Against Privatisation As Such' [2006] *OJLS* 400, 419.

[98] Ibid., 420.

seemingly support the notion that APB rulemaking and private rulemaking are comparable phenomena.[99] I share that conviction for three main reasons.

First, both private and public autonomous actors represent a transfer of heteronomy to autonomy. The heteronomous chain of legitimacy, starting from the people (Rousseau) or from the nation (Sieyès), which reaches all the way up to the decision-maker, is apparently disconnected.[100] This feature of autonomy, which is sometimes described as the 'crisis of democratic legitimacy', surfaces in what may be called 'public' and 'private' autonomous actors.[101]

Second, constitutions do not generally[102] enshrine autonomous public, private, and hybrid actors as potential holders of rulemaking authority. If we assume that (written) constitutions exhaustively stipulate the actors that can exercise governmental powers, autonomous public, private, and hybrid actors would not be entitled to any legislative authority.[103] *Expressio unius est exclusio alterius*: to include the one, is to exclude the other. Nevertheless, in reality, both autonomous public bodies and private lawmakers receive rulemaking competences. It is no coincidence that they are described, each independently of the other, as the fourth branch of government.[104]

Third, it is not always easy to make a clear distinction between APBs and private rulemakers. A relatively recent US Supreme Court case attests to their overlap.[105] The 2008 Passenger Rail Investment and Improvement Act (PRIIA) gave joint authority to Amtrak (the US Passenger Railroad Corporation created by Congress) and the Federal Railroad Administration (FRA) to set standards to regulate the division between passenger traffic and freight traffic on the national railroads. The two main constitutional questions were: (1) whether Amtrak was a private entity that had received rulemaking powers; and (2) if so, whether the transfer of authority ran counter to the US non-delegation doctrine. The US Supreme Court

[99] Marc Joassart, Laurent Jans, Claudine Mertes, and Marc Oswald, 'Le Conseil d'Etat—Chronique de légisprudence 2013' [2015] *Revue belge de droit constitutionnel* 107–19; Belgian Constitutional Court, no. 166/2011, 10 November 2011, as discussed in Pierre Nihoul, 'Les autorités administratives indépendantes en Belgique' [2013] *RFDA* 897, fn. 21.

[100] Robert Baldwin, Martin Cave, and Martin Lodge, 'Introduction: Regulation—The Field and the Developing Agenda' in Robert Baldwin, Martin Cave, and Martin Lodge, *The Oxford Handbook of Regulation* (Oxford University Press 2010) 17; Walter Van Gerven and Steven Lierman, *Beginselen van Belgisch Privaatrecht—Algemeen Deel Veertig jaar later—Privaat- en Publiekrecht in een Meergelaagd Kader van Regelgeving, Rechtsvorming en Regeltoepassing* (Kluwer 2010) 274.

[101] Karen Yeung, 'The Regulatory State' in Robert Baldwin, Martin Cave, and Martin Lodge (eds), *The Oxford Handbook of Regulation* (Oxford University Press 2010) 77.

[102] See, for partial exceptions, the Netherlands, Sweden, and Sudan.

[103] This, however, is not uncontested: Filip Dorssemont, 'De rechtspositie van de representatieve werknemersorganisatie', PhD dissertation, University of Antwerp (2000) 183.

[104] Respectively, Francesco Bavagnoli, 'Independent Regulators in Italy' in Claude Henry, Michel Mathieu, and Alain Jeunemaître (eds), *Regulation of Network Utilities: The European Experience* (Oxford University Press 2001) 192; Martino Maggetti, 'Legitimacy and Accountability of Independent Regulatory Agencies: A Critical Review' [2010] *Living Reviews in Democracy* 2 and Hans Lindahl, 'Privaatrecht is publiekrecht: Vranken en de privatisering van het burgerlijk recht' [2005] *NJB* 1892, 1892.

[105] *Department of Transport v. Association of American Railroads*, 575 US 576 (2015).

eventually defused the problem because it did not consider Amtrak to be a private entity. Nevertheless, this case demonstrates that apparent public bodies might receive such a high degree of autonomy that, over time, it is no longer clear whether they are still public entities.

Some authors have described autonomous public, private, and hybrid actors as repositories of rulemaking powers that have replaced traditional democratic legitimacy with substantive autonomy.[106] This autonomy works in two directions: on the one hand, the rulemaker needs to 'legislate' independently of political intervention;[107] on the other, the rulemaker must not be led by selfish interests.[108] If the autonomous public, private, and hybrid actor manages to make decisions with full autonomy, its legitimacy ties into the consensual model of democracy more than the representative model.[109] One would therefore be jumping the gun to denominate autonomous public, private, and hybrid actors as 'non-democratically legitimized actors'.

Finally, I have also decided against the notion of 'non-majoritarian institutions',[110] which is often used in the political sciences to describe bodies that are isolated from the traditional democratic process. The concepts are not completely synonymous. Contrary to non-majoritarian *institutions*, this research focuses on private actors. Moreover, contrary to this book's study object, non-majoritarian institutions can even consist of objects such as a written constitution.[111]

1.3 Hypotheses

As already referred to in the formulation of the problem, this monograph addresses one key research query, which consists of two research hypotheses. Section 1.3.1 first spells out the research query and hypotheses, Section 1.3.2 then discusses the importance of constitutional provisions and principles for both research hypotheses, and, finally, Section 1.3.3 defends the independent value of both research hypotheses.

[106] Dagmar Schiek, 'Private Rule-Making and European Governance—Issues of Legitimacy' [2007] *E. L. Rev.* 443, 465.

[107] Imre Kovalovszky, 'À propos du pouvoir réglementaire' [1995–6] *Administration publique trimestriel* 301, 305.

[108] Dagmar Schiek, 'Private Rule-Making and European Governance—Issues of Legitimacy' [2007] *E. L. Rev.* 443, 444.

[109] Patricia Popelier, *Democratisch regelgeven* (Intersentia 2001) 61.

[110] Dietmar Braun and Fabrizio Gilardi, 'Introduction' in Dietmar Braun and Fabrizio Gilardi (eds), *Delegation in Contemporary Democracies* (Routledge 2006) 9; Mark Thatcher and Alec Stone Sweet, 'Theory and Practice of Delegation to Non-Majoritarian Institutions' [2002] *West Eur. Politics* 1.

[111] Giandomenico Majone, *Temporal Consistency and Policy Credibility. Why Democracies Need Non-Majoritarian Institutions* (Robert Schuman Centre 1997) 18.

1.3.1 Two related research hypotheses

The overarching issue that I address in this monograph is made apparent in its title: *Outsourcing Rulemaking Powers*. In other words, how does (comparative constitutional) law condition the outsourcing of rulemaking power, especially in Belgium, France, Germany, the UK, and the US?[112]

This overarching research query consists of two, more precise, research hypotheses as shown in the monograph's subtitle: *Constitutional Limits and National Safeguards*. Both research hypotheses will be systematically analysed and addressed throughout this monograph. While they are related and supplement each other, it is still useful to approach them separately.

1.3.1.1 Comparative limits on outsourcing rulemaking powers

This first hypothesis concerns the limits to a Legislature or Executive outsourcing rulemaking power.[113] Constitutional provisions or constitutional principles may allow for some powers to be transferred to other actors or institutions while obliging the Legislature and/or the political Executive to exercise other powers themselves. Apart from some rare exceptions,[114] autonomous public, private, or hybrid actors are not mentioned in constitutions, let alone the previously mentioned techniques for outsourcing rulemaking powers to them. It might, therefore, be asserted that any type of outsourcing of rulemaking powers should be strictly forbidden. However, Schwärzel has countered that argument as follows: 'just as the tradition of cooperative law-making does not testify to its lawfulness; the smallest inclination to move away from the constitutional ideal does not prove its unlawfulness'.[115] Rather than strict prohibitions, I thus focus on the precise limits that the researched countries set on the transfer of rulemaking powers via their constitutional principles.

[112] The research therefore does not focus on competition law concerns when outsourcing rulemaking powers. See for this: e.g. Mislav Mataija, *Private Regulation and the Internal Market: Sports, Legal Services, and Standard Setting in EU Economic Law* (Oxford University Press 2016) 246–7; Judit Szoboszlai, 'Delegation of State Regulatory Powers to Private Parties—Towards an Active Supervision Test' (2006) 29 *World Comp.* 84; Michel Bazex and Sophie Blazy, 'Droit de la concurrence et extension des conventions collectives' [June 2003] *Droit Administratif* comm. 123.

[113] Bogdan Iancu established there was an erosion of rulemaking limits for the traditional delegation in his researched countries: Bogdan Iancu, *Legislative Delegation The Erosion of Normative Limits in Modern Constitutionalism* (Springer-Verlag 2012) ch. 4. The question remains whether this applies for outsourcing to autonomous public, private, and hybrid actors as well. Furthermore, if so, where do the eroded borders lie in contemporary global societies?

[114] Article 134.2 of the Dutch Constitution, e.g., for delegation of powers to a type of autonomous public, private, and hybrid actor.

[115] Katrin Schwärzel, 'Die kooperierende rechtserzeugende Gewalt in der kompetenzrechtlichen, legitimatorischen und instrumentellen Krise?' *HFR* 4/2007, 37.

1.3.1.2 Comparative safeguards after outsourcing rulemaking powers

A mere glance at the current practice of outsourcing rulemaking powers shows that regardless of the constitutional hurdles, Legislatures will still outsource some of their rulemaking powers.[116] The second research hypothesis, therefore, introduces the idea that there are standards and guarantees that rules made by autonomous public, private, or hybrid actors must heed in order to comply with the principles of good rulemaking in a similar manner to traditional rulemakers. This hypothesis aims to lay bare principles of good rulemaking normally protected by traditional rulemakers which has also remained largely unexplored. Evidently, the study cannot advance without a descriptive analysis of how proactive or reactive mechanisms within states have outlined these guarantees. Nevertheless, it also leaves more room for a normative approach. Normative theory helps institutions to act more effectively within the constraints that they face.[117]

1.3.2 Constitutional provisions or principles, and principles of good rulemaking

The first research hypothesis focuses on the current impact of constitutional provisions and principles on ceding rulemaking powers, while the second research hypothesis focuses on the principles of good rulemaking that must be respected by an autonomous public, private, or hybrid actor that subsequently exercises this power in the rules it creates.

The five researched countries have their own constitutions, although the UK constitution is not written or codified. The clearest source of constitutional authority can be found in the articles of these constitutions: their *provisions*. The provisions of a constitution tend to leave leeway to ulterior evolutions because they cannot anticipate the exact future relationship between the state and its citizens.[118] Constitutions provide evolving limits that have to be achieved to the fullest by governmental actors, both legally and factually.[119] In a multilevel society, it has become increasingly important to establish these boundaries.

[116] J. E. Kersell, *Parliamentary Supervision of Delegated Legislation* (Stevens & Sons 1960) 4. See for the US: e.g. Bogdan Iancu, *Legislative Delegation: The Erosion of Normative Limits in Modern Constitutionalism* (Springer-Verlag 2012) 9.

[117] David Landau, 'Report on IACL Roundtable on the "New" Separation of Powers', UK Constitutionbal Law Blog (16 June 2015) no. 126.

[118] George Letsas, 'The ECHR as a Living Instrument. Its Meaning and Legitimacy' in Andreas Follesdal, Birgit Peters, and Geir Ulfstein (eds) *Constituting Europe: The European Court of Human Rights in a National, European and Global Context*, (Cambridge University Press 2013) 107; Amrita Mukherjee, 'The ICCPR as a "living Instrument": The Death Penalty as Cruel Inhuman and Degrading Treatment' [2004] *J. Crim. L.* 507.

[119] Andreas Engels, *Die Verfassungsgarantie kommunaler Selbstverwaltung* (Mohr Siebeck 2014) 132.

If constitutional provisions do not suffice to provide a satisfactory answer, it will be necessary to resort to the concept of *constitutional principles*.[120] In this monograph, it was often necessary to dig down to the foundations of the national constitutions to test the research hypotheses. 'When the constitution is silent, the acceptability of delegation can only be ascertained by constitutional notions and concepts.'[121]

The notion of 'constitutional principles' consists of two combined, yet autonomous, concepts: principles and the constitution. As US President, Franklin D. Roosevelt, famously said during his 1937 Constitution Day Address: 'The *Constitution* of the United States was a layman's document, not a lawyer's contract … [It] was a charter of general *principles*, completely different from the "whereases" and the "parties of the first part" and the fine print which lawyers put into leases and insurance policies and instalment agreements.'[122] Constitutional principles are 'principles'. Ronald Dworkin famously resisted Hart's positivist legal views and considered both rules and principles to be part of the law. Moreover, principles are not 'all or nothing' standards.[123] They may conflict and they often do. The interpreter of the principle—often ultimately a judge—must choose the principle with the highest aggregated weight.[124] Inspired by Dworkin, the German philosopher, Robert Alexy, calls constitutional principles 'Optimierungsgebote' or 'optimization commandments'.[125] Nevertheless, constitutional principles are not solely aspirations because they are derived from the constitution itself.

Constitutional principles appear in many forms, especially when analysing and comparing them across national borders. For the purpose of this research, four constitutional principles are especially relevant because of their significance to the exercise of rulemaking powers: (1) democracy; (2) the rule of law; (3) the separation of powers; and (4) the legality principle.[126] Commendable attempts to define these principles have reached the following results.

[120] Constitutional values are also influential throughout this research. A value is 'the quality of a thing or action by virtue of which it deserves esteem or is the object of a desire'. (Édouard Dubout, 'Les règles ou principes inhérents à l'identité constitutionnelle de la France: une supra-constitutionnalité?' [2010] *Revue française de droit constitutionnel* 461). The key difference between principles and values appears to be that principles are an integral part of the law, whereas values reside at the axiological level of morals and thus on the periphery of the law (Robert Alexy, *Theorie der Grundrechte* (Suhrkamp 1985) 71–80 and 125–32); Pietro Perlingieri, 'Legal Principles and Values' [2017] *Italian LJ* 125, 126; Gary Jeffrey Jacobsohn, 'Constitutional Values and Principles' in András Sajó and Michel Rosenfeld (eds), *The Oxford Handbook of Comparative Constitutional Law* (Oxford University Press 2012) 786–7).

[121] Carl Schmitt, 'Vergleichender überblick über die neueste Entwicklung des Problems der gesetzgeberischen Ermächtigungen (Legislative Delegationen)' [1936] *ZaöRV* 252, 253.

[122] Franklin D. Roosevelt, 'Address on Constitution Day', Washington DC, 17 September 1937 (emphasis added).

[123] Ronald Dworkin, 'The Model of Rules I', Yale Law School Faculty Scholarship Series Paper 3609 (1967) 24.

[124] Scott J. Shapiro, 'The Hart–Dworkin debate: a short guide for the perplexed', Michigan Law School Working Paper No. 77 (2007) 9.

[125] Robert Alexy, *Theorie der Grundrechte* (Suhrkamp 1985) 75–6.

[126] Partly based on a statute of the Council of Europe, 5 May 1949, preamble and Article 3.

- First, democracy is 'a method through which the highest will of the state is composed by those people who are subjected to that will'.[127] More specifically, 'democracy … concerns the role of the people in their governance: the right of persons in a political community to participate meaningfully in the process by which they define and implement values, priorities and policies'.[128] The democracy principle is closely linked to both procedural democracy (in which predefined electoral procedures are respected) and substantive democracy (in which the results of elections are representative of the people). It consists of several theories, such as the sovereignty of the people, the national sovereignty, liberal democracy, and the sovereignty of Parliament. In all these theories, a central role is reserved to Parliament. However, as discussed in the problem formulation, this central role of Parliament seems to be diminishing through the outsourcing of rulemaking powers.
- Second, the rule of law implies that 'all persons and authorities within the state, whether public or private, should be bound by and entitled to the benefit of laws, publicly made, taking effect (generally) in the future and publicly administered in the courts'.[129] The rule of law is a broad notion but it can be concretized by the constitutional principles that give shape to it. This principle makes its appearance in different forms throughout various countries, through similar, yet not synonymous, concepts such as 'Rechtsstaat' or 'l'état de droit'.[130] As a constitutional principle that sets limits and safeguards on the exercise of governmental power, it is essential to the research hypotheses, especially the second one.
- Third is the principle of separation of powers, or checks and balances. The present-day idea of the separation of powers dates back to both John Locke and Charles-Louis de Secondat, Baron de La Brède et de Montesquieu.[131] However, their accounts of the separation of powers differ. Locke did not consider the courts to be one of the three branches that he distinguished.[132] Montesquieu's division between the Legislative, Executive, and Judicial branches is one that the five researched countries currently uphold to a greater or lesser degree and it has held sway in traditional constitutionalism for more than two centuries. Nevertheless, many scholars criticize the canonized

[127] Pieter Vonk, *Autocratie, aristocratie, democratie* (Van Gorcum 1951) 97.

[128] Thomas M. Franck, 'Democracy, Legitimacy and the Rule of Law: Linkages' in Norman Dorsen and Prosser Gifford (eds), *Democracy and the Rule of Law* (CQ Press 2001) 169.

[129] Tom Bingham, *The Rule of Law* (Penguin 2011) part 1, p. 8. The concept of the rule of law is very closely linked to principles such as *Rechtsstaat* or *Etat de droit*: Geranne Lautenbach, *The Concept of the Rule of Law and the European Court of Human Rights* (Oxford University Press 2013) 15. See also: Martin Krygier, 'Rule of Law' in Michel Rosenfeld and András Sajó (eds), *The Oxford Handbook of Comparative Constitutional Law* (Oxford University Press 2012) 242.

[130] Belgian Constitutional Court no. 67/2013, 16 May 2013, B.7.2.

[131] Patricia Popelier, *Democratisch regelgeven* (Intersentia 2001) 26.

[132] John Locke, *Second Treatise of Government* (Project Gutenberg 2010) ch. XII: legislative, executive, and federative.

interpretation of this tradition. First, Montesquieu never used the expression 'separation of powers'. Second, the book, *De l'esprit des lois*, in which he described a triad of powers, was descriptive of the ideal common law state structure, rather than normative for all future state structures.[133] Third, in this book what he appears to be describing resembles more a 'mutual check of powers' than a 'separation of powers'. The rejection of an absolute separation of powers has been reflected in a large number of countries across the globe.[134] Even though the separation of powers is not absolute, it still exerts an institutional and functional influence on the exercise of rulemaking powers in the researched states.

- Fourth, the legality principle. This principle aims to protect the regulated from the whims of the regulator.[135] If the rule of law can be summarized by the maxim, *sub lege* (under the law), then the legality principle can be summarized by the maxim, *per legem* (by the law).[136]Actions of the Executive must be based on a statutory foundation and must be in accordance with that basis.[137] It is possible to categorize the legality principle under the rule of law and the democracy principle. On the one hand, it structures the relationship between public actors by establishing the primary rulemaking role of the Legislature (rule of law).[138] On the other hand, the Legislature receives those powers in certain areas of competence precisely because it is democratically legitimized (democracy). The legality principle is one that flows from the rule of law in a broad sense within a democratic state with the potential to limit the transfer of powers.[139]

Democracy and the rule of law are not 'separately available'.[140] Nevertheless, they are globally accepted as being key principles of constitutional law.[141]

[133] Charles-Louis de Secondat, Baron de La Brède et de Montesquieu, *L'Esprit des Lois* (A. Belin 1817) 129.

[134] See for, amongst others, South Africa, Canada, and Ireland: Eoin Carolan, *The New Separation of Powers* (Oxford University Press 2009) 20.

[135] Ybo Buruma, 'Het legaliteitsbeginsel in een veranderende democratische rechtsstaat' in P. C. Bogert and T. Kooijmans (eds), *Over de grens van het legaliteitsbeginsel* (Goud Quint 2000) 65.

[136] Tom Duijkersloot, 'The Principle of Legality and the "Soft Law" Regulation and Supervision of Financial Markets' in Leonard F. M. Besselink, Frans Pennings, and Sacha Prechal (eds), *The Eclipse of the Legality Principle in the European Union* (Kluwer Law International 2011) 175.

[137] Jan Theunis, 'Behoorlijke wetgeving in de rechtspraak van het Grondwettelijk Hof 2007–2008' [2009] *Tijdschrift voor Wetgeving* 59–63; Frank Van Ommeren, 'Het legaliteitsbeginsel als hoeksteen van het staats- en bestuursrecht' [2010] *Ars Aequi* 6.

[138] Patricia Popelier and Koen Lemmens, *A Constitution of Belgium* (Hart Publishing 2015) 18; Jeffrey Jowell, 'The Rule of Law and its Underlying Values' in Jeffrey Jowell and Dawn Oliver, *The Changing Constitution* (Oxford University Press 2011) 17–18.

[139] Patricia Popelier, *Democratisch regelgeven* (Intersentia 2001) 258; Jeroen Van Nieuwenhove, 'Delegatie van regelgevende bevoegdheid in België' [2017] *Tijdschrift voor Wetgeving* 196.

[140] Ernst Hirsch Ballin, 'De rechtsstaat: wachten op een nieuwe dageraad' [2011] *Nederlands Juristenblad* 73; Geranne Lautenbach, *The Concept of the Rule of Law and the European Court of Human Rights* (Oxford University Press 2013) 67.

[141] Christian Tomuschat, 'Democracy and the Rule of Law' in Dinah Shelton (ed.), *The Oxford Handbook of International Human Rights Law* (Oxford University Press 2013) 469 and 473.

Internationally, they are referred to in the preamble to the ECHR and the preamble to and article 2 of the Treaty on European Union (TEU). Also, the preamble to the EU Charter of Fundamental Rights states that 'the Union ... is based on the principles of *democracy* and the *rule of law*'.[142]

At the national level, article 1 of the Norwegian Constitution, article 1 of the Czech Constitution, the preamble to and article 10 of the Spanish Constitution, articles 1 and 2 of the Swedish Constitution, and Chapter 1 of the Finnish Constitution all protect these constitutional principles. The Norwegian Constitution, for example, 'shall ensure *democracy*, a state based on the *rule of law* and human rights'.[143] Some other European countries, such as the Netherlands, also wished to introduce these constitutional principles into their constitutional preambles.[144] Emphasizing their importance, the Dutch Constitutional State Commission—mandated to examine constitutional reform—even advised against integrating any other broad-ranging values or historical facts into the constitution.[145] Many other countries' constitutions explicitly guarantee at least one of the principles. Germany, France, Italy, Canada, and Switzerland are only a few examples.[146] Despite the UK Constitution being uncodified, Lord Judge also identifies democracy and the rule of law as key UK constitutional principles.[147]

Finally, this research makes a selection from the ample lists of principles of good rulemaking to frame quality requirements of rules. This is done in order to find an answer to the second research hypothesis. I begin from the five principles of good governance in the EU Commission's White Paper, as adapted to national constitutional law and the research subject. These five EU principles of good governance are: openness, coherence, accountability, participation, and effectiveness.[148] The European Commission developed these principles in reply to the criticism that the EU would be insufficiently legitimized because of a lack of political accountability. This criticism greatly resembles the challenges that autonomous public, private, and hybrid actors face at a national level, and thus provides fertile ground for addressing this monograph's second research hypothesis. In the context of this monograph, I opted to rephrase these concepts as: principles of good rulemaking in 'transparency'; an established position within the 'hierarchy of rules', 'judicial review'; 'representativeness'; and 'efficiency and effectiveness', respectively.

[142] Emphasis added.

[143] Emphasis added.

[144] 'The Constitution guarantees democracy, the rule of law and human rights'. Dutch Government, *Memorie van toelichting algemene bepaling Grondwet*, 22 August 2014.

[145] Dutch Constitutional State Commission, *Report*, November 2010, 37.

[146] Dutch government, *Memorie van toelichting algemene bepaling Grondwet*, 22 August 2014, 5.

[147] Lord Judge, 'Ceding Power to the Executive: The Resurrection of Henry VIII', speech at King's College London (12 April 2016) 1.

[148] European Commission, 'European Governance: A White Paper', Communication of 25 July 2001, COM(2001) 428, C 287.

Here, it is sufficient to say that the *evaluation* of rules will depend on their acceptance by the people. In other words, from where do autonomous public, private, and hybrid actors derive their legitimacy? Scharpf's division between input legitimacy and output legitimacy, supplemented by the subsequent addition of throughput legitimacy, has propelled the legal and social debate on this topic for the past five decades.[149] It is possible to explain this triad through a variation on Abraham Lincoln's famous Gettysburg Address and his description of American representative democracy. Legitimacy can only be attained by the people (input legitimacy), for the people (output legitimacy), and with the people (throughput legitimacy).[150] One could say that the principle of representativeness ensures *input legitimacy*; that efficiency and effectiveness attain *output legitimacy*; and that transparency, the hierarchy of rules, and judicial review safeguard *throughput legitimacy*.

The application of these constitutional provisions, constitutional principles, and principles of good rulemaking to the outsourcing of rulemaking powers sheds new light on the conditions under which the countries researched may outsource (first research hypothesis) and how autonomous public, private, and hybrid actors should exercise their new-found powers (second research hypothesis).

1.3.3 Complementarity of both research hypotheses

One could argue that the possibility of outsourcing rulemaking powers, on the one hand, and the guarantees that have to be maintained by rulemakers, on the other, derive from one and the same obligation, which is negative or positive depending on how it is phrased. 'Do not outsource unless' would be a negative obligation, whereas 'only outsource if' would be a positive obligation. According to this argument, both formulations of obligations would be two sides of the same coin.

However, the research hypotheses prove independently significant and even complementary for three reasons.

- First, both research hypotheses focus on different entities. The first research hypothesis describes the existing constitutional limits for traditional rulemaking *actors* to outsource. The second research hypothesis concentrates on the rule of law safeguards that need to be present within all *rules*. Respect for these safeguards can involve both the obligations of traditional rulemakers when they outsource rulemaking powers and the requirements of autonomous public, private, and hybrid actors when they receive

[149] Fritz W. Scharpf, *Demokratietheorie zwischen Utopie und Anpassung* (Konstanz 1970).

[150] Vivien A. Schmidt, 'Democracy and Legitimacy in the European Union Revisited: Input, Output and "Throughput"' [2013] *Political Studies* 4.

rulemaking powers. In the transfer of powers, it would be inadequate to place limits on the principals alone if the aim is to chart the outsourcing process as a whole.[151]

- A second reason to distinguish the research hypotheses is that they target different constitutional principles. The first research hypothesis is primarily tied to the legality principle, the separation of powers, and the democracy principle, limiting the instances in which rulemaking powers can be exercised. The second research hypothesis predominantly inquires into the role of the rule of law in outsourcing rulemaking powers. The rule of law traditionally requires certain qualitative guarantees of rules. However, the rule of law does not suffice to explain all of the relevant qualitative guarantees of rules. In this research, I selected the following principles of good rulemaking: transparency, established place in the hierarchy of rules, judicial review, representativeness, and efficiency/effectiveness. To some extent, this dual approach fits the dual questions that were put before the US Supreme Court in the previously mentioned *Amtrak* case.[152] The US Supreme Court was first asked to hold the presumed private rules against articles I and II of the US Constitution, which concretize the powers of the Legislature and the Executive (legality principle, democracy principle, and separation of powers). Second, the presumed private rules were argued to transgress the Due Process Clause of the Fifth Amendment which contains the guarantee of a person's rights (of liberty) by the federal state and is the legal ground against 'delegations made to biased decision-makers' (rule of law).[153] This approximate matching of the democracy principle with the first research hypothesis and the rule of law with the second research hypothesis will be further corroborated in Chapters 4 and 5.
- Third, this distinction between the two research hypotheses themselves is not bereft of implicit support by the national institutions of the researched countries. As the Belgian Council of State Legislative Section stated in one of its advisory opinions on the WADA Code (a topic that I will revisit): 'The Legislature may not … grant binding force to rules of which the content is not yet known, given that it would thus cede from (1) its constitutional rulemaking powers in combination with (2) the guarantees that ordinarily apply when rules are created.'[154] With its choice of words, the Belgian Council of State creates room for both: (1) the prohibition to depart from its constitutionally defined powers;

[151] Guan Baoying, 'The Legal Basis of Delegation of Governmental Powers in a Changing Society' [2015] *Social Sciences in China* 108.

[152] *Department of Transport v. Association of American Railroads*, 575 US 576 (2015); Dina Mishra, 'An Executive-Power Non-Delegation Doctrine for the Private Administration of Federal Law' [2015] *Vanderbilt L. Rev.* 1513–14.

[153] Ibid., 1513.

[154] Belgian Council of State Legislative Section, Advisory opinion no. 50.723/3 of 17 January 2012, section 4. *Numbers added.*

and (2) the need to safeguard the constitutional guarantees that exist when constitutionally defined actors make rules.

In conclusion, the first research hypothesis probes the obligations of traditional rulemakers, the Legislature in particular, not to relinquish rulemaking authority. Therefore, case law and jurisprudence on delegations to the Executive are the best-developed framework to unravel the most poignant constitutional principles.[155] For the second research hypothesis, it remains crucial that autonomous public, private, and hybrid actors have a different constellation than traditional rulemakers, which will impose alternative difficulties with which to comply. Typical safeguards that are constitutionally enshrined for branches of the *Trias Politica* are often presumed to be out of reach for autonomous public, private, and hybrid actors. Their rules may at first sight seem barely accessible, unclear with respect to the hierarchy of rules, more difficult to challenge before a court of law, subject to little participation, and questionably effective. Throughout this monograph, I have evaluated whether that preconception is justified.

1.4 Methodology

The methodology chosen for this research is qualitative doctrinal desk analysis. Doctrinal research can be defined as: 'research that aims to give a systematic exposition of the principles, rules and concepts governing a particular legal field or institution and analyses the relationship between these principles, rules and concepts with a view to solving unclarities and gaps in the existing law'.[156] Moreover, the study is comparative in nature, given that it draws on the legal practice of multiple national jurisdictions. In order to establish an appropriate benchmark, five countries with their respective constitutional principles have been selected.

1.4.1 Originality 'inside the box'

Current research on the relationship between constitutional law and outsourcing cannot escape the influence of modern theories on topics such as regulation and

[155] Other authors used the same premise: e.g. Dimitri Yernault, 'Constitution, privatisations et pouvoirs spéciaux: un débat oublié' [2001] *CRISP* 70–90.

[156] Jan Smits, 'What is Legal Doctrine' in Rob van Gestel, Hans-W. Micklitz, and Edward L. Rubin (eds), *Rethinking Legal Scholarship: A Transatlantic Dialogue* (Cambridge University Press 2017) 210; Ian Dobinson and Francis Johns, 'Qualitative Legal Research' in Mike McConville and Wing Hong Chui (eds), *Research Methods for Law* (Edinburgh University Press 2007) 28; Terry Hutchinson, 'Doctrinal Research: Researching the Jury' in Dawn Watkins and Mandy Burton (eds), *Research Methods in Law* (Routledge 2013) ch. 1.

governance,[157] global administrative law/constitutionalism,[158] and transnational constitutionalism.[159] All of them share a degree of disdain for 'outdated' national and doctrinal constitutional law. They pursue a more holistic and interdisciplinary approach to contemporary legal issues and the governance of global society.[160] They especially take issue with doctrinal research due to its: (1) state-centred approach (too provincial); (2) embeddedness in positive law (too narrow); and (3) monopoly of legal scientists (not creative enough).[161] Researchers in various scientific disciplines, such as the political sciences, sociology, and political philosophy, have shown an interest in the rulemaking powers of autonomous public, private, and hybrid actors and analyse these actors from the viewpoint of their subject area. Specifically, with respect to regulation, Baldwin, Cave, and Lodge have described their interaction as an example of transdisciplinary research, with various research disciplines and traditions communicating with each other and being influenced by one another.[162]

However, I support the claims that legal scholarship has underestimated the capacities of national public law to adapt to changing societal circumstances.[163] It might actually be refreshing to think 'inside the box'[164] of legal structures as well.[165] Doctrinal legal science risks being marooned in the social sciences to which it will structurally seem inferior because of its weaker methodology. This research attempts to derive overarching insights from doctrinal constitutional law through a comparative interpretation of constitutional principles.

157 David Levi-Faur, 'Regulation and Regulatory Governance' in David Levi-Faur (ed.), *Handbook on the Politics of Regulation* (Edward Elgar 2011) 3–25.

158 Petra Dobner, 'More Law, Less Democracy? Democracy and Transnational Constitutionalism' in Petra Dobner and Martin Loughlin (eds), *The Twilight of Constitutionalism* (Oxford University Press 2010) 142.

159 Peer Zumbansen, 'Carving Out Typologies and Accounting for Differences Across Systems: Towards a Methodology of Transnational Constitutionalism' in Michel Rosenfeld and András Sajó (eds), *The Oxford Handbook of Comparative Constitutional Law* (Oxford University Press 2012) 77; Neil Walker, 'Taking Constitutionalism Beyond the State' [2008] *Political Studies* 540.

160 Catherine Durose, Jonathan Justice, and Chris Skelcher, 'Governing at Arm's Length: Eroding or Enhancing Democracy?' [2015] *Pol'y & Politics* 146.

161 Jan Smits, 'What is Legal Doctrine' in Rob van Gestel, Hans-W. Micklitz, and Edward L. Rubin (eds), *Rethinking Legal Scholarship: A Transatlantic Dialogue* (Cambridge University Press 2017) 201 and 228; Ralf Michaels, 'Transnationalizing Comparative Law' [2016] *MJ* 352–8.

162 Robert Baldwin, Martin Cave, and Martin Lodge, 'Introduction: Regulation—The Field and the Developing Agenda' in Robert Baldwin, Martin Cave, and Martin Lodge, *The Oxford Handbook of Regulation* (Oxford University Press 2010) 12.

163 Daniel Mockle, 'Le débat sur les principes et les fondaments du droit administratif global' [2012] *Cahiers de Droit* 45; Armin von Bogdandy, Philipp Dann, and Matthias Goldmann, 'Developing the Publicness of Public International Law: Towards a Legal Framework for Global Governance Activities' [2008] *German LJ* 1376; Danielle Hanna Rached, 'Doomed Aspiration of Pure Instrumentality: Global Administrative Law and Accountability' [2014] *Global Constitutionalism* 354.

164 Scott J. Shapiro, *Legality* (Harvard University Press 2011) 398.

165 *Contra* Gunther Teubner, 'Fragmented Foundations: Societal Constitutionalism Beyond the Nation State' in Petra Dobner and Martin Loughlin (eds), *The Twilight of Constitutionalism* (Oxford University Press 2010) 328.

Westerman cleverly described legal desk research as similar to rearranging a cupboard or an office. An outsider will not know or recognize the methodology utilized, as opposed to the methodology in the exact or social sciences, but he or she will notice in the results whether a clarifying methodology has been applied.[166] Too often, domestic constitutional lawyers ignore the evolutions in transnational private regulations and, too often, transnational private regulation scholars underrate the ability of traditional public law to face the challenges of a changing society. Importantly, this research recognizes the strength and flexibility of domestic constitutional law on the one hand, and of global administrative law and/or self-regulation on the other. It constitutes a bridge between these two apparently different worlds.[167] Domestic public law is equipped to recognize and even utilize bottom-up rulemaking projects.

1.4.2 Sources and structure

The obligations that rest on (European) lawmakers subsequent to outsourcing rulemaking powers can be deduced from various sources. A common denominator of four of the five researched countries (Belgium, France, Germany, and the UK) is that they have been part of two emphatically successful types of *international* cooperation: the EU[168] and the Council of Europe. Both institutions have exerted considerable pressure on their Member States to abide by the rules of their respective treaties. It could be argued that the TEU and the Treaty on the Functioning of the European Union (TFEU), in combination with the EU Charter of Fundamental Rights, constitute a European Constitution. Furthermore, the ECHR, created under the auspices of the Council of Europe, forms—if not a constitution in itself—the agglomerate of European constitutions. The unifying function of the ECHR has been further enhanced by the European Commission for Democracy through Law (also known as the Venice Commission) and its striving towards shared constitutional principles. These constitutional principles might not be explicitly phrased in the various national constitutions, although they sometimes have a constitutional or quasi-constitutional status. The keystone documents of the EU and the Council of Europe should therefore be scrutinized.

Apart from the sources within the scope of the EU or the Council of Europe, this research primarily ventures into constitutional provisions, constitutional principles, and principles of good rulemaking that are shared outside the purview of

[166] Pauline Westerman, *Outsourcing the Law* (Edward Elgar 2018) 122–3.

[167] Matthias Kötter and Gunnar Folke Schuppert, 'Applying the Rule of Law to Contexts Beyond the State' in James Silkenat, James Hickey Jr, and Peter Barenboim (eds), *The Legal Doctrines of the Rule of Law and the Legal State (Rechtsstaat)* (Springer 2014) 85.

[168] For the UK until 31 January 2020.

these treaties. These sources can be found in national constitutions but also in constitutional practices, statutes,[169] and case law.

In order to unravel the relevant constitutional principles on the outsourcing of rulemaking powers to autonomous public, private, and hybrid actors, it is imperative to point out the idiosyncrasies of the researched countries' constitutional and institutional set-ups. All constitutional principles scrutinized under the first research hypothesis, namely legality, separation of powers, and democracy, are especially sensitive to country-specific differences. The sovereignty of Parliament principle, for example, has been and remains unique to the UK system. Moreover, it is impossible to fathom the existing limits to the outsourcing of rulemaking powers in any given state without first scrutinizing the limits to the outsourcing of rulemaking powers by the Legislature to the Executive. It is possible to test the research hypotheses from a bird's-eye perspective on all of the researched countries. Especially in Chapter 3 'Comparative Delegation Framework by Constitutional Provisions', Chapter 4 'Comparative Outsourcing Limits by Constitutional Principles', and Chapter 5 'Comparative National Outsourcing Safeguards', I will thus perform integrated comparative research.

1.4.3 Country selection

In order to establish common constitutional principles and principles of good rulemaking on the outsourcing of rulemaking powers in contemporary democracies, substantial comparative studies of selected legal systems are required. Belgium, France, Germany, the UK, and the US function as the elected researched countries. This research opts to systematically compare their similarities and differences for four reasons: their lingering involvement in international treaties; their focus on constitutional principles; their approach to delegation and decentralization via historically interwoven legal cultures; and my personal capacity to consult their authentic sources.

First, the five researched countries are all experiencing strong decentralizing vectors. In particular, the presence of upward-facing vectors was an important reason for their selection. The exercise of powers within the US is influenced by international pressure, as shown by the example of ICANN. The other four researched countries even ceded part of their sovereignty to the Council of Europe and the EU.[170] These four researched countries have been parties to the EU Treaties and the ECHR.

[169] Carl Schmitt, 'Vergleichender überblick über die neueste Entwicklung des Problems der gesetzgeberischen Ermächtigungen (Legislative Delegationen)' [1936] *ZaöRV* 253.

[170] The recent exit of the UK from the EU has obviously somewhat altered that, but it does not diminish the impact that EU law had on the UK for the previous forty-six years.

- The EU has created a strong impetus towards implementation, interpretation, and coordination of various types of regulations.[171] At the same time, however, these four researched countries, as traditional European democracies, have maintained a solid focus on their constitutional identities.[172] These constitutional identities will be further researched in the analysis of the first research hypothesis.
- The ECHR is another international treaty to which these four researched countries have transferred some of their sovereignty. When Contracting States are awarded a large margin of appreciation by the ECtHR, legal cross-fertilization remains limited. This margin of appreciation may differ significantly depending on the political history of the Contracting State. Well-established democracies can undergo stricter scrutiny than transitional systems.[173] Those traditional democracies might therefore offer more defined results. For a similar reason, it is also not uncommon for the European Commission and the Organisation for Economic Co-operation and Development (OECD) to compare the 'old European states' with regard to better regulation.[174]

Second, the strong theoretical focus on constitutional principles within the selected countries is particularly interesting for this research project's principle-based approach to outsourcing rulemaking powers. The principles of legality and the separation of powers are particularly strong in France and the US. This has obviously had a significant impact on the primary locus of rulemaking power in these countries. In contrast, the Belgian Constitution testifies to a strong degree of trust between the branches of government. The separation of powers and checks and balances have never been literally enshrined in a constitutional text. Furthermore, the Executive has always been part of the Legislature in several stages of Belgian history. The Executive may design statutes, propose them, and—after Parliament has voted on the content—ratify, promulgate, and publish these statutes. The division between the Legislature and the Executive has continued to be eroded due to governments enjoying the loyal support of the majority in Parliament.[175] In

[171] Walter Van Gerven and Steven Lierman, *Beginselen van Belgisch Privaatrecht—Algemeen Deel Veertig jaar later—Privaat- en Publiekrecht in een Meergelaagd Kader van Regelgeving, Rechtsvorming en Regeltoepassing* (Kluwer 2010) 275.

[172] Tiina Randma-Liiv, 'Comparing Agencification in Central and Eastern Europe' in Koen Verhoest, Geert Bouckaert, Per Lægreid, and Sandra Van Thiel (eds), *Government agencies: Practices and Lessons in 30 Countries* (Palgrave Macmillan 2012) 337.

[173] Sergey Golubok, 'Right to Free Elections, Emerging Guarantees or Two Lawyers of Protection' [2009] *NQHR* 376.

[174] OECD, 'Better regulation in Europe—The EU 15 Project' <http://www.oecd.org/gov/regulatory-policy/better-regulation-in-europe-the-eu-15-project.htm> (last accessed May 2021); Flemish Government, *Strategisch beleidskader: kwaliteitsvolle regelgeving en administratieve vereenvoudiging* (2009–14) 3.

[175] This continuous interplay between branches explains why this research refers to 'Legislature' rather than 'Parliament'.

Germany, the trust between government institutions is also deeply engrained in the constitutional system.[176] The German Bundesverfassungsgericht strongly developed the democracy principle as enshrined in article 20 of the German Basic Law. Finally, the most important constitutional principle in the UK is parliamentary sovereignty.[177] This principle has lost some of its sting but still leaves legislative action largely unchecked. Parliamentary sovereignty implies a different take on democracy than sovereignty of the people or sovereignty of the nation.[178] In addition, apart from the sovereignty of Parliament, the rule of law is the second strongest British constitutional principle because of the nation's emphasis on freedom.[179]

The other researched countries are also familiar with an approximate type of rule of law, namely 'Rechtsstaat' (Germany), 'état de droit' (France), and 'rechtsstaat/ état de droit' (Belgium). Each one of the chosen countries has its own strongly developed priority principles which may feed this research project's fusion of constitutionally shared concepts. Many younger democracies have had less time to develop their constitutional principles. In addition, former Soviet Union countries have had a 'clean break' with the previous regime and could thus be more extensive in their constitutions. This strengthens the force of constitutional provisions but decreases the impact of constitutional principles.[180]

Third, the first research hypothesis applies and expands on the constitutional framework developed for the *outsourcing* of rulemaking powers to the Executive in the five countries.

In the first instance, despite differences in method, there is an alignment in the legal approach to delegation and the outsourcing of rulemaking powers. Both the French and the German constitutions provide for explicit provisions that attach conditions to the delegation of rulemaking powers in general. In the US, Belgium, and the UK, the existing constitutional documents provide fewer guidelines on the delegation of rulemaking powers. Especially in the UK with its common law system, the emphasis is therefore on judicial interpretation of the possibility of outsourcing rulemaking powers.[181] Moreover, Dicey has described the Belgian

[176] Daniel Halberstam, 'The Promise of Comparative Administrative Law: A Constitutional Perspective on Independent Agencies' in Susan-Rose Ackerman and Peter L. Lindseth (eds), *Comparative Administrative Law* (Edward Elgar 2010) 196.

[177] As mentioned, the UK has an uncodified constitution. The consequences of this have repercussions on the topic of outsourcing governmental powers (Catherine Donnelly, *Delegation of Governmental Power to Private Parties: A Comparative Perspective* (Oxford University Press 2007) 151).

[178] Patricia Popelier, *Democratisch regelgeven* (Intersentia 2001) 26.

[179] Albert Venn Dicey, *The Law of the Constitution* (Macmillian 1965) 189–95.

[180] Jeffrey Jowell, 'Publication Review: *The New British Constitution* (Vernon Bogdanor)' [2010] *Public Law* 627.

[181] On the importance of comparing common and civil law countries with each other, see Stephen Gardbaum, 'How do and should we compare constitutional law?', UCLA Public Law & Legal Theory Research Paper No. 16-15 (2016) 7.

Constitution as a fitting mix between the UK and French constitutional principles.[182] Hence, the mix between textually and judicially developed delegation doctrines allows this monograph to shed more light on the transfer of rulemaking powers in general. Countries which do not yet have 'a systemic body of law regulating the delegation of governmental powers' would therefore fit less naturally into the research framework.[183]

In the second instance, the benefit of juxtaposing the researched countries in this respect can also be traced back to their historically and socially comparable stance towards decentralization. Belgium shares a strong Napoleonic administrative tradition with France. According to this tradition, rulemaking authority should be centralized within the state. This tradition would leave little room for autonomous actors; definitively so, if they were private actors.[184] Nevertheless, outsourcing legislation has had a long history in France (e.g. with the *autorités administratives indépendantes*) and the US (e.g. with 'Commissions') as in the UK (e.g. with its 'Boards').[185] In Belgium, despite deontology codes and collective labour agreements, and in Germany, despite the 'Selbstverwaltungskammern', this practice has emerged more recently but has in the meantime also become widespread.[186]

Fourth, comparative legal research will always be flawed because of the figurative translation of foreign legal systems to the legal framework of the author.[187] This threshold, however, can be lowered by a certain familiarity with the legal culture of the comparative countries and the aptitude to read legal texts in their original language.[188] An ultimate, pragmatic reason for the country selection is thus my personal proficiency in Dutch, German, French, and English and my studies

[182] Albert Venn Dicey, *Introduction to the Study of the Law of the Constitution* (Liberty Fund 1915) 38–9; Emilio Santoro, 'The Rule of Law and the "Liberties of the English": The Interpretation of Albert Venn Dicey' in Pietro Costa and Danilo Zolo (eds), *The Rule of Law* (Springer 2007) 167 and Gustavo Gozzi, 'Rechsstaat and Individual Rights in German Constitutional History' in Pietro Costa and Danilo Zolo (eds), *The Rule of Law* (Springer 2007) 239.

[183] See e.g. for China:Baoying Guan, 'The Legal Basis of Delegation of Governmental Powers in a Changing Society' [2015] *Social Sciences in China* 108.

[184] Edoardo Ongaro, *Public Management Reform and Modernization* (Edward Elgar 2009) 247.

[185] Daniel Halberstam, 'The Promise of Comparative Administrative Law: A Constitutional Perspective on Independent Agencies' in Susan-Rose Ackerman and Peter L. Lindseth (eds), *Comparative Administrative Law* (Edward Elgar 2010) 185; *Carter v. Carter Coal Co.*, 298 US 311 (1936). See also *A. L. A. Schechter Poultry Corp. v. United States*, 295 US 495 (1935).

[186] Daniel Halberstam, 'The Promise of Comparative Administrative Law: A Constitutional Perspective on Independent Agencies' in Susan-Rose Ackerman and Peter L. Lindseth (eds), *Comparative Administrative Law* (Edward Elgar 2010) 185. This also applies to independent agencies, see Stéphanie De Somer, 'The creation of autonomous public bodies from a European comparative legal perspective: international impulse, national restraint and how to reconcile these trends', PhD thesis, University of Antwerp (2015) 48.

[187] See, for the importance of an objective selection, Pierre Legrand, 'Negative Comparative Law' [2016] *J. Comp. L.* 411; Guillaume Tusseau, 'Sur le métalangage du comparatiste' [2013] *Revus: J. Const. Theory & Philos. L.* 105–7 and 111.

[188] About the inherent flaws of translations, see François R. Van der Mensbrugghe, 'Traverser les états. Traduire le droit' in Pierre d'Argent, David Renders, and Marc Verdussen (eds), *Les visages de l'Etat Liber Amicorum Yves Lejeune* (Bruylant 2017) 754.

in Belgium, France, Germany, the UK, and the US at the outset of the country selection.

Despite the active choice to compare the legal systems of these five countries, telling examples and principles of other jurisdictions also surface throughout the research by means of functional comparative law.[189]

1.5 Conclusion

Tasks that were previously thought to be governmental are increasingly being exercised by actors that fall outside the traditional *Trias Politica*. Conversely, governments are increasingly integrating private agreements so that they bind citizens to a far-reaching extent. This hybrid zone of governmental action on a national level calls for comprehensive legal research.

I first framed this legal problem here in this introduction (*Chapter 1*). I have introduced the issue of the Legislature and the Executive investing their rulemaking powers in autonomous public, private, and hybrid actors. More specifically, I have explained that the research will address how rulemaking powers are utilized in five researched states. Rulemaking powers are powers to enact, accept, or establish abstract, general, and obligatory rules that have the purpose and effect of altering legal rights, duties, and relations between persons. Outsourcing, as defined earlier, may consist of three techniques: delegation to, referral to, and reception of external documents. The recipients of rulemaking powers can be autonomous public or private actors that fall outside the *Trias Politica*.

The overarching issue of this monograph is how comparative constitutional law conditions the outsourcing of rulemaking powers. Two, more specific, research hypotheses will be addressed in the following.

First, I will scrutinize the constitutional limits to the outsourcing of rulemaking powers. These limits will primarily be derived from constitutional provisions and constitutional principles. Given the fact that national constitutions do not ordinarily consider autonomous public, private, and hybrid actors as rulemakers, it is a promising first hypothesis that constitutional principles will eventually provide limits. The three main constitutional principles analysed in this regard are the legality principle, the separation of powers, and the democracy principle.

Second, if these powers are outsourced, the question arises as to which standards those rules must respect in order to comply with the safeguards that ordinarily rest on rules made by the Legislature and the Executive. For the purpose of this research, I selected five principles of good rulemaking that derive mainly from the rule of law principle: transparency, an established position within the hierarchy of

[189] See for that use, e.g. Ron Harris, 'Is it Time for Non-Euro-American Legal History?' [2016] *Am. J. Legal Hist.* 60.

rules, judicial review, representativeness, and efficiency/effectiveness. The second research hypothesis is that *all* rules need to comply with these principles.

Both research hypotheses have independent significance, since they respectively: (1) concern actors and their rules; (2) with a focus on different constitutional principles; and (3) with some basis for the distinction in positive law.

Through a comparative doctrinal analysis, the two research hypotheses are posed in the light of the constitutional systems of five specific countries. They are in alphabetical order: Belgium, Germany, France, the UK, and the US. These five countries were selected because of the influence of international law that that they all experience; because of their shared emphasis on constitutional principles; because of their strongly interwoven histories and legal systems with regard to transferring rulemaking powers; and because I could consult the primary sources in their original languages.

In *Chapter 2*, I set out the international framework on the outsourcing of rulemaking powers.

At the same time, each researched country has its own constitutional idiosyncrasies with regard to transferring rulemaking powers. In the light of these characteristics that determine the constitutional limits to the outsourcing of rulemaking powers, it proves vital that the first research hypothesis is answered via the traditional division of powers (*Chapter 3*) and its application to autonomous public, private, and hybrid actors (*Chapter 4*). The national replies to the second research hypothesis are casuistic and serve as good practices. *Chapter 5* is thus equally based on integrated comparative research.

Finally, a case study on anti-doping regulation (*Chapter 6*) and an overarching concluding *Chapter 7* will distil the most important insights from the comparative analyses of the two research hypotheses.

2
International Framework

Principles of international law on the outsourcing of rulemaking powers frame how national parliaments and executives can outsource rulemaking powers. In addition to national constitutions, constitutional principles may also emanate from international law. National jurisdictions look to international courts for principled guidance in respecting international obligations.[1]

2.1 Introduction

Chapter 2 aims to pinpoint both the limits set by international law and the requirements that international law demands with respect to the outsourcing of rulemaking power in comprehensive treaties that enshrine human rights (first and second research hypothesis). Classic free trade agreements, for example, are not sufficiently comprehensive to influence national delegation doctrines.[2] While it would be possible to analyse the impact of specific human rights, such as discrimination and privacy laws, on the outsourcing of rulemaking powers,[3] for the

[1] Elaine Mak, *Judicial Decision-Making in a Globalised World: A Comparative Analysis of the Changing Practices of the European Highest Courts* (Hart Publishing 2013) 162.

[2] More modern free trade agreements, such as the Canada–EU Trade Agreement and—if it eventually is adopted—the Transatlantic Trade and Investment Partnership, also fall outside the scope of this research.

[3] After all, dishonest innuendos have been ascribed to the outsourcing practice (Dietman Braun and Fabrizio Gilardi, *Delegation in Contemporary Democracies* (Routledge 2006) 14). Parliaments may want to avoid taking tough decisions, as they are afraid of the public backlash (Tony Prosser, 'The Powers and Accountability of Agencies and Regulators' in David Feldman (ed.), *Oxford Principles of English Law* (Oxford University Press 2009) 279). See also Belgian Council of State Legislative Section, Advisory opinion no. 50.763/3 of 17 January 2012.

Outsourcing Rulemaking Powers. Cedric Jenart, Oxford University Press. © Cedric Jenart 2022.
DOI: 10.1093/oso/9780192897831.003.0002

purpose of this book I approach the limits imposed by comprehensive (human rights) treaties from a bird's-eye perspective. Even in the absence of a concrete human rights violation, constitutional principles within human rights treaties still have the potential to restrict the ability of parliaments (and/or governments) to outsource rulemaking power. Therefore, Chapter 2 juxtaposes democracy and legality as constitutional principles that emanate from these international treaties.

(1) First, democracy is a key constitutional principle. Given the timing and context of several international treaties that focus on human rights, it is barely possible to identify attention to democracy in a single clause. The European Convention on Human Rights (ECHR), for example, contains democratic warranties in its conceptualization of a 'combative democracy',[4] while all limitations on the ECHR's relative human rights must be 'necessary in a democratic society'. However, both concerns are of limited interest to our first research hypothesis, namely to what extent the Legislature and the Executive are restricted in outsourcing rulemaking powers. First, this is because the theory of combative democracy is usually applied in order to increase the deference of national parliaments and to lift limits *not* to decrease that deference and impose limits. Second, and in the same vein, if Contracting States manage to demonstrate that the limitation they have placed on relative human rights is 'necessary in a democratic society', it allows them to supersede a human right limit through their margin of appreciation.[5]

Nevertheless, in a number of human rights treaties the democracy principle is safeguarded in a formal democracy clause[6] which may impose an obligation of democratic representation in two relevant ways.[7] First, democratic representation could boil down to the basic right to vote during regular and fair elections (*democratic representation in a strict formal sense*). Second, democratic representation may be considered present when lawmakers materialize the 'will of the people'. The latter would then bind and constrain the Legislature. This could be achieved by having a Parliament that genuinely decides on policy matters (*democratic representation in a broad formal sense*). This second definition in particular—of democratic representation in a broad formal sense—will be further expounded here

[4] Article 17 ECHR. See for a national application: Belgian Constitutional Court, no. 10/2001, 7 February 2001.

[5] Yutaka Arai-Takahashi, *The Margin of Appreciation Doctrine and the Principle of Proportionality in the Jurisprudence of the ECHR* (Intersentia 2001) 11.

[6] e.g. article 3, Protocol 1 ECHR and article 25(b) ICCPR. Johan Schaffer, 'The Co-Originality of Human Rights and Democracy in an International Order' [2015] *International Theory* 96–101.

[7] In a third way, the will of the people can also be respected by scrutinizing whether the rules substantively coincide with what the people wanted (*democratic representation in a material sense*). However, this approach is not relevant to either of the research hypotheses.

to verify whether it holds promise as a limiting principle on transferring rulemaking power from the Legislature or the Executive.[8] In doing so, the research tests the internationally shared intuition that increased power requires increased accountability.[9]

(2) Second, comprehensive human rights treaties also guarantee the legality of domestic governance in various provisions.[10] Sometimes one overarching clause stipulates that limitations on human rights must be 'provided for by law'.[11] In other instances, the distinct human rights clauses provide for their possible limitation 'by law'.[12] Later, I will explain to what extent comprehensive human rights treaties require a formal statute—or, rather, qualitative guarantees—to comply with the international principle of legality. It will become apparent that the interpretation that the courts (of human rights) researched have attributed to the international legality principle in fact more strongly resembles domestic guarantees of the rule of law than the domestic legality principle.[13] A study of the international legality principle thus underlies the shared groundwork for testing the second research hypothesis throughout this monograph.

Chapter 2 attempts to provide insights from an international perspective with respect to the two research hypotheses which can be specifically formulated here as: (1) Did the Member States subject to these human rights treaties incorporate a right to democratic representation in a broad formal sense, which would limit the possibility of outsourcing their rulemaking powers? (2) Does the international legality principle in these treaties place an obligation on autonomous public bodies and private actors to draft their rules in conformity with certain guarantees? The monograph examines these notions of democratic representation and legality in four treaty constellations that influenced the researched countries: the Inter-American Convention on Human Rights (IACHR), the International Covenant on Civil and Political Rights (ICCPR), the European Convention on Human Rights (ECHR), and the Human Rights Charter of the European Union (EU Charter).[14]

[8] Sergey Golubok, 'Right to Free Elections, Emerging Guarantees or Two Lawyers of Protection' [2009] *NQHR* 361, 390: 'There is still huge potential behind the brief wording of article 3, protocol 1 ECHR.'

[9] Claude Rochet, 'Strategic planning and reporting among French public establishments', OECD Conference Devolving and Delegating Power to More Autonomous Public Bodies and Controlling Them: The Governance of Public Agencies and Authorities (22–23 November 2001) 10–11.

[10] Bardo Fassbender, 'Der Gesetzesvorbehalt in internationalen Menschenrechtsverträgen' in Eckart Klein (ed.), *Gewaltenteilung und Menschenrechte* (Berliner Wissenschafts Verlag 2006) 99.

[11] Article 52(1) EU Charter; article 29(2) Universal Declaration on Human Rights 1948.

[12] ICCPR 1966; ECHR 1950 (see later).

[13] The legality principle is indeed accepted as part of the rule of law: Commission for Democracy through Law (Venice Commission), 'Report on the rule of law', CDL-AD(2011)003 rev., 86th plenary session (25–26 March 2011) 10.

[14] The US signed, but did not ratify, the IACHR. It has signed and ratified the ICCPR but has altered its domestic law the least of the countries researched as a result of comprehensive human rights treaties.

Monist countries have developed ways of receiving international law that differ from dualist countries. Chapter 2 will not focus on the national consequences of the international case law described; it merely develops the democracy framework and the legality framework that may have inspired national jurisdictions.

2.2 Inter-American Convention on Human Rights

A first example of how these constitutional principles might be intertwined as limits to the outsourcing of rulemaking powers can be found in the application of the IACHR. According to the Inter-American Court of Human Rights (IACtHR), the word 'law' in derogation clauses necessitates 'normative [or rulemaking] acts directed towards the general welfare, passed by a democratically elected Legislature and promulgated by the executive branch'.[15] Delegation as a type of outsourcing is permitted, continues the Court, if the exercise of powers is subject to effective control, the delegation does not impair the fundamental nature of guaranteed basic rights, and it stays within the boundaries of the national constitution.[16] All three of these conditions could become problematic in the case of outsourcing rulemaking powers. These recipients sometimes receive broad-ranging powers, are subject to decreased control, and often remain unaddressed by national constitutions.

2.3 United Nations: International Covenant on Civil and Political Rights

A second major comprehensive treaty on human rights that has the potential to limit and frame the outsourcing of rulemaking powers is the ICCPR. The ICCPR's weaker enforcement mechanism explains why domestic lawyers appear only mildly concerned with its guarantees of democratic representation and legality. Nevertheless, this UN treaty still contributes to the debate, not least because it appears to be more sceptical towards the outsourcing of rulemaking power than the other treaties discussed (e.g. the ECHR and the EU Treaties mentioned later).

[15] IACtHR, the word 'laws' in article 30 IACHR (Advisory Opinion OC-06/86, 9 May 1986) § 35; Christian Tomuschat, 'Democracy and the Rule of Law' in Dinah Shelton (ed.), *The Oxford Handbook of International Human Rights Law* (Oxford University Press 2013) 492.

[16] IACtHR, the word 'laws' in article 30 IACHR (Advisory Opinion OC-06/86, 9 May 1986) § 36.

2.3.1 First research hypothesis: democracy and the will of the people

The ICCPR also emulates the principle of democratic representation, mainly in article 25. It ensures that every citizen has the right 'to vote and to be elected at genuine periodic elections which shall be by universal and equal suffrage and shall be held by secret ballot, guaranteeing the free expression of the will of the electors'.

Article 25 ICCPR expressly grants a right to individuals; it is not just an agreement between states. Additionally, article 25 is not obstinately limited to the election of the 'Legislature' but applies to all types of democratic elections. In the ICCPR, the explicit phrasing of article 25 leans towards a broad, formal concept of democratic representation. The provision safeguards 'free expression of the will' rather than 'free expression of the opinion' as in the ECHR. The words were not chosen haphazardly as is shown by the vivid discussion about precisely where those words should be inserted into article 25.[17] The right thus seems to transcend events that take place on election day.

A system with representative elections but with unrepresentative bodies that can block decisions does not pass muster. The Human Rights Committee (HRC) made these remarks with regard to Chile, where members of the former military regime held a decisive position in the Senate and the National Security Council.[18] In its general comment to article 25, the HRC strikingly demands that 'those [elected] representatives do in fact exercise governmental power and that they are accountable through the electoral process for their exercise of that power'.[19] This comment reveals the major democratic stumbling block in relation to the outsourcing of rulemaking powers. If a Legislature outsourced all its rulemaking powers, the elected representatives would not 'in fact' exercise governmental power. They might still exercise that governmental power in theory because they could overturn their own decision, but again a complete reversal is in fact unrealistic. The law may not confer unrestricted powers on those charged with its execution.[20] Even in less extreme examples when the Legislature only outsources part of its rulemaking powers, the question remains whether the representatives are still accountable through the electoral process. When expert or bottom-up entities develop policy, politicians do not have to directly face the proverbial music. Therefore, commentators on the ICCPR proclaim that state representatives should either play a vital role in policymaking or control the body that does so.[21] Nevertheless, although the

[17] Marc Bossuyt, *Guide to the 'Travaux Preparatoires' of the International Covenant on Civil and Political Rights* (Martinus Nijhoff 1987) 475.

[18] HRC, 'Concluding observations Chile', CCPR/C/79/Add.104 (30 March 1999) § 8.

[19] HRC, 'General Comment 25', UN Doc. CCPR/C/21/Rev.1/Add.7 (1996) § 7.

[20] Sarah Joseph and Melissa Castan, *The International Covenant on Civil and Political Rights: Cases, Materials, and Commentary* (3rd edn, Oxford University Press 2014) 605.

[21] Ibid., 732–3. Nahuel Maisley, 'Right to Take Part in International Law-Making' [2017] *Eur. J. Int'l L.* 89–113.

HRC voices a lucid concern, the principle of democracy in article 25 ICCPR does not provide a 'sufficiently sophisticated mechanism' to set clear national boundaries on the outsourcing of rulemaking powers.

2.3.2 Second research hypothesis: the legality principle and guarantees of quality

The legality principle in the ICCPR is scattered throughout the various human rights that are protected. Initially, the literature was not overly interested in the legality principle of the ICCPR, apart from the potential meaning in the difference between various phrasings of the principle.[22] For example, articles 12, 19, and 21 have derogation clauses with the key requirements of being 'provided by law' or 'in conformity with the law'.

The HRC was unconvinced by a strictly formal reading of the legality principle and inquired into the quality of the law. In *Pinkney v. Canada*, Mr Pinkney, a former prison inmate, protested against the control and censorship that could be exercised on the letters he wrote in prison. There was a broad legislative provision which at first sight would have fulfilled the formal requirements of the restriction clause. The HRC gave substantive content to the limitation clause and stated that 'a legislative provision in the very general terms of this section did not, in itself provide satisfactory legal safeguards against arbitrary application'.[23] The rule had to be enacted with sufficient accessibility and foreseeability, which was highly questionable in that case. Unfortunately for him, however, Mr Pinkney lost the case on the basis of another issue: he could not prove that he was personally harmed therefore it was found that Canada had not infringed the ICCPR.

As a general rule of thumb, the quality of the law requires that legal rules restraining the exercise of fundamental rights are clear and accessible to everyone.[24] Again, the HRC leaves much to the national level in reviewing the quality of law. In *Ross v. Canada*, a teacher was sanctioned for badgering his Jewish students about their religious beliefs and for writing provocative books. The teacher felt unduly restricted in his right to freedom of religion and expression. The HRC noted that the legal basis of the Canadian decision—a broad legal framework to remove teachers—did, indeed, seem vague. Nevertheless, given the legal framework in

[22] Sarah Joseph, Jenny Schultz, and Melissa Castan, *The International Covenant on Civil and Political Rights: Cases, Materials, and Commentary* (2nd edn, Oxford University Press 2004) 525.

[23] *Pinkney v. Canada* no. 27/1977 (UN HRC, 29 October 1981) § 34.

[24] UN Sub-Commission on Prevention of Discrimination and Protection of Minorities, 'Siracusa Principles on the Limitation and Derogation of Provisions in the International Covenant on Civil and Political Rights', UN Doc. E/CN.4/1985/4, Annex (1985) § 17.

combination with the thorough review of the Canadian Supreme Court, the HRC did not deem itself fit 'to re-evaluate the findings of the Supreme Court [against the legality principle]'.[25] The restriction was provided for by law.

Perhaps the clearest limit to the outsourcing of rulemaking powers is stipulated in General Comment 34 on freedom of expression: restrictions may not be enshrined in traditional, religious, or customary law.[26] Yet again, the effect of these limitations appears minimal because any type of legal framework will exert a curative influence on the outsourcing of rulemaking powers that is based on traditional, religious, or customary law. This framework is almost always in place for the outsourcing of rulemaking powers.

In other words, whether it be by strict procedural requirements (such as demonstrating personal harm in *Pinkney*), by extensive trust in the quality of domestic laws (through court review in *Ross*), or by practically unrelated limitations (prohibition of traditional, religious, or customary restrictions in General Comment 34), the Member States enjoy a great deal of freedom under the ICCPR in the elaboration of their political agendas under the legality principle. Such a broad margin of appreciation leaves considerable leeway for outsourcing within a legal framework. Neither the democracy principle, via article 25 ICCPR, nor the legality principle in the scattered restriction clauses, seem to exclude delegation of rulemaking powers, referral to private standards, or the reception of agreements as long as they are imbedded within a clear legislative framework.

2.4 Council of Europe and the European Convention on Human Rights

The High Contracting Parties of the ECHR provided for a specific democracy clause, albeit delayed, in article 3, Protocol 1 ECHR. When we analyse the textual and interpretative history of this article, we find a broader interpretation than is usually attributed to it. Additionally, there is no single provision on the legality principle in the Convention; instead, the principle of legality is again dispersed through the Convention in limiting provisions. Here, I first clarify the potential of article 3, Protocol 1 ECHR before discussing the meaning and extent of the legality provisions of the Convention.

[25] *Ross v. Canada* no. 736/1997 (UN HRC, 18 October 2000) §§ 11.3 and 11.4.
[26] HRC, 'Comment 34', No. CCPR/C/GC/34 (11–29 July 2011) § 24.

2.4.1 First research hypothesis: democracy and the will of the people?

Article 3, Protocol 1 ECHR states that: 'The High Contracting Parties undertake to hold free elections at reasonable intervals by secret ballot, under conditions which will ensure the free expression of the opinion of the people in the choice of the legislature.'

At first glance, article 3, Protocol 1 ECHR only contains an obligation for Contracting States. However, there is more to the article than meets the eye. In the 1987 case of *Mathieu-Mohin and Clerfayt v. Belgium*, the plenary European Court of Human Rights (ECtHR) confirmed that 'the inter-State colouring of the wording of Article 3 [Protocol 1] does not reflect any difference of substance from the other substantive clauses in the Convention and Protocols'.[27] Individuals could thus invoke article 3, Protocol 1 ECHR against their state. Therefore, negative and positive obligations rest on Belgium, France, Germany, and the UK to respect, protect, and fulfil the requirement of this provision on democracy in the ECHR.[28]

Only the selection of the Legislature is protected by article 3, Protocol 1 ECHR. The provision is not applicable to referenda,[29] to the composition of parliamentary committees,[30] regional councils with limited economic competences,[31] or professional organizations.[32] Here, the question arises as to which criteria the Court applies to recognize a Legislature.[33] First, the enactor of the rule must act on a matter that is usually reserved for a Legislature. Second, the rule needs to be generally binding. Third, the competence in question has to be far-reaching. Fourth, the action of the presumed Legislature should be treated domestically as an ordinary statute. Finally, the authority to make rules should originate from a source which is hierarchically higher than an ordinary statute.[34] Ultimately, the ECtHR

[27] *Mathieu-Mohin and Clerfayt v. Belgium* no. 9267/81 (ECtHR, 2 March 1987) §§ 46–50. Sophie de Cacqueray, 'La Convention européenne des droits de l'homme et le droit des élections: entre patrimoine européen et suprématie étatique' [2016] *Constitutions*, I.B.

[28] Jean-François Akandji-Kombe, *Positive Obligations under the European Convention on Human Rights* (Council of Europe 2007) 48; Johan Vande Lanotte and Yves Haeck, *Handboek EVRM Deel II* (Intersentia 2004) 456. Although the intensity of review towards article 3, Protocol 1 is more lenient than towards articles 8–11 ECHR. *Zdanoka v. Latvia* no. 58278/00 (ECtHR, 16 March 2006) § 115; Yannick Lécuyer, *The Right to Free Elections* (Council of Europe Publishing 2014) 32.

[29] *Castelli and Others v. Italy* nos 35790/97 and 38438/97 (European Commission of Human Rights, 14 September 1998) fourth last paragraph.

[30] Tribunal Administratif de Paris 15 June 2006 (*AJDA* 2006) 1960.

[31] *Alain Malarde v. France* no. 46813/99 (ECtHR, 5 September 2005) § 1 on the law.

[32] *Warmerdam v. Netherlands* no. 9926/82 (European Commission of Human Rights, 1 March 1983) § 2 on the law.

[33] Bernadette Duarte, 'Le chef de l'État: un "corps législatif" au sens de l'article 3 du Protocole no. 1 de la Convention européenne des droits de l'homme?' (2009) 3 *Revue française de droit constitutionnel* 477, 488–95.

[34] Sergey Golubok, 'Right to Free Elections, Emerging Guarantees or Two Lawyers of Protection' [2009] *NQHR* 361, 368.

decides what is or is not a Legislature.[35] In some instances, the Court exercises this task rather pragmatically. In the case of *Matthews*, for example, the ECtHR treated the European Parliament as a Legislature even though the European Parliament did not yet have any official legislative power within the EU.[36] Ordinarily, petitioners go to great lengths to convince the Court that the enactor of a certain rule is a Legislature. National governments and their ministers are not regulated by article 3, Protocol 1 ECHR and are therefore not limited by the provision when they outsource rulemaking powers. National parliaments, however, are accepted as Legislatures and thus fall under the purview of article 3, Protocol 1 ECHR. If they outsource rulemaking powers, article 3, Protocol 1 ECHR could therefore potentially condition that transfer of rulemaking powers.

If citizens of a Contracting State rely on article 3, Protocol 1 ECHR to elect their Legislature, this begs the question of the objective of the provision. Ultimately, the High Contracting Parties aimed to 'ensure the free expression of the opinion of the people'. The aim of the ECHR's democracy clause seems different from those enshrined in other human rights treaties. Usually, the principle of democracy is tied to the will of the people, not the expression of their opinion. However, contrary to the exact wording of the text, we can assume that the Convention also protects the will of the people as a requirement for fair elections. The *travaux préparatoires* contain various references to the will of the people; however, such phrasing was omitted from the final text. The omission has been attributed to the British concern for its non-proportional electoral system.[37] The first-past-the-post electoral system, in which the winner takes all, contravenes one possible interpretation of 'the will of the people'. Nevertheless, the French representative to the consultative assembly of the ECHR, Pierre-Henri Teitgen, adamantly linked the will of the people to the democracy clause.[38] Over the years, more emphasis was put on this concept in the interpretation of the ECHR. As is the case for all ECHR rights, the interpretational theory of the covenant as a living and evolving instrument heavily influenced article 3, Protocol 1 ECHR. Over time, the Copenhagen Document[39]

[35] Gerhard Van der Schyff, 'Het concept van democratie in het EVRM' in Maurice Adams and Patricia Popelier (eds), *Recht en democratie. De democratische verbeelding in het recht* (Intersentia 2004), Johan Vande Lanotte, Geert Goedertier, Yves Haeck, Jurgen Goossens, and Tom De Pelsmaeker, *Belgisch Publiekrecht* (Die Keure 2015) 717.

[36] Sébastien Van Drooghenbroeck, *Cour européenne des droits de l'homme trois années de jurisprudence* (Bruylant 2006) 255; Bernadette Duarte, 'Le chef de l'État: un "corps législatif" au sens de l'article 3 du Protocole no. 1 de la Convention européenne des droits de l'homme?' (2009) 3 *Revue française de droit constitutionnel* 477, 491.

[37] Council of Europe, 'Preparatory work on article 3 of Protocol 1 to the European Convention on Human Rights', Strasbourg (5 September 1986) Cour (86) 36, 4 and 23.

[38] 'to hold free elections with universal suffrage and secret ballot at reasonable intervals, as to ensure that Government action and legislation is *in fact an expression of the will of the people*': Pierre-Henri Teitgen in the Committee on Legal and Administrative Questions, 'Presentation of a report', Seventeenth Sitting (7 September 1949) 1146 (emphasis added).Sergey Golubok, 'Right to Free Elections, Emerging Guarantees or Two Lawyers of Protection' [2009] *NQHR* 361, 365.

[39] Article 6 Conference on Security and Cooperation in Europe 1990; Golubok, ibid., 363.

and the case law of the ECtHR corroborated the pre-eminence of the will of the people. The Copenhagen Document declared the will of the people to be the basis of authority and legitimacy of all governments. The ECtHR emphasized, especially in *Py v. France*, that the 'will of the people' should triumph through free, fair, and regular elections.[40]

Finally, the question arises as to what enforceable impact the will of the people has on the outsourcing of rulemaking powers to autonomous public or private actors. Article 3, Protocol 1 ECHR sets formal conditions on electing a Legislature. The Convention necessitates free, regular, and secret elections. However, answering the British concerns mentioned earlier, votes do not have to be given equal substantive weight. Nevertheless, the assumption that the framers of the Convention professed only a limited, formal interpretation of democracy is not set in stone. Article 3, Protocol 1 needs to be read 'in the best interest of democracy'.[41] I argue that the provision does not merely enshrine a 'light concept' of democracy therefore its impact does not necessarily fade as soon as national citizens have had their 'freely expressed' say during elections. It would seem of little avail if free, regular, and secret elections were held only for the Legislature to outsource all or a substantial part of its powers.[42]

In the same vein, the European Commission for Democracy through Law (Venice Commission) defended a related position in its advisory opinion on cardinal laws in Hungary. Cardinal laws cannot be undone by a future parliament with a simple majority; they require a two-thirds super-majority. When the constitutional majority that backed Hungarian Prime Minister Viktor Orban also enacted a flood of policy decisions[43] in the form of cardinal laws rather than ordinary laws, the Venice Commission criticized the practice of entrenching ordinary policy in extraordinary laws under article 3, Protocol 1 ECHR:

> Elections, which, according to Article 3 of the First Protocol to the ECHR, should guarantee the 'expression of the opinion of the people in the choice of the legislator', would become meaningless if the legislator would not be able to change important aspects of the legislation that should have been enacted with a simple majority. When not only the fundamental principles but also very specific and 'detailed rules' on certain issues will be enacted in cardinal laws, the principle of democracy itself is at risk.[44]

[40] *Py v. France* no. 66289/01 (ECtHR, 11 January 2005) § 46.

[41] *Hirst v. United Kingdom* no. 74025/01 (Concurring Opinion Judge Caflisch of the ECtHR, 6 October 2005) § 3.

[42] See for a similar argument the German Federal Constitutional Court with regard to article 38 of the German Basic Law (see later), BVerfG, 2 BvR 2728/13, 2 BvR 2729/13, 2 BvR 2730/13, 2 BvR 2731/13, 2 BvE 13/13, § 81.

[43] e.g. family policy, right of nationality and police services, etc.

[44] Commission for Democracy through Law (Venice Commission), 'Opinion on the New Constitution of Hungary', 87th plenary session (17–18 June 2011) 6.

The criticism of the Venice Commission, derived from article 3, Protocol 1, is directed to the level of the national constitution itself. Every time the drafters of a revised or new constitution decide to create a new constitutional or organic provision, they should avoid cutting Parliament off from 'detailed rules' on important policy considerations.

One could argue that the outsourcing of rulemaking powers also limits the Legislature in its ability to 'change important aspects of the legislation that should have been enacted with a simple majority'.

Admittedly, statutory limits are a far lower threshold than constitutional limits. In theory, the Legislature would never be as powerless as in a system dominated by cardinal laws. The same Legislature or a subsequent one can always overturn the outsourcing decision. However, that is not always the case. The outsourcing of rulemaking power will also have legal ramifications; sometimes it might even prevent the legal exercise of legislative powers. For example, whenever a Legislature transfers rulemaking power in a treaty, the nation is legally obliged to respect its treaty obligations. On those occasions, the Legislature is even stripped of its own power to overrule the outsourced rules (without legal international repercussions). It might also be possible for a Legislature to turn back a decision of the repository of rulemaking powers, but that is often too little too late. In that event, citizens could have already been temporarily or permanently harmed by the immediate effect of an autonomous public or private actor's actions. Furthermore, in matters of democratic representation, practical limitations can lead to legal impediments. Technical or strategic considerations will hinder a Legislature in effectively reversing outsourced rulemaking powers.[45] For example, the Belgian Council of State forbade nationwide referenda even if they were merely advisory.[46] It argued that the people, organized in referenda, were not a constitutionally recognized power such as the Legislature, the Executive, or the Judiciary. Certainly, any advisory referendum could be overturned by the Legislature, but the democratic pressure on Parliament would be irresistible, making the referendum the de facto deciding event.[47] The 2016 Brexit referendum in the UK, and the ensuing legal debate on whether the royal prerogative sufficed to renounce the EU Treaties, has buttressed the way in which de facto events can influence legal status. In such instances, practical pressure overpowered the Legislature's legal discretion. In a similar vein, outsourced rules could be overturned by the Legislature, but the

[45] Daniel Halberstam, 'The Promise of Comparative Administrative Law: A Constitutional Perspective on Independent Agencies' in Susan-Rose Ackerman and Peter L. Lindseth (eds), *Comparative Administrative Law* (Edward Elgar 2010) 189.

[46] Belgian Council of State Legislative Section, Advisory opinion (Parliamentary Preparation 2000–1, Chamber of Representatives no. 792/2) 13–14. André Alen and Koen Muylle, *Handboek van het Belgisch Staatsrecht* (Kluwer 2011) 123.

[47] Belgian Council of State Legislative Section, Advisory Opinion (Parliamentary Preparation 2000–1, Chamber of Representatives no. 792/2) 15. For a critical appraisal of this argument, see Patricia Popelier, *Democratisch regelgeven* (Intersentia 2001) 266.

pressure of technical policy areas on Parliament would be irresistible, making the rule the de facto deciding event. In addition, if an autonomous public or private body has been established as an economic or moral buffer against political meddling, a new democratic majority would seem overly politicized if it overturned the outsourced rule. Often the ECtHR reiterates that the rights enshrined in the Convention cannot remain illusory.[48] The national parliament 'is vested with the legislative power and plays a primordial role in the democratic state'.[49] A constitutional democracy could thus find inherent value in having the Legislature make the de facto laws in the first place.

Finally, even if the theoretical possibility of a Legislature fully reversing its own decision to outsource rulemaking powers remains present, it would do little to safeguard the 'will of the people'. According to Van Dijk, it follows from the tenor of article 3, Protocol 1 that legislative power is also vested in the body that has been constituted as a result of free, regular, and secret elections.[50] Likewise, some authors argue that the ECtHR would thwart any national attempt to (self) rob a Legislature of all its powers.[51] The ECtHR is indeed adamant on one barrier: it is not allowed 'for a legal discretion granted to the executive to be expressed in terms of unfettered power'.[52] This is in line with the philosophy of a 'combative democracy'. The Legislature should determine the extent of the delegated power with sufficient precision.[53] This fits into an evolving understanding of democracy in international law, whereby proper elections are just one step in the quest to implement the people's will.[54]

In conclusion, article 3, Protocol 1 does not provide any strict contemporary limits on the outsourcing of rulemaking powers. According to Velu and Ergec, one cannot derive the conclusion from the sole applicability of article 3, Protocol 1 to the legislative branch of government that another branch of government could not be mandated with legislative powers.[55] Nevertheless, the wording and

[48] *Tahirov v. Azerbaijan* no. 31953/11 (ECtHR, 11 June 2015) § 67; *Podkolzina v. Latvia* no. 46726/99 (ECtHR, 9 April 2002) § 35; Sergey Golubok, 'Right to Free Elections, Emerging Guarantees or Two Lawyers of Protection' [2009] *NQHR* 361, 373.

[49] *Podkolzina v. Latvia* no. 46726/99 (ECtHR, 9 April 2002) § 35.

[50] Pieter Van Dijk, *Theory and Practice of the European Court on Human Rights* (2nd edn, Kluwer 1990) 479. From the 3rd edition onwards, the necessary 'parliamentary basis' for delegation changed to the necessary 'parliamentary mandate'. E.g. Pieter Van Dijk, *Theory and Practice of the European Court on Human Rights* (4th edn, Intersentia 2006) 913.

[51] Sian Lewis-Anthony, 'Autonomy and the Council of Europe—With Special Reference to the Application of Article 3 of the First Protocol of the European Convention on Human Rights' in Markku Suksi (ed.), *Autonomy: Applications and Implications* (Martinus Nijhoff 1998) 341.

[52] *Hasan and Chaush v. Bulgaria* no. 30985/96 (ECtHR, 26 October 2000) § 84; Patricia Popelier, 'The Court as Regulatory Watchdog. The Procedural Approach in the Case Law of the European Court of Human Rights' in Patricia Popelier, Armen Mazmanyan, and Werner Vandenbruwaene (eds), *The Role of Constitutional Courts in Multilevel Governance* (Intersentia 2012) 256.

[53] *Gillow v. United Kingdom* no. 9063/80 (ECtHR, 24 November 1986) § 51; Rusen Ergec and Jacques Velu, *Convention européenne des droits de l'homme* (Bruylant 2014) 186.

[54] Guy S. Goodwin-Gill, *Free and Fair Elections* (Inter-Parliamentary Union 2006) 167.

[55] Rusen Ergec and Jacques Velu, *Convention européenne des droits de l'homme* (Bruylant 2014) 830; Johan Vande Lanotte and Yves Haeck, *Handboek EVRM Deel II* (Intersentia 2004) 481.

jurisprudential interpretation of article 3, Protocol 1 suggest a predominant role for the Legislature in any European democracy. Delegations could prove increasingly more problematic from a democratic point of view than delegations to the Executive branch. If it becomes less and less feasible to overturn the outsourcing of rules because of political strategy and augmented technicality, the true decision-making process will be shielded from the will of the people. I would thus argue that the outsourcing of unfettered power by a Contracting State, especially without the possibility of expediently overturning that decision, could constitute a forbidden impairment of the very essence[56] of the evolved right to free, fair, and regular elections. Whenever the ECtHR decides to protect core democratic values against the outsourcing of rulemaking powers, it has—with article 3, Protocol 1 ECHR—a sharp arrow in its quiver.

2.4.2 Second research hypothesis: the legality principle and guarantees of quality

The legality principle also has the capacity to limit the transfer of rulemaking powers in Contracting States. Here, the legality principle will be approached from three angles. First, a preliminary step is taken to determine to what degree private or autonomous public actors can trigger a Contracting State's responsibility before the ECtHR when they exercise rulemaking powers. Second, the specific features of the legality test will be reiterated. Third, I develop the idea that the ECtHR sometimes disfavours rules made by private and autonomous public bodies, not because of their democratic status but because of their comparatively premature guarantees of legal certainty.

2.4.2.1 When can autonomous public and private actors trigger a Contracting State's responsibility

At the outset, a key difference between potential restrictions on outsourcing derived from democratic representation and potential restrictions on outsourcing derived from the legality principle is the applicable 'state actor'. For democratic representation, article 3, Protocol 1 ECHR restricts any protection to actions of a Legislature. The ECtHR has expanded human rights protection under the legality clause against actions of other state actors. If such an actor infringes the Convention rights of an individual, the Contracting State itself can experience the consequences of that action and can be held responsible.

There is a tension between private and autonomous public actors and the legal standing requirements of article 34 ECHR.[57] When is such an actor a state actor?

[56] *Tahirov v. Azerbaijan* no. 31953/11 (ECtHR, 11 June 2015) § 54.

[57] 'The Court may receive applications from any person, nongovernmental organization or group of individuals claiming to be the victim of a violation *by one of the High Contracting Parties* of the rights

The ECtHR stipulated several requirements of state responsibility in the case of *Van der Mussele v. Belgium*. Van der Mussele was a trainee attorney who protested against the pro bono obligations created by his bar association. The ECtHR accepted that the rules of bar associations could engage the Belgian state's responsibility under the Convention. I discern three criteria in the Court's motivation. These categories resurface in the subsequent case law of the ECtHR.

2.4.2.1.1 International obligation

First, an international obligation would have forced the Belgian state to legislate on the same topic. If the bar association had not adopted rules on free legal assistance in *Van der Mussele*, the Belgian state should have done so under article 6 ECHR.[58] Therefore, Belgium's responsibility was triggered. One of the milestone cases on positive state obligations in human rights law, *Costello Roberts v. United Kingdom*, is actually an example of a private actor that engaged state responsibility. Disciplinary sanctions in privately organized schools endangered the physical integrity and procedural rights of pupils. A state can, likewise, not absolve itself from protecting these human rights by outsourcing its educational responsibilities to private actors.[59] Equally, a state cannot evade its obligation to protect the right to physical integrity that its citizens in psychiatric private hospitals enjoy under article 8 ECHR.[60] In *Aizpurua v. Spain* and *Evaldsson v. Sweden*, labour unions made agreements on acquired property rights which the state is obligated to preserve under article 1, Protocol 1 ECHR.[61] In *Aizpurua*, a collective labour agreement changed the annual payments of an early retirement pension into a lump sum. The ECtHR considered Spain's responsibility in the labour agreement but ultimately rebuffed any violation of article 1, Protocol 1 ECHR on the merits of the case. *Evaldsson* also concerned a collective agreement that covered eight employees of the same company. Three employees were members of trade unions, while five employees were not. Under the collective agreement, the union was entitled to monitor wage payments. The employer needed to withhold a percentage of the employees' wages to compensate the trade union. Here, the Court not only considered Sweden's responsibility but also found a violation of article 1, Protocol 1 and held

set forth in the Convention or the Protocols thereto. The High Contracting Parties undertake not to hinder in any way the effective exercise of this right' (emphasis added). The extent to which non-state actors can have human rights obligations outside the state's immediate sphere of influence falls outside the scope of this research, but see e.g. Wouter Vandenhole and Mark Gibney, 'Transnational Human Rights Obligations' in Mark Gibney and Wouter Vandenhole (eds), *Litigating Transnational Human Rights Obligations* (Routledge 2014) 3–5.

[58] *Van der Mussele v. Belgium* no. 8919/80 (ECtHR, 23 November 1983) § 29.

[59] *Costello Roberts v. United Kingdom* no. 13134/87 (ECtHR, 25 March 1993) § 27.

[60] *Storck v. Germany* no. 61603/00 (ECtHR, 16 June 2005) § 103.

[61] *Aizpurua Ortiz and Others v. Spain* no. 42430/05 (ECtHR, 2 October 2010) § 49; *Evaldsson and others v. Sweden* no. 75252/01 (ECtHR, 13 February 2007) § 63; *Vörður Ólafsson v. Iceland* no. 20161/06 (ECtHR, 27 April 2010) § 35.

Sweden accountable for its infringement of the property rights of the employees without a union; in other words, by the labour union. When it would otherwise be up to the state to protect the fundamental right to a fair trial, physical integrity, or property rights because of an international human rights obligation, the state cannot escape its responsibility by outsourcing its authority.

2.4.2.1.2 Basis in domestic legislation

Second, if the rules of a private or autonomous public actor have their basis in national legislation, the Contracting State can also be held accountable. In *Van der Mussele*, for example, the Belgian state put an obligation on the bar associations, under article 455 of the Civil Procedure Code, to provide pro bono legal assistance.[62] In other words, the second criterion for a private or autonomous public actor's actions to trigger state responsibility is whether the state has incorporated that action in its legislation. Another example flows from the Polish government's consent to a foundation to compensate for prison labour during the Second World War. The ECtHR concluded: 'Once a compensation scheme is put in place by a government or *with a government's consent* … issues of compliance with article 6 § 1 or article 1 of Protocol 1 may arise.'[63] Put differently, if the state brings the actions (such as rules) of a private or autonomous public actor into a national framework, that state can be brought before the ECtHR under article 34 ECHR.

2.4.2.1.3 Connection to one of the three branches of government

Third, the task of a private or autonomous public actor could tie into one of the three branches of government. According to the ECtHR in *Van der Mussele*, the Belgian bar associations could be associated with the exercise of judicial power.[64] *Buzesco v. Romania* was another case before the ECtHR in which a professional association influenced the legal position of a citizen.[65] Mr Buzesco was a Romanian lawyer who moved to the US in 1981 and was henceforth removed from the members list of the Constanța Bar. When the Iron Curtain came down, Mr Buzesco moved back to Romania. The Constanța Bar reinstated Mr Buzesco but the Romanian Union of Lawyers (UAR) annulled the decision on the basis of the rules governing the legal profession issued by the UAR. Mr Buzesco eventually lodged a complaint in the Strasbourg Court. The ECtHR accepted that the Romanian state's responsibility was engaged because 'the UAR is legally constituted by Law no. 51/1995',[66] and is invested with administrative and rulemaking prerogatives.[67] The

[62] *Van der Mussele v. Belgium* no. 8919/80 (ECtHR, 23 November 1983) § 29.
[63] *Woś v. Poland* no. 22860/02 (ECtHR, 8 June 2006) § 72.
[64] *Van der Mussele v. Belgium* no. 8919/80 (ECtHR, 23 November 1983) § 29.
[65] *Buzescu v. Romania* no. 61302/00 (ECtHR, 24 May 2005) § 78.
[66] See also the previous title: (2) Basis in domestic law.
[67] *Buzescu v. Romania* no. 61302/00 (ECtHR, 24 May 2005) § 78. Matthias De Groot, 'Het private beheer van overheidstaken in mensenrechtelijk perspectief. De verdeling van mensenrechtelijke verantwoordelijkheid en aansprakelijkheid in het licht van het stelsel van rechtsbescherming van het EVRM' [2018] *TBP* 79.

UAR was listed as a public authority exercising a public service role. In that configuration, its functions were so intertwined with state functions that Romania could be held accountable.

Very often the outsourcing of rulemaking power will: (1) touch on internationally protected human rights; (2) have a basis in domestic law; and (3) will connect with a branch of government. Private and autonomous public actors do not automatically escape the application of human rights.[68] The more a state outsources rulemaking power, the more likely it will become that the state will be held accountable for a situation in which its *Trias Politica* only had a limited role. Equally, a private or autonomous public actor that exercises outsourced rulemaking powers can thus trigger the responsibility of a Contracting State.

Indications of this conclusion can also be found in section 6(3)(b) of the UK Human Rights Act 1998. Private bodies can be public authorities and thus must respect Convention rights if they exercise a public function. Public functions are those granted by statutory powers, that are publicly funded, or that the private body performs as a substitute for governmental action.[69] If private entities exercise public functions, they are described as hybrid bodies or functional public bodies and they need to comply with the obligations derived from the Human Rights Act 1998. Certainly, the exercise of rulemaking powers would qualify as a public function.

2.4.2.2 Safeguards when private or autonomous public actors make rules

The legality requirements that may therefore also rest on autonomous public or private actors are spread throughout the Convention in various limitation clauses. Articles 5, 7,[70] and 8–11[71] and article 2, Protocol 4 contain clear examples. Although the ECHR differs from some other human rights treaties in lacking one overarching legality limitation clause, the ECtHR interprets these provisions in an analogous manner.[72] When a human rights limitation must be provided 'by law', the Convention does not require a formal act of Parliament unless it concerns

[68] Sébastien Van Drooghenbroeck and Isabelle Hachez, 'Les limites à la privatisation déduites des droits fondamentaux' in Bruno Lombaert (ed.), *Les partenariats public-privé (P.P.P.): un défi pour le droit des services publics* (La Charte 2005) 128.

[69] *Poplar Housing and Regeneration Community Association Ltd v. Donoghue* [2002] QB 48; Clive Lewis, *Judicial Remedies in Public Law* (5th edn, Sweet & Maxwell 2014) 2-054; Stephanie Palmer, 'Privatization and Human Rights in the United Kingdom' in Tsvi Kahana and Anat Scolnicov (eds), *Boundaries of State, Boundaries of Rights* (Cambridge University Press 2016) 238–9; Paul Craig, 'Contracting Out: The Human Rights Act and the Scope of Judicial Review' [2002] *Law Quarterly Review* 551–4.

[70] Valsamis Mitsilegas, 'Article 49. Principles of Legality and Proportionality of Criminal Offences and Penalties' in Steve Peers, Tamara Hervey, Jeff Kenner, and Angela Ward (eds), *The EU Charter of Fundamental Rights* (Hart/Beck 2014) 1355.

[71] *Silver and others v. United Kingdom* nos 5947/72, 6205/73, and 7052/75 (ECtHR, 25 March 1983) § 85; *Veniamin Tymoshenko and Others v. Ukraine* no. 48408/12 (ECtHR, 2 October 2014) § 80.

[72] Berend Hovius, 'The Limitation Clauses of the European Convention on Human Rights: A Guide for the Application of Section 1 of the Charter?' (1985) 17 *Ottawa L. Rev.* 213, 225.

access to justice or domestic formal requirements.[73] Usually, this broad reading of 'law' is explained by the traditional idiosyncrasies of common law countries in the Council of Europe.[74] The entire system of *stare decisis* and precedent would be threatened if the ECtHR were to require actual acts of parliaments to impose restrictions on human rights.[75] It would attest to little respect for the common law constitutional tradition if the ECtHR reserved the realm of human rights to the Legislature alone. Nevertheless, the ECtHR not only adopted this flexible interpretation of the legality principle for common law countries but applies it equally to civil law countries.[76] In the past decades, the Court has approved enactments of lower rank than statutes, and even unwritten law, as *substantive laws* to justify human rights limitations.[77] Only when the rule was too vague or indeterminate did the ECtHR disregard it.[78] The ECtHR developed a three-pronged test to establish the legality of a rule: (1) it should be in accordance with domestic law; (2) it should be readily accessible; and (3) it should be foreseeable. The last two requirements are sometimes referred to as the 'quality of the law' which safeguards citizens from arbitrariness.[79]

2.4.2.2.1 In accordance with domestic law

The case of *Silver v. United Kingdom* explicitly introduced compliance with domestic law as a necessary initial step.[80] 'Step zero' embodies a '*Patere legem quam ipse fecisti*' principle: one has to abide by self-made rules. Deference to the domestic level is the zenith of this test.[81] Originally, some commentators on the ECHR were convinced that Contracting States need only avoid blatant infringements of domestic law to survive the legality test.[82] Eventually, the ECtHR rejected

[73] *Coëme and others v. Belgium*, nos 32492/96, 32547/96, 32548/96, 33209/96, and 33210/96 (ECtHR, 22 June 2000) § 98. Christoph Grabenwarter, *European Convention on Human Rights* (Beck/Hart 2014) 263; Christian Tomuschat, 'Democracy and the Rule of Law' in Dinah Shelton (ed.), *The Oxford Handbook of International Human Rights Law* (Oxford University Press 2013) 492–3; Patricia Popelier, 'La loi aujourd'hui (le principe de légalité)' in Philippe Gérard, François Ost, Michel Van de Kerchove, Isabelle Hachez, Yves Cartuyvels, and Hugues Dumont (eds), *Les sources du droit revisitées tôme II* (Anthemis 2012) § 19.

[74] Rusen Ergec and Jacques Velu, *Convention européenne des droits de l'homme* (Bruylant 2014) 183.

[75] Geranne Lautenbach, *The Concept of the Rule of Law and the European Court of Human Rights* (Oxford University Press 2013) 85.

[76] *Kruslin v. France* no. 11801/85 (ECtHR, 24 April 1990) § 29.

[77] Ibid.; *Kopp v. Switzerland* no. 23224/94 (ECtHR, 25 March 1998) § 59.

[78] Christoph Grabenwarter, *European Convention on Human Rights* (Beck/Hart 2014) 263. But some degree of vagueness is always to be expected: *Michaud v. France* no. 12323/11 (ECtHR, 6 December 2012) § 94.

[79] Berend Hovius, 'The Limitation Clauses of the European Convention on Human Rights: A Guide for the Application of Section 1 of the Charter?' (1985) 17 *Ottawa L. Rev.* 213, 236.

[80] *Silver and others v. United Kingdom* nos 5947/72, 6205/73, and 7052/75 (ECtHR, 25 March 1983) § 86.

[81] Berend Hovius, 'The Limitation Clauses of the European Convention on Human Rights: A Guide for the Application of Section 1 of the Charter?' (1985) 17 *Ottawa L. Rev.* 213, 225.

[82] Richard Clayton and Hugh Tomlinson, *The Law of Human Rights* (2nd edn, Oxford University Press 2009) 382; Rusen Ergec and Jacques Velu, *Convention européenne des droits de l'homme* (Bruylant 2014) 183.

that interpretation. Nevertheless, authors criticize the deference that the ECtHR grants to the Contracting States with this first criterion.[83] Often the ECtHR will validate the domestic law on which the limitation rests.[84] The ECtHR fears that too much attention to domestic affairs would discourage Contracting States from further integrating human rights. Nevertheless, in a number of cases the ECtHR has found a violation if there is no domestic law that governs the matter. In *Halford v. United Kingdom*, for example, the Court noted that a domestic UK Act did not apply to interception of telephone calls and that no other provision filled that gap. A violation of the legality principle in article 8 ECHR was thus the only possible outcome.[85]

2.4.2.2.2 Quality of the law

The milestone case on the legality condition of human rights limitations is *Sunday Times v. United Kingdom*.[86] *The Sunday Times* had held a 'trial by newspaper' in a product liability case concerning deformed babies. The Court of Appeal issued an injunction (which was confirmed by the then House of Lords) to prevent the media from publishing details about thalidomide children in relation to actions which were pending or imminent against the drug manufacturer. According to the applicant, the law of contempt of court was excessively vague and uncertain. The ECtHR ruled that the legality requirement was fulfilled.[87] It did so on the basis of two key arguments:[88] the law on contempt of court was sufficiently accessible and foreseeable.

First, citizens must be aware that a rule is in place. *The Sunday Times* had an indication of the 'pressure principle' that gives content to contempt of court.[89] Its lawyer even referred to the principle in the domestic proceedings. Accessibility is rarely the stumbling block for domestic rules because most of the rules reviewed by the Commission and the Court have been adequately published.[90] In general,

[83] Anika Logemann, *Grenzen der Menschenrechte in Demokratischen Gesellschaften, Die demokratische Gesellschaft als Determinante der Grundrechtsschranken der Europäischen Menschenrechtskonvention* (Nomos 2004) 308; Geranne Lautenbach, *The Concept of the Rule of Law and the European Court of Human Rights* (Oxford University Press 2013) 123.

[84] e.g. *Sanoma Uitgevers BV v. Netherlands* no. 38224/03 (ECtHR, 14 September 2010) § 84; *De Wilde, Ooms and Versyp v. Belgium* nos 2832/66, 2835/66, and 2899/66 (ECtHR, 18 June 1971) § 93.

[85] *Halford v. United Kingdom* no. 20605/92 (ECtHR, 25 June 1997) § 50.

[86] *Sunday Times v. United Kingdom* no. 6538/74 (ECtHR, 26 April 1979) § 49.

[87] The UK was eventually held responsible for a breach of article 10 ECHR since it had limited the freedom of expression disproportionally.

[88] Geranne Lautenbach recognizes 'judicial safeguards' as a third argument in later case law, but admits that the ECtHR sometimes derives that argument from accessibility and foreseeability and does not consistently refer to it: *The Concept of the Rule of Law and the European Court of Human Rights* (Oxford University Press 2013) 101–2.

[89] The pressure principle means that public pressure is developed to force the counterparty into a settlement.

[90] Berend Hovius, 'The Limitation Clauses of the European Convention on Human Rights: A Guide for the Application of Section 1 of the Charter?' (1985) 17 *Ottawa L. Rev.* 213, 228; Geranne Lautenbach, *The Concept of the Rule of Law and the European Court of Human Rights* (Oxford University Press 2013) 87.

publication appears to be the key element for accessibility because if rulemaking documents are not published, they cannot form the legal basis for authorities' actions.[91] Unpublished non-statutory directives have been held to be insufficiently accessible.[92] The Belgian Court of Cassation also viewed the deontology code of the professional order of pharmacists sufficiently 'precise and accessible' in the light of the ECHR without explicitly investigating how it had been published.[93] In fact, even the ECtHR does not consider that its task is to decide which publication method a Contracting State should apply.[94] In fact, publication in a financial bulletin (other than the official gazette) that is sold to subscribers in retail units of a private company connected to the government may suffice.[95] In exceptional cases, such as extraordinary technicality or the publication of related documents, the rule might not even be published at all.[96]

Second, in addition to being accessible, a rule also needs to be formulated with sufficient precision to allow citizens to adapt their conduct. Citizens should be capable of foreseeing the consequences of their actions.[97] Whenever a rule is too vague, it either takes the citizen by surprise or has a chilling effect on their fundamental freedoms.[98] Initially, the European Commission of Human Rights and the ECtHR rarely applied this requirement.[99] However, it has since become essential for the general quality of the law that it is enacted and applied in a foreseeable manner.[100] The ECtHR will scrutinize the precision of the law with due regard to the specific circumstances, the content of the rule, the legal domain, and the people to whom the rule is directed.[101] Moreover, the manner in which individuals and enterprises keep abreast of rulemaking changes influences compliance with the principle of legal certainty.[102] Clarifying the law is not the monopoly of

[91] *Silver and others v. United Kingdom* nos 5947/72, 6205/73, and 7052/75 (ECtHR, 25 March 1983) § 87; Berend Hovius, 'The Limitation Clauses of the European Convention on Human Rights: A Guide for the Application of Section 1 of the Charter?' (1985) 17 *Ottawa L. Rev.* 213, 233.

[92] Richard Clayton and Hugh Tomlinson, *The Law of Human Rights* (2nd edn, Oxford University Press 2009) 387.

[93] Belgian Court of Cassation 27 September 2012, *D. J. v. Président du conseil national de l'Ordre des pharmaciens*, D.11.0013.F, § 2.

[94] *Spacek SRO v. Czech Republic* no. 26449/95 (ECtHR, 9 November 1999) § 57.

[95] Ibid., § 58.

[96] *Groppera Radio AG and Others v. Switzerland* no. 10890/84 (ECtHR, 28 March 1990) § 68.

[97] *Silver and others v. United Kingdom* nos 5947/72, 6205/73, and 7052/75 (ECtHR, 25 March 1983) § 88.

[98] Olivier De Schutter, *International Human Rights Law: Cases, Materials and Commentary* (Cambridge University Press 2014) 345.

[99] Berend Hovius, 'The Limitation Clauses of the European Convention on Human Rights: A Guide for the Application of Section 1 of the Charter?' (1985) 17 *Ottawa L. Rev.* 213, 230.

[100] *RTBF v. Belgium* no. 50084/06 (ECtHR, 29 March 2011) § 116. *Sanoma Uitgevers BV v. Netherlands* no. 38224/03 (ECtHR, 14 September 2010) § 98.

[101] *Michaud v. France* no. 12323/11 (ECtHR, 6 December 2012) § 97; Patricia Popelier, 'Behoorlijke wetgeving in de rechtspraak van het Europese Hof voor de Rechten van de Mens (2012–2013)' [2014] TvW 104, § 20.

[102] Patricia Popelier, 'Legal Certainty and the European Courts' in Mark Fenwick, Mathias Siems, and Stefan Wrbka (eds), *The Shifting Meaning of Legal Certainty in Comparative and Transnational Law* (Hart 2017) 50.

majoritarian state actors. Courts—and even academics—can also inform the expectations of citizens.[103]

2.4.2.3 Legal certainty protection by traditional v. non-traditional rulemakers

Finally, the question arises as to whether the application of the legality test on the outsourcing of rulemaking powers leads to a preference for rules being enacted by the Legislature or the Executive over autonomous public or private actors. I have already pointed out the lenient legality approach of the ECtHR towards enactments of a lower rank than statutes.

Similarly, the Court readily accepts *delegated* legislation that limits human rights.[104] This was recently confirmed in the *FNASS* case, where the AFLD—a French anti-doping regulator—had drafted rules on how athletes could be checked for doping violations. The rules made by this autonomous public body were swiftly considered to have been 'provided by law'.[105] Moreover, the Court expressly accepts 'regulatory measures taken by professional regulatory bodies under independent rulemaking powers delegated to them by Parliament' as being prescribed by law.[106] The Contracting Parties thus enjoy a sizeable margin of appreciation.

In its 2020 advisory opinion—only the second under Protocol 16 ECHR—concerning the use of the 'blanket reference' or 'legislation by reference' technique in the definition of a criminal offence, the ECtHR gave guidance on the quality of law requirements for the *referral* technique. It did so in the context of criminal law; however, the quality of law requirement is similar throughout the ECHR.[107] After applying the general principles of the quality of law review to referenced legislation, the ECtHR stated that 'the referenced provisions may not extend the scope of criminalisation as set out by the referencing provision'.[108] This consideration appears to leave little room for dynamic referrals—whereby the referenced provision

[103] *Kopp v. Switzerland* no. 23224/94 (ECtHR, 25 March 1998) § 59; *Kruslin v. France* no. 11801/85 (ECtHR, 24 April 1990) § 29.

[104] *Peck v. United Kingdom* no. 44647/98 (ECtHR, 28 January 2003) §§ 66–7; Berend Hovius, 'The Limitation Clauses of the European Convention on Human Rights: A Guide for the Application of Section 1 of the Charter?' (1985) 17 *Ottawa L. Rev.* 213, 234.

[105] *Fédération Nationale des Associations et des Syndicats Sportifs (FNASS) ea v. France* nos 48151/11 and 77769/13 (ECtHR, 18 January 2018) §§ 160–2. Dellaux criticized this part of the judgment because—in his view—the ECtHR accepted that the human rights limitation was prescribed by law because the AFLD rule was in conformity with the World Anti-Doping Code (WADC) (Julien Dellaux, 'La réglementation de la lutte contre le dopage à l'aune de la jurisprudence de la Cour européenne des droits de l'homme, ou quand la pratique sportive justifie des restrictions importantes au droit au respect de la vie privée' [2018] *Revue trimestrielle des droits de l'homme* 889). However, the ECtHR only establishes that the rule was 'in conformity with the provisions of the WADC' in a short *obiter dictum*. As a consequence, the ECtHR also recognized the delegation of rulemaking powers to the AFLD as an entity of the French state.

[106] *Sanoma Uitgevers BV v. Netherlands* no. 38224/03 (ECtHR, 14 September 2010) § 83.

[107] *Del Río Prada v. Spanje* no. 42750/09 (ECtHR, 21 October 2013) § 91.

[108] Advisory opinion P16-2019-001 (ECtHR, 29 May 2020) § 74.

can inherently extend the scope of the referencing provision—unless sufficient political control can be exercised on the referenced standard.

Outsourcing through the *reception* of professional conduct rules and collective labour agreements should also be read with a 'reasonable approach in assessing statutory precision'.[109]

The ECtHR does not formally apply a different tier of scrutiny for rules made by state actors and rules made by non-state actors because—as it stated in *Verein gegen Tierfabriken v. Switzerland*—it does not meddle in the means that states utilize to perform their treaty obligations.[110]

Nevertheless, a historical analysis of the broad legality interpretation within Europe shows that the Legislature, the Executive, and the Judiciary, as the three branches of government, were the powers that the ECtHR originally envisioned to justly limit human rights. The emergence of other actors with rulemaking powers has posed new problems for some rules in achieving the necessary degree of legal certainty. The ECtHR has, on several occasions, established the principle of legal certainty.[111] However, the Court can encounter more difficulty in relation to the interference of such newer types of rules with a basic right because their accessibility and foreseeability are not as institutionalized and thus may not be of the same quality as the rules made by traditional rulemakers. As a result, the Court sometimes seems to prefer that not only is a legal framework in place to limit a human right but also that this framework consists of statutory laws or state regulations.

Three cases exemplify this evolution. First, in *Gross v. Switzerland*, the ECtHR criticized ethical guidelines issued by an NGO which did not have the formal quality of law. The Court required 'state-approved guidelines' about the circumstances in which medical practitioners could issue prescriptions to end the life of patients. The majority opinion was aware of the controversy that could arise within state Legislatures, but 'these difficulties are inherent in any democratic process and cannot absolve the authorities from fulfilling their task therein'.[112] Second, in *Copland v. United Kingdom*, a university had monitored the internet use, emails, and telephone conversations of Lynette Copland, one of its employees. A complaint was filed under article 8 ECHR. The ECtHR established a limitation of article 8 ECHR but it did not even reach the level of the legitimacy test or the proportionality test. According to the Court, a national statute creating public bodies—that could take all expedient and necessary measures regarding education—was a limitation not 'in accordance with the *law*'.[113] Finally, in *Shimovolos v. Russia*,

[109] *Oleksandr Volkov v. Ukraine* no. 21722/11 (ECtHR, 9 January 2013) § 178; *Barthold v. Germany* no. 8734/79 (ECtHR, 25 March 1985) § 46; Filip Dorssemont, Klaus Lörcher, and Isabelle Schömann (eds), *The European Convention on Human Rights and the Employment Relationship* (Hart 2013) 390.

[110] *Verein gegen Tierfabriken v. Switzerland* no. 24699/94 (ECtHR, 28 June 2001) § 78.

[111] e.g. in the recent Grand Chamber case *Lupeni Greek Catholic Parish and Others v. Romania* no.76943/11 (ECtHR, 29 November 2016) § 108.

[112] *Gross v. Switzerland* no. 67810/10 (ECtHR, 14 May 2013) § 66.

[113] *Copland v. United Kingdom* no. 62617/00 (ECtHR, 3 April 2007, §§ 47–9 (emphasis added).

the Court stated that for secret surveillance and data retention cases specifically, 'the following minimum safeguards should be set out in *statute law* [sic] to avoid abuses: the nature, scope and duration of the possible measures, the grounds required for ordering them, the authorities competent to permit, carry out and supervise them, and the kind of remedy provided by the national law'.[114]

This inclination towards rules made by the Legislature or the Executive materializes in the margin of appreciation that the ECtHR grants to Member States. Recent case law has assigned a specific function to state (statutory) law. In *Animal Defenders v. United Kingdom*, a commercial supporting primate's rights was declined by the Broadcast Advertising Clearance Centre because it was—contrary to section 321(2) of the Communications Act 2003—'wholly or mainly of a political nature'. The Court declared the Act in compliance with article 10 ECHR (freedom of speech). It opined that the '*quality of the parliamentary and judicial review* of the necessity of the measure is of particular importance in this respect, including to the operation of the relevant margin of appreciation'.[115] This judgment substantively contradicted previous case law, had only a narrow majority, and was criticized in legal scholarship.[116] Nevertheless, the opinion formally confirmed the Court's dedication to 'procedural rationality'. The Court refers to famous cases such as *Hirst v. United Kingdom* (prisoner's right to vote), *Evans v. United Kingdom* (consent withdrawal for storage of and use of embryos), and *SAS v. France* (the 'burqa prohibition') in which the thorough process employed by the national parliaments was an important element to be weighed for or against human rights violations.[117] The ECtHR increasingly scrutinizes the committee and plenary sessions of parliaments for elements of democratic representation and domestic expertise to establish the breadth of a state's margin of appreciation.[118] Generally, the better these parliamentary processes, the greater the margin of appreciation. The purpose of procedural rationality for this research lies not in the precise extent of the margin of appreciation for the national versus the international level. Rather, it lies in the fact that the ECtHR's scrutiny may evolve following the parliamentary procedure. The ECtHR has expressly mentioned 'democratic representation' and its vital role

114 *Shimovolos v. Russia* no. 30194/09 (ECtHR, 21 June 2011) §§ 67–8 (emphasis added). This case law has not been repeated since then. Most recently: *Big Brother Watch ao v. United Kingdom* nos. 58170/13, 62322/14, and 24960/15 (ECtHR, 25 May 2021) §§ 332–3. See on the special treatment of wiretapping and surveillance cases: Christian Tomuschat, 'Democracy and the Rule of Law' in Dinah Shelton (ed.), *The Oxford Handbook of International Human Rights Law* (Oxford University Press 2013) 493.

115 *Animal Defenders International v. United Kingdom* no. 48876/08 (ECtHR, 22 April 2013) § 108 (emphasis added).

116 Tom Lewis, '*Animal Defenders International v United Kingdom*: Sensible Dialogue or a Bad Case of Strasbourg Jitters?' [2014] *Modern Law Review* 467–9. See also Patricia Popelier and Catherine Van De Heyning, 'Subsidiarity Post-Brighton: Procedural Rationality as Answer?' [2017] *Leiden J. Int'l L.* 18–20.

117 Matthew Saul, 'The European Court of Human Rights' Margin of Appreciation and the Processes of National Parliaments' [2015] Human Rights Law Review 754–7.

118 Ibid., 762–6.

'in matters of general policy'.[119] Autonomous public or private actors do not go through a parliamentary process to enact their rules. Moreover, their degree of democratic representation and expertise is very diverse and—at times—doubtful. Such actors may thus encounter an inherent disadvantage, as opposed to national parliaments, when their rules are subjected to the procedural rationality review of the ECtHR.

Examples of the ECtHR's case law demonstrate that the legality principle also offers a modest theoretical and practical opportunity to exercise increased scrutiny on outsourced rulemaking powers. Moreover, the ECtHR will always look for both substantive and procedural safeguards against discretionary power (in the repository of outsourced rulemaking powers).[120] In this regard, substantive safeguards are inherent in the test of the quality of the law. Procedural safeguards take the form of evidence and consultations but also adversarial proceedings before an independent body which may create rules as a result of the transfer of powers.

2.5 European Union and the Charter of Fundamental Rights

The fourth influential set of international agreements with potential reverberations for the outsourcing of rulemaking powers are the EU Treaties and the EU Charter.

Articles 290 and 291 of the Treaty on the Functioning of the European Union (TFEU) require that the lawmaking institutions set the 'objectives, content, scope and duration' and other controlling 'conditions' respectively when they delegate non-essential aspects of legislative powers in relation to delegated acts.[121] They also introduce 'mechanisms for control' when they delegate executive powers in relation to implementing acts. All these limits refer to some kind of democratic supervision on the traditional delegation of rulemaking powers to the European Commission. Articles 290 and 291 do not mention many EU bodies, such as European regulatory agencies,[122] as recipients of rulemaking powers. Until 2010, it was sometimes believed that there were no European regulatory agencies with

[119] *SAS v. France* no. 43835/11 (ECtHR, 1 July 2014) § 129; Patricia Popelier and Catherine Van De Heyning, 'Subsidiarity Post-Brighton: Procedural Rationality as Answer?' [2017] *Leiden J. Int'l L.* 9.

[120] *Oleksandr Volkov v. Ukraine* no. 21722/11 (ECtHR, 9 January 2013) § 181; *Hasan and Chaush v. Bulgaria* no. 30985/96 (ECtHR, 26 October 2000) § 85; Patricia Popelier, 'Behoorlijke wetgeving in de rechtspraak van het Europese Hof voor de Rechten van de Mens (2012-2013)' [2014] TvW 104, § 15.

[121] The ECJ distinguishes between the essentialness test (i.e. 'non essential') and the preciseness test (i.e. with determined 'objectives, content, scope and duration'). Case C-696/15 P *Czech Republic v. Commission* ECLI:EU:C:2017:595, §§ 81–2; Merijn Chamon, 'Limits to Delegation under Article 290 TFEU: The Specificity and Essentiality Requirements Put to the Test' [2018] MJ 11–12.

[122] The European Commission defined a European Regulatory Agency as 'an independent legal entity created by the legislator in order to help regulate a particular sector at European level and help implement a particular Community policy': European Commission, 'Draft Interinstitutional Agreement on the operating framework for the European regulatory agencies', COM(2005) 59 final, 5.

rulemaking powers.[123] However, in the 2014 *ESMA* case, the rulemaking powers of a European public body were put before the European Court of Justice (ECJ).[124] The European Securities and Markets Authority (ESMA) is one of the financial agencies that the EU established in 2012 in the aftermath of the economic and financial crisis. The ESMA can 'in exceptional circumstances' adopt 'measures' to prohibit natural or legal persons from short-selling (i.e. selling a security that is not owned by the seller).[125] The UK argued that this amounted to the transfer of 'quasi-legislative measures of general application'.[126] The ECJ eventually accepted that 'a possibility exists' of delegating rulemaking powers to autonomous public bodies regardless of the framework of articles 290 and 291 TFEU.[127] Despite autonomous public actors not being mentioned as recipients of rulemaking powers in the 'constitutional' document, the highest EU judicial body thus deems them suitable to exercise rulemaking powers as a whole.

Prior to this, the ECJ had already recognized that governmental powers could be delegated to external private actors in the infamous 1958 *Meroni* case. In that case, the High Authority (today the European Commission) had entrusted the ferrous scrap equalization bodies (two companies under Belgian private law) with making financial arrangements on ferrous scrap equalization.[128] Although the ECJ would eventually disallow this delegation of powers, it declared that 'the possibility of entrusting to bodies established under private law—having a distinct legal personality and possessing powers of their own—the task of putting into effect certain "financial arrangements common to several undertakings" ... cannot be excluded'.[129] The test that the *ESMA* case introduces is different to that applied by the ECJ in the *Meroni* case. European scholarship has derived at least three main conclusions from *Meroni*: (1) to begin with, discretionary or non-executive powers may not be delegated; (2) furthermore, the delegation should flow from an explicit act; and (3) finally, the delegator cannot delegate more powers than it holds itself by evading ordinary institutional procedures such as a duty to state reasons, to publish

[123] Stefan Griller and Andreas Orator, 'Everything Under Control? The "Way Forward" for European Agencies in the Footsteps of the Meroni Doctrine' [2010] E. L. Rev. 35.

[124] Case C-270/12 *United Kingdom v. European Parliament and the Council of the European Union* ECLI:EU:C:2014:18; Megi Medzmariashvili, 'Delegation of Rulemaking Power to European Standards Organizations: Reconsidered' [2017] *LIEI* 359; Paul Craig, 'Comitology, Rulemaking, and the Lisbon Settlement Tensions and Strains' in Carl Fredrik Bergström and Dominique Ritleng (eds), *Rulemaking by the European Commission: The New System for Delegation of Powers* (Oxford University Press 2016) 178–9.

[125] Article 28 EU Regulation 236/2012.

[126] Case C-270/12 *United Kingdom v. European Parliament and the Council of the European Union* ECLI:EU:C:2014:18, § 56. Linda Senden, 'The Constitutional Fit of European Standardization Put to the Test' [2017] *LIEI* 347.

[127] Case C-270/12 *United Kingdom v. European Parliament and the Council of the European Union* ECLI:EU:C:2014:18, § 79.

[128] Joined Cases C-9 and 10/56 *Meroni v. High Authority* [1957/8] ECR 133; Koen Lenaerts, 'Regulating the Regulatory Process: "Delegation of Powers" in the European Community' [1993] *E. L. Rev.* 40–2.

[129] Joined Cases C-9 and 10/56 *Meroni v. High Authority* [1957/8] ECR 151.

a yearly report and other data, and to be subjected to review by the ECJ.[130] The *ESMA* case strongly nuanced the first condition because: (1) ESMA's competences are substantial;[131] in addition, the ECJ in *ESMA* put forward a test that resembles *Meroni* by checking whether the delegated powers (2) 'are precisely delineated and' (3) 'amenable to judicial review in the light of the objectives established by the delegating authority'.[132] Some legal scholars also defend the position that the European Parliament, European Commission, or the Council should maintain a strong grip on safeguarding representativeness by, for example, influencing the appointment of directors and senior officials of EU agencies.[133] In *ESMA*'s dual test, one can recognize the concern from the point of view of both the 'constitutional limits' (precise delineation by lawmaking EU institutions—first research hypothesis) and the 'internal safeguards' (such as transparency, representativeness, and judicial review—second research hypothesis).[134]

The EU is thus familiar with the issue of outsourcing rulemaking powers to autonomous public actors and to private actors within the EU institutions. From the milestone cases of *Meroni* and *ESMA*, it is possible to derive the conclusion that the transfer of rulemaking powers is permitted as long as it is sufficiently controlled by politically accountable actors and it upholds rulemaking safeguards. Next, I describe the evolution that occurred in the EU to enable more outsourcing despite the democracy principle. Subsequently, the limits that the Charter sets on outsourcing will be discussed in the light of the legality principle.

2.5.1 First research hypothesis: democracy and EU impetus on outsourcing

The EU has exerted an undeniable influence on the existence of national regulators, especially for network industries, within Member States. The push for independent regulators without political influence was especially responsible for creating a strong branch of autonomous public bodies.[135] From the outset, the EU Charter demonstrates that national autonomous public or private actors have a specific role and status.

[130] Marta Simoncini, *Administrative Regulation Beyond the Non-Delegation Doctrine* (Hart 2018) 26–7; Joined Cases C-9 and 10/56 *Meroni v. High Authority* [1957/8] ECR 149.

[131] Megi Medzmariashvili, 'Delegation of Rulemaking Power to European Standards Organizations: Reconsidered' [2017] *LIEI* 366.

[132] Case C 270/12 *United Kingdom v. European Parliament and the Council of the European Union* ECLI:EU:C:2014:18, § 53.

[133] Stefan Griller and Andreas Orator, 'Everything Under Control? The "Way Forward" for European Agencies in the Footsteps of the *Meroni* Doctrine' [2010] *E. L. Rev.* 29.

[134] Supporting this thesis in the *Meroni* doctrine: Griller and Orator, ibid., 3–4 and 28–9.

[135] Koen Muylle, 'Het grondwettelijke delegatieverbod en het EU recht' in André Alen and Jan Theunis (eds), *Leuvense staatsrechtelijke standpunten* (3rd vol., die Keure 2012) 332.

Article 8 of the Charter states that 'Everyone has the right to the protection of personal data concerning him or her. . . . Compliance with these rules shall be subject to control by *an independent authority*.' The ECJ monitors this obligation in the Charter[136] and has indeed rendered some interesting judgments on national data protection supervisory authorities set up by the General Data Protection Regulation and its predecessor Directive 95/46/EC. These authorities 'shall act with *complete independence* in exercising the functions entrusted to them'.[137] In *Commission v. Austria*, the ECJ unequivocally declared that 'those independent authorities must remain free from any external influence, direct or indirect, which is liable to have an effect on their decisions'.[138]

Germany has vehemently defended its system of governmental supervision of regulatory authorities, deriving its main line of argument from the preambles and article 2 in conjunction with article 6(3) TEU on the democracy principle. The EU is founded on the values of democracy and human rights which are interpreted in line with the constitutional traditions of the Member States. Germany, being domestically sensitive to the democracy principle, deemed political monitoring of the legality or substance of agency decisions absolutely necessary.[139] The ECJ ultimately applies a flexible interpretation of the democracy principle. National parliaments can still *influence* the independent authorities by outlining the delegated powers, appointing the officials leading such authorities, and requiring accountability reports.[140] Such secondary influence meets the conditions of the EU democracy principle for outsourcing rulemaking powers.

Advocate General (AG) Pitruzzella summarized the EU's approach towards such autonomous public bodies as follows in a 2021 opinion:

> NRAs [national regulatory authorities] in the electricity and gas sectors operate, as we have seen, within the sphere of competence reserved to them, applying EU law without interference from national political bodies, even by way of formal or substantive laws. EU legislation takes the place that laws enacted by parliament under the national government model had in order to reconcile them with the principle of democracy. The decision-making process which produces EU legislation is a democratic process involving the participation of the European Parliament, which is elected by Union citizens, and the Council, in which are

136 Case C-131/2012 *Google Spain SL, Google Inc. v. Agencia Española de Protección de Datos (AEPD), Mario Costeja González* ECLI:EU:C:2014:317, § 69 and Consolidated Version of the Treaty on European Union [2008] OJ C115/13, article 6.

137 Article 28(1) GDPR (emphasis added).

138 Case 614/10 *Commission v. Austria* ECLI:EU:C:2012:631, § 42. The Court referred to Case C-518/07 *Commission v. Germany* ECLI:EU:C:2010:125, § 42 and more recently continued this line of reasoning in Case C-288/12 *Commission v. Hungary* ECLI:EU:C:2014:237, § 48.

139 AG Mazák had originally followed Germany in its opinion: Case C-518/07 *Commission v. Germany* ECLI:EU:C:2013:816, Opinion of AG Mazák.

140 Case C-518/07 *Commission v. Germany* ECLI:EU:C:2014:237, §§ 42–4.

present the interests of the Member States through democratically elected governments and, in this way, NRAs are brought back within the circuit of democratic legitimacy.[141]

2.5.2 Second research hypothesis: legality principle and guarantees of quality for Member States

The legality principle could equally have reverberations for the guarantees with which autonomous public and private actors must comply when they exercise rulemaking power.[142] Any such guarantees would apply when Member States implement EU law. There are few formal requirements for this implementation process as long as it occurs efficiently. For example, a Member State is not obliged to transpose directives through a formal statute; it merely has to ensure that the transposition is mirrored in a binding provision.[143] Non-binding circular letters or an adapted administrative practice would not meet the requirements.[144]

Because of a resurgence of human rights interest in the EU, the material legality requirements for restrictions on fundamental rights have also arisen in the EU. Since 2009, the EU Treaties explicitly incorporate the EU Charter.[145] This Charter applies to the EU institutions and—under certain conditions—to the Member States. In *Åkerberg Fransson*, the ECJ opted for a broad applicability of the Charter, namely whenever a national measure restricted EU law and thus fell within the scope of EU law.[146] Mr Fransson accused Sweden of violating the *non bis in idem* principle by punishing him twice for defrauding the value added tax (VAT) system. On the basis of Council Directive 2006/112 EC and article 4(3) TEU, every Member State is obliged to ensure VAT collection. The facts of the case did not amount to a straightforward implementation of EU law but, nevertheless, the ECJ deemed the Charter applicable. 'The applicability of European Union law entails applicability of the fundamental rights guaranteed by the Charter.'[147] Given the broad reach of

[141] Case C-718/18 *European Commission v. Federal Republic of Germany* ECLI:EU:C:2021:20, Opinion of AG Pitruzzella, § 140.

[142] This research is not concerned with the type of legality principle that limits the power of the EU to the competences which have been explicitly attributed to it. Tom Eijsbouts, *Europees Recht/Algemeen deel* (Europa Law Publishing 2010) 15.

[143] Belgian Council of State, *Beginselen van wetgevingstechniek* (*Manual for Making Statutory and Executive Legislation*) (2008) 116.

[144] Linda Senden, *Soft Law in European Community Law* (Hart 2004) 51.

[145] Consolidated Version of the Treaty on European Union [2008] OJ C115/13, article 6.1.

[146] Case C-617/10 *Åkerberg v. Fransson* ECLI:EU.C.2013:280. The Court affirmed its case law in Case C-390/12 *Robert Pfleger, Autoart s, Mladen Vucicevic, Maroxx Software GmbH, Hans-Jörg Zehetner* ECLI:EU:C:2014:281. See also: Anne Pieter van der Mei, 'The Scope of Application of the EU Charter of Fundamental Rights "ERT Implementation"' (2015) 22 *MJ* 432–9. Case C-260/89 *Elliniki Radiophonia Tiléorassi AE and Panellinia Omospondia Syllogon Prossopikou v. Dimotiki Etairia Pliroforissis and Sotirios Kouvelas and Nicolaos Avdellas and others (ERT)* ECLI:EU:C:1991:254, §§ 41–3; Theodore Konstadinides, *The Rule of Law in the European Union* (Hart 2017) 31–2.

[147] Case C-617/10 *Åkerberg v. Fransson* ECLI:EU:C:2013:280, § 21.

EU law, it will become increasingly difficult for Members States to escape the ECJ's review under the Charter.

When the EU Charter is applicable, it does not provide a separate (legality) derogation clause for each basic right. Article 52(1) of the Charter establishes, in general, that any limitation on the exercise of the rights and freedoms recognized by it must be *provided for by law* and must respect the essence of those rights and freedoms. Concerning the justification for such interference, the requirement as established in article 52(1) of the Charter, that any limitation on the exercise of fundamental rights must be provided for by law, implies that the legal basis which permits that interference with those rights must itself define the scope of the limitation on the exercise of the right concerned.[148]

Moreover, through AG Cruz Villalón's application of the legality principle in a privacy case on harmonizing Directive 2006/24/EC regarding data retention, a parallel can be found between, on the one hand, delegation from the EU to the Member States in this case and, on the other hand, delegation from a Member State to an autonomous public or private actor in this research. AG Cruz Villalón required the EU to define, at the very least, in its harmonizing Directive 2006/24/EC, the principles which must govern the definition, establishment, application, and review of observance of the relevant human rights guarantees by the Member States.[149] He deemed this necessary to live up to the quality of law requirement of the legality principle in article 52 of the Charter. His approach should resonate with the relationship between a Member State and an autonomous public or private actor.

In general, the ECJ has recognized that the principles of protection of legitimate expectations and legal certainty form part of the EU legal order when national authorities implement EU law.[150] Moreover, it substantively applies the legality principle of the Charter in a very similar manner to the way that the ECtHR does for the ECHR.[151] Generally, the legality principle does not require formal statutes by national parliaments to limit fundamental rights.[152] 'It follows from that case-law that the concept of "law" ("droit") … corresponds to "law" ("loi") used in other

[148] Cases C-511, 512, and 520/18 *La Quadrature du Net* ECLI:EU:C:2020:791, § 175; Case C-311/18 *Facebook Ireland and Schrems* ECLI:EU:C:2020:559, § 175; *Opinion 1/15* (EU–Canada PNR Agreement) ECLI:EU:C:2017:592, § 139.

[149] Case C-293/12 *Digital Rights Ireland Ltd* ECLI:EU:C:2013:845, Opinion of AG Cruz Villalón, § 120.

[150] Case C-181/04 *Elmeka NE v. Ypourgos Oikonomikon* ECLI:EU:C:2006:563, § 31. Patricia Popelier, 'Legal Certainty and the European Courts' in Mark Fenwick, Mathias Siems, and Stefan Wrbka (eds), *The Shifting Meaning of Legal Certainty in Comparative and Transnational Law* (Hart 2017) 38.

[151] Valsamis Mitsilegas, 'Article 49. Principles of Legality and Proportionality of Criminal Offences and Penalties' in Steve Peers, Tamara Hervey, Jeff Kenner, and Angela Ward (eds), *The EU Charter of Fundamental Rights* (Hart/Beck 2014) 1360.

[152] *Opinion 1/15* (EU–Canada PNR Agreement) ECLI:EU:C:2017:592, §§ 137–47 referring to *Opinion 1/15* of AG Mengozzi in ECLI:EU:C:2016:656, §§ 190–3. The exception in the ECHR for the independence and impartiality of judges, which requires a formal statute, is also present in the EU Charter: Case C-216/18 PPU *LM* ECLI:EU:C:2018:586, § 66.

provisions of the ECHR and encompasses both law of legislative origin and that deriving from case-law.'[153] The ECJ still falls short of requiring legislative measures, even in highly sensitive cases such as general data retention, despite the suggestion by AG Saugmandsgaard Øe that 'it would appear desirable for the essential content of the regime in question, and in particular the safeguards surrounding the obligation, to be laid down in a measure adopted by the legislative authority and to leave the executive authority with responsibility for the detailed rules governing its implementation.'[154] Only in very limited instances, such as the Dublin III Regulation, has the ECJ ruled that the criteria for detention must be established in a binding provision of general application and that settled case law cannot suffice in that regard,[155] which intensifies the ordinary formal legality requirement.

Nevertheless, the ECJ, as does the ECtHR, mainly looks for sufficient quality of the law.[156] A rule needs to be at least accessible and foreseeable.

To begin with, the ECJ recognizes the value of publication for the *accessibility* of a rule.[157] In the past, the ECJ emphasized, in *Skoma-Lux sro* and *AS Pimix*, that EU rules have to be published in the printed version of the *Official Journal of the European Union* and in the native language of the economic actor concerned in order for those rules to bind that actor.[158] Even knowledge of the rules through the publication of the electronic version or through other means was not adequate.[159] For three reasons, I do not believe that the ECJ would now have such high demands for implementing legislation (by autonomous public or private actors) through the Member States—as is of interest to this research. First, the case that required publication in the printed version of the *Official Journal* dates back almost fifteen years and the impact of technology has grown exponentially since that time. Even the ECJ left the door ajar for an evolution in *Skoma-Lux*: 'the only version of a Community regulation which is authentic, *as Community law now stands*, is that which is published in the Official Journal of the European Union.'[160] Second, the

[153] Joined Cases C-189, 202, 205–8/02, and 213/02 P *Dansk Roerindustri* ECLI:EU:C:2005:408, §§ 215–16. This would apply *mutatis mutandis* to other (relative) Convention rights.

[154] Joined Cases C-203 and 698/15, *Tele2 Sverige AB* ECLI:EU:C:2016:572, Opinion of AG Saugmandsgaard Øe, § 152; Joined Cases C-203 and 698/15 *Tele2 Sverige AB* ECLI:EU:C:2016:572 and ECLI.EU:C:2016:970, § 94. The same AG does not repeat this consideration in the *Schrems II* case: Case C 311/18 *Facebook Ireland and Schrems* ECLI:EU:C:2019:1145, Opinion of AG Saugmandsgaard Øe, §§ 263–71.

[155] Case C-528/15 *Al Chodor* ECLI:EU:C:2017:213, §§ 42–5.

[156] Joined Cases C-189, 202, 205–8, and 213/02 P *Dansk Roerindustri* ECLI:EU:C:2005:408, § 219.

[157] Patricia Popelier, 'Legal Certainty and the European Courts' in Mark Fenwick, Mathias Siems, and Stefan Wrbka (eds), *The Shifting Meaning of Legal Certainty in Comparative and Transnational Law* (Hart 2017) 52.

[158] Case C-161/06 *Skoma-Lux sro v. Celní ředitelství Olomouc* ECLI:EU:C:2007:773, §§ 45–8; Case C-146/11 *AS Pimix v. Maksu- ja Tolliameti Lõuna maksu- ja tollikeskus and Põllumajandusministeerium* ECLI:EU:C:2012:450, § 47.

[159] Case C-161/06 *Skoma-Lux sro v. Celní ředitelství Olomouc* ECLI:EU:C:2007:773, §§ 47–8; Case C-146/11 *AS Pimix v. Maksu- ja Tolliameti Lõuna maksu- ja tollikeskus and Põllumajandusministeerium* ECLI:EU:C:2012:450, §§ 43–4.

[160] Case C-161/06 *Skoma-Lux sro v. Celní ředitelství Olomouc* ECLI:EU:C:2007:773, § 50 (emphasis added).

ECJ rendered these judgments with regard to acts adopted by EU institutions[161] which are different from national public or private actors. It is logical that at least the language requirements for EU institutions are stricter than for national public or private actors. Third, both cases concerned the question of whether prior EU legislation could be applied to economic actors of new Member States after their accession to the EU in 2004.[162] The ECJ thus arguably focused on the equality of languages in an inter-European context. This is contrasted to the probable freedom of a Member State to prefer one language in its implementation of an EU rule, as an 'internal affair'.

Moreover, whether a rule is *foreseeable* is influenced by the content of the matter, the area of legislation, and the number and capacity of the addressees, as in the ECtHR context.[163] Citizens and corporations need to follow up on evolutions in the regulatory framework that could influence their legitimate expectations.[164] In the *Plantanol* case, a German court referred the following preliminary question to the ECJ: 'Do the general principles of legal certainty and the protection of legitimate expectations within EU law preclude a Member State from prematurely withdrawing a tax exemption scheme which applied to a fuel that contained a blend of vegetable oil, fossil gas oil and specific additives?'[165] In particular, the German court wondered whether such a withdrawal required exceptional circumstances. The ECJ placed the final responsibility for the decision on whether those principles had been respected in the hands of the national court. The national judge should take into account all relevant circumstances relating to the case. Some authors applaud this kind of deferential review of the quality of the law because national courts are in a better position to evaluate whether a law is foreseeable.[166] However, one of the relevant circumstances that the ECJ has already established is whether the legal change could be predicted through coalition agreements, draft legislation, and parliamentary debates.[167] When autonomous public or private actors make rules, these ordinary legislative safeguards are absent. In practice, the quality of law requirements, derived from the legality principle, will thus also be harder to fulfil for autonomous public or private actors than for traditional politically accountable actors.

[161] Ibid., § 37.

[162] The Czech Republic, Estonia, Cyprus, Latvia, Lithuania, Hungary, Malta, Poland, Slovenia, and Slovakia.

[163] Joined Cases C-189, 202, 205–8, and 213/02 P *Dansk Roerindustri* ECLI:EU:C:2005:408, § 219.

[164] Patricia Popelier, 'Legal Certainty and the European Courts' in Mark Fenwick, Mathias Siems, and Stefan Wrbka (eds), *The Shifting Meaning of Legal Certainty in Comparative and Transnational Law* (Hart 2017) 45 and 53.

[165] Case C-201/08 *Plantanol GmbH & Co. KG v. Hauptzollamt Darmstadt* ECLI:EU:C:2009:539, § 32.

[166] Steve Peers and Sacha Prechal, 'Scope and Interpretation of Rights and Principles' in Steve Peers, Tamara Hervey, Jeff Kenner, and Angela Ward (eds), *The EU Charter of Fundamental Rights* (Hart/Beck 2014) § 52.47.

[167] Case C-201/08 *Plantanol GmbH & Co. KG v. Hauptzollamt Darmstadt* ECLI:EU:C:2009:539, § 63.

To conclude, on the one hand, the national democracy principle is put under additional pressure by the EU's preference for independent regulators and the ECJ's flexible interpretation of the European democracy principle. On the other hand, the ECJ leaves a substantial margin of appreciation at the national level when it fleshes out the legality principle. Nevertheless, by emulating the ECtHR case law on the ECHR, the ECJ case law on the Charter of Fundamental Rights appears to impose some mild guarantees—through the quality of law—on Member States when they outsource rulemaking powers. This may influence the possibilities of recipients of outsourced rulemaking powers.

2.6 Conclusion

This chapter had the crucial objective of verifying how the international law framework influences the national constitutional frameworks on the topic of outsourcing rulemaking powers. Two of the constitutional principles, as set out in this monograph's introduction, have proven to be instrumental here. In the first instance, the democracy principle has the potential to set the clearest limits on the outsourcing of rulemaking powers. In the second instance, there is the international legality principle, which more resembles the domestic rule of law principle since it sets certain qualitative requirements on all rules, including those made by autonomous public or private actors. In relation to these principles, four comprehensive treaties that are important branches of human rights protection were investigated: the IACHR, the ICCPR, the ECHR, and the European Union and the EU Charter of Fundamental Rights.

First, I want to reiterate that none of the judicial bodies watching over the ECHR, the EU, or the ICCPR has been as concrete in formulating limits to delegation as the IACtHR. According to the IACtHR, delegation is allowed if the delegation does not impair the fundamental nature of the guaranteed basic rights, the exercise of powers is subject to effective control, and it stays within the boundaries of the national constitution.[168] Both the Court's audacity to formulate a definition and its scientific precision must be applauded.

Second, the ICCPR contains a provision (article 25) that directly installs a basic right to have the electoral will of the people respected. However, no clear case law suggests that article 25 ICCPR would prioritize rules made by Legislatures rather than by autonomous public or private actors. Nevertheless, a degree of legal certainty is guaranteed by the HRC through, amongst other things, its attention to the quality of the outsourced rules created.

[168] IACtHR, the word 'laws' in article 30 IACHR (Advisory Opinion OC-06/86, 9 May 1986) § 36.

Third, within the ECHR the democracy principle appears to have only a narrow influence on limiting the possibility to outsource rulemaking powers. Only article 3, Protocol 1 has developed over the years into a potential bar on outsourcing rulemaking powers, because it now grants an individual right against the national Legislature to abide by the will of the people. This will of the people is generally seen in the context of elections but may be read more broadly, to the effect that the Legislature should remain in control of the rulemaking process.

Because of the fact that autonomous public or private actors can often be seen as state actors within the context of the ECHR, the case law of the ECtHR can also teach us how the legality principle places certain safeguards on outsourced rules that limit fundamental rights. Just like other rules, they must comply with domestic law and be sufficiently accessible and foreseeable. The ECtHR, in principle, does not prefer rules made by the Legislature or the Executive over rules made by other actors. This is confirmed by the case law of the ECtHR which stated in the case of *Silver* that 'in accordance with the law' does not mean that 'the safeguards must be enshrined in the very text which authorises the imposition of restrictions'.[169] In other words, autonomous public and private actors can also provide these safeguards in their rules. Nevertheless, the Court's case law suggests that the safeguards set by traditional rulemakers have a comparative advantage over rules made by other actors because the former can rely on more institutionalized procedures to attain the required quality of law and procedural rationality.

Fourth, the democracy principle enshrined in the primary legislation of the EU appears to set few limits on the national Legislature or Executive to outsource rulemaking powers. On the contrary, the EU Charter grants special status to autonomous public bodies that have the capacity to exercise rulemaking powers in relation to data protection. Moreover, the case law of the ECJ suggests a low threshold for obtaining sufficient parliamentary influence to comply with the democracy principle when outsourcing rulemaking powers. However, due to the fact that the ECJ refers to the case law of the ECtHR for the interpretation of the legality principle in the EU Charter, we encounter some influence of the legality principle, comparable to the legality principle in the ECHR, regarding the quality of the rule that is drafted by autonomous public or private actors.

The IACtHR should serve as an example to other treaty bodies under the ECHR, EU Treaties, and the ICCPR on how to delineate national discretion to delegate rulemaking powers without transgressing provisions and principles enshrined in comprehensive human rights treaties. The ECHR, the EU Charter, and the ICCPR do not offer clear-cut protection to the citizens of Contracting States against a decision by a state's Legislature or Executive to outsource rulemaking powers. The first research hypothesis, concerning the limits to the outsourcing of rulemaking

[169] *Silver and others v. United Kingdom* nos 5947/72, 6205/73, 7052/75, 7061/75, 7107/75, 7113/75, and 7136/75 (ECtHR, 25 March 1983) § 90.

powers, is thus left unconfirmed by comprehensive human rights treaties. In relation to the democracy principle, based on the inclusive overview earlier it is possible to derive only one outer restriction on national Legislatures, namely to stop them from divesting unfettered powers. With respect to the second research hypothesis concerning the safeguards with which outsourced rules need to comply, these comprehensive treaties largely leave this issue unregulated. The international legality principle only places some qualitative standards on autonomous public or private actors that draft rules.

All of the treaty bodies leave a sizeable margin of appreciation to the Contracting State to interpret both issues formulated in the two research hypotheses. This chapter on the international limits to the outsourcing of rulemaking power proved a necessary, yet insufficient exercise. The ultimate responsibility for dealing with the phenomenon of outsourcing rulemaking powers lies with nation-states. Article 53 ECHR and article 53 of the EU Charter both encourage Member States to provide increased protection for human rights.[170] Assuming that the transfer of rulemaking powers can affect the human rights of individuals, the focus of this monograph now shifts to national limits and safeguards.

[170] Rusen Ergec and Jacques Velu, *Convention européenne des droits de l'homme* (Bruylant 2014) 186.

3
Comparative Delegation Framework by Constitutional Provisions

Based on constitutional provisions, Chapter 3 inquires into the traditional, constitutional framework to delegate rulemaking powers that exists in the countries researched.

3.1 Rulemaking powers exercised by the Executive

The most familiar example of the delegation of rulemaking powers benefits the Executive in the various countries researched.

3.1.1 Belgium

As in most legal systems, the Belgian federal Legislature primarily exercises lawmaking authority. It is said in Belgium that the federal Legislature disposes of 'full authority' (French *plénitude de compétence*, Dutch *volheid van bevoegdheid*).[1] This authority consists of explicitly attributed (rulemaking) powers and residuary (rulemaking) powers; that is, all powers not assigned to another branch of government.[2]

[1] Marnix Van Damme, *Overzicht van het grondwettelijk recht* (die Keure 2014) 85; Jan Velaers, *De Grondwet en de Raad van State Afdeling Wetgeving* (Maklu 1999) 229.

[2] This residuary competence is primarily based on articles 33, 36, and 105 of the Belgian Constitution. Article 33 states that all powers derive from the nation and that they will be 'exercised in

Outsourcing Rulemaking Powers. Cedric Jenart, Oxford University Press. © Cedric Jenart 2022.
DOI: 10.1093/oso/9780192897831.003.0003

In three separate cases, the King [read: government plus head of state] or the governments of the federated entities can create their own rules independently.

First, the Executive can have its own—constitutionally reserved—rulemaking powers. On the federal level, the King exercises the executive power according to article 37 of the Belgian Constitution. It is debated whether a distinct police power, including rulemaking powers, could derive from this provision. Following the related article 108 of the Belgian Constitution, the King makes regulations required for the execution of laws.[3] In its 1924 milestone judgment *Mertz*, the Belgian Supreme Court (the Court of Cassation) defined the extent of executive powers. The case reviewed the executive decree according to which every Belgian citizen needed to carry an identification card while outdoors. The exercise of executive powers was solely based on a statute regulating censuses and civil registers. According to the Court of Cassation, the executive decree was still 'executing' the aforementioned statute because it 'derived from the statute's principle and from its general implication the events that had inspired it and the goals that it envisaged'.[4] More recently, the Belgian Council of State Administrative Litigation Section stressed that the Legislature first had to determine the 'goal and the spirit' of the rule.[5] Despite this broad and lenient interpretation of executive powers, they are not limitless. By definition, executive powers need to execute abstract, general, or binding legal bases previously made by the Legislature. Furthermore, according to article 107 of the Belgian Constitution, the King appoints civil servants to positions in the general and foreign affairs administrations of the state. In this capacity, the King can make rules on the status, the rights, and the obligations of federal civil servants and cabinet employees concerning rules on recruitment, appointment conditions, training, and mobility.[6]

Second, the Legislature can delegate rulemaking powers to the Executive that are not explicitly reserved to the Legislature but which it can wield due to its residuary powers. Until recently, the Council of State Legislative and Administrative Sections were convinced that a legislative statute needed to regulate core policy matters, even those matters for which the Constitution did not explicitly require

a constitutionally defined manner'. Article 36 identifies the federal legislative power as exercising legislative authority (and as being different from federal executive power and the federal judiciary power). Article 105 of the Belgian Constitution explicitly states that the King may *only* exercise explicitly attributed powers; it flows from this that the Legislature may also exercise other (residuary powers).

[3] See article 20 of the Special Majority Act of 8 August 1980 pertaining to the Reform of State Institutions for the federated entities.

[4] Belgian Court of Cassation 18 November 1924, *Pas.* 1925, 25. In the original French: 'dégager du principe de celle-ci et de son économie générale les conséquences qui a présidé à sa conception et les fins qu'elle poursui': Ingrid Opdebeek and Stéphanie De Somer, *Algemeen bestuursrecht. Grondslagen en beginselen* (Intersentia 2017) 334.

[5] Belgian Council of State Administrative Litigation Section, no. 114.688, 20 January 2003, 5–6.

[6] Jan Velaers, *De Grondwet, een artikelsgewijze commentaar* (die Keure 2019) article 107, §§ 7–10; André Alen and Koen Muylle, *Handboek van het Belgisch Staatsrecht* (Kluwer 2011) 669.

rules made by statute.[7] In the controversial judgment 31/2004, the Constitutional Court seemed to reciprocate the Council of State's reticence towards the delegation of essential elements of *non-reserved* powers through its anti-discrimination case law.[8] Soon after that judgment, however, the Constitutional Court once again started to show increasing leniency towards delegating non-reserved powers.[9] At present, however, the dust has settled in favour of constitutional permission to delegate non-reserved rulemaking powers.[10] In 2012, the Constitutional Court proclaimed that it could only invalidate the delegation of non-reserved powers if the delegation would be: (1) 'manifestly unreasonable'; or (2) 'would infringe disproportionally on rights of the involved people';[11] and (3) the Constitutional Court could also intervene when delegation would infringe on the vertical division of powers between the federal state and the federated entities.[12] This current status of the court's case law leaves a considerable margin of appreciation to the Legislature.[13]

Third, the Legislature may even delegate (parts of) its explicitly reserved rulemaking powers to the King. If a rulemaking power is reserved to the Legislature, then the essential elements of the policy have to be determined by the Legislature. In that event, rulemaking power cannot be outsourced when the outsourced measures are central or essential.[14] What exactly constitutes an 'essential aspect' is generally unclear and unfortunately differs from competence to competence. In tax matters, for instance, tax rates, the tax base, and tax exemptions are essential aspects, whereas the control and levying of taxes are deemed to be non-essential.[15] Even when the Legislature has not established the essential elements, it can still delegate reserved rulemaking powers to the Executive.[16] If the Legislature needs to

[7] Belgian Council of State Administrative Litigation Section, no. 201.859, 15 March 2010, § 14; Koen Muylle, 'Het grondwettelijk delegatieverbod en het Unierecht' in André Alen and Jan Theunis (eds), *Leuvense Staatsrechtelijke Standpunten 3* (die Keure 2012) 319.

[8] Belgian Constitutional Court no. 31/2004, 3 March 2004, B.5.2; see also Belgian Council of State Legislative Section, Advisory opinion no. 60.350/4 of 28 November 2016, 3–4.

[9] Daan Bijnens, Peter Schollen, and Jan Theunis, 'Behoorlijke wetgeving in de rechtspraak van het Grondwettelijk Hof 2013–2014' [2015] *Tijdschrift voor Wetgeving* § 33.

[10] Belgian Constitutional Court no. 8/2009, 15 January 2009, B.6.2; Belgian Constitutional Court no. 36/2012, 8 March 2012, B.5–B.6.2; Belgian Constitutional Court no. 107/2013, 18 July 2013, B.10.2; and Belgian Constitutional Court no. 86/2015, 11 June 2015, B.8; Jeroen Van Nieuwenhove, 'Delegatie van regelgevende bevoegdheid in België' [2017] *Tijdschrift voor Wetgeving* 207.

[11] Belgian Constitutional Court no. 36/2012, 8 March 2012, B.6.2.

[12] Belgian Constitutional Court no. 2011/71, 10 May 2011, B.9; Belgian Constitutional Court no. 2010/56, 12 May 2010, B.5. André Alen and Koen Muylle, *Handboek van het Belgisch Staatsrecht* (Kluwer 2011) 490.

[13] Marnix Van Damme, *Overzicht van het grondwettelijk recht* (die Keure 2014) 86.

[14] Frank Meersschaut, 'Overzicht van rechtspraak. De rechtspraak van het Arbitragehof ten behoeve van de private rechtspraktijk 1992–1997' [1998] *Tijdschrift voor Privaatrecht* 15.

[15] Belgian Constitutional Court no. 90/2015, 18 June 2015, B.5.2. The Legislature also decides on the essential aspects of selecting the army by allowing the Executive to make a list based on which 'the attitude of the candidates' can be assessed.

[16] This delegation occurs primarily with regard to tax law. Jeroen Van Nieuwenhove, 'Delegatie van regelgevende bevoegdheid in België' [2017] *Tijdschrift voor Wetgeving* 202. See also Heidi Bortels and Peter Heyvaert, 'Het legaliteitsbeginsel in de rechtspraak van het Grondwettelijk Hof: een variërende

delegate reserved competences on essential policy decisions, this is accepted if: (1) it occurs in exceptional circumstances; (2) explicitly; (3) the Executive's rule is later ratified by the Legislature as set out in the enabling statute; and (4) the rule retroactively disappears from the legal order if ratification does not occur.[17]

Next, article 33 of the Belgian Constitution is key to determining the possibility of outsourcing rulemaking powers further on towards ministers and the central administration.[18] The Belgian Constitution does not expressly confer (rulemaking) powers to individual ministers; nevertheless, the Belgian Court of Cassation had already allowed for this at the end of the nineteenth and the beginning of the twentieth centuries. In principle, the powers are inalienable and not transferable, which may prohibit the delegation of broad powers to ministers[19], but does not exclude every delegation to them.[20] Moreover, the Belgian Council of State explicitly accepts the delegation of rulemaking powers to ministers and civil servants.[21]

Under a double condition, ministers may receive rulemaking powers through delegation from the King or federated governments.[22] The delegation of rulemaking powers is subject to stricter conditions than the sub-delegation of individual decision-making or administrative tasks of management. According to the principal case law and scholarship, the delegation of rulemaking power is permitted when the following condition is met:[23] the exercise of rulemaking powers by ministers can only concern accessory matters or details and not the essence of

intensiteit van de toetsing' [2011] *TBP* 353; André Alen and Koen Muylle, *Handboek van het Belgisch Staatsrecht* (Kluwer 2011) 33 and 737.

[17] Belgian Constitutional Court no. 195/2004, 1 December 2004, B.16.3; Belgian Constitutional Court no. 145/2005, 21 September 2005, B.4.3; Patricia Popelier, 'La loi aujourd'hui (le principe de légalité)' in Philippe Gérard, François Ost, Michel Van de Kerchove, Isabelle Hachez, Yves Cartuyvels, and Hugues Dumont (eds), *Les sources du droit revisitées tôme I* (Anthemis 2012) § 44; Koen Muylle, 'Het grondwettelijk delegatieverbod en het Unierecht' in André Alen and Jan Theunis (eds), *Leuvense Staatsrechtelijke Standpunten 3* (die Keure 2012) 323; Bruno Peeters, 'Het fiscaal legaliteitsbeginsel in de Belgische Grondwet: verstrakking of erosie?' in Bruno Peeters and J. Velaers (eds), *De Grondwet in groothoekperspectief. Liber amicorum discipulorumque Karel Rimanque* (Intersentia 2007) 538; Wouter Pas and Brecht Steen, 'Met het nodige voorbehoud. Het grondwettelijk voorbehoud aan de formele en aan de federale wetgever - Deel 1' [2004] *Tijdschrift voor Wetgeving* 375–80.

[18] 'All powers emanate from the Nation. These powers are exercised in the manner laid down by the Constitution.'

[19] Belgian Court of Cassation, 6 February 1891 [1891] *Pas.* I, 59.

[20] Belgian Court of Cassation, 3 May 1921 [1921] *Pas.* I, 362. The court in this case accepted the outsourced power of a minister to fix bread prices but not the power to create further rules that impeded the freedom of commerce and industry. In Belgian Court of Cassation, 13 May 1935 [1935] *Pas.* I, 246, the court also accepted the ministerial competence to determine to which countries' livestock could be transferred.

[21] e.g. the Belgian Council of State Administrative Litigation Section, no. 2436, 8 May 1953, *Ansion*; Belgian Council of State Legislative Section, Advisory opinion no. 67.490/3 of 26 June 2020, § 4.

[22] Council of State, *Beginselen van Wetgevingstechniek* (Raad van State 2008) 24–6; Marc Joassart, Laurent Jans, Claudine Mertes, and Marc Oswald, 'Le Conseil d'Etat—Chronique de légisprudence 2014' [2016] *Revue belge de droit constitutionnel* 263–6.

[23] Patricia Popelier, *Democratisch regelgeven* (Intersentia 2001) 188–90; Patrick Goffaux, *Dictionnaire de droit administratif* (Bruylant 2015) 206.

the rulemaking competence.[24] Delegations to civil servants must additionally be of a technical nature.[25]

When the Legislature wishes to delegate rulemaking powers to a minister or the administration, the Belgian Council of State Legislative Section adheres to a steadily cascading chain of delegation.[26] The rulemaking power that a minister might receive should originate from the Executive not directly from the Legislature.[27] In particular, a legislative delegation cannot hinder the Executive in exercising its—constitutionally granted—powers.[28] In other words, the Council of State Legislative Section does not permit fetters on the chain of delegation. According to the Council, only in exceptional cases, namely where 'urgent' action is required, can the delegation of rulemaking powers skip one shackle on the legitimacy chain and permit the Legislature to delegate directly to ministers.[29] This was most recently affirmed by a 2021 general assembly opinion on a Belgian 'pandemic statute'.[30]

3.1.2 France

Historically, the Legislature had been the *primus inter pares* of the French *Trias Politica*. French legal theorists, such as Carré de Malberg, convincingly argued that the Legislature embodied the expression of the general will.[31] Delegations in France have been described as the 'open wound of public law'.[32] The grant of public powers appears to go against the *delegatus delegare non potest* principle.

[24] Belgian Council of State Administrative Litigation Section, no. 208.462, 26 October 2010, 11; Belgian Council of State Administrative Litigation Section, no. 85648, 28 February 2000, *T'Heist Best*, 5; Belgian Council of State Administrative Litigation Section, no. 31.584, 14 December 1988, *Wauthier*; Belgian Council of State Administrative Litigation Section, no. 25.595, 30 July 1985, *Wauthier*; Belgian Council of State Legislative Section, Advisory opinion (Parliamentary Documents Chamber of Representatives 2005–6, no. 51-2491/001) 9–10; Belgian Council of State Legislative Section, Advisory Opinion no. 28.343/1 of 7 January 1999 (*Parl. St.* Kamer 1998–9, no. 49-2003/1-2004/1) 37.

[25] e.g. Belgian Council of State Legislative Section, Advisory opinion no. 67.490/3 of 26 June 2020, § 4.

[26] Belgian Council of State Legislative Section, Advisory opinion no. 55.268/4 of 5 March 2014, § 2; Belgian Council of State Legislative Section, Advisory opinion no. 53.230/4 of 22 May 2013, § 2; Belgian Council of State Legislative Section, Advisory opinion no. 53.229/4 of 22 May 2013, § 2; Belgian Council of State Legislative Section, Advisory opinion no. 52.128/1 of 25 October 2012, § 22; Belgian Council of State Legislative Section, Advisory opinion no. 38.577/2 of 17 June 2005, § 3.

[27] Jan Velaers, *De Grondwet en de Raad van State Afdeling Wetgeving* (Maklu 1999) 375.

[28] Belgian Council of State Legislative Section, Advisory opinion no. 44.607/1 of 12 June 2008, § 1.

[29] Belgian Council of State Legislative Section, Advisory opinion no. 39.272/3 of 29 November 2005, § 4; Koen Muylle, 'Het grondwettelijk delegatieverbod en het Unierecht' in André Alen and Jan Theunis (eds), *Leuvense Staatsrechtelijke Standpunten 3* (die Keure 2012) 319.

[30] Belgian Council of State Legislative Section, Advisory opinion no. 68.936/AV of 7 April 2021, § 66.

[31] Laurent Depussay, 'Hiérarchie des normes et hiérarchie des pouvoirs' [2007] *RDP* 421, fn. 28; Pierre Le Mire, *La loi et le règlement: articles 34, 37 et 38 de la Constitution de 1958* (Documentation Française 1994) 3; Nadine Poulet-Gibot Leclerc, *La place de la loi dans l'ordre juridique interne* (Presses universitaires de France 1992) 1.

[32] French private law also strongly deals with delegation. Ludovic Maupas, 'La délégation de pouvoirs au sein des associations' [30 October 2004] *Defrénois* 1351.

Competences should not be exercised in any way other than their constitutional attribution[33] because those powers are in principle 'inalienable'.[34] Article 45 of the French 1795 Constitution had already stipulated that in no event could 'the legislative body ... delegate to one of its members, or to whomever, any of the competences attributed to it in that Constitution'. Subsequently, the position towards delegations softened in political practice. Yet, after an excess of delegations in the Third Republic (between 1870 and 1940),[35] article 13 of the French Constitution of 27 October 1946 again expressly prohibited Parliament from delegating legislative powers in the Fourth Republic (1946–58).[36]

This conviction seems to have flipped within the current French Constitution, as introduced in 1958, due to the large number of enabling statutes over which the Executive had factually taken over control in the previous decades.[37] The Legislature only has competences explicitly mentioned in the French Constitution. Article 34 provides a strikingly clear description of the rulemaking powers of the Legislature. On the one hand, statutes shall *determine the rules* concerning civil liberties, fundamental issues of family law, criminal law, tax law, etc. On the other hand, statutes shall *lay down the basic principles* of national defence, territorial decentralization, education, environment, property rights, and labour law. At first sight, article 34 of the French Constitution thus appears to represent a closed shop of rulemaking competences with an 'exclusive' category of rulemaking and a 'basic principles' category of rulemaking. However, article 34 is not exhaustive. Its final section allows for the extension of competences of the Legislature through an (explicit) Organic Statute. Also other constitutional provisions refer to Parliament or statutes to regulate certain competences.[38] Moreover, the exclusive competence of the Legislature in article 34 itself has still been sufficiently broadly phrased, such as the exercise of civil liberties and freedom, so that it may be difficult to find rulemaking provisions that do not touch upon it at all.[39]

[33] Joseph Barthélemy and Paul Duez, *Traité de droit constitutionnel* (Editions Panthéon Assas 2004) 722–3; Anne-Marie Le Pourhiet, *Les ordonnances* (LGDJ 2011) 42; Michel Degotte, 'Constitution et compétences normatives économiques des "autorités de régulation"' [22 January 2009] *Issu de Petites affiches* 18.

[34] Philippe Azouaou, *L'indisponibilité des compétences en droit public interne* (Marc & Martin 2012) 19 and 28–9.

[35] Anne-Marie Le Pourhiet, *Les ordonnances* (LGDJ 2011) 41; Jean-Marc Sauvé, 'Allocution d'ouverture' in Philippe Lauvaux and Jean Masset (eds), *La législation déléguée* (Société de Legislation Comparée 2014) 7.

[36] Pierre le Mire, *La loi et le règlement: articles 34, 37 et 38 de la Constitution de 1958* (Documentation Française 1994) 5; Francis Hamon and Michel Troper, *Droit constitutionnel* (LGDJ 2015–16) 723.

[37] Ibid., 680; Nadine Poulet-Gibot Leclerc, *La place de la loi dans l'ordre juridique interne* (Presses universitaires de France 1992) 6; Sophie Boyron, *The Constitution of France: A Contextual Analysis* (Hart 2012) 48.

[38] Francis Hamon and Michel Troper, *Droit constitutionnel* (LGDJ 2015–16) 681; Cathérine Boyer-Mérentier, *Les ordonnances de l'article 38 de la Constitution de 1958* (Presses universitaires d'Aix-Marseille 1996) 255.

[39] Anne-Marie Le Pourhiet, *Les ordonnances* (LGDJ 2011) 54.

The French Council of State and Constitutional Council used this leeway and have not followed the dichotomy that was suggested by the letter of the French Constitution. Article 34 was interpreted as a unity; none of the competences listed there had to be exclusively regulated by the Legislature. Rather, the Legislature must always determine the fundamental or essential principles (*mise en cause*) of any competence, whereas the Executive will adopt the rules that apply and concretize (*mise en oeuvre*) those fundamental principles.[40]

The rulemaking competences of the Executive in France mainly derive from article 37 of the French Constitution, even though that provision actually grants no such general power. Article 37 attributes the residuary (rulemaking) competences to the Executive. The provision broadly states that 'matters other than those coming under the scope of statute law shall be matters for regulation'. The French Constitutional Council accepted that article 37 vested general 'executive' competence in the Executive to implement previously made legislative rules;[41] moreover, the Executive maintained its general policing power.[42] This refusal to compartmentalize various aspects of the executive competence between the Legislature and the Executive has been described as the French version of the 'unity of executive power'.[43]

There is a provision in the French Constitution that invests extraordinary powers in the Executive.[44] Article 38 institutionalizes the historically polemic *décret-loi*, endowing the Executive with conditional legislative powers.[45] The provision stipulates that 'in order to implement its programme, the government may ask Parliament for authorization, for a limited period, to take measures by ordinance [*ordonnance*] that are normally the preserve of statute law'. The Legislature is no longer allowed to legislate on a matter for the duration of it having granted the Executive the power to create an ordinance.[46] This last element does not imply that the ordinance itself is hierarchically equivalent or even paramount to a statute.

[40] Ferdinand Mélin-Soucramanien and Pierre Pactet, *Droit constitutionnel* (Sirey 2017) 623; Pierre le Mire, *La loi et le règlement: articles 34, 37 et 38 de la Constitution de 1958* (Documentation Française 1994) 12–13; Francis Hamon and Michel Troper, *Droit constitutionnel* (LGDJ 2015–16) 683.

[41] French Constitutional Council no. 61-631, 3 May 1961; Nadine Poulet-Gibot Leclerc, *La place de la loi dans l'ordre juridique interne* (Presses universitaires de France 1992) 42; Laurent Depussay, 'Hiérarchie des normes et hiérarchie des pouvoirs' [2007] *RDP* 421, II A.

[42] French Council of State, 22 December 1978, *Union des chambres syndicales d'affichage et de publicité extérieure* as confirmed in the decision of the French Constitutional Council no. 87-149 L of 20 February 1987, § 7. Pierre le Mire, *La loi et le règlement: articles 34, 37 et 38 de la Constitution de 1958* (Documentation Française 1994) 34.

[43] Nadine Poulet-Gibot Leclerc, *La place de la loi dans l'ordre juridique interne* (Presses universitaires de France 1992) 41–3.

[44] Pierre le Mire, *La loi et le règlement: articles 34, 37 et 38 de la Constitution de 1958* (Documentation Française 1994) 35.

[45] Cathérine Boyer-Mérentier, *Les ordonnances de l'article 38 de la Constitution de 1958* (Presses universitaires d'Aix-Marseille 1996) 202; Sophie Boyron, *The Constitution of France: A Contextual Analysis* (Hart 2012) 48.

[46] Francis Hamon and Michel Troper, *Droit constitutionnel* (LGDJ 2015–16) 726; Ferdinand Mélin-Soucramanien and Pierre Pactet, *Droit constitutionnel* (Sirey 2017) 635.

Contrary to Spanish or Italian legislative decrees,[47] for example, the French ordinances under article 38 of the French Constitution still have to be ratified and maintain an inferior legal status until that point.[48] There is one exception to this rule with regard to the French overseas territories. According to article 74-1, the ordinances that the French government can enact for the overseas areas do have the same status as a statute. The article states that 'in the Overseas territorial communities ... the government may ... extend by ordinance ... the statutory provisions applying in mainland France, or *adapt the statutory provisions* applying, to the specific organization of the community in question, provided statute law has not expressly excluded the use of this procedure for the provisions involved'.[49] However, because of even stricter procedural conditions in article 74-1 (e.g. automatic lapse of an ordinance if it is not ratified within eighteen months of its publication), ordinances concerning the overseas areas are still mainly adopted following the procedure of article 38.[50]

Individual ministers do not ordinarily retain rulemaking powers.[51] However, the Council of State recognized in its *Jamart* case that ministers could autonomously exercise rulemaking powers to take measures necessary for the functioning of public services.[52] Moreover, rulemaking powers can be delegated to individual ministers. This delegation can be done either by the Legislature or the Prime Minister, representing the government. Four conditions apply specifically when the *Legislature* delegates rulemaking competences to ministers: (1) it should concern a technical matter; (2) with a limited extent; (3) for which an advisory opinion of the Council of State would not be useful; and (4) which is not politically controversial since the Prime Minister cannot fulfil his mediating function if an individual minister exercises rulemaking powers.[53] When the *Prime Minister* (i.e. the government) delegates executive rulemaking powers to an individual minister, no stringent barriers exist since article 21, 2 of the French Constitution explicitly allows for that possibility: '[the Prime Minister] may delegate certain of his powers

[47] Articles 76 and 77 Italian Constitution and article 82 Spanish Constitution. Guillaume Tusseau, 'La législation déléguée' in Michel Troper and Dominique Chagnollaud (eds), *Traité international de droit constitutionnel, Tome 2* (Dalloz 2012) 647.

[48] Pierre le Mire, *La loi et le règlement: articles 34, 37 et 38 de la Constitution de 1958* (Documentation Française 1994) 37. After ratification, ordinances retroactively attain legislative value. Guillaume Tusseau, 'La législation déléguée' in Michel Troper and Dominique Chagnollaud (eds), *Traité international de droit constitutionnel, Tome 2* (Dalloz 2012) 649; Cathérine Boyer-Mérentier, *Les ordonnances de l'article 38 de la Constitution de 1958* (Presses universitaires d'Aix-Marseille 1996) 202.

[49] Anne-Marie Le Pourhiet, *Les ordonnances* (LGDJ 2011) 107 (emphasis added).

[50] Jean-Marc Sauvé, 'Allocution d'ouverture' in Philippe Lauvaux and Jean Masset (eds), *La législation déléguée* (Société de Legislation Comparée 2014) 15.

[51] Jean-François Lachaume, *Droit administratif* (Thémis 2002) 213.

[52] French Council of State, 7 February 1936, *Lebon* 172; Pierre Brunet, 'Les normes législatives et administratives' in Pascale Gonod, Fabrice Melleray, and Philippe Yolka (eds), *Traité de Droit Administratif* (Dalloz 2011) 520; Jean-François Lachaume, *Droit administratif* (Thémis 2002) 213.

[53] Prime Minister and Council of State, *Guide de légistique* (3rd edn, La documentation française 2017) 326.

to ministers'. One overriding condition applies when a competence that was originally delegated from the Legislature to the Executive is being sub-delegated to ministers. The sub-delegation may not comprise the full authority and must be sufficiently precise.[54]

3.1.3 Germany

Legal scholarship of the Kingdom of Prussia (1701–1870) prohibited any type of legislative delegation.[55] Subsequently, opinions evolved and during the old German Empire (1871–1918) the delegation of rulemaking powers was generally deemed permissible.[56] Legal jurist and philosopher Heinrich Triepel and Professor Woldemar Friedrich Poetzsch-Heffter resuscitated the discussion after the First World War by espousing that delegations should not be permitted unless for specific competences and with a specific objective.[57] As a response, Carl Schmitt famously defended a flexible interpretation of delegations.[58] He indicated that the degree to which a delegation is specified should not influence its permissibility: either the cession of rulemaking powers by the Legislature is allowed or it is not. The authoritarian regime that proliferated during the Interbellum internalized this approach to delegations by adopting the enabling statute (*Ermächtigungsgesetz*) on 23 March 1933. The statute enabled Chancellor Adolf Hitler and his cabinet to amend other statutes and even the Constitution.[59] Germany's history is heavily influenced by the atrocities that took place during the Second World War as a result of the deficiencies in the rule of law and democracy. The German Basic Law of 1949 was shaped to prevent such broad delegation.[60]

Article 76, 1 of the Basic Law names the Bundestag, the Bundesrat, and the federal government as the exclusive actors in the legislative process based on the legislative initiative. The Legislature is the leading power[61] of democratic legitimacy

[54] French Council of State no. 210412 of 30 June 2000, § 5; French Council of State no. 28467 of 28 September 1984; Prime Minister and Council of State, *Guide de légistique* (3rd edn, La documentation française 2017) 333.

[55] Carl Schmitt, 'Vergleichender Überblick über die neueste Entwicklung des Problems der gesetzgeberischen Ermächtigungen' [1936] *ZaöR* 260.

[56] Sidney Jacoby, 'Delegation of Powers and Judicial Review: A Study in Comparative Law' [1936] *Colum. L. Rev.* 884.

[57] Ibid., 885.

[58] Carl Schmitt, 'Vergleichender Überblick über die neueste Entwicklung des Problems der gesetzgeberischen Ermächtigungen' [1936] *ZaöR* 267.

[59] Werner Heun, *The Constitution of Germany* (Hart 2011) 110.

[60] Gerhard Leibholz and Hans-Justus Rinck, *Grundgesetz für die Bundesrepublik Deutschland* (Otto Schmidt 1971) 621; Hermann Pünder, 'Democratic Legitimation of Delegated Legislation—A Comparative View on the American, British and German Law' [2009] *ICLQ* 363; Werner Heun, *The Constitution of Germany* (Hart 2011) 152.

[61] Christoph Degenhart, *Staatsorganisationsrecht* (Müller 2013) 114.

in the federation.[62] Far-reaching socio-political decisions thus have to be made by Parliament and not solely by the Executive.[63]

The German Basic Law, which creates a parliamentary system with a President as head of state, does not grant any rulemaking power directly to the President. Articles 54, 59, and 60 of the Basic Law merely give the President, powers with regard to international representation, the appointment of civil servants and the ability to pardon individual offenders. The German President ratifies statutes, by which he or she confirms the existence of the rule. The President cannot veto rulemaking acts based on opportunistic considerations and is deemed to have veto powers solely based on reasons of formal legality.[64]

The federal government, on the other hand, may be authorized by law to issue statutory instruments on policy matters, based on and limited by article 80, 1 of the Basic Law.[65] The rules made as a consequence of a legislative delegation to the Executive are coined 'executive regulations' (*Rechtsverordnungen*).[66] At least following a strict reading of article 80, 1 of the Basic Law, the Legislature can only delegate the power to make executive regulations directly to the federal government, a federal minister, or a government of a federated entity.[67] However, these three types of actors can subdelegate their authority—by adopting a regulation—if the enabling statute so allows.

With regard to their ability to receive delegations, individual ministers can also obtain rulemaking powers under article 80, 1 of the Basic Law. Federal ministers represent the bridge between the federal government and the administration. Article 65 of the Basic Law obliges each federal minister to conduct the affairs of his/her department independently and on his/her own responsibility.[68] As a result,

[62] Konrad Hesse, *Grundzüge des Verfassungsrechts der Bundesrepublik Deutschland* (Müller 1975) 205; Florian Becker, *Kooperative und konsensuale Strukturen in der Normsetzung* (Mohr Siebeck 2005) 351.

[63] Harald Eberhard, 'Das Legalitätsprinzip im Spannungsfeld von Gemeinschaftsrecht und nationalem Recht' [2008] *ZöR* 84

[64] Hartmut Bauer, 'Artikel 82 GG' in Horst Dreier (ed.), *Grundgesetz Kommentar* (Mohr Siebeck 2004) 1902.

[65] '1. The federal government, a federal minister or the Land governments may be authorised by a law to issue statutory instruments. The content, purpose and scope of the authority conferred shall be specified in the law. Each statutory instrument shall contain a statement of its legal basis. If the law provides that such authority may be further delegated, such subdelegation shall be effected by statutory instrument.'

[66] Christoph Degenhart, *Staatsorganisationsrecht* (Müller 2013) 131.

[67] That is consistent with the paradigm that there is an inherent difference between the Legislature or these three other politically accountable actors and autonomous public, private or hybrid actors. Konrad Hesse, *Grundzüge des Verfassungsrechts der Bundesrepublik Deutschland* (Müller 1975) 211; Hartmut Bauer, 'Artikel 80 GG' in Horst Dreier (ed.), *Grundgesetz Kommentar* (Mohr Siebeck 2004) 1844–5 and 1854.

[68] Daniel Halberstam, 'The Promise of Comparative Administrative Law: A Constitutional Perspective on Independent Agencies' in Susan Rose-Ackerman and Peter Lindseth (eds), *Comparative Administrative Law* (Edgar Elgar 2010) 191.

they have historically steered the administration in such a way that it has minimal administrative discretion.[69]

The federal administration is an extension of this federal government. According to article 86 of the Basic Law, the federal government arranges the establishment of the administration. Indirectly, the limitations on the federal government to receive rulemaking powers will also apply to the entire federal administration.

3.1.4 United Kingdom

The UK does not have a written or codified constitution with constitutional provisions. Arguably, though, the most important constitutional principle in the UK is the sovereignty of Parliament.[70] Dicey defined this principle as: 'Parliament can legally legislate on any topic whatever which, in the judgment of Parliament, is a fit subject for legislation.'[71] The famous description of this principle by De Lolme, echoed by Dicey, is that Parliament can do everything but turn a man into a woman.[72] Popelier correctly jests that Parliament can actually turn a man into a woman simply by amending the legal definition of each gender.[73] The principle of sovereignty of Parliament has been nuanced during the past three decades. Nevertheless, in its most modest form the principle still means that Parliament should remain at the apex of exercising governmental powers and that it retains residual rulemaking power.[74] As a result, the UK Legislature is encumbered with the task of making generally binding, abstract rules.

The UK Executive has autonomous competences since it is invested with the royal prerogative. This prerogative is often defined in a circular manner as granting the Executive the powers that it alone can exercise.[75] As a result, the royal prerogative expands and shrinks on a case-by-case basis. The prerogative power was primarily aimed at regulating external relations with foreign nations. The milestone case of *Proclamations* of 1610 clarified that the UK Executive principally

[69] Tobias Bach, 'Delegated governance in Germany: agencies and other autonomous bodies in a Rechtsstaat', paper presented at the Third Meeting of COST Action IS0601, 'Comparative Research into Current Trends in Public Sector Organization' (CRIPO) (2008) 4.

[70] Jeffrey Goldsworthy, *Parliamentary Sovereignty. Contemporary Debates* (Cambridge University Press 2010) 106; Halsbury's Laws *of England* (5th edn, LexisNexis 2010) 'Doctrine of parliamentary sovereignty', § 98.

[71] Albert Venn Dicey, *The Law of the Constitution* (Macmillian 1965) 69–70; David Pollard, Neil Parpworth, and David Hughes, *Constitutional and Administrative Law* (Oxford University Press 2007) 49.

[72] Lord Hewart of Bury, *The New Despotism* (London Ernest Benn 1929) 19.

[73] Patricia Popelier, *Democratisch regelgeven* (Intersentia 2001) 39.

[74] Paul Craig, *Administrative Law* (Sweet & Maxwell 2016) 72; Hansard Society, 'Report: The Challenge for Parliament: Making government accountable (2001) xi; Oliver Dawn, 'The Challenge for Parliaments' [2001] *Public Law* 667.

[75] Clive Lewis, *Judicial Remedies in Public Law* (5th edn, Sweet & Maxwell 2014) 2-019 and 2-020; John McEldowney, *Public Law* (Sweet & Maxwell 2016) 235.

has no inherent and autonomous legislative or rulemaking powers.[76] This general prohibition has been confirmed, for example, with regard to the lack of power to make immigration rules solely based on the royal prerogative.[77] Nevertheless, the Executive can create rules on martial law, the civil service, and—in previous times—the British Colonies.[78] The prerogative can also contain the power to confer financial benefits.[79] One could argue that under its common law emergency powers the Executive even has the power to create rules on all matters independently of Parliament in exceptional circumstances. However, this position remains debatable, as recently attested to in practice by the Coronavirus Act 2020.[80]

In fact, due to the UK's delegation doctrine, it has become increasingly irrelevant whether the Executive can make rules through the royal prerogative. English legal practice has not followed through on the axiom of the English legal philosopher, John Locke, who said that the Legislature should make laws not legislators through delegation.[81] For more than a century, the UK Legislature has been progressively ceding significant powers to the Executive via legislative delegations. The category of rules made subsequent to such delegation is described as subordinate or secondary legislation.[82] If the delegating statute explicitly refers to the 1946 Statutory Instruments Act, the delegated rules are categorized as statutory instruments and must comply with the conditions listed in that statute. The nomenclature for the resulting statutory instruments is not uniform. The Executive's rules materialize as 'Orders', 'Regulations', 'Warrants', 'Schemes', etc.[83]

The rulemaking powers that the Legislature delegates to the Executive should preferably be detailed and technical in nature,[84] expressly adding something to primary legislation[85] and limited by predefined parameters.[86] This was underlined by

[76] William Wade and Christopher Forsyth, *Administrative Law* (Oxford University Press 2014) 737.

[77] *R (Munir) v. Home Secretary* [2012] UKSC 32; Anthony Bradley, Keith Ewing, and Christopher Knight, *Constitutional and Administrative Law* (16th edn, Pearson 2014) 599.

[78] Alex Carroll, *Constitutional and Administrative Law* (Pearson 2015) 278–9; Andrew Le Sueur, Maurice Sunkin, and Jo Eric Khushal Murkens, *Public Law* (Oxford University Press 2016) 465.

[79] Anthony Bradley, Keith Ewing, and Christopher Knight, *Constitutional and Administrative Law* (16th edn, Pearson 2014) 581.

[80] Alex Carroll, *Constitutional and Administrative Law* (Pearson 2015) 274, William Wade and Christopher Forsyth, *Administrative Law* (Oxford University Press 2014) 730–1; *Halsbury's Laws* (5th edn, LexisNexis 2010) 'The principle of legality', § 7.

[81] John Locke, *Second Treatise of Government* (Project Gutenberg 2010) ch. XI, section 141.

[82] Andrew Le Sueur, Maurice Sunkin, and Jo Eric Khushal Murkens, *Public Law* (Oxford University Press 2016) 462.

[83] Anthony Bradley, Keith Ewing, and Christopher Knight, *Constitutional and Administrative Law* (16th edn, Pearson 2014) 588; Paul Craig, *Administrative Law* (Sweet & Maxwell 2016) 436; Andrew Le Sueur, Maurice Sunkin, and Jo Eric Khushal Murkens, *Public Law* (Oxford University Press 2016) 463; Neil Parpworth, *Constitutional and Administrative Law* (Oxford University Press 2016) 204; William Wade and Christopher Forsyth, *Administrative Law* (Oxford University Press 2014) 731.

[84] Anthony Bradley, Keith Ewing, and Christopher Knight, *Constitutional and Administrative Law* (16th edn, Pearson 2014) 583; Aileen McHarg, 'What is Delegated Legislation?' [2006] *Public Law* 557.

[85] Anthony Bradley, Keith Ewing, and Christopher Knight, *Constitutional and Administrative Law* (16th edn, Pearson 2014) 595.

[86] Mark Elliott and Robert Thomas, *Public Law* (Oxford University Press 2017) 138.

the House of Lords Select Committee on the Constitution in its report of November 2018 on 'The Legislative Process: The Delegation of Powers'. However, there are no strict constitutional limits to the amount of power that the Legislature can transfer to the Executive. Any such limit would hamper parliamentary sovereignty. It is perfectly possible to draft only skeleton legislation and enable the Executive to give substance to the rulemaking framework.[87]

One category of delegated legislation reveals the far-reaching results of this practice, namely rules made in application of Henry VIII powers, which take their name from the king who personified executive autocracy.[88] They imply that the Executive can not only enact generally binding rules but that it can also supersede prior rules that the Legislature had enacted through statute.[89] Henry VIII powers are highly controversial since they infringe on the primacy of statutory rules. Nevertheless, here there are also no clear constitutional limitations. The House of Lords Constitutional Commission merely defended the position that these powers could only be given 'where a full and clear explanation and justification is provided'.[90] A number of high-profile UK statutes have received Henry VIII clauses.[91] The UK Executive can amend statutes if a UK court declares them incompatible with the European Convention on Human Rights through the Human Rights Act 1998. A Henry VIII clause could also be found in the repealed European Communities Act 1972 to ensure proper implementation of EU law. Henry VIII clauses have been inserted in the European Union (Withdrawal) Act 2018.[92] Despite fierce criticism on its extensive use,[93] Brexit has proven to be a suitable political circumstance to resort to Henry VIII powers. To that effect, Lord Pearson had already quipped in 1997 that 'Henry VIII' powers should be renamed 'Moses' powers in the context of the UK leaving the EU because they would help to lead the British people out of Brussels' captivity.[94] It is unclear whether Lord Pearson expected the British people to wander for forty years through the desert before reaching their final destination.

[87] Hermann Pünder, 'Democratic Legitimation of Delegated Legislation—A Comparative View on the American, British and German Law' [2009] *ICLQ* 353, 360; *contra*: Aileen McHarg, 'What is Delegated Legislation?' [2006] *Public Law* 557.

[88] Alex Carroll, *Constitutional and Administrative Law* (Pearson 2015) 169.

[89] Anthony Bradley, Keith Ewing, and Christopher Knight, *Constitutional and Administrative Law* (16th edn, Pearson 2014) 581; Paul Craig, *Administrative Law* (Sweet & Maxwell 2016) 434; Mark Elliott and Robert Thomas, *Public Law* (Oxford University Press 2017) 143. These types of regulations are e.g. prohibited in the Netherlands (Rob van Gestel, 'The Deparliamentarisation of Legislation: Framework Laws and the Primacy of the Legislature' (2013) 9 *Utrecht L. Rev.* 114).

[90] House of Lords, 'Constitution Committee 6th Report', HL 51, 2010-11, para. 6.

[91] Anthony Bradley, Keith Ewing, and Christopher Knight, *Constitutional and Administrative Law* (16th edn, Pearson 2014) 586.

[92] Section 8A of the revised European Union (Withdrawal) Act 2018.

[93] Bingham Centre for the Rule of Law, 'Briefing Paper: Parliament and the Rule of Law in the Context of Brexit' (29 September 2016) 1, recommendation 3.

[94] Sionaidh Douglas-Scott, 'The "Great Repeal Bill": Constitutional Chaos and Constitutional Crisis?', UK Constitutional Law Blog (10 October 2016), available at <https://ukconstitutionallaw.org/>.

The Executive needs to be subjected to continuous and effective parliamentary control in the exercise of its rulemaking and other powers.[95] Through a three-pronged approach, Parliament manages to oversee and supervise the adoption of delegated legislation. First, the UK Parliament can utilize its ordinary tools to keep the Executive in check, namely parliamentary questions and debates.[96] Second, both houses of Parliament have developed select committees to keep abreast of delegated legislation. The House of Lords created the Parliamentary Committee on Delegated Powers and Regulatory Reform to especially scrutinize Henry VIII powers[97] and the House of Commons retains both the Regulatory Reform Committee and the Select Committee on Statutory Instruments, which examine regulations and statutory instruments respectively.[98] Third, usually the parent statutes that allow for delegated legislation grant a continuing role to Parliament when the Executive creates its rules. The delegated legislation can be subject to an affirmative, super-affirmative, or negative resolution by Parliament through which the legislators can accept, condone, or veto secondary legislation.[99]

Individual ministers can receive delegated rulemaking powers from the Legislature in the same way—and with just as few constitutional impediments—as the Executive as a whole.[100] Delegations to ministers may equally contain Henry VIII clauses. For example, section 1(1) and (2) of the Legislative and Regulatory Reform Act 2006 grants this type of broad delegation of powers to individual ministers.

The subsequent delegation of rulemaking power—which originated from the Legislature—by the Queen in Council or the Prime Minister to individual ministers or further is not allowed in principle.[101] Wade, Forsyth, Elliott, and Varuhas, however, suggest three exceptions.[102] First, the parent statute itself might have

[95] Mark Elliott and Jason N. E. Varuhas, *Administrative Law: Text and Materials* (Oxford University Press 2017) 678; Paul Craig, *Administrative Law* (Sweet & Maxwell 2016) 60.

[96] Alex Carroll, *Constitutional and Administrative Law* (Pearson 2015) 176; Peter Leyland and Gordon Anthony, *Textbook on Administrative Law* (Oxford University Press 2016) 25–6.

[97] Aileen McHarg, 'What is Delegated Legislation?' [2006] *Public Law* 556; Anthony Bradley, Keith Ewing, and Christopher Knight, *Constitutional and Administrative Law* (16th edn, Pearson 2014) 589.

[98] K. C. Wheare, 'Controlling Delegated Legislation: A British Experiment' [1949] J. Politics 748; Anthony Bradley, Keith Ewing, and Christopher Knight, *Constitutional and Administrative Law* (16th edn, Pearson 2014) 592. The House of Commons and House of Lords even joined forces in the Joint Committee on Statutory Instruments. Mark Elliott and Robert Thomas, *Public Law* (Oxford University Press 2017) 148.

[99] Ibid.; Andrew Le Sueur, Maurice Sunkin, and Jo Eric Khushal Murkens, *Public Law* (Oxford University Press 2016) 479–81; Mark Elliott and Jason N. E. Varuhas, *Administrative Law: Text and Materials* (Oxford University Press 2017) 682–4.

[100] Anthony Bradley, Keith Ewing, and Christopher Knight, *Constitutional and Administrative Law* (16th edn, Pearson 2014) 587.

[101] Mark Elliott and Jason N. E. Varuhas, *Administrative Law: Text and Materials* (Oxford University Press 2017) 686. See, for a case from New Zealand with a similar outcome for invalidation: *Hawk's boy raw milk* as referred to in Paul Craig, *Administrative Law* (Sweet & Maxwell 2016) 458.

[102] William Wade and Christopher Forsyth, *Administrative Law* (Oxford University Press 2014) 748; Mark Elliott and Jason N. E. Varuhas, *Administrative Law: Text and Materials* (Oxford University Press 2017) 691.

allowed for sub-delegation, as occurred in the British Emergency Powers (Defence) Act 1939 leading up to the Second World War. Second, even without such statutory interpretation, emergency cases for national security could likewise warrant sub-delegating rulemaking powers to ministers. Third, if the Crown transfers powers -originally derived from the royal prerogative—to ministers via an Order in Council this is also within the discretion of the Executive.[103] As an autonomous and inherent power of the Executive, the transfer of the prerogative does not actually concern a subsequent delegation, but an original delegation.

3.1.5 United States

In the US Constitution, no clear reference can be found to the delegation of rulemaking powers. According to article I, § 1 of the US Constitution, 'all legislative Powers herein granted shall be vested in a Congress of the United States, which shall consist of a Senate and House of Representatives.' According to article I, § 8, cl. 18, 'The Congress shall have Power … To make all Laws which shall be necessary and proper for carrying into Execution the foregoing Powers, and all other Powers vested by this Constitution in the Government of the United States, or in any Department or Office thereof.' It is said that the cited 'necessary' (*pro* delegation) and 'proper' (*contra* delegation) clause balances itself out, leaving no constitutional guidance on the permissibility of delegation.

Still, as a matter of principle, 'the legislative power of Congress cannot be delegated', which the US Supreme Court considered to be 'clear'.[104] US Supreme Court Chief Justice Taft even referred to the maxim: *delegata potestas non potest delegari* (what has been delegated may not be delegated).[105] In *Wayman v. Southard*, the US Supreme Court had previously stated more precisely that Congress could delegate powers which it could rightfully exercise itself but is not allowed to delegate powers that are strictly and exclusively legislative.[106] In practice, since its acceptance of the New Deal, the Court has been extremely lenient in allowing various sorts of delegation, including of rulemaking power, to the Executive with only few exceptions.[107] If Congress lays down an intelligible principle with which the delegatee is directed to conform, such action is not a forbidden delegation of legislative power.[108]

The rich case law of the US Supreme Court has also allowed for the direct transfer of rulemaking powers by the Legislature to members of the Cabinet on the

[103] Subject to judicial review: *Council of Civil Service Unions v. Minister for the Civil Service* [1984] UKHL 9.

[104] *United States v. Shreveport Grain & Elevator Co.*, 287 US 77, 85 (1932).

[105] *J. W. Hampton, Jr. & Co. v. United States*, 276 US 394, 405 (1928).

[106] *Wayman v. Southard*, 23 US (10 Wheat.) at 42.

[107] Cornell Legal Information Institute, US Constitution Annotated, Article I., Legislative department, Section I, Delegation of legislative power.

[108] *J. W. Hampton, Jr. and Co. v. United States*, 276 US 394 (1928).

condition that they are not excessive (*filling in the details*).[109] It is possible to reference the delegation to the Commissioner of Internal Revenue, the Secretary of the Treasury, etc.[110]

Moreover, 3 USC § 302 concerning delegation of authority by the President to members of the Cabinet, states that 'nothing herein shall be deemed to require express authorization in any case in which such an official would be presumed in law to have acted by authority or direction of the president', confirming the wide leeway the President has in delegating rulemaking powers to members of the Cabinet in line with article II, § 1, cl. 1 of the US Constitution.

The bulk of the legal literature and case law still endorses the non-delegation doctrine but, regardless, delegation of rulemaking powers occurs on a regular basis. Merrill described this counter-legal practice as 'a low-level but persistent crisis of legitimacy'.[111] In 2002, Posner and Vermeule wrote an influential article which 'interred' the non-delegation doctrine.[112] They found no 'roots of the doctrine in history, tradition, and legislative or judicial precedent'.[113] The non-delegation doctrine has not resulted in the striking down of any important delegation by the US Supreme Court since the New Deal.[114]

3.2 Rulemaking powers exercised by autonomous public and private actors

Rulemaking powers are also being transferred beyond the traditional Executive to autonomous public and private actors within the countries researched. Again this phenomenon is first approached through the existing constitutional provisions of those countries.

3.2.1 Belgium

Article 33 of the Belgian Constitution declares that all powers 'emanate from the Nation' and that they should be 'exercised in the manner *laid down in the*

[109] *United States v. Grimaud*, 220 US 506 (1911).

[110] *In re Kollock*, 165 US 526 (1897); *Buttfield v. Stranahan*, 192 US 470 (1904). Other examples are: *United States v. Bailey*, 34 US. (9 Pet.) 238 (1835); *Caha v. United States*, 152 US 211 (1894); *ICC v. Goodrich Transit Co.*, 224 US 194 (1912).

[111] Thomas W. Merrill, 'Rethinking article I, section 1: From Nondelegation to Exclusive Delegation' (2004) 104 *Colum. L. Rev.* 2097, 2100.

[112] Eric Posner and Adrian Vermeule, 'Interring the Non-Delegation Doctrine' (2002) 69 *U. Chi. L. Rev.* 1721–62.

[113] Ibid., 1732–3.

[114] Eoin Carolan, 'Democratic Accountability and the Non-Delegation Doctrine' [2011] *Dublin U. LJ* IV (i) The American Non-delegation Doctrine.

Constitution'.[115] The delegation of rulemaking powers to the traditional Executive at least still complies with articles 105 and 108 of the Constitution, which respectively give the King a derived and autonomous authority to exercise rulemaking powers.[116] No similar powers were invested in ministers or the central administration, but they are still named in Title III (The Powers) of the Belgian Constitution; however, autonomous public or private actors are not named in that title. As a result of article 33 of the Belgian Constitution—read in conjunction with articles 36, 37, 105, and 108—the outsourcing of rulemaking powers to autonomous public or private actors is thus constitutionally problematic.[117]

One suprastatutory provision mentions the existence of autonomous public actors in general. Article 9 of the 1980 federal Special Majority Act pertaining to the Reform of State Institutions proclaims that: 'For the matters within their competence, the Communities and the Regions may establish *decentralized services, institutions and undertakings*'.[118] This provision does not have constitutional value, yet hierarchically trumps statutory provisions. It lays out the groundwork for the Belgian federated entities to receive governmental (also rulemaking) powers. It further posits that 'the *statute* [of the Community or the Region] regulates [the] establishment, composition, *authority, operation and supervision* of the [decentralized services, institutions and undertakings]'.[119] This provision implies a specific legality principle and could have been construed as a strict limit to the outsourcing of rulemaking powers within the federated entities. However, the Constitutional Court and the Council of State Legislative Section do not appear to apply a stricter scrutiny of delegations to federated autonomous public or private entities than those of delegations to federal autonomous public or private entities.[120]

Article 24 of the Constitution, which enshrines the right to education, is the only Belgian constitutional provision that explicitly refers to an 'autonomous body'. More precisely, article 24, §§ 2 and 5 of the Belgian Constitution states that:

> § 2. If a community, in its capacity as an organising authority, wishes to delegate powers [regarding education] to one or several *autonomous bodies*, it

[115] Emphasis added.

[116] Belgian Council of State Legislative Section, Advisory opinion no. 54.536/2/2 of 19 December 2013, § 3.

[117] Jeroen Van Nieuwenhove, 'Delegatie van regelgevende bevoegdheid in België' [2017] *Tijdschrift voor Wetgeving* 209; Pierre Nihoul, 'Les autorités administratives indépendantes en Belgique' [2013] *RFDA* 897, fn. 11; André Alen, *Handboek van het Belgisch Staatsrecht* (Mechelen, Kluwer 1995) 224.

[118] Emphasis added.

[119] Emphasis added.

[120] See later and compare, e.g., Belgian Constitutional Court no. 24/98, 10 March 1998 (federated entity) with Belgian Constitutional Court no. 86/2015, 11 June 2015 (federal). See also Sven Baeten and Frederik Vandendriessche, 'Oprichting van rechtspersonen en participaties' in Bruno Seutin and Geert van Haegendoren (eds), *De transversale bevoegdheden in het federale België* (die Keure 2017) 296–8; Jan Velaers, *De Grondwet en de Raad van State Afdeling Wetgeving* (Maklu 1999) 812–14.

can only do so by federate (federated entity) law adopted by a two-thirds majority of the votes cast.

§5. The organisation, the recognition and the subsidising of education by the community are regulated by the law or federate (federated entity) law.

These paragraphs, adopted in 1988, contain a constitutional permission to outsource governmental power.[121] However, article 24 of the Belgian Constitution is believed not to enable delegations of *rulemaking* powers to autonomous educational bodies.[122] This was already apparent from the preparatory comments of the Belgian constitutional drafters.[123] In particular, one Constitutional Court case addressed the powers of the autonomous education bodies. In this case, the Flemish Autonomous Council of Public Education wished to forbid students wearing headscarves in schools. The question arose as to whether the Autonomous Council was competent to do so. The Constitutional Court affirmed the Autonomous Council's competence because it was not exercising any rulemaking function; rather, it had adopted a code of 'internal order'.[124] According to the court, the prohibition on headscarves did not bind third parties in a general and abstract manner. Arguably, the court wished to maintain the parallel between, on the one hand, the public school system and, on the other hand, the private school system with clear codes of internal order. This contrived argument can be criticized. Pupils wishing to wear headscarves in public schools appear to be clear third parties bound in a general and abstract manner by the Autonomous Council's code of 'internal order', thus making it a 'rule'.

Article 23 of the Belgian Constitution enshrines social, economic, and cultural rights in Belgium. The joint legislative declaration of 12 April 1995 had marked this provision for revision with the aim of amending it and introducing a right to minimum service for postal services, communications, and mobility.[125] Some Members of Parliament had even urged the extension of the declaration to a minimum right to energy.[126] If article 23 of the Belgian Constitution had been amended accordingly, this human rights provision could have been used as a limit

[121] Jan De Groof, 'Hoe bijzonder is het bijzonder decreet in uitvoering van artikel 24, §2 GW' [1995–6] *TORB* 1.

[122] e.g. Jan Velaers, *De Grondwet, een artikelsgewijze commentaar* (die Keure 2019) article 24, §§ 5, 8; Eddie Clybouw, 'Een evaluatie van artikel 24, § 2 GW en de bijzondere onderwijsdecreten ter uitvoering daarvan' [2005] *TBP* 643.

[123] Parliamentary preparation as mentioned in judgment Belgian Constitutional Court no. 40/2011, 15 March 2011, B.17.1: Constitutional Drafters, *Herziening van artikel 17 van de Grondwet met uitzondering van de woorden 'Het onderwijs is vrij, elke preventieve maatregel is verboden' (Maximale toekenning van de bevoegdheid inzake onderwijsbeleid aan de Gemeenschappen)* (Acts of the Belgian Senate *B.Z.* 1988, no. 100/1, 14 June 1988) 520 and with regard to the Autonomous Council of Community Education: Draft Flemish Statute, *Ontwerp van bijzonder decreet betreffende de Autonome Raad voor het Gemeenschapsonderwijs* (Parliamentary Documents Flanders 1988–9, no. 161/1) 9.

[124] Belgian Constitutional Court no. 40/2011, 15 March 2011, B.17.2.

[125] Parliamentary preparation federal Chamber of Representatives 1994–5, no. 1740/1, 5.

[126] Ibid., 19–21.

to the outsourcing of rulemaking powers in network industry sectors.[127] However, the constitutional amendment was not eventually adopted.

According to article 34 of the Constitution the exercise of specific powers can be assigned by a treaty or by a law to institutions of public international law. This provision was introduced in the Belgian Constitution in 1971 to meet the challenges of European integration. The Constitutional Court established that the absence of hierarchical or administrative supervision of the national energy regulator's (CREG's) competence to establish administrative fines was not contrary to the Belgian Constitution. Yet, as if to anticipate any criticism of its ruling, the court offered a potential trump card to allow delegations to autonomous public bodies, even if the national test was not met. By means of an *obiter dictum*, it recalled that—to the extent that CREG would be excessively independent of the Executive—the transfer of powers was still acceptable under article 34 of the Constitution because the EU obliged its independence.[128] Belgian scholarship was not at all impressed with the interpretation of article 34 as a master key to open all locks on internationally inspired governmental bodies.[129] It appeared that the Constitutional Court had unprecedentedly sacrificed Belgian constitutional provisions and principles to the benefit of EU and international law. However, in a 2016 judgment on the Stability and Growth Pact (62/2016), the court clarified through one more *obiter dictum* that article 34 of the Belgian Constitution was not a blank cheque to transfer powers to the international level.[130] According to the Constitutional Court, it would prevent the "Belgian national identity, enshrined in political or constitutional basic structures, and core values of constitutional protection for the constituency" being infringed (even by international law with direct effect).[131] Any transfer of powers to internationally inspired autonomous public or private actors could thus also run against those limits. As attested to by its then acting president, André Alen, the Belgian Constitutional Court had been influenced by the vehement criticism on its *obiter dictum* regarding article 34 in judgment 130/2010.[132]

[127] Dimitri Yernault, 'Les limitations constitutionnelles a la privatisation—Rapport belge', XVth International Congress of Comparative Law, Bristol (26 July–1 August 1998, unpublished) 44. This argument, as has been made in Germany, was nipped in the bud in Belgium, maintaining constitutional silence.

[128] Belgian Constitutional Court no. 130/2010, 18 November 2010, B.8.1. Philippe Gérard and Willem Verrijdt, 'Belgian Constitution Court Adopts National Identity Discourse. Belgian Constitutional Court No. 62/2016, 28 April 2016' [2017] *Eur. Const. L. Rev.* 186.

[129] Stéphanie De Somer, 'The creation of autonomous public bodies from a European comparative legal perspective: international impulse, national restraint and how to reconcile these trends', PhD thesis, University of Antwerp (2015) 329–30; Michel Pâques, 'Décentralisation, régulation et contrôle démocratique: l'arrêt 130/2010 en question' in David D'Hooghe, Kurt Deketelaere, and Anne Mie Draye (eds), *Liber amicorum Marc Boes* (die Keure 2011) 411 and 423; Emmanuel Slautsky, 'Droit européen, Constitution et autorités administratives indépendantes: commentaire de l'arrêt de la Cour constitutionnelle du 18 novembre 2010, no. 130/2010 et de l'arrêt du Conseil d'État du 7 avril 2011, Ville de Wavre, no. 212.557' [2012] Administration Publique—Trimestriel 112.

[130] Belgian Constitutional Court no. 62/2016, 28 April 2016.

[131] Ibid., B.8.7.

[132] André Alen, 'De nationale identiteit—Slotwoord' [2017] *Tijdschrift voor Bestuurswetenschappen en Publiekrecht* 367.

At least thirteen Belgian authors have explicitly pleaded for the introduction of a new or amended constitutional provision to regulate the outsourcing of rulemaking powers.[133] In fact, the 2010 and 2014 declarations to amend the Belgian Constitution declared Title III of the Belgian Constitution amendable to insertion of a provision on 'functional decentralisation'. However, no constitutional amendment was eventually adopted.

3.2.2 France

Charles Ganilh declared on 24 ventôse of the year VIII (14 March 1800): '[If the branches of the Legislature could delegate rulemaking powers to one and another] they could [transfer rulemaking powers] to *all*; they could dispose of the power, which they merely hold and safeguard. *A monstrous system* that no one will doubtlessly attempt to establish nor justify.'[134] The transfer of rulemaking powers beyond the traditional branches of government was thus the standard of what should be avoided in governance.

No indication is currently present in the French Constitution of an aim to vest rulemaking powers in private actors. However, a lot of ink has been spilled on autonomous public actors, the *autorités administratives indépendantes* (AAIs). This designation was invented by Professor Maisl and later adopted by Parliament in the lead-up to the first French AAI in 1978: the National Committee on Information and Liberties (CNIL).[135] Initially, these autonomous public actors were established

[133] Valérie De Schepper and Emmanuel Slautsky, 'Decentralisering en privatisering van regelgevende bevoegdheid: naar een grondwettelijke verankering?' in *Leuvense Staatsrechtelijke Standpunten* (Die Keure 2019) III.b; Laura De Deyne, Markttoezicht in de energiesector (Intersentia 2017) 122; Pierre Nihoul, 'Les autorités administratives indépendantes en Belgique' [2013] *RFDA* 902; Patricia Popelier and Jeroen Van Nieuwenhove, 'Decentralisering en privatisering van wetgeving' in Jef De Mot (ed.), *Vrank en vrij: liber amicorum Boudewijn Bouckaert* (Die Keure 2012) 284–5; Koen Muylle, 'Het grondwettelijk delegatieverbod en het Unierecht' in André Alen and Jan Theunis (eds), *Leuvense Staatsrechtelijke Standpunten 3* (die Keure 2012) 352; M. Nihoul, 'Les affres de la législation en matière d' "autorité administrative" et le respect de la Constitution' [2008] *JT* 71–3; Pierre Nihoul, 'Pouvoir réglementaire dérivé et dérives du pouvoir réglementaire' in Robert Andersen (ed.), *En hommage à Francis Delpérée. Itinéraires d'un constitutionnaliste* (Bruylant 2007) 1135; Hugues Dumont, 'La Constitution et le contrôle parlementaire des délégations de pouvoirs aux autorités administratives. Pour un renouveau du régimes parlementaire belge à l'heure de la gouvernance' in André Alen, Arnold Rainer, and Marc Bossuyt (eds), *De Grondwet: verleden, heden en toekomst* (Bruylant 2006) 66; Xavier Delgrange and Luc Detroux, 'Les limites constitutionnelles à la privatisation' in Bruno Lombaert (ed.), *Les partenariats public-privé (PPP): un défi pour le droit des services publics* (La Charte 2005) 84–5; Genevieve Cerexhe, 'Les ministres disposent-ils d'un pouvoir réglementaire?' [1984] *Administration publique* 183; Jean Laguesse, 'La participation des organisations professionnelles à l'exercice du pouvoir réglementaire' [1966] *Recueil de jurisprudence du droit administratif et du Conseil d'Etat* 94.

[134] Philippe Azouaou, *L'indisponibilité des compétences en droit public interne* (Marc & Martin 2012) 27 (emphasis added).

[135] Martine Lombard and Gilles Dumont, *Droit administratif* (Dalloz 2003) 115; Stéphanie Dubiton, *La protection des libertés publiques par les autorités administratives indépendantes, une solution démocratique?* (LGDJ 2016) 9; Jean-Marc Sauvé, 'Les autorités administratives indépendantes' in *Transcription d'intervention Comité d'évaluation et de contrôle des politiques publiques (CEC) sur les autorités administratives indépendantes* (Conseil d'État 2010) fnn. 1 and 2; soon after, other AAIs such

by statute without a legal basis in the Constitution or Organic Statutes. This equally led to a high degree of hybridity within the various AAIs with, for example, a myriad number of ways to assign their members.[136] Only one AAI was eventually explicitly named in the French Constitution in 2008: the Defender of Rights (*Défenseur des Droits*).[137] Article 71-1 of the French Constitution declares that the Defender of Rights 'shall ensure the due respect of rights and freedoms by state administrations, territorial communities, public legal entities, as well as by all bodies carrying out a public service mission or by those that the Organic Statute decides that fall within his remit'. He or she thus acts as a type of public ombudsman with reinforced competences.[138] At one point, the constitutionalization of the Superior Council of the Audiovisual (CSA) was also seriously considered but was eventually not carried out.[139]

The constitutionalization of AAIs as a general category had been suggested by President Mitterrand but was discarded by the advisory Vedel Committee in 1993.[140] Three reasons explain why a general provision on AAIs was never introduced in the French Constitution.[141] First, AAIs had already become widespread—it is easier to build on pre-existing foundations than to insert foundations under a dwelling already in situ. Moreover, some legislators feared that a constitutional embedding would decrease the flexibility with which the actions of AAIs were usually accompanied. If the exercise of all powers of AAIs had to fit into a

as CADA and CASA would follow suit; French Council of State, 'Considérations générales. Les autorités administratives indépendantes' in Renaud Denoix de Saint Marc (ed.), *Reports French Council of State* (Conseil d'État 2001) 261.

[136] Merryl Hervieu, *Les autorités administratives indépendantes et le renouvellement du droit commun des contrats* (Dalloz 2012) 8.

[137] Jean-Louis Autin and Emmanuel Breen, *Autorités Administratives Indépendantes* (JurisClasseur Administratif 75, 4 April 2017) § 29; Pierre de Montalivet, 'Constitution et autorités de régulation' [2014] *RDP* 316, II.A.2. Other constitutional indications that would lay the foundations for the development of AAIs are implicit at most. Some argue that the independent commission defining the election constituencies of article 25, 3 of the French Constitution—albeit not constituting an AAI itself—embodies a constitutional confirmation of independence that is so central to AAI (Pierre de Montalivet, 'Constitution et autorités de régulation' [2014] *RDP* 316, II.A.2). Ultimately, article 37-1 allowing for experimental statutes and executive regulations has been construed as a possible basis for (functional?) decentralization (Bertrand Foure, 'L'intégration de l'expérimentation au droit public français' in Franck Moderne (ed.), *Mélanges en l'honneur de Franck Moderne* (Dalloz 2004) 178–9).

[138] Even though it does not have financial autonomy, since it does not count as a *pouvoir public constitutionnel*: French Constitutional Council no. 2011-626 of 29 March 2011. Stéphanie Dubiton, *La protection des libertés publiques par les autorités administratives indépendantes, une solution démocratique?* (LGDJ 2016) 234.

[139] Tanneguy Larzul and Pierre de Montalivet, *Droit constitutionnel de l'administration* (JurisClasseur Administratif 2017) § 31; Jean-Philippe Feldman, 'Les "autorités administratives indépendantes" sont-elles légitimes? Sur les AAI en général et le Conseil supérieur de l'audiovisuel en particulier' [2010] *Recueil Dalloz* 2852 etc., last paragraph.

[140] Ibid., last paragraph; French Council of State, 'Considérations générales. Les autorités administratives indépendantes' in Renaud Denoix de Saint Marc (ed.), *Reports French Council of State* (Conseil d'État 2001) 297; Jean-Louis Autin and Emmanuel Breen, *Autorités Administratives Indépendantes* (JurisClasseur Administratif 75, 4 April 2017) § 30.

[141] Pierre de Montalivet, 'Constitution et autorités de régulation' [2014] *RDP* 316, II.A.1.

predetermined straitjacket, the AAI would lose part of its attraction and the competence might as well have been exercised by a traditional branch of government. Third, the case law of the Constitutional Council had already embraced the existence of AAIs without a constitutional provision.

Indeed, the French Constitutional Council did not question the constitutionality of AAIs when it was asked to review their creation or the transfer of governmental powers to a number of them.[142] The Council mustered remarkable pragmatism. Over the last three decades it has never invalidated (the independence of) an AAI.[143] The Constitutional Council even suggested that the French Constitution could require the existence of an AAI. The replacement of officials of the High Authority of the Audiovisual through the creation of a new AAI, the National Committee of Communications and Liberties (CNCL), could only occur if this 'does not take away legal guarantees from constitutional requirements'.[144] The French Constitutional Council did not eventually apply its test stringently in the CNCL case itself, since it condoned the disguised overturning of the High Authority of the Audiovisual by the CNCL.[145] The Constitutional Council thus clearly allows for AAIs but it does not oblige their (continued) existence for the protection of constitutional freedoms.

After various scholarly calls to amend the French Constitution or to adopt new legislation in order to streamline the system of AAIs,[146] Organic Statute 2017-54 on AAIs and APIs (*autorités publiques indépendantes*) was eventually adopted on 20 January 2017, together with an ordinary statute (2017–55). This (organic) statute mainly provides a common framework for all autonomous public actors in France, even though it is currently exclusively applicable to the twenty-five autonomous authorities that the ordinary statute lists. The French Constitutional Council declared these statutes on AAIs and APIs to be in conformity with the French Constitution.[147] Organic Statutes, as discussed in article 46 of the French Constitution, are hierarchically inferior to the Constitution but superior to

[142] French Constitutional Council no. 84-173 of 26 July 1984 with regard to the *Haute autorité de la communication audiovisuelle*; French Constitutional Council no. 86-217 of 18 September 1986 with regard to the *Commission nationale de la communication et des libertés*; French Constitutional Council no. 86-224 of 23 January 1987 with regard to the *Conseil de la concurrence*; French Constitutional Council, no. 88-248 of 17 January 1989 with regard to the *Conseil supérieur de l'audiovisuel*; French Constitutional Council no. 89-260 of 28 July 1989 with regard to the *Commission des opérations de bourse*; Tanneguy Larzul and Pierre de Montalivet, *Droit constitutionnel de l'administration* (JurisClasseur Administratif 2017) § 13; Jacques Chevalier, 'Autorités administratives indépendantes et État de droit' [2016] *Civitas Europa* 144.

[143] Pierre de Montalivet, 'Constitution et autorités de régulation' [2014] *RDP* 316.

[144] French Constitutional Council no. 86-217 of 18 September 1986 with regard to the *Commission nationale de la communication et des libertés*, § 82.

[145] Tanneguy Larzul and Pierre de Montalivet, *Droit constitutionnel de l'administration* (JurisClasseur Administratif 2017) § 15.

[146] e.g. Roland Drago, 'Pour ou contre les autorités administratives indépendantes' in Robert Andersen (ed.), *En hommage à Francis Delpérée. Itinéraires d'un constitutionnaliste* (Bruylant 2007) 476; Pierre de Montalivet, 'Constitution et autorités de régulation' [2014] *RDP* 316.

[147] X, 'La réforme des AAI conforme à la Constitution' [2017] AJDA 142.

ordinary statutes.[148] The Constitutional Council can henceforth review ordinary statutes against Organic Statute 2017-54 through article 34, 8 of the Constitution. The last provision (reserving powers to the Legislature) internalizes organic statutes in the French Constitution by stating that 'the provisions of this article may be further specified and completed by an Organic Statute'.[149] Article 1 of Organic Statute 2017-54 determines that AAIs and APIs have to be established by statute and that a statute regulates their composition, competences, and the essentials of their organization or functioning.[150] The Organic Statute thus claims the establishment of AAIs and APIs as the exclusive competence of the Legislature.[151] This important statutory link with AAIs could not previously be derived from article 34 of the Constitution since it did not mention them.[152] As a result of this Organic Statute, autonomous public actors have been semi-introduced in the French Constitution.

It is one matter to establish an autonomous public actor; it is an entirely different matter to grant rulemaking powers to it. These apparent problems emanate from the constitutional provisions themselves. When rulemaking powers were being transferred to the CNIL, Senator M. Tinguy vehemently argued that 'the attribution of "reglementary" power to a commission, a group or an organization independent from the Executive poses problems'.[153] First, article 3 of the Declaration of the Rights of Man and of the Citizen states that the principle of sovereignty resides primarily in the nation: 'No corporate body and no individual may exercise any authority that does not expressly derive from the nation.' Given the constitutional silence on autonomous public actors, it is not a straightforward matter whether the 'nation' expressly grants autonomous public actors (rulemaking) powers.[154] Equally, article 13 that stipulates the powers of the President and article 20 that appoints the government to determine and conduct the policy of the nation, seem to contradict rulemaking powers within autonomous public actors.[155] Article 20, 2 of the Constitution equally proclaims that the government has the administration

[148] Sophie Boyron, *The Constitution of France: A Contextual Analysis* (Hart 2012) 47.

[149] French Constitutional Council no. 60-8 of 11 August 1960, § 3.

[150] Jean-Louis Autin and Emmanuel Breen, *Autorités Administratives Indépendantes* (JurisClasseur Administratif 75, 4 April 2017) § 1; Philippe Bachschmidt, ' Première extension "authentique" du domaine de la loi par le législateur organique' [2017] *Constitutions* 55; Vincent Tchen, *Domaines de la loi et du règlement* (JurisClasseur Administratif 106, 4 April 2017) § 57.

[151] Jacques Chevalier, 'Autorités administratives indépendantes et État de droit' [2016] *Civitas Europa* 153.

[152] Merryl Hervieu, *Les autorités administratives indépendantes et le renouvellement du droit commun des contrats* (Dalloz 2012) 8.

[153] Stéphanie Dubiton, *La protection des libertés publiques par les autorités administratives indépendantes, une solution démocratique?* (LGDJ 2016) 91.

[154] French Council of State, 'Considérations générales. Les autorités administratives indépendantes' in Renaud Denoix de Saint Marc (ed.), *Reports French Council of State* (Conseil d'État 2001) 284.

[155] Thomas Perroud, *La fonction contentieuse des autorités de régulation en France et au Royaume-Uni* (Dalloz 2013) 85; Bertrand Marais, 'Convergence entre télécommunications et audiovisuel en France' [9 August 2008] *Gazette du Palais* 5, I.1.2; Pierre de Montalivet, 'Constitution et autorités de régulation' [2014] *RDP* I.B.1.

at its disposal, which would at first sight not allow for the independent rulemaking powers of AAIs.[156] The strongest objections against the outsourcing of rulemaking powers arguably derive from article 21 of the French Constitution, in general terms granting the 'reglementary' (rulemaking) powers to the Prime Minister.[157] However, according to the established case law of the Constitutional Council, article 21 does not 'form an impediment for the Legislature to transfer to a *state authority, other than* the Prime Minister, the competence to fix rules enabling to execute a statute'.[158]

Private actors may in some circumstances have a specific constitutional basis to receive rulemaking powers, especially in the area of social law. The Constitutional Council explicitly invoked the eighth paragraph of the preamble to the 1946 Constitution as a basis for employers and employees to concretize and execute statutes.[159] This provision ensures that all workers can participate in the collective determination of their conditions of work and in the management of their workplace through the intermediary of their representatives. Furthermore, article 1 of the Constitution purposefully describes France as an indivisible, secular, democratic, and *social* Republic. Admittedly, article 34 reserves the power to determine the basic principles of employment law, trade union law, and social security to the Legislature, but this does not impede the execution of these basic principles by collective labour agreements.[160]

Ultimately, the entry into force of the Maastricht Treaty triggered article 88-1 of the Constitution, which incorporated the EU Treaties into the French Constitution[161] and increased the impact of EU law in the national legal order. Originally introduced in 1992, this provision states that 'the Republic shall participate in the European Union ... by virtue of the Treaty on the European Union and of the Treaty on the Functioning of the European Union'. The Constitutional Council in its *TECE22* case[162] recognized article 88-1 as the internalization of EU

[156] Tanneguy Larzul and Pierre de Montalivet, *Droit constitutionnel de l'administration* (JurisClasseur Administratif 2017) § 8; Pierre de Montalivet, 'Constitution et autorités de régulation' [2014] *RDP* I.A.2; Jean-Philippe Feldman, 'Les "autorités administratives indépendantes" sont-elles légitimes? Sur les AAI en général et le Conseil supérieur de l'audiovisuel en particulier' [2010] *Recueil Dalloz* 2852 etc., I.

[157] Arnaud Haquet, 'Le pouvoir réglementaire des autorités administratives indépendantes. Reflexion sur son objet et sa légitimité' [2008] *RDP* 394; Catherine Teitgen-Colly, 'Les instances de régulation et la Constitution' [1990] *RDP* 175.

[158] French Constitutional Council no. 86-217 of 18 September 1986, § 58 (emphasis added), Jean-Louis Autin and Emmanuel Breen, *Autorités Administratives Indépendantes* (JurisClasseur Administratif 75, 4 April 2017) § 88; Tanneguy Larzul and Pierre de Montalivet, *Droit constitutionnel de l'administration* (JurisClasseur Administratif 2017) § 17.

[159] French Constitutional Council no 89-257 of 25 July 1989, §§ 10–11; French Constitutional Council no. 99-423 of 13 January 2000, § 28, French Constitutional Council no. 2004-494 of 29 April 2004, § 8.

[160] French Constitutional Council no. 89-269 of 22 January 1990, § 20.

[161] Emmanuel Decaux, 'France' in Dinah Shelton (ed.), *International Law and Domestic Legal Systems* (Oxford University Press 2011) 237.

[162] Sylvie Peyrou, 'Cour constitutionnelle allemande et pouvoirs de la Banque centrale européenne: le premier renvoi préjudiciel à la Cour de Justice de l'Union européenne (décision du 14 janvier 2014)' [2015] *Revue française de droit constitutionnel* 149.

law. The provision can thus be seen as the constitutional recognition of the primacy of EU law. However, the Constitutional Council made a reservation to this primacy. In line with article 88-1, EU law has prevalence over national law except in the case where it infringes 'on a rule or a principle inherent to the constitutional identity of France'.[163] At least three provisions, related to the transfer of rulemaking powers to autonomous public actors, could potentially be perceived as part of France's constitutional identity. First, 'no one doubts' that article 16 of the Declaration, enshrining the separation of powers, is a part of the national constitutional identity.[164] This can be derived from the Council's aforementioned habit of referring to the 'French version of the separation of powers'. Second, article 34 itself, listing the legislative competences, may belong to the national constitutional identity because it enshrines a 'modern' idea of the separation of powers and defends the French republican form of government.[165] Third, article 2 of the Declaration also describes resistance against oppression as a natural and imprescriptible right of man. It can certainly be argued that this right, which is one of the guarantees against limitless delegations, resides in France's constitutional identity.

3.2.3 Germany

More clearly than Belgium and France, the German Basic Law conceives of autonomous public actors within its Basic Law. They are recognized in its article 87, 3: 'autonomous federal higher authorities as well as new federal corporations and institutions under public law may be established by a federal law for matters on which the Federation has legislative power'.

European integration inspired some constitutional amendments to introduce autonomous public bodies, such as the Federal Bank (Bundesbank, article 88 of the Basic Law) in German society. Other autonomous public or private actors have been explicitly introduced into the Basic Law because of the privatization of the railways and post/telecommunications services through, respectively, article 87E (1993) and article 87F (1994). The latter article even provides that federal

[163] French Constitutional Council no. 2006-540 of 27 July 2006. Before this case, the constitutional reserve was only triggered by express contradictory provisions of the French Constitution: Martin Quesnel, *La protection de l'identité constitutionnelle de la France* (Dalloz 2015) 48; Édouard Dubout, '"Les règles ou principes inhérents à l'identité constitutionnelle de la France": une supra-constitutionnalité?' [2010] *Revue française de droit constitutionnel* 452; François-Xavier Millet, *L'Union Européenne et l'identité constitutionnelle des états membres* (LGDJ 2013) 37.

[164] Édouard Dubout, '"Les règles ou principes inhérents à l'identité constitutionnelle de la France": une supra-constitutionnalité?' [2010] *Revue française de droit constitutionnel* 459 and 474.

[165] Bertrand Mathieu, '"Les règles et les principes inhérents à l'identité constitutionnelle de la France": une catégorie juridique fonctionnelle, à définir' in Robert Andersen (ed.), *En hommage à Francis Delpérée. Itinéraires d'un constitutionnaliste* (Bruylant 2007) 986–7; Édouard Dubout, '"Les règles ou principes inhérents à l'identité constitutionnelle de la France": une supra-constitutionnalité?' [2010] *Revue française de droit constitutionnel* 474–5.

administrative authorities part with their sovereign functions in the area of post and telecommunication. One could venture an *a contrario* reasoning and claim that other types of (rulemaking) privatization should be forbidden as a result of the express recognition of autonomous public or private actors in the policy areas of railways and post/telecommunications. This theory, though, disregards the fact that the Basic Law previously explicitly stated that the railways and the postal service had to be arranged by the federal administration. An explicit recognition in the Basic Law of autonomous public or private actors within this policy field was thus considered necessary to justify their validity.

Despite its recognition of autonomous public or private actors, the German Basic Law does not explicitly allow for the delegation of rulemaking powers to them; it has no constitutional provision that clearly sets out the possible rulemaking competences of private and autonomous public bodies.[166]

For some time, there was debate on whether article 80, 1 of the Basic Law was applicable to the outsourcing of rulemaking powers.[167] That provision merely mentions that the federal government, a federal minister, or the Land governments may be authorized by law to issue statutory instruments. Autonomous public or private actors have thus been textually ignored with regard to the transfer of rulemaking powers, begging the question whether a delegation of rulemaking powers could ever be permitted by a constitutional provision such as article 80. According to some authors, article 80 was also applicable to the outsourcing of rulemaking powers because the fourth sentence of article 80, 1 broadly states that (if the law provides that such authority may be further delegated) sub-delegations shall be effected by statutory instrument. The provision appears to leave the door ajar for delegations to autonomous public or private actors. Others disagreed with that position and argue that article 80 is only applicable to delegations between the Legislature and the Executive and not to outsourced rules as a result of, for example, delegations, referrals, rules adopted by statutory corporations (*Satzungen*), or declarations of general applicability.[168] This interpretation is supported by a contextual analysis of article 80, 1 sentence 4 of the Basic Law, according to which the provision is meant for sub-delegations within the administration and not for (sub-)delegations outside the administration.[169] The German Constitutional

[166] Thomas Holzner, *Konsens im Allgemeinen Verwaltungsrecht und in der Demokratietheorie* (Mohr Siebeck 2016) 498, 509. For private actors, Anne Röthel, 'Lex mercatoria, lex sportiva, lex technica Private Rechtsetzung jenseits des Nationalstaates?' [2007] *JZ* 762.

[167] Florian Becker, *Kooperative und konsensuale Strukturen in der Normsetzung* (Mohr Siebeck 2005) 425.

[168] Thomas Züll, *Regulierung Im Politischen Gemeinwesen* (Mohr Siebeck 2014) 166; Arnd Uhle, 'Artikel 80 GG' in Volker Epping and Christian Hillgruber (eds), *Grundgesetz GG* (32nd edn, Beck 2017) § 1; Bodo Pieroth, 'Artikel 80 GG' in Hans Jarass and Bodo Pieroth, *Grundgesetz für die Bundesrepublik Deutschland Kommentar* (Beck 2012) 881.

[169] Klaus Rennert, 'Beleihung zur Rechtsetzung' [2009] *Juristenzeitung* 981.

Court (FCC) sided with the latter position that article 80 should not be considered for the outsourcing of rulemaking powers.[170]

As a result, article 33, 4 of the German Basic Law seems to come closest to establishing a framework for public powers exercised by autonomous public or private actors.[171] The provision potentially offers a fascinating constitutional bar on outsourcing rulemaking powers:[172] 'The exercise of sovereign authority on a regular basis shall, as a rule, be entrusted to members of the public service who stand in a relationship of service and loyalty defined by public law.' The limitation of article 33, 4 is only strengthened whenever basic rights are threatened.[173] At first sight, article 33, 4 would prohibit the transfer of rulemaking powers to autonomous public or private actors.[174] Private rulemakers are arguably not members of the public service and thus not allowed to exercise sovereign authority. The requirement of article 33, 4 of the Basic Law to stand in a relationship of service would become problematic for autonomous public bodies that receive rulemaking powers because they do not stand in a hierarchical relation with the rest of the administration.[175] Still, despite its absolute phrasing, the German courts do not forbid autonomous public or private actors from performing governmental tasks through article 33, 4.[176]

Finally, some authors argue that the modern applications of outsourcing rulemaking powers merely occur because of other specific constitutional provisions. The FCC explicitly stated that 'the declaration of general applicability of a [collective labour agreement] is ... a legal act of its own kind residing between

[170] BVerfG 44, 322 § 53; BVerfGE 33, 125, § 120. *Satzungen*: see Christoph Degenhart, *Staatsorganisationsrecht* (Müller 2013) 136; Fritz Ossenbühl, 'Satzung' in Josef Isensee and Paul Kirchhof (eds), *Handbuch des Staatsrechts der Bundesrepublik Deutschland*, vol. V (Beck 2005) 373. Collective labour agreements: BVerfG 33, 125; Florian Becker, *Kooperative und konsensuale Strukturen in der Normsetzung* (Mohr Siebeck 2005) 437.

[171] Thomas Holzner, *Konsens im Allgemeinen Verwaltungsrecht und in der Demokratietheorie* (Mohr Siebeck 2016) 498; Florian Becker, 'Privatisierung (*Contracting out*) von Leistungsverwaltung' in Klaus Hopt, Thomas von Hippel, and Rainer Walz (eds), *Nonprofit Organisationen in Recht, Wirtschaft und Gesellschaft* (Mohr Siebeck 2005) 352–3; Johannes Masing, 'Artikel 33 GG' in Horst Dreier (ed.), *Grundgesetz Kommentar* (Mohr Siebeck 2004) 848–9.

[172] Alexander Volokh, 'Privatization and the Constitutional Delegation of Coercive Power in Germany', Reason Foundation Blog, § 3 (last accessed January 2019); Karin Bieback, *Zertifizierung und Akkreditierung* (Nomos 2008) 322; Steffen Detterbeck, *Allgemeines Verwaltungsrecht mit Verwaltungsprozessrecht* (Beck 2015) 334.

[173] Johannes Masing, 'Artikel 33 GG' in Horst Dreier (ed.), *Grundgesetz Kommentar* (Mohr Siebeck 2004) 853.

[174] Karin Bieback, *Zertifizierung und Akkreditierung* (Nomos 2008) 324.

[175] This research sides with the view that article 33, 4 of the Basic Law could also apply to rulemaking powers. Britta Beate Wiegand, *Die Beleihung mit Normsetzungskompetenzen. Das Gesundheitswesen als Exempel* (Duncker & Humblot 2007) 255. See for context or *contra*: Klaus Rennert, 'Beleihung zur Rechtsetzung' [2009] *Juristenzeitung* 980; Steffen Detterbeck, *Allgemeines Verwaltungsrecht mit Verwaltungsprozessrecht* (Beck 2015) 334; Thomas Holzner, *Konsens im Allgemeinen Verwaltungsrecht und in der Demokratietheorie* (Mohr Siebeck 2016) 491.

[176] BVerfG 130, 76, 12 January 2012, § 142; BVerfG 15, 235, § 24; . Reinhard Hendler, 'Das Prinzip Selbstverwaltung' in Josef Isensee and Paul Kirchhof (eds), *Handbuch des Staatsrechts der Bundesrepublik Deutschland*, vol. IV (Beck 2005) 1128.

autonomous regulation and state regulation, finding its independent basis in Article 9, 3 Basic Law'.[177] According to the court, the fundamental right on which this rulemaking power is based is the right to collective bargaining following article 9, 3 of the Basic Law. The provision literally protects 'the right to form associations safeguarding and improving economic and work conditions'.[178] This constitutional validation for outsourcing is, for example, also argued with regard to academic freedom and the freedom of the press, which would allow for more political independence for universities and publishers (article 5).[179]

In Chapter 2 on the international limits that are put on outsourcing rulemaking powers, we have already encountered the *Commission v. Germany* case law, in which the German state unsuccessfully invoked its democracy principle in order to question the independence of EU-inspired independent regulators.[180] One could assume that the word of the EU Legislature is final when it comes to the independence of regulators. This can be derived from the EU supremacy case law dating back to the *Costa v. ENEL* judgment of the European Court of Justice.[181] Also article 23, 1 of the Basic Law seems to suggest primacy of at least primary EU law in Germany.[182] However, for several decades the FCC had already conditioned the EU's supremacy on a German *ultra vires* and national identity test.[183] According to this test, EU legislation does not trump national law if the EU is regulating outside its actual competences or within the most central core of national authority. In the *Honeywell* judgment, this case law was finetuned.[184] *Ultra vires* review would only be triggered in the case of a sufficiently qualified breach of competences.[185] More specifically, the breach had to be *manifest* and create a structurally significant shift in the Member State's competences. The *ultra vires* doctrine has the potential to set a precisely determined limit on this type of delegation. The *OMT* case attested

[177] BVerfG 44, 322, § 55.

[178] Article 9, 3 of the Basic Law: 'The right to form associations to safeguard and improve working and economic conditions shall be guaranteed to every individual and to every occupation or profession.' Florian Becker, *Kooperative und konsensuale Strukturen in der Normsetzung* (Mohr Siebeck 2005) 434–5. See in a similar vein, article 20 of the Basic Law: Florian Becker, 'Privatisierung (*Contracting out*) von Leistungsverwaltung' in Klaus Hopt, Thomas von Hippel, and Rainer Walz (eds), *Nonprofit Organisationen in Recht, Wirtschaft und Gesellschaft* (Mohr Siebeck 2005) 352–3.

[179] Horst Dreier, 'Artikel 20 GG' in Horst Dreier (ed.), *Grundgesetz Kommentar* (Mohr Siebeck 2004) 97.

[180] Case C-518/07 *Commission v. Germany* ECLI:EU:C:2010:125, §§ 41–6.

[181] Case 6/64 *Costa v. ENEL* ECLI:EU:C:1964:66.

[182] It says that 'with a view to establishing a *united Europe*, the Federal Republic of Germany shall participate in the development of the European Union that is committed to democratic, social and federal principles, to the rule of law, and to the principle of subsidiarity, and that guarantees a level of protection of basic rights essentially comparable to that afforded by this Basic Law. To this end, the Federation *may transfer sovereign powers* by a law with the consent of the Bundesrat ...' (emphasis added).

[183] Adam Lazowski and Steven Blockmans, *Research Handbook on EU Institutional Law* (Edgar Elgar 2016) 70.

[184] BVerfGE 126, 286, *Honeywell*.

[185] Sylvie Peyrou, 'Cour constitutionnelle allemande et pouvoirs de la Banque centrale européenne: le premier renvoi préjudiciel à la Cour de Justice de l'Union européenne (décision du 14 janvier 2014)' [2015] *Revue française de droit constitutionnel* 161–2.

to the relevance of the democracy principle for *ultra vires* review.[186] The FCC interpreted the right to vote of article 38 of the Basic Law not merely formally, but also substantively. In the court's opinion, the provision entitles citizens 'to influence the formation of political will and to make an impact with their choices'.[187] This influence of citizens clearly decreases when autonomous public bodies exercise rulemaking powers. Certainly, if the EU required a clearer transfer of state powers—especially rulemaking powers—the FCC could establish a (manifest) breach of the EU's competences that led to a structurally significant shift in its own competences.

3.2.4 United Kingdom

A UK constitutional framework could encompass constitutional recognition of autonomous public or private actors or express constitutional provisions on the limits to the outsourcing of rulemaking powers to them. However, given that the UK has no written or codified constitution,[188] these express provisions cannot be found in one centralized and hierarchically superior document. There is no codified UK constitution that determines which bodies can be created to exercise governmental functions.[189] Legal scholars have repeatedly debated the introduction of a codified UK Constitution and lengthy lists of advantages and disadvantages have been drafted, of which increased transparency is an oft-cited trump card.[190] Commentators tend to lament this lack of constitutional structuring of autonomous public or private actors.[191] Arguably, the 2005 Constitutional Reform Act was a missed chance to bring more structure to various types of constitutional issues, including the existence of autonomous public or private actors.[192] A number of statutes, such as the Public Bodies Act 2011, regulate aspects of the functioning of autonomous public actors but they are not harmonized. One UK government document—'Guidance: Public Bodies'—possibly approached a constitution for them because it gave a valuable overview of all types of autonomous public actors

[186] BVerfG 134, 366, *OMT-Beschluss*. Sylvie Peyrou, 'Cour constitutionnelle allemande et pouvoirs de la Banque centrale européenne: le premier renvoi préjudiciel à la Cour de Justice de l'Union européenne (décision du 14 janvier 2014)' [2015] *Revue française de droit constitutionnel* 145.

[187] BVerfG, 2 BvR 2728/13, 2 BvR 2729/13, 2 BvR 2730/13, 2 BvR 2731/13, 2 BvE 13/13, § 81.

[188] Barry Winetrobe, 'Next Steps and Parliamentary Scrutiny' in Philip Giddings (ed.), *Parliamentary Accountability. A Study of Parliament and Executive Agencies* (Palgrave Macmillan 1995) 34.

[189] John Alder, *Constitutional & Administrative Law* (Palgrave 2015) 349.

[190] Robert Blackburn, 'Enacting a Written Constitution for the United Kingdom' [2015] *Statute L. Rev.* 1–3; John Alder, *Constitutional & Administrative Law* (Palgrave 2015) 9; R. C. Van Caenegem, *Introduction in Western Constitutionalism* (Cambridge University Press 2012) 199.

[191] Ian Harden, 'A Constitution for Quangos?' [1987] *Public Law* 27–8.

[192] Alex Carroll, *Constitutional and Administrative Law* (Pearson 2015) 48.

that had been created, reviewed, merged, and abolished. However, the document was only directed to civil servants and has no formal legal status.[193]

Therefore, the provisions structuring this debate are statutory. These statutes can either be overarching for various applications or ad hoc for the specific transfer of powers.

First, the 1946 Statutory Instruments Act was originally designed with the aim of transferring rulemaking powers to the Executive. Section 1(1) of the Act only mentions [Her] Majesty in Council or any minister of the Crown as receiving rulemaking powers. Nevertheless, it could also serve as a 'constitutional' act for the outsourcing of rulemaking. There is no reason why the Statutory Instruments Act could not apply to rulemaking powers of autonomous public or private actors, certainly when Her Majesty in Council or a minister retains the power to approve or confirm a secondary rule.[194] The Statutory Instruments Act is, for example, applicable to regulations or orders drafted by such an autonomous public actor, namely the British Hallmarking Council.[195]

Second, exact limitations can also be set on outsourcing rulemaking powers through the parent statute, the terms of a royal charter, or the memorandum of a company through which rulemaking powers are transferred.[196]

3.2.5 United States

Autonomous agencies are not incorporated in the US Constitution and yet their rulemaking powers are commonplace today. The aforementioned intelligible principle is also applied to the transfer of rulemaking powers to independent agencies. As such, the US Supreme Court upheld a statute authorizing the Federal Communications Commission (US FCC)to issue regulations as public convenience, interest, or necessity requires,[197] a statute empowering the US FCC to regulate broadcasters in the public interest,[198] and a statute authorizing the Federal Power Commission (FPC) to set just and reasonable rates for power,[199] etc.

Moreover, the canon of US constitutional law is especially clear on the prohibition of delegating rulemaking powers to private actors. It is useful to reiterate the infamous cases of *Schechter Poultry* and *Carter Coal*, in which the US Supreme

[193] UK Government, 'Guidance: Public Bodies' <https://www.gov.uk/guidance/public-bodies-reform> (last accessed January 2019); see previously, Ian Harden, 'A Constitution for Quangos?' [1987] *Public Law* 28.

[194] Paul Craig, *Administrative Law* (Sweet & Maxwell 2016) 437.

[195] Section 21(2) and (3) in conjunction with section 13 of the Hallmarking Act 1973: 'Any such power to make regulations [and orders] under this Act shall be exercisable by statutory instrument.'

[196] Paul Craig, *Administrative Law* (Sweet & Maxwell 2016) 104; Ian Harden, 'A Constitution for Quangos?' [1987] *Public Law* 33–4.

[197] *United States v. Southwestern Cable Co.*, 392 US 157 (1968).

[198] *National Broadcasting Co. v. United States*, 319 US 190 (1943).

[199] *FPC v. Hope Nat. Gas Co.*, 320 US 591 (1944).

Court flatly denounced the possibility of delegating rulemaking powers to private actors.[200] It even called the outsourcing of rulemaking powers, 'legislative delegation in its most obnoxious form'. More recently, the DC Circuit Court of Appeals reaffirmed an absolute ban on delegating rulemaking powers to private entities in the *Amtrak* case. Justice Alito endorsed this position in a separate decision of the ensuing Supreme Court judgment. However, Justice Kennedy's majority opinion avoided the issue altogether by denying that Amtrak was a private actor: 'Amtrak is a governmental entity'.[201] Increasingly, legal scholarship approves of or condones private actors exercising rulemaking powers.[202] In practice, this has resulted in a number of instances in which private actors have de facto received rulemaking powers. For example, in the US Kenneth Feinberg was tasked—as a private attorney—to set binding rules on the remuneration of executives of entities receiving Troubled Asset Relief Program (TARP) bailout funds during the latest financial and economic crisis.[203]

3.3 Conclusion

Four of the five countries researched, namely Belgium, France, Germany, and the US, attach a lot of importance to their written constitutions and the limits they set on the sovereignty of Parliament. As the French scholar, Léon Duguit, phrases it: 'a limit that can be created, modified or suppressed at the discretion of those to whom it is applied, is no limit at all'.[204] However, the research was given further depth by also including the UK, which does not have a written and codified constitution that sets clear and insurmountable limits to the exercise or transfer of powers. The combination of constitutional approaches to delegation in these countries leads to some interesting outcomes.

As can be found in numerous scholarly writings, the countries studied here historically had a general delegation prohibition. However, this historical truism often finds no backing in the explicit texts of their constitutions or constitutional practices.

Article 80 of the German Basic Law most exhaustively stipulates the delegation of powers that are limited in their content (*Inhalt*), purpose (*Zweck*), and extent (*Ausmaß*). Not all delegation doctrines are as precisely spelled out in other

200 *ALA Schechter Poultry Corp. v. United States*, 295 US 495 (1935); *Carter v. Carter Coal Co.*, 298 US 238 (1936).

201 *Department of Transport v. Association of American Railroads*, 575 US 576 (2015); Dina Mishra, 'An Executive-Power Non-Delegation Doctrine for the Private Administration of Federal Law' [2015] *Vanderbilt L. Rev.* 1588.

202 Kimberly N. Brown, 'We the People, Constitutional Accountability, and Outsourcing Government' (2013) 88 *Ind. LJ* 1347, 1403; Harold J. Krent, 'The Private Performing the Public: Delimiting Delegations to Private Parties' (2011) 65 *U. Miami L. Rev.* 507, 523.

203 Ibid., 508 and 517.

204 As translated and cited in Alain Laquièze, 'Etat de droit and national sovereignty in France' in history' in Pietro Costa and Danilo Zolo (eds), *The Rule of Law* (Springer 2007) 266.

constitutions. In Belgium, for instance, article 105 of the Constitution merely implies that rulemaking powers can be transferred to the Executive. In France, articles 34–7 of the Constitution stipulate the exercise of rulemaking by the Legislature and the Executive. Moreover, article 38 explicitly regulates the limited-in-time transfer of powers from the Legislature to the Executive via ordinances. Delegation of powers is thus generally constitutionally allowed.

However, courts have interpreted these constitutional provisions in highly flexible and at least three ways.

First, the universal way in which rulemaking power is regarded as cascading from the Legislature to the Executive appears so engrained in the minds of courts and legal scholars that it erodes the rough cornerstones of literal constitutional provisions. For example, the French articles 34–7 of the Constitution have been read counter-textually by the French Constitutional Council to grant a general rulemaking power to the Legislature and an implementing power to the Executive.

Second, the Legislature may well be the theoretical protagonist, but the Executive is the actual powerhouse. Article 105 of the Belgian Constitution was actually created to circumscribe the powers of the Executive. However, in its current interpretation, this very provision has become the legal foundation for rulemaking delegations. Even without a written constitution, a similar evolution has occurred in the UK.

Third, even a literal text of constitutional provisions can easily be flattened out in a judicial balancing exercise. Iancu has established that there is a judicial weakening of seemingly strict delegation limitations within legal systems in modern constitutionalism.[205] Indeed, as will be elaborated further, the explicit limits in article 80 of the German Basic Law have turned into a judicial test of essentialness. In a similar fashion, the French Constitutional Council is flexible in allowing legislative decrees, in seeming contrast to the actual text of article 38 of the Constitution. Likewise, article I of the US Constitution and the US non-delegation principle have been hollowed out by the courts with the lenient intelligible principle test.

The traditional prohibition of the delegation of powers theoretically applies to the outsourcing of rulemaking powers—if not *a fortiori*. Earlier texts and opinions in all of the countries researched disapproved of outsourcing rulemaking powers. For example, the French Council of State called AAIs 'institutional UFOs'.[206]

Unfortunately, there is an emphatic lack of constitutional provisions on autonomous public and private actors and their potential to receive rulemaking powers within the countries researched.

[205] Bogdan Iancu, *Legislative Delegation: The Erosion of Normative Limits in Modern Constitutionalism* (Springer 2012) ch. 4.

[206] As referred to by Yoan Vilain, 'Demokratische Legitimität und Verfassungsmäßigkeit unabhängiger Regulierungsbehörden. Von den ursprünglichen Bedenken bis zur richterlichen Eingliederung in das französische Verwaltungssystem' in Johannes Masing and Gérard Marco (eds), *Unabhängige Regulierungsbehörden* (Mohr Siebeck 2010) 12.

Such constitutional embodiments are not unheard of. They can also be found in countries that were not central to our comparative study. For example, Portugal inserted a clear constitutional prerogative for the Legislature to create autonomous public bodies in article 267.3 of its Constitution.[207] A similar constitutional provision is present in the Netherlands. According to article 134 of the Dutch Constitution, public bodies for the professions and trades, and other public bodies, may be established and dissolved by or pursuant to a statute. Analogous constitutional provisions can be found in Greece (article 101a), South Africa (article 181), Egypt (article 215), Kosovo (article 142), Sudan (article 115), and Sweden (Instrument of Government 8.4.10).

In contrast, Germany, France, and Belgium have only partially and quasi-constitutionally entrenched autonomous public and private actors, through article 87 of the German Basic Law, the French Organic Statute 2017-54, and article 9 of the Belgian Special Majority Act 1980 pertaining to the Reform of State Institutions. Furthermore, autonomous public bodies have been implemented case by case in the French and German constitutions for particularly important bodies or public regulators.[208] Finally, the German and French cases have demonstrated that German and French constitutional theory attaches great importance to the fact that autonomous public or private actors are installed in order to fulfil a constitutional right, such as the right of collective bargaining and the freedom of the press and the media.[209] There are thus some explicit or implicit references to them in the constitutions of some of the countries researched, but they remain comparatively weak. The UK—for obvious reasons—and the US do not contain a single reference to them or their rulemaking powers in a constitutional text.

Nevertheless, all of the countries studied have found ways to outsource a degree of rulemaking powers. Constitutional or high courts have accepted them and their ability to receive governmental powers. A prohibition based on traditional scholarship or case law and on a lack of constitutional entrenchment of rulemaking powers for autonomous public or private actors does not reflect the legal reality. Instead of maintaining the 'obligatory' statement that, in principle, outsourcing of rulemaking powers is prohibited, it is much more fruitful to focus on the clear delineation of limits to the delegation of rulemaking powers.[210] This approach is ultimately more practical and candid and is followed in the rest of this monograph, moving beyond constitutional provisions towards constitutional principles.

[207] 'A lei pode criar entidades administrativas independentes'; András Sajó, 'Les autorités indépendantes' in Michel Troper and Dominique Chagnollaud (eds), *Traité international de droit constitutionnel, Tome 2* (Dalloz 2012) 330.

[208] Pierre de Montalivet, 'Constitution et autorités de régulation' [2014] *RDP* 316, II.a.2.

[209] Eva Krodel, *Öffentlich-rechtliche und privatrechtliche Rundfunkorganisation in Großbritannien im Lichte der Rundfunkfreiheit* (Verlag Dr. Kovač 2015) 258.

[210] Harold J. Krent, 'The Private Performing the Public: Delimiting Delegations to Private Parties' (2011) 65 *U. Miami L. Rev.* 507, 525.

4
Comparative Outsourcing Limits by Constitutional Principles

Given the lack of clear constitutional provisions on outsourcing rulemaking powers, the research has analysed constitutional principles. The Belgian Constitutional Court or Council of State Legislative Section, the French Constitutional Council, the German Constitutional Court, the UK House of Lords/Supreme Court, and the US Supreme Court reconciled the lack of explicit constitutional provisions with the apparent need to outsource rulemaking powers through criteria and standards derived from constitutional principles. Through constitutional principles, the highest national courts can responsibly steer constitutional law into the twenty-first century for matters that do not appear to rank high on the priority list of possible constitutional amendments.[1]

Across the countries researched, the limits to the outsourcing of rulemaking powers were found to derive most notably from the legality principle, the separation of powers, and the democracy principle.

4.1 Legality principle

In the context of outsourcing rulemaking powers, the legality principle has been fittingly summarized using a famous quotation from John Locke to the effect that the Legislature has the power to make laws, not to make legislators.[2] I distinguished two versions of the legality principle, namely a specific legality principle for specific

[1] Despite the fact that in 2010 and 2014, Title III of the Belgian Constitution was marked as constitutionally amendable to introduce an article on functional decentralization (2010-1472). Koen Muylle, 'Het grondwettelijk delegatieverbod en het Unierecht' in André Alen and Jan Theunis (eds), *Leuvense Staatsrechtelijke Standpunten 3* (die Keure 2012) 353.

[2] John Locke, *Second Treatise of Government* (Project Gutenberg 2010) ch. XI, section 141.

Outsourcing Rulemaking Powers. Cedric Jenart, Oxford University Press. © Cedric Jenart 2022.
DOI: 10.1093/oso/9780192897831.003.0004

competences spelled out in the constitution and the general legality principle for all rules. The effects of both types of legality principle are similar: it remains the ultimate responsibility of the Legislature to at least create the essence of its rules. The countries researched that adhere to a version of the legality principle have adopted some type of essentialness test with a court deciding whether the Legislature determines the essence of the matter. As a result, it will always be easier to outsource detailed, technical, implementing, or temporary rules from the Legislature than fundamental policy decisions.[3]

4.1.1 Specific legality principle

In Belgium, France, and Germany, all of which have a written and codified constitution, I encountered examples of the specific legality principle. This implies that explicit constitutional provisions—often scattered throughout the national constitution—reserve the exercise of some competences to the Legislature.

In the first instance, a number of constitutional provisions have been interpreted as endowing the Belgian Legislature with reserved powers.[4] For example, the core of criminal law (articles 12 and 14 of the Belgian Constitution), the organization of the educational system (article 24, § 5),[5] tax law (article 170),[6] rights and duties of soldiers (article 182), the organization of the police force (article 184), etc. have to be provided for by statute.[7] For social, economic, and cultural rights (article 23), the Executive can only execute the measures of which the object has been predefined by the Legislature.[8] Contrary to the Dutch situation, this interpretation was judicially developed after the adoption of the Constitution.[9] The textual

[3] Paul Kirchhof, 'Artikel 3, Abs. 1 GG' in Theodor Maunz and Günter Dürig (eds), *Grundgesetz* (Beck 2015) 244, rn. 229.

[4] Jan Velaers, *De Grondwet, een artikelsgewijze commentaar* (die Keure 2019) article 105, §10; Jan Velaers, 'Het "recht op de wetgever": beschouwingen over de voorbehouden en de residuaire bevoegdheden' in Robert Andersen (ed.), *Itinéraires d'un constitutionnaliste: en hommage à Francis Delpérée* (Bruylant 2007) 1634–8; Wouter Pas and Brecht Steen, 'Met het nodige voorbehoud. Het grondwettelijk voorbehoud aan de formele en aan de federale wetgever—Deel 1' [2004] *Tijdschrift voor Wetgeving* 362–72.

[5] Brecht Steen, 'Streng, strenger, strengst!? De verhouding tussen de rechtspraak van het Arbitragehof en de adviezen van de Afdeling wetgeving van de Raad van State in constitutionele onderwijsaangelegenheden. Het legaliteitsbeginsel als casus' [2006–7] *Tijdschrift voor Onderwijsrecht en Onderwijsbeleid* 213–22.

[6] e.g. Belgan Constitutional Court no. 142/2010, 16 December 2010, B.4.1–B.4.6.

[7] Patricia Popelier, *Democratisch regelgeven* (Intersentia 2001) 136; Koen Muylle, 'Het grondwettelijk delegatieverbod en het Unierecht' in André Alen and Jan Theunis (eds), *Leuvense Staatsrechtelijke Standpunten 3* (die Keure 2012) 323.

[8] Belgian Constitutional Court nos 77/2018 and 86/2018, 21 June 2018 and 5 July 2018, B.5.4. and B.14.1. However, see Belgian Council of State Legislative Section, Advisory opinion no. 63.964/4/VR of 16 October 2018, 44–9.

[9] The eventual outcome in the Netherlands is also diametrically opposed to the Belgian interpretation. In the Netherlands, competence is not reserved when the Constitution allows for regulation 'by' or 'through' the law. Jeroen Van Nieuwenhove and Luc Verhey, 'Delegatie en de gevolgen voor de wetgevingspraktijk in België en Nederland' [2017] *Tijdschrift voor Wetgeving* 175.

tell-tale sign of whether constitutional competence is reserved for the Legislature is whether or not that competence needs to be exercised 'by' or 'through' a statute. Even for reserved competences to which the stricter legality principle applies, such as criminal law, the Belgian Constitutional Court apparently sees political accountability as an element that could justify the delegation of essential aspects of reserved rulemaking powers. Municipal administrative fines (*Gemeentelijke Administratieve Sancties*) represent a system whereby the municipalities can sanction people for the infraction of a municipal rule. In a much-anticipated judgment on the legality of municipal administrative fines, the court stressed that a municipality was a 'democratically elected deliberating assembly' before condoning the practice.[10] This system seems to nuance the strict nature of the delegation requirements in criminal matters.

A textual interpretation of the French Constitution would point to the existence of a 'specific legality principle' in article 34 of the French Constitution with a centralized list of policy matters that need to be regulated by statute. For example, the taxing competence that article 34 reserves to the Legislature means that the Executive is not allowed to subject taxpayers to a fiscal measure not foreseen by the Legislature.[11] This centralized list of reserved competences is supplemented by Organic Statutes and various other provisions of the Constitution reserving competence to the Legislature, such as articles 3 (voting right), 35 (war declaration), 47 (finance statutes), 53 (ratification of certain treaties), 66 (arbitrary detention), 72 (administration and creation of territorial communities), etc.[12] Moreover, article 1 of Organic Statute 2017-54 reserved the determination of competences of autonomous public actors to the Legislature. In principle, only the Legislature can thus delegate rulemaking powers to them.[13] If the Executive wishes to subdelegate rulemaking powers to them, it can only do so if this is permitted in the original delegating statute.[14]

Policy matters that are subject to the specific legality principle are scattered throughout the provisions of the German Basic Law. Whenever an article of the Basic Law itself refers to a formal statute as the sole rule for regulating a competence or a right, that obligation must be observed (*Gesetzesvorbehalt*). Any other conclusion would contravene the hierarchy of rules within the German system. If the Legislature does not legislate exhaustively, it can delegate its authority only insofar as it has established the essence of the policy matter or right. Provisions of the Basic Law that specifically require a formal statute traditionally deal with

[10] Belgian Constitutional Court no. 44/2015, 23 April 2015, B.18.4.

[11] French Council of State no. 37529 of 7 November 1960; Ministère de finance, *Pouvoir réglementaire* (no. 13 O1112, 30 April 1996).

[12] Cathérine Boyer-Mérentier, *Les ordonnances de l'article 38 de la Constitution de 1958* (Presses universitaires d'Aix-Marseille 1996) 254–5; Anne-Marie Le Pourhiet, *Les ordonnances* (LGDJ 2011) 56.

[13] Prime Minister and Council of State, *Guide de légistique* (3rd edn, La documentation française 2017) 334.

[14] French Council of State no. 320827 of 17 November 2010, *Société Arthus Consulting*.

infractions on basic freedom and property (*Eingriffe in Freiheit und Eigentum*).[15] The most notable examples of this specific legality principle are expropriation (article 14, III, 2 and 3 of the Basic Law), access to a lawful judge (article 101, I, 2), and criminal law (article 103, II and article 104, I, 1).[16] Regarding the latter provision, the German Federal Constitutional Court (FCC) proclaimed that it 'requires the Legislature ... to define the conditions of punishable offenses in such a concrete fashion that the scope and ambit of the offences can be recognized and determined by interpretation'.[17] The court applied this strict legality principle, for example, in its *Rindfleischetikettierungsgesetz* judgment.[18] § 10, 1 of the beef meat labelling statute delegated the authority to establish a punishable offence to the Executive. The FCC found this to be a transgression of the specific legality principle because the statutory framework clearly defined the type or degree of criminal punishment but not the (essential) punishable offence.[19] Sometimes the specific legality principle also appears in more institutional provisions of the Basic Law such as article 24. Sovereign powers may only be transferred to international organizations through a statute; as a consequence, regulations or administrative guidelines can never delegate rulemaking powers to international organizations.[20]

The specific legality principle will continue to form the minimum requirement for all legislative delegations.[21] This means in practice that a *Satzung*, as a rule made by a statutory corporations, cannot impose a criminal sanction without having a statutory basis in accordance with the specific legality principle in article 103, 2 of the Basic Law.[22] This constitutional provision equally implies that dynamic referrals to standards made by standardization organizations will never be allowed in the field of criminal law.[23]

A 'specific legality principle' is absent in the US and the UK.

[15] Peter Axer, *Normsetzung der Exekutive in der Sozialversicherung* (Mohr Siebeck 2000) 315; Bardo Fassbender, 'Der Gesetzesvorbehalt in internationalen Menschenrechtsverträgen' in Eckart Klein (ed.), *Gewaltenteilung und Menschenrechte* (Berliner Wissenschafts-Verlag 2006) 72. See recently Thüringer Verfassungsgerichtshof no. 110/20, 19 May 2021.

[16] See for a broader overview, Fritz Ossenbühl, 'Vorrang und Vorbehalt des Gesetzes' in Josef Isensee and Paul Kirchhof (eds), *Handbuch des Staatsrechts der Bundesrepublik Deutschland*, vol. V (Beck 2005) 201.

[17] BVerfG 71, 108, § 16. See also Christian Bumke and Andreas Voßkuhle, *Casebook Verfassungsrecht* (Mohr Siebeck 2015) 623; Guido Ernst, *Blankettstrafgesetze und ihre verfassungsrechtlichen Grenzen* (Springer 2018) 73.

[18] BVerfGE 2 BvL 1/15, 21 September 2016.

[19] Ibid., §§ 39 and 64.

[20] Thorsten Reinhardt, *Delegation und Mandat im öffentlichen Recht* (Duncker & Humblot 2006) 108.

[21] Hans-Ulrich Karpen, *Die Verweisung als Mittel der Gesetzgebungstechnik* (De Gruyter 1970) 130; Thomas Holzner, *Konsens im Allgemeinen Verwaltungsrecht und in der Demokratietheorie* (Mohr Siebeck 2016) 491.

[22] Fritz Ossenbühl, 'Satzung' in Josef Isensee and Paul Kirchhof (eds), *Handbuch des Staatsrechts der Bundesrepublik Deutschland*, vol. V (Beck 2005) 371.

[23] Alfred G. Debus, *Verweisungen in Deutschen Rechtsnormen* (Duncker & Humblot 2008) 264–5; Hans-Ulrich Karpen, *Die Verweisung als Mittel der Gesetzgebungstechnik* (De Gruyter 1970) 203.

For the US, this can be ascribed to the succinct content of the US Constitution, as opposed to the other countries researched with a written constitution, and the fact that the US Constitution remains the oldest surviving constitution. Some examples of the specific legality principle in other countries is even derived from the political history of the US. Consider, for example, the specific legality principle in tax law which was inspired by the American political slogan 'No taxation without representation' during the American Revolution.

For the UK, without a written constitution to indicate the areas of competence that require specific statutory protection, it is not possible for the Judiciary to reserve the exercise of those powers to the Legislature. The Executive could make regulations in the UK on core topics of criminal and tax law, which are traditionally reserved for the Legislature in the other countries researched.[24] Nevertheless, even in the UK there are indications that these two policy matters are subject to stricter parliamentary and judicial control. At least three examples testify to this.

First, concerning criminal matters, the Executive is prohibited from adopting retroactive rules and from limiting access to the courts. This prohibition has been accepted in the case law, although partly under the influence of the European Convention on Human Rights which deprives rulemakers of the possibility of imposing heavier sanctions retroactively.[25]

Second, concerning tax matters, the imperative consent of Parliament to levy money is expressly enshrined in the 1689 British Bill of Rights. It would lead the American colonists to the aforementioned expression: no taxation without representation. Again, this principle does not lead to a constitutional bar against the Legislature from transferring aspects of its taxing power. Rather, it indicates a particular sensitivity to parliamentary influence. Parent statutes on public finances and taxes will regularly reserve delineated powers for the Legislature. For example, the *Legislature* has to establish an Annual Finance Act to create changes in revenue and direct taxation. Indirect taxation can also be regulated through delegated legislation because it has been considered more technical and more prone to change due to EU law influences.[26] Moreover, the exercise of these powers of taxation by the Executive is still subject to the control and/or consent of the Legislature.[27] In accordance with sections 13(2), 65(1), and 66 of the Tax Credits Act 2002, the House of Commons and the House of Lords can veto secondary legislation made by the

[24] Criminal law: Mark Elliott and Robert Thomas, *Public Law* (Oxford University Press 2017) 144. Tax law: Anthony Bradley, Keith Ewing, and Christopher Knight, *Constitutional and Administrative Law* (16th edn, Pearson 2014) 504, William Wade and Christopher Forsyth, *Administrative Law* (Oxford University Press 2014) 726.

[25] Article 7 ECHR; William Wade and Christopher Forsyth, *Administrative Law* (Oxford University Press 2014) 739.

[26] Alex Carroll, *Constitutional and Administrative Law* (Pearson 2015) 169.

[27] Adam Tucker, 'Tax Credits, Delegated Legislation, and Executive Power', UK Constitutional Law Blog (5 November 2015) <http://ukconstitutionallaw.org/>; William Wade and Christopher Forsyth, *Administrative Law* (Oxford University Press 2014) 739.

Treasury, as part of the Executive, defining thresholds for tax credits. Ultimately, the courts have developed a somewhat stricter review of powers of taxation. To this effect, Scrutton LJ declared in *Wilts United Dairies* that 'it is conceivable that Parliament, which may pass legislation requiring the subject to pay money to the Crown, may also delegate its powers of imposing such payments to the Executive. But in my view the clearest words should be required before the courts hold that such an unusual delegation has taken place.'[28] This last example further corroborates how courts can limit the rulemaking powers of the Executive by raising their expectations of how explicit and precise the Legislature should have been in order for those rules not to be vague or *ultra vires*.

Third, in relation to both criminal and tax matters, one need only refer to the Legislative and Regulatory Reform Act 2006 which transfers broad rulemaking powers to ministers for 'removing or reducing burdens' on any person as a result of that legislation. Sections 5 and 6 of that Act clarify that ministers may *not* exercise these rulemaking powers with regard to criminal or tax matters.[29] There is a general sense that those powers should be exercised as far as possible by a democratically elected Parliament.

4.1.2 General legality principle

Apart from the specific legality principle, a substantial number of the countries researched currently have a general legality principle through which the Legislature must exercise the core of all rulemaking power.

Germany most clearly embraces this general legality principle in article 80 of its Basic Law.[30] Even if the strict phrasing of the constitutional provision does not require a formal statute for essential policy matters, article 80 of the Basic Law offers a safety net to place essential rulemaking powers in the hands of the Legislature. This derivation of the legality principle is *general*, in the sense that it always applies when rulemaking power is being delegated to the federal government, a federal minister, or the German federated governments.

Article 80 of the Basic Law literally states that 'the federal government, a federal minister or the Land governments may be authorised by a law to issue statutory instruments. The content, purpose and scope of the authority conferred shall be specified in the law. Each statutory instrument shall contain a statement of its legal basis.' This enables the federal Legislature to delegate some of its powers to these actors if the Legislature has previously established the content (*Inhalt*), purpose

[28] Even when a company itself consents, it cannot be confronted with a tax without the consent of Parliament. *Attorney-General v. Wilts United Dairies Ltd* (1921) 39 TLB 781, (1922) 127 LT 822.

[29] Neil Parpworth, *Constitutional and Administrative Law* (Oxford University Press 2016) 206.

[30] Geranne Lautenbach, *The Concept of the Rule of Law and the European Court of Human Rights* (Oxford University Press 2013) 63.

(*Zweck*), and extent (*Ausmaß*) of the delegated competence.[31] Accordingly, article 80 manages to inhibit any unwarranted influence by the Executive.[32] The FCC can determine when these criteria are met. Sometimes the court has considered content, purpose, and extent to be three separate criteria. The content, purpose, and/or extent of a policy matter may be deemed insufficiently formulated through, respectively, a textual, teleological, or contextual analysis.[33] On other occasions, the FCC has subsumed the three elements into one overarching test.[34] In any event, a clear delegation does not require a completely exhaustive enabling statute. Enabling statutes may be interpreted against the backdrop of their history and purpose and will transgress article 80 when the delegation is so vague and undetermined that one cannot foresee[35] under which circumstances and in what manner it can be utilized.[36] The more substantial the transferred rulemaking powers and the more meaningful for the constituency or the heavier the potential impact on the rights of citizens, the more precise and clear an enabling statute needs to be.[37] It is therefore difficult to predict the outcome of a case before the FCC based on this general principle of legality.

Also other nations may have the general principle of legality spelled out in their constitutions. According to article 18, 1 of the Austrian Constitution, the entire public administration shall be 'based on law'. In addition, article 5 of the Swiss Constitution stipulates that all activities of the state are based on and limited by law. Sometimes courts determine this general legality principle despite the absence of such a provision in a clear constitutional text. In France, for example, the general legality principle seems to contravene the letter of the French Constitution and was only established after intervention by the French Constitutional Council. Equally, article 15.2.1 of the Irish Constitution states that 'the sole and exclusive power of making laws for the State is hereby vested in the Oireachtas [Legislature]'. In

[31] Hartmut Bauer, 'Artikel 80 GG' in Horst Dreier (ed.), *Grundgesetz Kommentar* (Mohr Siebeck 2004) 1850; Thomas Mann, 'Artikel 80 GG' in Michael Sachs (ed.), *Grundgesetz Kommentar* (Beck 2011) 1644.

[32] Roland Geitmann, *Bundesverfassungsgericht und 'offene Normen'* (Duncker & Humblot 1971) 68.

[33] Gerhard Leibholz and Hans-Justus Rinck, *Grundgesetz für die Bundesrepublik Deutschland* (Otto Schmidt 1971) 621; Britta Beate Wiegand, *Die Beleihung mit Normsetzungskompetenzen. Das Gesundheitswesen als Exempel* (Duncker & Humblot 2007) 229–30; Thomas Mann, 'Artikel 80 GG' in Michael Sachs (ed.), *Grundgesetz Kommentar* (Beck 2011) 1644.

[34] Bogdan Iancu, *Legislative Delegation: The Erosion of Normative Limits in Modern Constitutionalism* (Springer 2012) 263; Britta Beate Wiegand, *Die Beleihung mit Normsetzungskompetenzen. Das Gesundheitswesen als Exempel* (Duncker & Humblot 2007) 226–7.

[35] BVerfGE 14, 60; 2 BVerfGE 307, 334; 78 BVerfGE 249, 272; Susan Rose-Ackerman, Stefanie Egidy, and James Fowkes, *Due Process of Lawmaking* (Cambridge University Press 2014) 168.

[36] BVerfGE 19, 354; Gerhard Leibholz and Hans-Justus Rinck, *Grundgesetz für die Bundesrepublik Deutschland* (Otto Schmidt 1971) 628.

[37] Thomas Mann, 'Artikel 80 GG' in Michael Sachs (ed.), *Grundgesetz Kommentar* (Beck 2011) 1645; Antje von Münch, *Das Spannungsverhältnis zwischen funktionaler Privatisierung und demokratischer Legitimation* (Nomos 2014) 181.

practice, this has led to a test in which the principles and policies of a subject matter need to be established by statute.[38]

However, the explicit, general legality principle within article 80, 1 of the Basic Law is not applicable to autonomous public or private actors that received rulemaking powers because this provision does not apply to them.[39] Still, for these actors a judicially developed general legality principle was introduced in Germany in the 1960s and 1970s.[40] There are three theories about the legal underpinning of this legality principle. First, some scholars still want to apply article 80 to autonomous public and private actors in any event.[41] In their view, article 80 would be sidestepped and even undermined if all rulemaking powers were outsourced, not to the Executive with clear limitations but to other actors without limitations. Second, other scholars derive from the general legality principle in article 80 a general constitutional principle that also applies to actors outside the scope of that article.[42] Following a third theory, the FCC bases its increased review mainly on the constitutional principles of democracy and the rule of law.[43] This third theory appears most faithful to the German case law. According to the FCC, article 80 was merely a source of inspiration for the judicially developed general legality principle.[44]

The FCC devised the standard for the judicial legality threshold in its *Sexualkundeunterricht* judgment[45] which concerned the introduction of sex education in public schools. The German Federal Administrative Court sought the opinion of the FCC on whether § 28 of the Hamburg School Statute (SchulG) and § 2 (1) 1 and 2 of the Hamburg School Structure Statute (SchVG) were compatible with the Basic Law when they left the decision to introduce sex education to public school boards without any apparent statutory guidance. Even though the case did not concern a policy reserved to the Legislature through the specific legality principle or delegate the rulemaking power to a type of actor mentioned in article 80, the court still required Parliament to establish 'the essential core' (*wesentlichkeit*) of the delegated area of competence. In this case, the Parliament had sufficiently defined the scope because the sex education course as it was construed fell within

[38] Eoin Carolan, 'Democratic Accountability and the Non-Delegation Doctrine' [2011] *Dublin U. LJ* I, Introduction.

[39] Hartmut Bauer, 'Artikel 80 GG' in Horst Dreier (ed.), *Grundgesetz Kommentar* (Mohr Siebeck 2004) 1840.

[40] Fritz Ossenbühl, 'Vorrang und Vorbehalt des Gesetzes' in Josef Isensee and Paul Kirchhof (eds), *Handbuch des Staatsrechts der Bundesrepublik Deutschland*, vol. V (Beck 2005) 208.

[41] Gerhard Leibholz and Hans-Justus Rinck, *Grundgesetz für die Bundesrepublik Deutschland* (Otto Schmidt 1971) 623.

[42] Florian Becker, *Kooperative und konsensuale Strukturen in der Normsetzung* (Mohr Siebeck 2005) 373.

[43] SG Mainz Vorlagebeschluss 12 December 2014—S 3 AS 130/14; Werner Heun, *The Constitution of Germany* (Hart 2011) 57 and 111.

[44] D BVerfG 44, 322 § 53; BVerfGE 33, 125, § 120.

[45] BVerfGE 47, 46, 21 December 1977.

the ambit of the exact sciences and biology. If the course had not taken a scientific but a moral approach, a separate legislative statute would have been necessary to define the essential elements of the rule. It is subject to debate what exactly constitutes an essential aspect. The greater the impact on citizens' lives, the higher the required precision and vice versa. The seriousness of an interference with a fundamental right often defines the impact of measures on citizens.[46] A number of concrete factors further define the magnitude of the rule's impact on the lives of citizens: significant financial consequences, whether it concerns pilot legislation on which future legislation will be moulded, the impact on state structure, and the duration of the measure are all elements that would increase the burden of arranging essential elements through a statute.[47]

In the US and Belgium, the general legality principle has been derived from imprecise constitutional provisions, namely article I of the US Constitution and articles 33, 36, and 105 of the Belgian Constitution. In these two examples, the lack of clarity of the constitutional provision has led to an ever-decreasing relevance of the general legality principle with recent pushes for a revival.

In the US, this is shown by the introduction of the intelligible principle standard through which the Legislature must provide a delegatee with an intelligible principle for exercising the delegated authority.[48] Soon after its introduction, the intelligible principle would turn out to be toothless. Despite previous competing tests, the standard is currently still formally endorsed, although in 2019 a majority of the US Supreme Court indicated that they would be willing to revisit the theory: Chief Justice Roberts and Justices Thomas, Alito, Gorsuch (and Kavanaugh) in *Gundy v. United States* and its aftermath.[49] The 'new' test developed by Justice Gorsuch would provide a higher bar for legislative delegation: first, Congress could grant the authority to 'fill in the details' as already introduced in *Wayman v. Southard*. Second, Congress might make the application of a rule depend on Executive fact-finding. Third, Congress might assign the Executive and Judiciary certain non-legislative responsibilities.

In Belgium, every Executive regulation needs a constitutional or statutory basis.[50] The necessary adoption by the Legislature of the 'essence' of all rulemaking decisions was, for a long time, required by the Belgian Council of State Legislative

[46] Hans Jarass and Bodo Pieroth, 'Artikel 20 GG' in Hans Jarass and Bodo Pieroth (eds), *Grundgesetz für die Bundesrepublik Deutschland Kommentar* (Beck 2012) 519; Roland Geitmann, *Bundesverfassungsgericht und 'offene Normen'* (Duncker & Humblot 1971) 90.

[47] Florian Becker, *Kooperative und konsensuale Strukturen in der Normsetzung* (Mohr Siebeck 2005) 380–1.

[48] *J. W. Hampton, Jr & Co. v. United States*, 276 US 394, 405 (1928).

[49] *Gundy v. United States*, 588 US ___ (2019); *Paul v. United States*, 140 S. Ct. 342, 342 (2019) (mem.). Jonathan Hall, 'The Gorsuch Test: *Gundy v. United States*, Limiting the Administrative State, and the Future of Nondelegation' [2020] *Duke LJ* 175–215; Mila Sohoni, 'Opinion analysis: Court refuses to resurrect nondelegation doctrine', SCOTUSblog (20 June 2019).

[50] See article 108 of the Belgian Constitution and the notion '*rechtsgrond*'/'*fondement juridique*' in article 84, § 3, first section of the coordinated statutes of 12 January 1973 on the Council of State.

Section; however, it was recently discontinued by the Constitutional Court and the Council of State Legislative Section. Nevertheless, in 2021 the general assembly of the Belgian Council of State Legislative Section endorsed legal scholarship, which claims that a heightened legality requirement exists whenever fundamental rights are at stake, regardless of the applicability of the specific legality principle.[51] This can require the Legislature to regulate more expansively with regard to an issue involving fundamental rights.

No such general legality principle can be found in the UK, without a written and codified constitution. There is no verifiable limit on the sovereignty of Parliament to delegate rulemaking power to the Executive.[52] Furthermore, limiting constitutional provisions such as article 80 of the Basic Law in Germany, or limiting superior court case law such as in France or originally in the US and Belgium, only has practical use when the respective courts of those countries can effectively test all outsourcing rules—including statutes—against the constitution. This is not the case in the UK. Nevertheless, UK constitutional law embraces a 'general legality principle' in practice. Parliamentary legislation should be 'the ultimate source' of rulemaking powers and constitute the foundations on which ulterior Executive actions are based.[53] This general legality principle is most clearly embraced in the 1689 British Bill of Rights: 'the pretended power of ... the execution of laws by regal authority without *consent of Parliament* is illegal'.[54] If the state sets limitations on freedom of persons or property, it should do so by statutory authority.[55]

When a specific or general legality principle rests on a competence, the Legislature must realize the core of that competence to the detriment of all other actors, including autonomous public or private actors. In other words, the legality principle presents a first general limit to the outsourcing of rulemaking powers.

[51] Belgian Council of State Legislative Section, Advisory opinion no. 68.936/AV of 7 April 2021, § 70. Sébastien Van Drooghenbroeck, Cécilia Rizcallah, Christine Horevoets, and Grégory Delannay, 'La loi, condition de licéité des restrictions aux libertés publiques' in Luc Detroux, Mathias El Berhoumi, and Bruno Lombaert (eds), *La légalité: un principe de la démocratie belge en péril* (Larcier 2019). See previously Belgian Council of State Legislative Section, Advisory opinion no. 62.592/3 of 3 January 2018, § 3.3.

[52] Mark Elliott and Jason N. E. Varuhas, *Administrative Law. Text and Materials* (Oxford University Press 2017) 668; William Wade and Christopher Forsyth, *Administrative Law* (Oxford University Press 2014) 725.

[53] Gerdy Jurgens, Maartje Verhoeven, and Paulien Willemsen, 'Administrative Powers in German and in English Law' in Leonard F. M. Besselink, Frans Pennings, and Sacha Prechal (eds), *The Eclipse of the Legality Principle in the European Union* (Kluwer Law International 2011) 52; Stéphanie De Somer, 'The creation of autonomous public bodies from a European comparative legal perspective: international impulse, national restraint and how to reconcile these trends', PhD thesis, University of Antwerpen (2015) 164; Sidney B. Jacoby, 'Delegation of Powers and Judicial Review. A Study in Comparative Law' [1936] *Colum. L. Rev.* 881.

[54] Emphasis added.

[55] *Entick v. Carrington* [1765] EWHC KB J98, 95 ER 807; Neil Parpworth, *Constitutional and Administrative Law* (Oxford University Press 2016) 43; *Halsbury's Laws of England* (5th edn, LexisNexis 2010) 'The principle of legality', § 7(1).

4.2 Separation of powers as a hidden limit

The separation of powers principle has been embraced in countries around the globe[56] but this does not hinder some cross-fertilization between the branches of government in the countries researched.

This research revealed perturbations of any notion of a 'strict' separation of powers. Article 80, 1 of the Basic Law debunks any claim of an absolute separation of powers (*absolute Trennung der Gewalten, Gewaltengliederung*) in Germany. The German Basic Law rather entails a control, inhibition, restraint, and fusion of powers (*Kontrolle, Hemmung, Mäßigung, Ineinandergreifen, Verschränkung und Verzahnung der Gewalten*).[57] The goal of separation of powers (or 'division of labour') is then not to separate the three powers but to moderate and control them.[58] The most salient example of this was the former UK jack of all trades, the Lord Chancellor, who convened the Executive, Legislature, and Judiciary in one. Nevertheless, there are still current examples of this 'unity' between the three branches, such as the Queen, the Queen in Parliament, and the Queen's Bench in the UK.

The influence of this principle in the UK, as in other countries researched, is contested. On the one hand, broad judicial statements emphasize the value of the separation of powers principle. Lord Diplock wrote this apology for the separation of powers in the *Duport Steel* case: 'The British Constitution, though largely unwritten, is firmly based upon the separation of powers.'[59] According to Lord Mustill in the *Fire Brigade Union* case: 'It is a feature of the peculiarly British conception of the separation of powers that Parliament, the executive and the courts have each their distinct and largely exclusive domain.'[60] On the other hand, all commentators agree that the UK constitutional system does not adhere to a rigorous interpretation of the separation of powers.[61] They contribute this to the strength of the sovereignty of Parliament principle and to the flexible UK constitution.[62]

[56] Wen-Chen Chang, Li-ann Thio, Kevin Y. L. Tan, and Jiunn-rong Yeh, *Constitutionalism in Asia: Cases and Materials* (Hart 2014) 144.

[57] BVerfGE 95, 1 (43); Hans Jarass and Bodo Pieroth, 'Artikel 20 GG' in Hans Jarass and Bodo Pieroth (eds), *Grundgesetz für die Bundesrepublik Deutschland Kommentar* (Beck 2012) 506, Roland Geitmann, *Bundesverfassungsgericht und 'offene Normen'* (Duncker & Humblot 1971) 67 and 80; Florian Becker, *Kooperative und konsensuale Strukturen in der Normsetzung* (Mohr Siebeck 2005) 352.

[58] Gerhard Leibholz and Hans-Justus Rinck, *Grundgesetz für die Bundesrepublik Deutschland* (Otto Schmidt 1971) 387.

[59] *Duport Steels Ltd v. Sirs* [1980] WLR 142, 157; William Wade and Christopher Forsyth, *Administrative Law* (Oxford University Press 2014) 17; Roger Masterman, *The Separation of Powers in the Contemporary Constitution* (Cambridge University Press 2010) 10.

[60] *R v. Secretary of State for the Home Department, ex p. Fire Brigades Union* [1995] 2 AC 513.

[61] Mark Elliott and Robert Thomas, *Public Law* (Oxford University Press 2017) 64, 97, and 98; Andrew Le Sueur, Maurice Sunkin, and Jo Eric Khushal Murkens, *Public Law* (Oxford University Press 2016) 430.

[62] Roger Masterman, *The Separation of Powers in the Contemporary Constitution* (Cambridge University Press 2010) 17 and 25; Roger Masterman and Se-shauna Wheatle, 'Unpacking Separation of Powers: Judicial Independence, Sovereignty and Conceptual Flexibility in the UK Constitution' [2017] *Public Law* 484.

This research opted to focus on the separation of powers principle in the countries studied. It generally distinguished between an institutional perception of the separation of powers (Section 4.2.1) and a functional perception of the separation of powers (Section 4.2.2).

4.2.1 Institutional separation of powers

In the light of the institutional separation of powers, governmental powers must be exercised such that they do not infringe on the powers of other branches of government. The separation of powers principle is most clearly embedded in the French Constitution through article 16 of the Declaration of the Rights of Man and of the Citizen.[63] Article 16 of the declaration provides that 'any society in which no provision is made for guaranteeing … the separation of powers, has no Constitution'. A 1971 decision of the Constitutional Council, which added the *Déclaration* to the review rules, paved the way for the Council to recognize the separation of powers as (an autonomous) constitutional principle in France.[64] The Council explicitly recognized that this principle was applicable to the Executive (the President and the government) and the Legislature.[65]

The relevance of the institutional separation of powers for the theory of the unitary executive in the US has been well established, granting the President a strong grip on the administration as a whole since the 1980s.[66] This principle has equally inspired the French 'unity of executive power', which in its turn gave the Executive a general competence to execute rules in apparent contrast to the letter of the French Constitution.[67] In Belgium, the separation of powers is exclusively invoked by the Council of State, as well as legal scholarship, together with the 'unity of executive power' when it concerns rulemaking powers. More clearly than in Belgium but similarly to France and the US, the 'division of labour' works from both sides in Germany via the unity of the Executive (*Einheit der Verwaltung*).[68] For example, the German separation of powers doctrine calls for a hard core of competences

[63] 'Any society in which the guarantee of rights is not assured, nor the separation of powers determined, has no Constitution.'

[64] Cathérine Boyer-Mérentier, *Les ordonnances de l'article 38 de la Constitution de 1958* (Presses universitaires d'Aix-Marseille 1996) 254–5; Nina Le Bonniec, 'L'appréhension du principe de la séparation des pouvoirs par la Cour européenne des droits de l'homme' [2016] *Revue française de droit constitutionnel* 336.

[65] French Constitutional Council no. 76-72 of 12 January 1977; Philippe Blachèr, 'Le président de la République et le Gouvernement dans la jurisprudence du Conseil constitutionnel' [2016] *Les Nouveaux Cahiers du Conseil constitutionnel* 33.

[66] Lawrence Lessig and Cass Sunstein, 'The President and the Administration' [1994] *Colum. L. Rev.* 5, etc.

[67] Nadine Poulet-Gibot Leclerc, *La place de la loi dans l'ordre juridique interne* (Presses universitaires de France 1992) 41–3.

[68] Bettina Süsskind, *Die autorités administratives indépendantes* (Nomos 2010) 207.

of the Executive that even the Legislature cannot touch. The FCC calls this the *Kernbereich exekutiver Eigenverantwortung*.[69] In the same vein, it does not allow the Legislature to encroach on the powers of the Executive without a clear motivation.[70] Even in the UK where the separation of powers principle is arguably the weakest because of the sovereignty of Parliament, the House of Lords and the Supreme Court have clarified that parliamentary sovereignty is not absolute. Thus, there is a lingering presence of a separation of powers thinking.

There is an intrinsic separation of powers value in exercising rulemaking power precisely in the manner drafted in the constitution. In the US, the *Chadha* case emphasized this potential sensitivity.[71] Section 244(c)(2) of the Immigration and Nationality Act authorized either of the Houses of Congress to invalidate the Attorney General's (AG) decision to suspend an alien's deportation. The AG had received this authority by means of delegation. The House of Representatives or the Senate could, through a simple resolution, overturn the AG's decision. The US Supreme Court deemed this one-House veto unconstitutional. In the first instance, the majority established that the decision to suspend deportation was legislative.[72] This stance was debatable,[73] but the second step of the Supreme Court's reasoning is most relevant to us: it ruled that Congress cannot circumvent stringent constitutional procedure by effectively delegating power to one House under the pretext of delegating to the Executive (AG). One House of Congress did not have the authority to legislate in the first place, rather both Houses of Congress were constitutionally required. Therefore, Congress was perfectly allowed to delegate but, if it wished to overrule the AG's decision, both Houses would have to agree. It was all or nothing. Members of Parliament are only legislators when they act in accordance with constitutional procedures. As the US Supreme Court itself posited in *Loving*: 'Another strand of our separation-of-powers jurisprudence, the delegation doctrine, has developed to prevent Congress from forsaking its duties.'[74] This case law shows that constitutional issues can arise when the delegation of governmental powers eludes ordinary legislative procedures.

When we apply this reasoning to the outsourcing of rulemaking powers, the institutional separation of powers can limit the transfer of rulemaking powers even beyond the traditional three branches of government.

Despite it not being possible to categorize autonomous public bodies under one of the traditional branches of government, the exercise of any governmental power will influence the *Trias Politica*.[75] Outsourcing rulemaking powers at least

69 BVerfGE AZ 2 BvE 11, 15/83, 17. July 1984, § 3c.
70 Alfred G. Debus, *Verweisungen in Deutschen Rechtsnormen* (Duncker & Humblot 2008) 114.
71 *INS v. Chadha*, 462 US 952 (1983).
72 Ibid.
73 Ibid., 964.
74 *Loving v. United States*, 517 US 758 (1996).
75 Eric Barendt, 'Separation of Powers and Constitutional Government' [1995] *Public Law* 599, 606–7.

threatens the unity of executive power, which should lie with the Executive and is shredded to the benefit of the other branches of government. Transferring rulemaking powers to autonomous public or private actors contravenes the unity of the Executive and its civil service in the US and the UK.[76] The same finding applies in Belgium since the autonomous public actors and their powers are not envisaged in constitutional provisions.[77] A national court could rule that by establishing an autonomous public actor, the Legislature goes into too many (executive) details, thereby infringing the institutional separation of powers. Jacques Rigaud argued this transgression of the separation of powers principle for the CSA (the French audiovisual regulatory authority).[78]

Equally, the unique independent role of the Judiciary to interpret rules may be thwarted by autonomous public and private actors. Legal practitioners and commentators must at least consider the institutional separation of powers when they discuss the competences of autonomous public and private actors. This issue has been discussed with regard to the German Judiciary (Title IX of the Basic Law). The separation of powers principle can be considered threatened if the Legislature or the Executive refers dynamically to external documents so that the Judiciary's power to interpret state rules diminishes.[79] This fear is strengthened by the idea that the Judiciary is the only national branch of government that is 'independent' according to the clear text of the Basic Law (article 97).[80] The Legislature and Executive are not independent but autonomous public or private actors are. When the latter exercise rulemaking powers, the Judiciary can no longer claim a unique position of independence. In other words, autonomous public or private actors

[76] United States: *Free Enterprise Fund v. Public Company Accounting Oversight Board*, 561 US 497 (2010); Dina Mishra, 'An Executive-Power Non-Delegation Doctrine for the Private Administration of Federal Law' [2015] *Vanderbilt L. Rev.* 1580; Ryan J. Barilleaux and Christopher S. Kelley, 'What Is the Unitary Executive?' in Ryan J. Barilleaux and Christopher S. Kelley (eds), *The Unitary Executive and the Modern Presidency* (Texas A&M University Press 2010) 1–3; Melanie Marlowe, 'The Unitary Executive and Review of Agency Rulemaking' in Barilleaux and Kelley, ibid., 96–7; Harold J. Krent, 'The Private Performing the Public: Delimiting Delegations to Private Parties' (2011) 65 *U. Miami L. Rev.* 507, 523. United Kingdom: Andrew Le Sueur, Maurice Sunkin, and Jo Eric Khushal Murkens, *Public Law* (Oxford University Press 2016) 282.

[77] Belgian Council of State Legislative Section, Advisory opinion (Parliamentary Documents Flanders 90–91, no. 428/1, 21 November 1990) 621. Also when the Executive outsources rulemaking powers to autonomous public or private actors: Belgian Council of State Legislative Section, Advisory opinion no. 56.941/3 of 21 January 2015, § 14; Belgian Council of State Legislative Section, Advisory opinion no. 42.986/4 of 30 May 2007, § 1.2. See specifically for outsourcing powers to private actors: Dimitri Yernault, 'Constitution, privatisations et pouvoirs spéciaux: un débat oublié' [2001] *CRISP* 6 and Xavier Delgrange and Luc Detroux, 'Les limites constitutionnelles à la privatisation' in Bruno Lombaert (ed.), *Les partenariats public-privé (PPP): un défi pour le droit des services publics* (La Charte 2005) 84–5.

[78] Jacques Rigaud, 'Le Conseil supérieur de l'audiovisuel ou la difficulté d'être' [1992] *Commentaire* 650.

[79] Eberhard Baden, 'Dynamische Verweisungen und Verweisungen auf Nichtnormen' [1979] *NJW* 626.

[80] Bettina Süsskind, *Die autorités administratives indépendantes* (Nomos 2010) 207.

could diminish the authority of the Judiciary, thus changing the equilibrium within the *Trias Politica*.

Furthermore, there is even a role for the separation of powers doctrine to play outside the classical triad of powers.[81] Independent regulatory agencies or private power-wielders may constitute a fourth branch of government.[82] They serve as independent centres of authority and decision-making, in some sense comparable to the free press or academia.[83] The French Constitutional Council has invoked the institutional separation of powers principle with regard to autonomous public actors, even though it did not apply it substantively to the exercise of rulemaking powers. In reviewing the control by the ordinary French courts of the executive Competition Council (*Conseil de la Concurrence*), the Constitutional Council eventually found no transgression of the 'French conception of the separation of powers'.[84]

4.2.2 Functional separation of powers

In addition to the institutional separation of powers, there is also a functional separation of powers, which focuses on the division of governmental *functions* and not institutions or branches of government. Legal scholars have been discussing functional interpretations of the separation of powers for centuries.[85] The functional separation of powers contests the centralization of various functions within one body. This perception of the separation of powers, or checks and balances, primarily aims to enhance efficiency and to avoid arbitrariness within one powerful actor.[86]

The risk that the functional separation of powers will be violated is certainly present if autonomous public or private actors also receive powers other than rulemaking powers. The combination of rulemaking and adjudicative powers seems especially problematic because the autonomous public or private actor would become both the creator and judge of its own rules.

[81] András Sajó, 'Les autorités indépendantes' in Michel Troper and Dominique Chagnollaud (eds), *Traité international de droit constitutionnel—Tome 2* (Dalloz 2012) 353.

[82] Catherine Durose, Jonathan Justice, and Chris Skelcher, 'Governing at Arm's Length: Eroding or Enhancing Democracy?' [2015] *Pol'y & Politics* 141; Antonia Baraggia, Luca Pietro Vanoni, and Giovanni Bognetti, *Dividing Powers: A Theory of the Separation of Powers* (CEDAM 2017) 115.

[83] Lord Steyn, 'Democracy Through Law' [2002] *EHRLR* 735.

[84] French Constitutional Council no. 86-224 DC of 23 January 1987, §§ 15–23.

[85] As discussed in Michael Racky, *Die Diskussion über Gewaltenteilung und Gewaltentrennung im Vormärz* (Peter Land 2005) 193–5. Even before the institutional separation of powers, there was a debate on the functional separation of powers as indicated by Florian Becker, 'The Development of German Administrative Law' [2017] *George Mason L. Rev.* 459–60.

[86] Geranne Lautenbach, *The Concept of the Rule of Law and the European Court of Human Rights* (Oxford University Press 2013) 49–50.

Various, especially French, authors warn that autonomous public actors could become problematic from the perspective of a functional separation of powers because they combine numerous functions such as the executive, adjudicative, and rulemaking one.[87] The Constitutional Council established in 1988 and reaffirmed in 1989 that the functional separation of powers principle does not principally object to the combination of rulemaking powers and individual sanctioning powers exercised by autonomous public actors.[88] Over the years, the Constitutional Council has finetuned this principled permission to combine functions within an autonomous public actor by stressing that 'defence rights ... must be respected'.[89] The Constitutional Council derives defence rights, such as the independence and impartiality of judges, from article 16 of the *Déclaration*[90] which contains the separation of powers principle. This limit to the combination of functions, as cited by the Constitutional Council, can thus also be seen to derive from the separation of powers principle. The French Council of State had previously clarified that the combination of rulemaking powers with adjudicative powers does not generally infringe on article 6 of the European Convention on Human Rights and its safeguards of the right to a proper defence, the right to confront arguments during the legal proceedings, and the right to an impartial decision.[91] In its judgment 2013-331, the Constitutional Council found a violation of the separation of powers as enshrined in article 16 of the *Déclaration* because the competence to prosecute and to investigate, on the one hand, and the competence to adjudicate, on the other hand, resided within the same autonomous public actor, the Authority for the Regulation of Electronic Communication and Post.[92]

Arguably, the combination of rulemaking and adjudicative powers would also be invalidated if an autonomous public body thereby monopolized incompatible functions, as was also suggested by a judgment of the Belgian Council of State.[93] Andersen took offence at the combination of powers (rulemaking, advising, individual decision-making, controlling, sanctioning, and adjudicating)

[87] Bertrand Marais, 'Convergence entre télécommunications et audiovisuel en France' [9 August 2008] *Gazette du Palais* 5, I.1.2.; Jacques Chevalier, 'Autorités administratives indépendantes et État de droit' [2016] *Civitas Europa* 148; Pierre de Montalivet, 'Constitution et autorités de régulation' [2014] *RDP* 316, I; Jean-Philippe Feldman, 'Les "autorités administratives indépendantes" sont-elles légitimes? Sur les AAI en général et le Conseil supérieur de l'audiovisuel en particulier' [2010] *Recueil Dalloz* 2852 etc. I.

[88] See French Constitutional Council no. 88-248, 17 January 1989, § 27; French Constitutional Council no. 89-260 of 28 July 1989, § 6; Stéphanie Dubiton, *La protection des libertés publiques par les autorités administratives indépendantes, une solution démocratique?* (LGDJ 2016) 88; Jean-Philippe Feldman, 'La séparation des pouvoirs et le constitutionnalisme. Mythes et réalités d'une doctrine et de ses critiques' [2010] *Revue française de droit constitutionnel* 488; François-Xavier Millet, *L'Union Européenne et l'identité constitutionnelle des états membres* (LGDJ 2013) 126.

[89] French Constitutional Council no. 2012-280 QPC of 12 October 2012, § 16.

[90] Ibid.

[91] French Council of State no. 238169 of 30 July 2003, *Banque d'escompte et Wormser Frères réunis*.

[92] French Constitutional Council no. 2013-331 QPC of 5 July 2013, § 5.

[93] Council of State Administrative Litigation Section, no. 91.998, 8 January 2001, 3.1.1.

in many autonomous public bodies.[94] The author also rightly points out that the Belgian Constitutional Court should at least recognize the weight of the separation of powers principle in the balancing exercise of whether the Legislature or the Executive should outsource powers.[95]

In the other countries researched, the case law and influence of the functional separation of powers has not yet developed to such an extent.

In the light of the functional separation of powers, autonomous public or private actors regularly combine various governmental functions in the UK. This applies, for example, to the Civil Aviation Authority which combines executive, advisory, adjudicative, and regulatory functions.[96] This accumulation of functions may be dangerous in younger and smaller entities (as they often are) that have fewer internal mechanisms to avoid the abuse of power.

4.3 Democracy principle as the main limit

The democracy principle has received various definitions in the countries researched. However, its essence always reflected the description given in the research. Democracy implies the role of the people in their governance: the right of people in a political community to participate meaningfully in the process by which they are governed.[97] This definition is broad, yet not so broad as to also encapsulate other recognized constitutional principles, such as the rule of law.[98] This basically means that the people and, thus, the Legislature, must control the most important decisions.[99]

However, when the Legislature and the Executive outsource rulemaking powers further downstream, the democracy principle will require a form of compensation to continue to ensure that the people control who governs them.

In this regard, I already analysed to what extent the Belgian, French, German, UK, and US Legislatures can grant power to the Executive to make executive regulations at the hierarchical level of statutes—meaning that they can change prior

[94] In some cases, it is even debated whether a delegated power is rulemaking or individual decision-making such as in the Brussels Court of Appeals Case where the court eventually rejected the claimant's (bpost) assertion that the Belgian Post and Telecommunications Regulator had exercised rulemaking powers when refusing bpost's request to raise postal tariffs (Brussels Court of Appeals 18th Chamber no 2017/AR/873, 11 October 2017, 26, registry 379).

[95] Robert Andersen, 'Les autorités administratives indépendantes en droit belge' [2008] *Annuaire européen d'administration publique* 26.

[96] Ian Harden, 'A Constitution for Quangos?' [1987] *Public Law* 29–30.

[97] Thomas M. Franck, 'Democracy, Legitimacy and the Rule of Law: Linkages' in Norman Dorsen and Prosser Gifford (eds), *Democracy and the Rule of Law* (CQ Press 2001) 169.

[98] Geranne Lautenbach, *The Concept of the Rule of Law and the European Court of Human Rights* (Oxford University Press 2013) 62–3.

[99] Antje Von Ungern-Sternberg, 'Parliaments—Fig Leaf or Heartbeat of Democracy?' [2012] *Eur. Const. L. Rev.* 320.

statutes. In the UK, legal scholars and the House of Lords Constitution Committee frown on Henry VIII powers—through which the Executive can amend statutes—but examples still remain plentiful. In Germany, such types of statutory executive regulations are principally not allowed. In Belgium, such a 'special power' transferred to the Executive must be exceptional and clearly described. Moreover, the Legislature must subsequently ratify the special power executive regulations, otherwise they are retroactively removed. In France, article 38 of the French Constitution allows for the creation of ordinances if the Executive requests that power, it is restrictive and limited in its extent, it remains of a limited duration, and it is backed up by legislative ratifications. The US predominantly has examples of contingent legislation in which a statute can be changed when an executive or administrative officer establishes a predetermined fact.[100]

Delegations from the national Legislatures to ministers also came under scrutiny in this research (Chapter 3). Ministers are still directly, politically accountable to the Legislature. However, Germany, Belgium, and France put considerable limits on the possibility of transferring rulemaking powers from the Legislature to individual ministers.[101] These limits are either inspired by the idea that the Legislature should exercise this rulemaking power itself (legality principle) or that the Legislature must not tread on the powers of the Executive by bypassing them to the benefit of individual ministers (separation of powers). In Germany, the limits of article 80 of the Basic Law—namely, a predetermined content, purpose, and extent—apply to legislative delegations to ministers. In Belgium, legislative delegations to ministers are principally prohibited unless the matter is highly urgent (older legisprudence, but recently reaffirmed) or technical (more recent legisprudence). In France, the competence that is transferred by the Legislature to individual ministers should be technical, of limited scope, would not benefit from an advisory opinion of the Council of State, and not be politically controversial.

Furthermore, the transfer of rulemaking powers from the government or Prime Minister to individual ministers or civil servants further downstream would appear to diminish the influence of Parliament in decision-making (legality principle) or the competitive strength of a unified Executive (separation of powers). The delegation from the US President to members of the Cabinet is not deemed problematic. For France and Germany, article 21, 2 of the French Constitution and article 80, 1 of the Basic Law, respectively, explicitly allow for this type of sub-delegation. However, they impose limits regarding the extent of the transfer: in France '[the Prime Minister] may delegate *certain* of his powers to Ministers'; while in Germany, '*if the law provides that such authority may be further delegated*, such subdelegation shall be effected by statutory instrument'.[102] In the UK, the delegation

[100] Cornell Legal Information Institute, US Constitution Annotated, Article I., Legislative department, Section I, Delegation of legislative power.
[101] With the exception of the US and the UK and its sovereignty of Parliament.
[102] Emphasis added.

of rulemaking powers from the Executive to ministers or civil servants would also only seem acceptable in the light of parliamentary sovereignty; if Parliament implicitly allowed rulemaking power to be passed along. Finally, in Belgium the delegation of rulemaking powers within the Executive can only occur for precisely described accessory matters that remain subject to political control.

These examples show that the limits that were inspired by the democracy principle can counterbalance apparent issues with the legality principle or the separation of powers, by stripping the transferred rulemaking powers of their discretionary rulemaking liberty and societal impact. We can categorize these limits on rulemaking discretion in especially Belgium, France, and Germany as: (1) preciseness; (2) a limited or technical extent; and/or (3) *ex post* demonstration of political control (e.g. through ratification).

As this research argues, these three limits, which are already present when the Legislature and the Executive transfer rulemaking powers between themselves, equally surface when they outsource rulemaking powers to autonomous public or private actors. These limits indeed revolve around political influence as an emanation of the democracy principle and materialize in the limits of: an express and concrete transfer of powers (Section 4.3.1), for technical or accessory matters that are therefore not policy-oriented (Section 4.3.2), and with sufficient political control (Section 4.3.3).

The Belgian Constitutional Court and Council of State Legislative Section expressly adopted these three limits to the outsourcing of rulemaking powers.[103] The French Constitutional Council also emphasized all three requirements, such that transfers of rulemaking powers to autonomous public actors may: 'only concern measures with a limited reach, both with regard to their application and with their content' and be subject to political control.[104] In Germany, the FCC primarily highlights the third requirement of sufficient parliamentary control for private rulemakers.[105]

A combination of one or more of these requirements is also ever-present in international and comparative law on autonomous public and private actors. On the international level, the milestone EU case of *Meroni* derived—from the building blocks of its Member States—an obligation for the rules of private actors to be express, limited in scope (i.e. not discretionary), and subject to political control.[106] In the more recent *ESMA* case, this case law was largely affirmed in relation

[103] Belgian Constitutional Court no. 86/2015, 11 June 2015, B.22.4.

[104] French Constitutional Council, no. 88-248 DC, 17 January 1989, § 15 and French Constitutional Council no. 96-370 of 23 July 1996, § 12.

[105] See BVerfGE 33, 125 (157) *Facharzt*; Case C-518/07 *Commission v. Germany* ECLI:EU:C:2010:125, §§ 41–6.

[106] Cases C-9 and 10/56 *Meroni v. High Authority* [1957/8] ECR 133; Stefan Griller and Andreas Orator, 'Everything Under Control? The 'Way Forward' for European Agencies in the Footsteps of the *Meroni* Doctrine' [2010] *E. L. Rev.* 3; Marta Simoncini, *Administrative Regulation Beyond the Non-Delegation Doctrine* (Hart 2018) 25–40; Merijn Chamon, 'Delegation Doctrine in the EU—Rulemaking and Enforcement Powers?', PP Presentation, Utrecht (24 November 2017) 5.

to the transfer of rulemaking powers to autonomous public actors in the EU, with a particular focus on the precise delineation of those powers.[107] On the comparative level, similar limits appear. In the Netherlands, the Dutch Council of State advised against rulemaking authority for autonomous public bodies that would exceed merely technical or internal matters.[108] Likewise, in Austria, the transfer of rulemaking powers to autonomous public or private actors is limited to express, non-essential transfers, with political control remaining.[109]

4.3.1 Preciseness

The first limit of an express and precise transfer of powers is necessary to avoid the transfer of discretionary powers. This limit is apparent in the three recognized outsourcing techniques.

4.3.1.1 Delegation

In Belgium, it clearly shows from case law and advisory practice that the delegation of powers needs to be well defined.[110] The Belgian Council of State Legislative Section took the lead in developing this standard of 'clarity and preciseness'.[111] The Council requires that the extent of the delegation is defined in a clear and accurate manner. Without this, the transfer of rulemaking power is not acceptable.[112]

When the Legislature delegates rulemaking powers to autonomous public actors, Belgium's Constitutional Court has accentuated this requirement over time. In the first landmark judgment on outsourcing rulemaking powers, the court accepted the delegation of the Brussels Legislature to the Brussels Housing Society (BHS) because it merely concerned ten *clearly defined tasks*.[113] Next, in the *FOSO* judgment, the Constitutional Court dealt with the delegation to the federal institution for the research of naval accidents (FOSO) of the competence

[107] Case C-270/12 *United Kingdom v. European Parliament and the Council of the European Union* ECLI:EU:C:2014:18.

[108] Dutch Council of State, *Advies over regels betreffende zelfstandige bestuursorganen (Kaderwet zelfstandige bestuursorganen)* (Dutch Parliament Tweede Kamer, vergaderjaar 2000–1, no. 27 426) A 4.

[109] András Sajó, 'Les autorités indépendantes' in Michel Troper and Dominique Chagnollaud (eds), *Traité international de droit constitutionnel—Tome 2* (Dalloz 2012) 357.

[110] Belgian Council of State Legislative Section, Advisory opinion of 8 April 1971 (Parliamentary Documents Senate 1970–1, no. 570) 112. This condition is strongly intertwined with the second requirement that outsourced powers can only be non-policy-oriented. Otherwise how would it be possible to identify the policy matter of which only an accessory part could be delegated? Such a test on accessory powers would become practically impossible.

[111] Belgian Council of State Legislative Section, Advisory opinion no. 54.536/2/3 of 19 December 2013, § 5.

[112] Belgian Council of State Legislative Section, Advisory opinion no. 39.272/3 of 29 November 2005, § 5; Belgian Council of State Legislative Section, Advisory opinion no. 27.965/3 of 24 November 1998, 4; Belgian Council of State Legislative Section, Advisory opinion no. 47.101/2/V of 26 August 2009, 6.

[113] Belgian Constitutional Court no. 24/98, 10 March 1998, B. 5.2.

to make security guidelines. Such guidelines were not binding. Nevertheless, the Constitutional Court explicitly confirmed that 'even if the recommendation would be binding [*which would make them rules*][114] the Constitution does not prevent the Legislature from entrusting specific rulemaking powers in a *precise* matter to an [autonomous public actor]'.[115] I equally wish to reiterate the consideration of the milestone *FSMA* case in which the Constitutional Court said that a transferred matter should be 'precise'.[116] In two other judgments, the Constitutional Court did not agree with the assertion of the claimants that the delegated powers were rulemaking. However, even here the court unremittingly stressed the importance of delegating powers in a precise fashion.[117]

When the Executive delegates rulemaking powers to autonomous public actors, the Council of State Administrative Litigation Section equally performs the preciseness test when scrutinizing 'unilateral administrative acts' (*eenzijdige bestuurlijke rechtshandelingen*). In the *CVBA t'Heist Best* case, the Flemish Legislature had granted rulemaking power to the Flemish Executive. The Legislature wanted the Executive to develop requirements for the recognition of social housing societies through mandatory bylaws. The Flemish government passed this competence on to the Flemish Housing Society. The Council of State first established that the initial 'grant of powers was broad'.[118] Next, the Council sanctioned the sub-delegation to a 'non-politically accountable actor' because it was insufficiently clear and well defined.[119] The Council of State Administrative Litigation Section ended up annulling the Flemish government's executive decree.

The French Constitutional Council has stressed that an unlimited rulemaking competence may not be delegated to an autonomous public actor.[120] In the *CNCL* case, the Constitutional Council ruled that the transfer of rulemaking powers could only occur within a determined domain and for the implementation of a statute.[121] The limit with regard to the determined domain or field of application

[114] See for this assumption: Sophie Adriaenssen, 'L'autorité des services et marchés financiers (FSMA) autorité administrative indépendante?' [2014] *Administration Publique Trimestriel* 316.

[115] Belgian Constitutional Court, no. 158/2013, 21 November 2013, B.14.4 (emphasis added).

[116] Belgian Constitutional Court no. 86/2015, 11 June 2015, B.22.4.

[117] Belgian Constitutional Court no. 130/2010, 18 November 2010, B.5. The Constitutional Court actually introduced the limiting test in that judgment for autonomous public or private actors' individual decision-making powers. Belgian Constitutional Court no. 166/2011, 10 November 2011, B.56.2.

[118] Belgian Council of State Administrative Litigation Section, no. 85648, 28 February 2000, *T'Heist Best*, 5.

[119] Ibid.

[120] Yoan Vilain, 'Demokratische Legitimität und Verfassungsmäßigkeit unabhängiger Regulierungsbehörden. Von den ursprünglichen Bedenken bis zur richterlichen Eingliederung in das französische Verwaltungssystem' in Johannes Masing and Gérard Marco (eds), *Unabhängige Regulierungsbehörden* (Mohr Siebeck 2010) 24; Michel Degoffe, 'Constitution et compétences normatives économiques des "autorités de régulation"' [22 January 2009] *Issu de Petites affiches* 18, I.B.

[121] French Constitutional Council no. 86-217 of 18 December 1986 § 58; Jean-Bernard Auby, 'Autorités administratives indépendantes—Les AAI encore et toujours' [2014] *Droit Administratif* § 1.

especially appears to buttress the preciseness of the delegation so that the transfer of competences is well framed.[122]

4.3.1.2 Referral

In relation to the referral technique, the Belgian Council of State Legislative Section equally calls for a clear rulemaking framework.[123] It specifically highlights this requirement in its advisory opinions on (private) corporate government codes. The Council had serious misgivings about an earlier attempt to refer to a corporate governance code[124] and again did not wholeheartedly agree with the technique. If a traditional rulemaker refers to such 'best practices published by the industry' it should at least clearly identify which good practice code it is referring to.[125] The Belgian Executive complied with this obligation in its Royal Decree of 6 June 2010: 'The Belgian corporate governance code 2009, as added in attachment, applies as the only corporate code'[126] for listed companies to observe, in fact making it a static referral. This corporate governance code is a private document; it is also referred to as the Code Buysse.

In France, the referral to a private standard needs to be sufficiently precise. External referrals to other traditional rules than the reviewable statute have been considered unconstitutional because they did not comply with the demands of legislating clearly and with precision.[127] *A fortiori* referrals to privately made standards should be—to the extent possible—sufficiently clear and precise.

In Germany, the static referral to privately made standards is unproblematic.[128] However, for a long time throughout the twentieth century it was unclear whether especially dynamic referrals to external private documents were in conformity with the democracy principle.[129] Three legal positions have competed in German scholarship.

First, some argued that the lack of democratic legitimacy of the referred-to standard would always exclude the validity of the external dynamic referral

[122] French Constitutional Council no. 89-260 of 28 July 1989, § 31; Tanneguy Larzul and Pierre de Montalivet, *Droit constitutionnel de l'administration* (JurisClasseur Administratif 2017) §§ 19–20; French Council of State, 'Considérations générales. Les autorités administratives indépendantes' in Renaud Denoix de Saint Marc (ed.), *Reports: French Council of State* (Conseil d'État 2001) 295.

[123] Belgian Council of State Legislative Section, Advisory opinion no. 52.704/1 of 8 February 2013, § 6.3.

[124] Belgian Council of State Legislative Section, Advisory opinion no. 40.492/2 of 12 June 2006, § 4.

[125] Belgian Council of State Legislative Section, Advisory opinion no. 38.642/4 of 13 July 2005, 5–6.

[126] Article 1, 6 June 2010, *Koninklijk besluit houdende aanduiding van de na te leven Code inzake deugdelijk bestuur door genoteerde vennootschappen*; Article 3:6, § 2 last sentence Belgian Company and Societies Code; Draft Statute *tot versterking van het deugdelijk bestuur bij de genoteerde vennootschappen en de autonome overheidsbedrijven en tot wijziging van de regeling inzake het beroepsverbod in de bank- en financiële sector* (Parliamentary Documents Chamber of Representatives no. 2336/001, 2009–10) 9.

[127] French Constitutional Council no. 2000-435 of 7 December 2000, § 53.

[128] Horst Dreier, 'Artikel 20 GG' in Horst Dreier (ed.), *Grundgesetz Kommentar* (Mohr Siebeck 2004) 90; Bernd Hartlieb, *Verweisung auf technische Normen in Rechtsvorschriften* (Beuth 1982) 13.

[129] Eberhard Baden, 'Dynamische Verweisungen und Verweisungen auf Nichtnormen' [1979] *NJW* 626; Peter Marburger, *Die Regeln der Technik im Recht* (Heymann 1979) 386.

technique.[130] The referred-to document could be fully amended, making the rulemaking process completely rudderless. One judicial stance agrees that one can never fully control a dynamic referral, which makes the referral necessarily unconstitutional. The Berlin Administrative Court basically stated that it was impossible for dynamic referrals to be sufficiently precise regarding the referral that had been made in § 22, I of the Regulation on the granting of aid in illness, nursing, childbirth and other cases (*Verordnung über die Gewährung von Beihilfen in Krankheits-, Pflege-, Geburts- und sonstigen Fällen*).[131]

Second, others have noted that the technique was lawful but limited by the same constitutional provisions that limit the delegation of rulemaking powers. Indeed, if in any given situation a delegation is possible, then a dynamic referral must also be allowed in that situation.[132] However, we have already seen that article 80, 1 of the Basic Law, which places constitutional limits on the delegation of rulemaking powers to traditional rulemakers, does not apply to the referral technique and privately made standards.

A third legal tenor thus debunks the previous two interpretations. Its authors indicate that the referral technique was always in accordance with the democracy principle because the politically accountable actor made the referral and could ultimately renounce the referral.[133] The final democratic responsibility remained—like always—with the referring actor. In an appeal of the judgment of the Berlin Administrative Court, the Bundesverwaltungsgericht confirmed the position that dynamic referrals are principally permitted—even to autonomous public or private actors.[134] Research has ultimately shown that German case law embraces dynamic referrals but that the technique always needs to be analysed on a case-by-case basis.[135]

We can synthesize a test at the moment when the Legislature or the Executive makes a dynamic referral.[136] A dynamic referral is unconstitutional if the rule as a whole is not sufficiently determinable (*bestimmbar*).[137] Following this test, it must

[130] Hans-Ulrich Karpen, *Die Verweisung als Mittel der Gesetzgebungstechnik* (De Gruyter 1970); Florian Becker, *Kooperative und konsensuale Strukturen in der Normsetzung* (Mohr Siebeck 2005) 558; Alfred G. Debus, *Verweisungen in Deutschen Rechtsnormen* (Duncker & Humblot 2008) 199, 203.

[131] VG Berlin 7 K 140.14—24 September 2014, 2.b.; for broader support of this argument, Florian Becker, *Kooperative und konsensuale Strukturen in der Normsetzung* (Mohr Siebeck 2005) 570; Michael Sachs, 'Die dynamische Verweisung als Ermächtigungsnorm' [1981] *NJW* 1652.

[132] Alfred G. Debus, *Verweisungen in Deutschen Rechtsnormen* (Duncker & Humblot 2008) 163; Thomas Clemens, 'Die Verweisung von einer Rechtsnorm auf andere Vorschriften' [1986] *AöR* 82.

[133] See Göbel and Manssen cited in Alfred G. Debus, *Verweisungen in Deutschen Rechtsnormen* (Duncker & Humblot 2008) 222.

[134] BVerwG 5 C 9.14, 26 March 2015, § 25.

[135] Alfred G. Debus, *Verweisungen in Deutschen Rechtsnormen* (Duncker & Humblot 2008) 205, 224.

[136] Inspired by: Thomas Clemens, 'Die Verweisung von einer Rechtsnorm auf andere Vorschriften' [1986] *AöR* 103 and 83. These limits boil down to having respect for the will of the people and the referring actor.

[137] Alfred G. Debus, *Verweisungen in Deutschen Rechtsnormen* (Duncker & Humblot 2008) 148.

be possible for the outsourcer to overlook the context and the extent of the complete rule.[138] This naturally does not mean that the referred-to standard cannot change; otherwise it would no longer be a dynamical referral. Rather, this limit of requires a structured regulatory framework (*strukturierten Regelungsbereich*) that encapsulates the referral.[139] In other words, a dynamic referral is only permissible to a specific extent (*nur in gewissem Rahmen zulässig*).[140]

The test of a statutory structural framework is further exemplified by the FCC's case law concerning former § 9 of the Nordrhein Westphalen miners pension scheme Act (*Bergmannsversorgungsscheingesetz*).[141] Paragraph 9 provided that retired coalminers were subject to the same health care programme as current miners. This was generally seen as a dynamic referral in the statutory rule for former miners to the collective labour agreement (CLA) that had been made on health care for current miners. The FCC declared this dynamic referral unconstitutional. First, the court warned that citizens could not be surrendered without boundaries to the rulemaking powers of representative organizations of employers and employees. It required an assurance that the rule could be ascribed to the will of the people.[142] 'Only to the extent that the content of the collective labour agreement is essentially certain, are we not dealing with an unlawful cession of the Legislature's rulemaking power.'[143]

In another milestone case tackling dynamic referrals to actors outside the *Trias Politica*, the FFC ruled on notary fees (*Notargebühren*). Article 12, I of the Basic Law requires a federal statute to regulate access to the professions. Paragraph 144 III of the Act on costs in matters of voluntary jurisdiction (*Gesetz über die Kosten in Angelegenheiten der freiwilligen Gerichtsbarkeit*) referred dynamically to standards that could increase the duty of notaries to lower their fees for the benefit of municipalities without any legislative control. This dynamic referral was deemed not to be in conformity with the Basic Law.[144] The FCC concluded that the regulatory framework was unclear.

[138] Georg Wegge, 'Zur verfassungsrechtlichen Abgrenzung unbestimmter Rechtsbegriffe von unzulässigen dynamischen Verweisungen am Beispiel der der "betriebswirtschaftlichen Grundsätze" nach § 6 Abs. 2 Satz 1 KAG NW, DVBl. 1997, 648 ff.' [1997] *DVBl.* 648.

[139] Conclusion Advocate-General Langemeijer Dutch High Council, no. 11/01017, 30 March 2012, 26; Alfred G. Debus, *Verweisungen in Deutschen Rechtsnormen* (Duncker & Humblot 2008) 221; Thomas Clemens, 'Die Verweisung von einer Rechtsnorm auf andere Vorschriften' [1986] *AöR* 109.

[140] BVerfG 1 BvR, 1 March 1978, BVerfGE 47, 285 (312).

[141] See Alfred G. Debus, *Verweisungen in Deutschen Rechtsnormen* (Duncker & Humblot 2008) 213.

[142] BVerfGE 64, 208 (214); Thomas Clemens, 'Die Verweisung von einer Rechtsnorm auf andere Vorschriften' [1986] *AöR* 102.

[143] BVerfG 64, 208. Throughout its motivation, it underlined the interconnectivity between this technique and the reception technique by citing the system of declaring collective labour agreements generally binding and the rulemaking system developed by professional physicians' organizations.

[144] BVerfGE 47, 285; Thomas Clemens, 'Die Verweisung von einer Rechtsnorm auf andere Vorschriften' [1986] *AöR* 103.

4.3.1.3 Reception

Ultimately, also for the reception technique, the Belgian Council of State Legislative Section emphasizes clarity of the framework which allows for the creation of private rules.[145] In fact, the reason why the federal Legislature decided to create a framework law for the existing practice of CLAs in 1968 was precisely because it wanted to create more clarity on the reach of such rulemaking agreements.[146] Furthermore, the Belgian Constitutional Court accepted the transfer of powers to the orders of attorneys to regulate, among other things, the deontology of their profession. The Legislature '*clearly described* the task it assigned to the ... orders as well as the duties of lawyers in society to accomplish'.[147] In the light of the use of sector protocols to gradually lift restrictions on public life that were set due to Covid-19 in Belgium, the general assembly of the Council of State Legislative Section ruled in 2021 that if these sector protocols are obligatory, and thus rulemaking, they have to be enacted through regulations by the competent government not outsourced on the basis of a flimsy legal basis.[148]

French enabling statutes or regulations that attach public power to past or future agreements between negotiating parties equally have to do so expressly and be sufficiently precise.[149] With regard to CLAs, the Constitutional Council determined that the Legislature could leave it to employers and employees or their representative organizations to specify the exact means of implementation. However, the Legislature could only do so *after defining the rights and obligations relating to the conditions and the employment relations*.[150]

In Germany, in its landmark *Facharzt* case, the FCC clarified that the Legislature had to set the status-determining (*status bildende*) rules of self-regulating professional organizations.[151] The FCC stressed that a statute had to set the status defining rules but any supplementary rules were subject to the discretion (*Ermessen*) of the professional group.[152] Thus, at least 'status-defining rules' should be regulated by a traditional rulemaker. These status-defining rules are at a minimum those rules relating to educational requirements, recognition of the profession, any professional qualifications granted, the minimum duration of training, the procedure for

[145] Belgian Council of State Legislative Section, Advisory opinion no. 40.116/1 of 20 April 2006, § 1.

[146] L. Servais, Statutory Motivation CLA Statute (Parliamentary preparation Senate 1966–7, no. 148) 1–2; Belgian Council of State Legislative Section (Parliamentary preparation Senate 1966–7, no. 148) 86.

[147] Belgian Constitutional Court no. 16/2003, 28 January 2003, B.6.2.2 (emphasis added).

[148] Belgian Council of State Legislative Section, Advisory opinion no. 69.253/AV of 23 April 2021, § 20.3

[149] Michel Lascombe, 'Les ordres professionnels', Doctoral thesis, University of Strasbourg (1987) 215.

[150] French Constitutional Council no 89-257 of 25 July 1989, §§ 10 and 11; French Constitutional Council no. 99-423 of 13 January 2000, § 28; French Constiutional Council no. 2004-494 of 29 April 2004, § 14.

[151] 33 BVerfGE 125, Decision of 9 May 1972, § 128.

[152] Decision of 9 May 1972. 33 BVerfGE 125, § 128.

recognition, the grounds for withdrawal of recognition, and the general position of doctors within the health-care system.[153]

4.3.2 Not policy-oriented

Second, in order for a rule to be outsourced, it should generally not lie at the heart of an important policy decision. The rules should be accessory and/or merely technical.

An accessory matter is one that does not concern the core or essential elements of a governmental policy decision. However, sometimes powers that appear to overreach this accessory nature are outsourced. This can principally only be defended in the light of the democracy principle if the competence is technical. As inspired by the *Oxford English Dictionary*, a 'technical' matter is complex; it requires a specific educational background or professional experience to fully fathom, especially with regard to applied, medical, and industrial sciences. In other words, mere *legal* complexity does not make a matter of competence 'technical'.

4.3.2.1 Delegation

According to the Belgian Council of State Legislative Section, only accessory or non-essential (*bijkomstige of detailmatige*) measures can be *delegated* to actors that are not constitutionally enumerated to wield rulemaking powers.[154] The Constitutional Court confirmed that autonomous public actors can receive rulemaking power for details and non-essential matters. In the aforementioned case 24/98, the Brussels Legislature had outsourced rulemaking powers to the Brussels Housing Society. The Constitutional Court allowed for this because there was 'no delegation of general rulemaking powers'.[155] Through an *a contrario* reasoning, one can derive from this judgment that the court will *not* accept delegations of '*general* rulemaking powers' to autonomous public actors.[156] In other words, the rulemaking powers may not be too broad; they have to be limited and accessory.

The Belgian Council of State Legislative Section and the Belgian Constitutional Court have also emphasized an alternative condition on whether rulemaking

[153] BVerfG 33, 125, § 128. Christoph Degenhart, *Staatsorganisationsrecht* (Müller 2013) 137; Britta Beate Wiegand, *Die Beleihung mit Normsetzungskompetenzen. Das Gesundheitswesen als Exempel* (Duncker & Humblot 2007) 176–7; Fritz Ossenbühl, 'Satzung' in Josef Isensee and Paul Kirchhof (eds), *Handbuch des Staatsrechts der Bundesrepublik Deutschland*, vol. V (Beck 2005) 368.

[154] Belgian Council of State Legislative Section, Advisory opinion of 23 March 2015 (Parliamentary document Flanders 2015–16, no. 336/1) 73; Belgian Council of State Legislative Section, Advisory opinion no. 54.536/2/2 of 19 December 2013, 84; Belgian Council of State Legislative Section, Advisory opinion no. 44.192/1 of 1 April 2008, 10; Belgian Council of State Legislative Section, Advisory opinion no. 42.605/3 11 April 2007, 7–8.

[155] Belgian Constitutional Court no. 24/98, 10 March 1998, B.5.2 and B.5.3. Also see Belgian Constitutional Court no. 162/2015, 19 November 2015, B.8.4.

[156] Belgian Constitutional Court no. 24/98, 10 March 1998, B.5.3.

powers can be outsourced, namely if the 'the delegations have a primarily technical extent'.[157]

The demarcation line of what constitutes a technical and/or accessory rule may seem thin. On the one hand, when the predecessor of the Belgian Financial Services and Markets Authority (FSMA) was permitted to exercise the outsourced authority to adopt maximum reference rates, the Council of State condoned the delegation. Fixing reference rates fits perfectly within the FSMA's task to supervise the financial and insurance sector and permits it to exercise its expertise.[158] On the other hand, when the same autonomous public actor received the competence to make rules on how long certain documents needed to be stored with institutions for occupational pensions (IOPs) or whether they could extend certain loans, the Belgian Council of State Legislative Section deemed that grant of powers too substantial.[159] In the same vein, the establishment of the administrative and pecuniary status of employees is not such a detailed or technical matter that can be delegated to an autonomous public actor.[160] Because of this difficulty in delineating between technical and/or accessory rules, the Belgian Council of State Legislative Section has recently opted to adopt the overarching notion that the decision cannot be 'policy-oriented'.[161]

The French Constitutional Council clarified in its *CSA* case that the transferred competences needed to be 'limited in their field of application and content' (*limitées tant par leur champ d'application que par leur contenu*).[162] The limit with regard to the established content confirms the requirement that the rules do not

[157] Belgian Council of State Legislative Section, Advisory Opinion of 21 November 2016 (Parliamentary documents Flanders 2016–17, 1047/1) 88. The Belgian Council of State occasionally uses 'and' instead of 'or': Belgian Council of State Legislative Section, Advisory opinion 18 October 2016 (Parliamentary documents Flanders 2016–17, 995/1) 99. Belgian Constitutional Court no. 86/2015, 11 June 2015, B.22.4.

[158] Belgian Council of State Legislative Section, Advisory opinion no. 40.698/1 of 6 July 2006, 3.

[159] Belgian Council of State Legislative Section, Advisory opinion no. 40024/1 of 28 March 2006, 10, articles 52–4. For other practical examples of unauthorized delegations, see e.g. Robert Andersen, Pierre Nihoul, and Marc Joassart, 'Le Conseil d'État. Chronique de Jurisprudence—2001' [2003] *Revue belge de droit constitutionnel* 191–4.

[160] Belgian Council of State Legislative Section, Advisory opinion of 18 October 2016 (Parliamentary Documents Flanders 2016–17, 995/1) 99.

[161] Belgian Council of State Legislative Section, Advisory opinion no 66.870/3 of 30 January 2020, § 14.2.

[162] French Constitutional Council no. 88-248 of 17 January 1989 § 15. Bertrand Marais, 'Convergence entre télécommunications et audiovisuel en France' [9 August 2008] *Gazette du Palais* 5, I.1.2; Tanneguy Larzul and Pierre de Montalivet, *Droit constitutionnel de l'administration* (JurisClasseur Administratif 2017) § 20; Jean-Marc Sauvé, 'Les autorités administratives indépendantes' for *Transcription d'intervention Comité d'évaluation et de contrôle des politiques publiques (CEC) sur les autorités administratives indépendantes* (Conseil d'État 2010) B.3; Jean-Louis Autin and Emmanuel Breen, *Autorités Administratives Indépendantes* (JurisClasseur Administratif 75, 2017) § 88; Jacques Chevalier, 'Autorités administratives indépendantes et État de droit' [2016] *Civitas Europa* 150; Pierre de Montalivet, 'Constitution et autorités de régulation' [2014] *RDP* 316, I.B.1; Jean-Philippe Feldman, 'Les "autorités administratives indépendantes" sont-elles légitimes? Sur les AAI en général et le Conseil supérieur de l'audiovisuel en particulier' [2010] *Recueil Dalloz* 2852 etc. I third last paragraph.

make an essential policy decision but remain limited to the (technical) implementation of determined legal, economic, or social decisions.[163]

A number of examples help to elucidate when the delegation of rulemaking powers is insufficiently circumscribed in its field of application or content: in the aforementioned *CSA* case in which the Constitutional Council developed this first tier of the democracy test,[164] it immediately deemed the delegation of rulemaking powers to the CSA to be excessive since it contained not only the power to make deontology codes but also the competence to create general rules on institutional communication.[165] A step further down the line, the Council of State may determine that the interpretation of the delegation by the autonomous public actor, in drafting its rule, has been too broad and not in conformity with the predefined framework. The adoption of a 'terminology note', defining various legal terms such as the notion of audiovisual oeuvre, by an autonomous public actor (CNCL) was not accepted because the statute did not reasonably allow for this.[166] Equally, in *Société civile des auteurs réalisateurs producteurs et autres* the statutory delegation had explicitly endowed the government with the competence to set the general principles of televised publicity. As a result, there was at most an insufficiently clear delegation to the CSA to determine internet news and distribution and for cinema companies to air televised advertisements.[167]

This outcome does not differ substantially from Justice Rehnquist's famous concurring opinion in the US Supreme Court *Benzene* case, albeit equally framed within the separation of powers principle, as Justice Harlan and others had done before him:[168]

> Congress may wish to exercise its authority in a particular field, but, because the field is sufficiently *technical*, the ground to be covered sufficiently large, and the Members of Congress themselves not necessarily expert in the area in which they choose to legislate, the most that may be asked under the separation of powers doctrine is that *Congress lay down the general policy and standards that animate*

[163] French Council of State, 'Considérations générales. Les autorités administratives indépendantes' in Renaud Denoix de Saint Marc (ed.), *Reports: French Council of State* (Conseil d'État 2001) 339.

[164] French Constitutional Council no. 88-248 of 17 January 1989.

[165] Ibid., § 16; Jean-Louis Autin and Emmanuel Breen, *Autorités Administratives Indépendantes* (JurisClasseur Administratif 75, 2017) § 89; French Council of State, 'Considérations générales. Les autorités administratives indépendantes' in Renaud Denoix de Saint Marc (ed.), *Reports: French Council of State* (Conseil d'État 2001) 295.

[166] French Council of State 16 December 1990, *SA La Cinq* as cited in Michel Degoffe, 'Constitution et compétences normatives économiques des "autorités de régulation"' [22 January 2009] *Issu de Petites affiches* 18, I.B. and fn. 16.

[167] French Council of State no. 218358 of 3 July 2000; French Council of State, 'Considérations générales. Les autorités administratives indépendantes' in Renaud Denoix de Saint Marc (ed.), *Reports: French Council of State* (Conseil d'État 2001) 337–8.

[168] *Arizona v. California*, 373 US 546, 625–6 (1963) (Justice Harlan dissenting in part); see also *Mistretta v. United States*, 488 US 361 (1989).

the law, leaving the agency to refine those standards, 'fill in the blanks,' or apply the standards to particular cases.[169]

4.3.2.2 Referral

The position of the Belgian Council of State Legislative Section towards technicality and essentiality with regard to dynamic referrals has been especially developed in its legisprudence on the World Anti-Doping Code.

According to the Belgian Council of State Legislative Section, dynamic referrals are unproblematic in two main scenarios. First, if they occur simultaneously with a delegation to the Executive (as a type of guideline to interpret that delegation) and, second, if they do not directly affect the rights of citizens.[170] The rights of citizens are least affected when World Anti-Doping Agency (WADA) standards, to which a Belgian Legislature would refer, are accessory. Moreover, anti-doping policy is without doubt technical. This applies both to the World Anti-Doping Code and the international standards. The latter are even described by article 2, 35nd of the Flemish Anti-Doping Statute as 'documents, adopted by WADA in support of the WADA Code, that serve to harmonize the various *technical* and operational aspects of the Code's provisions'.[171]

In Germany, the aforementioned Berlin case indicates that the referral is constitutional if it is tightly measured ('*eng bemessen*').[172] In practice, a judge will operationalize this test by taking into account the broad or strict use of language, the degree to which the referring rule and the referred-to standard cover the same content, practical-political, and financial restrictions to alter the referred-to standard, the standing customary or judicial organization of the matter, and the already recognized technical rules in order to determine whether the rulemaking framework is sufficiently circumscribed.[173]

Comparative legal scholarship deems the *dynamic* referral technique 'questionable' or even 'invalid' in the UK.[174] This principled prohibition cannot be derived from a clear statutory provision or case law but flows from the way in which secondary legislation frames its references. According to regulation A4(5)(c)(i) of the UK Building Regulations 1976, for instance, an undated reference to a standard must be interpreted as referring to the edition of the standard at the time the regulation was enacted. In other words, dynamic referrals are implicitly excluded from

[169] *Indus. Union Department v. American Petroleum Inst.*, 448 US 675 (1980) (emphasis added).
[170] Council of State Legislative Section, Advisory opinion (Documents Flemish Parliament 2014–15 no 161/1), 169.
[171] Emphasis added.
[172] BVerwG 5 C 9.14, 26 March 2015.
[173] Alfred G. Debus, *Verweisungen in Deutschen Rechtsnormen* (Duncker & Humblot 2008) 221.
[174] Ibid., 30; Peter Marburger and Rainald Enders, 'Technische Normen im Europäischen Gemeinschaftsrecht' in Peter Marburger (ed.), *Jahrbuch des Umwelt- und Technikrechts* (Decker 1994) 362, K204–5; Peter Marburger, 'Legal and Organizational Aspects of Technical Standardization at the National and European Level' in K. H. Lindackers (ed.), *Safety Aspects of Technical Standards* (Springer 1992) 204.

that regulation.[175] There are some examples that suggest that the UK *Legislature* condones the static referral technique to private standards. This is apparent in the provision of the Gambling Act 2005, through which primary or secondary legislation can refer to a provision of the Gambling Commission Code as a generally binding, exonerating rule.[176] However, this merely facilitates the use of the referral technique; it does not apply the technique itself. The UK *Executive* regularly uses static referrals to private standards in technical matters. The executive regulations using referrals also do not set limits, which is why static referrals to private standards in the UK appear unproblematic.

4.3.2.3 Reception

Interestingly, in relation to *reception* as a third outsourcing technique, the accessory or technical nature does not appear as important for its acceptability. On the contrary, CLAs, deontology codes for free professions, and miscellaneous categories of agreements (consumer agreements, health service agreements, and covenants regarding commercials for marketing of alcoholic beverages) sometimes concern core labour, trade, and commercial policies.

4.3.3 Political control

The third overarching limit of sufficient political control appears especially problematic for autonomous public and private actors for at least two reasons. First, because they remain actors that are not directly politically accountable through democratic elections. Second, because there must be sufficient tools to review delegated rulemaking effectively.

In relation to the first reason, this seeming paradox of providing political control for autonomous public or private actors needs to be addressed. A balance must be struck between the Legislature's aim of remaining aware of the activities of an autonomous public actor and the latter's continuing status as an 'autonomous' actor. Inspired by the evolution of the Osmotherly Rules in the UK,[177] officials or employees of those actors could, for example, be interviewed by Parliament on day-to-day or operational matters. Other examples, deriving specifically from Belgium, France, and Germany, include members of the Legislature or the Executive being

[175] However, dynamic referrals have not been as explicitly outlawed as, e.g., in Austria, where the Austrian Constitutional Court prohibited direct, dynamic referrals to other rulemaking organs (and thus also to standards made by autonomous public or private actors). Austrian *Verfassungsgerichtshof* no. 12947/1991 (G280/91; G281/91; G325/91 13 December 1991), § 5 on the referral technique to § 320 StGB.

[176] Section 24(8) of the Gambling Act 2005.

[177] The Osmotherly Rules, codified in 1980, stipulate that parliamentary select committees may not summon civil servants because they bear no political responsibility. Margaret L. Liu, 'Ministerial Responsibility and Constitutional Law' [2002] *Coventry LJ* 34–5.

appointed as officials of an autonomous public or private actor, requiring notification of new rulemaking, or requesting an annual report from the new rulemaker.

In relation to the second reason, the main motives for outsourcing rulemaking powers are the search for independent buffers against short-term thinking, technical expertise, and the involvement of stakeholders. Even if sufficient political mechanisms are established for the Legislature or the Executive to review the actions of autonomous public or private actors, those same motives may lead Legislatures and Executives to refrain from genuinely intervening. It is crucial that the actors which need to review outsourced rulemaking are effectively motivated to check this massive body of rules.[178]

Countries can develop an institutionalized system in which the Legislature and the Executive are incentivized to monitor all types of delegated rulemaking. For example, Standing Order 151 of the UK House of Commons establishes the Joint Committee on Statutory Instruments.[179] An added value of increased parliamentary scrutiny of delegated legislation in Belgium or France is that it could decrease the almost untenable workload for their respective Councils of State (Legislative Section), which perform an *a priori* review of legislative and executive rules.

However, even in the UK such commissions ultimately fail to substantially review the large majority of outsourced legislation. UK select committees are heavily understaffed to a degree that they can no longer effectively perform their work.[180] Moreover, the ruling majority in parliamentary systems arguably does not even want to perform thorough reviews. Bodies that review outsourced legislation should be established to oppose and criticize.

On the level of the Legislature, the UK Joint Committee on Statutory Instruments, therefore, has a chair from an opposition party. Moreover, the committee is equally constituted between the ruling and opposition parties. Given the unique counter-majoritarian and advisory function of a reviewing committee, one might even consider giving the opposition parties full majority in their search for unconstitutional delegations of rulemaking powers. The majority of legislators could still overrule these decisions in a plenary session.

On the level of the Executive, Wass even proposed the construct of a UK 'Department of the Opposition'[181] which would be part of the Executive and staffed by experienced civil servants whose sole purpose would be to find irregularities in the Executive. The idea could be metaphorically compared to antibodies in the blood which fight disease. An ideal central focus of reviews by such a Department

178 Rob Van Gestel, 'The Deparliamentarisation of Legislation: Framework Laws and the Primacy of the Legislature' [2013] *Utrecht L. Rev.* 113–14.

179 Mark Elliott and Jason N. E. Varuhas, *Administrative Law: Text and Materials* (Oxford University Press 2017) 682–3.

180 Douglas Wass, 'Checks and Balances in Public Policy Making' [1987] *Public Law* 183–4.

181 Ibid., 192. In the same vein on the dominance of the UK government: Editorial, 'Secondary Legislation and the Primacy of Parliament' [2016] *Statute L. Rev.* iii–iv.

of the Opposition could also be outsourced rulemaking. However, this idea undermines the unity of the Executive and thus the institutional separation of powers.

Only more forceful and adapted measures can thus provide the means to control autonomous public and private actors. Such political control could take place in various ways. Again, the inspiration for these modes of political control is found in existing mechanisms that the Legislature uses to control the Executive. General techniques to review *delegated* legislation could be applied to both executive rules and outsourced rules.

4.3.3.1 Delegation

Traditionally, the Belgian Council of State Legislative Section went even further than political control for the transfer of rulemaking powers to autonomous public actors. It said that the Legislature or the Executive must at least confirm through ratification that the outsourced power was exercised correctly when delegating to an autonomous public actor.[182] The Council of State Legislative Section was dismissive of an autonomous public body for the financial markets with rulemaking powers on deontology, for example, without a ratification requirement.[183] A statute that ratifies the sub-statutory rule can accomplish this. Also the Executive or even a minister can ratify the rulemaking decision of an autonomous public actor. The Council of State Legislative Section has authorized this ministerial ratification power, for example in its 1971 advisory opinion on the Autonomous Institution for Insurance Control as an agency that could control insurance.[184]

However, this ulterior ratification is arguably not (any longer) a requirement for delegating rulemaking powers to autonomous public actors. The traditional mantra of the Council of State Legislative Section and scholarship, promoting ulterior ratification within the delegation technique to autonomous public actors,[185] no longer complies with the practical reality. The Legislature and governments have not always responded to the Council's call to provide ratification of delegations to autonomous public actors.[186] In fact, the superfluousness of explicit ratifications could already be derived from the early case law of the Court of Cassation going back to 1920, which asserted that rulemaking powers could be delegated to

[182] Belgian Council of State Legislative Section, Advisory opinion no. 25.835/9 of 11 December 1996, 12–13. Sophie Adriaenssen, 'L'autorité des services et marchés financiers (FSMA) autorité administrative indépendante?' [2014] *Administration Publique Trimestriel* 314.

[183] Belgian Council of State Legislative Section, Advisory opinion of 6 March 1995 (L 24.188/2, Parliamentary Documents Senate *1994–5*, no. 1352/1) 242–5; Imre Kovalovszky, 'À propos du pouvoir réglementaire, avis avant CE arrêt no. 63.275 du 22 novembre 1996' [1996] *APT* 301–2.

[184] Belgian Council of State Legislative Section, Advisory opinion of 8 April 1971 (Parliamentary Documents Senate 1970–1, no. 570) 111–12. Marc Uyttendaele, *Trente leçons de droit constitutionnel* (Bruylant 2011) 80; Pierre Nihoul, Marc Joassart, and Vinciane Franck, 'Le Conseil d'Etat. Chronique de Jurisprudence—2006' [2007] *Revue belge de droit constitutionnel* 320.

[185] David De Roy, 'Le pouvoir réglementaire des autorités administratives indépendantes en droit belge' in *Rapports belges au Congrès de l'Académie de droit comparé à Utrecht* (Bruylant 2006) § 31.

[186] Jan Velaers, *De Grondwet en de Raad van State Afdeling Wetgeving* (Maklu 1999) 384.

'secondary authorities' charged with acting under the control and under the condition of *tacit* or explicit parliamentary consent.[187] In its judgment 97/2011, the Belgian Constitutional Court factually buried the ratification requirement with regard to the rulemaking powers of the federal energy regulator, CREG, as an autonomous public actor, to determine the methodology for fixing tariffs: 'the King can no longer fix the methodology for setting and approving tariffs by distribution system operators following the advice of the CREG since the CREG now disposes exclusively of this competence'.[188] Furthermore, even if ratification of a specific rule occurs, that does not fully prove parliamentary control. The Council of State Legislative Section has deemed a mere ratification authority for a minister alone to be inadequate because the minister (and the Executive as a whole) would still lose the right to initiate rules that would ordinarily reside with it.[189]

The Legislature or the Executive must thus possess an alternative resource to exert control on an autonomous public actor, through a type of injunction right, an annual report, or government commissioners. The Belgian Financial Services and Markets Authority is currently subject to a right of injunction by the Executive and a yearly report to the Chamber of Representatives. Moreover, the Chamber hears the regulator's president each year and the Chamber can also summon him or her or the entire board. The Constitutional Court condoned these safeguards as sufficient parliamentary control.[190] It also accepts that the Executive exercises sufficient control if it recognizes the autonomous public actor, determines its bylaws, and follows up on its activities.[191]

What eventually represents sufficient democratic control 'can vary according to the composition and the functioning' of the recipient of rulemaking powers.[192] The Belgian Council of State Legislative Section makes the extent of parliamentary influence dependent on the amount of discretionary power that the autonomous public actor possesses. 'When it comes to applying precise regulations to individual cases, leaving little discretion to the [recipient], the supervision by the [politically accountable actor] may be reduced. On the other hand, when the exercise

[187] And taking accessory measures. Belgian Court of Cassation, 4 May 1920 [1920] *Pas.* I, 137; Karel Rimanque, *De Grondwet gewikt en gewogen* (Intersentia 2003) 103.

[188] Belgian Constitutional Court no. 97/2011, 31 May 2011, B.9.4. See also: Belgian Constitutional Court no. 71/2016, 25 May 2016. As discussed more widely in Emmanuel Slautsky, 'Principe de légalité et attributions de pouvoirs à des autorités indépendantes: une relation équivoque' in La légalité: un principe de la démocratie belge en péril (Larcier 2019) title C.

[189] Belgian Council of State Legislative Section, Advisory opinion no. 21.755/2 of 29 October 1992, 5–6; Belgian Council of State Legislative Section, Advisory opinion of 6 March 1995 (L 24.188/2, Parliamentary Documents Senate 1994–5, no. 1352/1) 243; Xavier Delgrange, Luc Detroux, and Hugues Dumont, 'La régulation en droit public' in Benoit Jadot and François Ost (eds), *Elaborer la loi aujourd'hui, mission impossible?* (Publications des Facultés universitaires Saint-Louis 1999) 81.

[190] Belgian Constitutional Court no. 86/2015, 11 June 2015, B.22.5.

[191] Belgian Constitutional Court, no. 166/2011, 10 November 2011, B.58.4; Patrick Goffaux, *Dictionnaire de droit administratif* (Bruylant 2015) 79.

[192] Pierre Nihoul, Marc Joassart, and Elisabeth Willemart, 'Le Conseil d 'Etat. Chronique de Jurisprudence—2008' [2009] *Revue belge de droit constitutionnel* 289.

of powers, conferred on that [recipient] implies opportunity choices, it is necessary that this [recipient], which is not politically responsible, is subject to closer scrutiny of the [Legislature or the Executive].'[193]

In France, the Legislature or the Executive must exert some degree of control on the exercise of rulemaking powers by an autonomous public actor.[194] The Constitutional Council confirmed this in its judgment 96/378: 'Given that the rulemaking power vested in the autonomous public actor is exercised *under the supervision of the Minister*, the argument alleging the violation of Article 21 FC can only be dismissed.'[195] It is possible to discern three stages to politically check outsourced rulemaking processes: *ex ante*, through confirmation, and *ex post*.

Ex ante: autonomous public actors (*autorités administratives indépendantes* (AAIs) and *autorités publiques indépendantes* (APIs) need to be founded through a statute since this is mandated by article 1 of Organic Statute 2017-54 . By establishing and designing the basic structure of the autonomous public actor, Parliament exercises a fundamental *ex ante* influence on its functioning in the light of rulemaking. This has been described as a guarantee of containment (*garantie d'endiguement*).[196] A further *ex ante* control applies through the appointment of officials within the autonomous public actor by the President and/or the government. However, the supervision of Parliament on the appointment of these officials has been weak and has triggered additional criticism of a lack of democratic legitimacy.[197] After the introduction of the common framework in 2017, there is now a veto power for the parliamentary commissions on the executive appointment of the presidents of all but six listed AAIs and APIs.[198] The presidents of those AAIs have to be appointed by the President of the French Republic after nomination by the competent parliamentary commissions, which can only veto a presidential appointment through a 3/5 majority.[199]

Confirmation: a traditional rulemaker (parliament, government, minister) can confirm (*habilitation*) a rule and attach its democratic legitimacy to the rule. Some raise the concern that this confirmation could undermine the reason for the

[193] Belgian Council of State Legislative Section, Advisory opinion no. 44.544/2 of 9 June 2008, 3.

[194] Stéphanie Dubiton, *La protection des libertés publiques par les autorités administratives indépendantes, une solution démocratique?* (LGDJ 2016) § 455 etc.

[195] French Constitutional Council no. 96-378 of 23 July 1996, §12 (emphasis added); see also French Constitutional Council no. 86-217 of 18 December 1986, § 23; Stéphanie Dubiton, *La protection des libertés publiques par les autorités administratives indépendantes, une solution démocratique?* (LGDJ 2016) 93.

[196] Pascale Idoux, 'Le nouveau statut général des AAI et API' [2017] *AJDA* 1115, III.B.

[197] Anne Debet, 'Lois sur les autorités administratives indépendantes: quels changements pour la CNIL?' [2017] *Communication Commerce électronique*, comm. 56, 3; Jean-Louis Autin and Emmanuel Breen, *Autorités Administratives Indépendantes* (JurisClasseur Administratif 75, 2017) § 49.

[198] Statutory law no. 2010-838 of 23 July 2010 *relative à l'application du cinquième alinéa de l'article 13 de la Constitution* (1) jo. Article 13, 5 of the French Constitution; Pascale Idoux, 'Le nouveau statut général des AAI et API' [2017] *AJDA* 1115, III.B; Jean-Louis Autin and Emmanuel Breen, *Autorités Administratives Indépendantes* (JurisClasseur Administratif 75, 2017) § 35.

[199] Pierre de Montalivet, 'Constitution et autorités de régulation' [2014] *RDP* 316, A.2.

existence of autonomous public actors.[200] The French Council of State disagrees and sees no reason why confirmation should not be allowed.[201] Indeed, even if an outsourced rule is confirmed, that does not imply that the rule is made by the Legislature or the Executive. In other words, the rulemaking value of the act would not derive from the confirmation.[202]

Ex post: ultimately, various instruments are in place through which the Legislature and the Executive can evaluate the dealings of autonomous public actors. From a *personnel* point of view, a parliamentary commission can call in the officials of an autonomous public actor to answer for their decisions.[203] Moreover, the Statute 2017/55 on AAIs and APIs allows for the one-time renewal of the mandates of officials. This renewal leaves room for evaluation. After their first term, politically accountable actors have the *ex post* possibility of influencing the (rulemaking) direction of the autonomous public actor.[204] From an *institutional* point of view, autonomous public actors are periodically re-evaluated by the Legislature, which allows for *ex post* control. Traditionally, they draft an annual report in which they justify their decisions regarding their various competences, including rulemaking competences.[205] Article 21 of the Statute 2017/55 even makes this obligatory.[206] Ultimately, an AAI cannot autonomously decide on the level of its own financial resources. If the Legislature is dissatisfied by what it learns through its *ex post* control mechanisms, it can simply exercise the power of the purse because AAIs do not have full financial autonomy.[207] The Legislature can then vote on a new statute and annul or alter the AAI.[208]

In Germany, there are also at least four mechanisms through which Parliament (more specifically, the Bundestag) itself retains the delegated powers

[200] Stéphanie Dubiton, *La protection des libertés publiques par les autorités administratives indépendantes, une solution démocratique?* (LGDJ 2016) 226.

[201] French Council of State, 'Considérations générales. Les autorités administratives indépendantes' in Renaud Denoix de Saint Marc (ed.), *Reports: French Council of State* (Conseil d'État 2001) 339.

[202] French Council of State no. 270234 of 26 September 2005; Stéphanie Dubiton, *La protection des libertés publiques par les autorités administratives indépendantes, une solution démocratique?* (LGDJ 2016) 226–7.

[203] French Council of State, 'Considérations générales. Les autorités administratives indépendantes' in Renaud Denoix de Saint Marc (ed.), *Reports: French Council of State* (Conseil d'État 2001) 369; Gabriel Eckert, 'L'indépendance des autorités de régulation économique à l'égard du pouvoir politique' [2012] *Revue française d'administration publique* 641.

[204] Anne Debet, 'Lois sur les autorités administratives indépendantes: quels changements pour la CNIL?' [2017] *Communication Commerce électronique*, comm. 56, 3.

[205] Gabriel Eckert, 'L'indépendance des autorités de régulation économique à l'égard du pouvoir politique' [2012] *Revue française d'administration publique* 641; French Council of State, 'Considérations générales. Les autorités administratives indépendantes' in Renaud Denoix de Saint Marc (ed.), *Reports: French Council of State* (Conseil d'État 2001) 372.

[206] Anne Debet, 'Lois sur les autorités administratives indépendantes: quels changements pour la CNIL?' [2017] *Communication Commerce électronique*, comm. 56, 5; Pascale Idoux, 'Le nouveau statut général des AAI et API' [2017] *AJDA* 1115, III.B.

[207] See, however, article 18 of Statute 2017; Pascale Idoux, 'Le nouveau statut général des AAI et API' [2017] *AJDA* 1115, III.A.

[208] Gabriel Eckert, 'L'indépendance des autorités de régulation économique à l'égard du pouvoir politique' [2012] *Revue française d'administration publique* 640.

for the Executive in check. Some executive regulations need to be alerted to Parliament (*Kenntnisgabevorbehalte*), others need to be approved by Parliament (*Zustimmungsvorbehalte*), and yet others can be vetoed by Parliament (*Aufhebungsvorbehalte*). Ultimately, another type of executive regulations can be altered by Parliament (*Änderungsvorbehalte*).[209]

The FCC has confirmed that when a Legislature cedes its rulemaking powers (*sich seiner Rechtsetzungsbefugnis entäußert*), it is limited by the democracy principle.[210] Despite the permissible autonomy of autonomous public or private actors, the Legislature remains subject to 'the principle that it cannot completely dispense with its power to legislate and that it cannot entirely abandon its influence on the content of the rules [*Einfluß auf den Inhalt der Normen*] to be issued by' such autonomous public or private actors.[211] The FCC stated this consideration in the context of the *Facharzt* case in which two doctors had filed a constitutional complaint against sanctions they had received as a result of violating their deontology codes. The codes had been based on a very broad recognition of the competence of the professional organizations of physicians (*Landesärztekammern*). The FCC also limited the outsourcing of rulemaking powers to the water corporation for the Lippe river under the democracy principle as follows: 'From a constitutional viewpoint, decisions as a result of binding action by functional self-regulating bodies is ... only permissible ... insofar as the People ... maintain a decisive influence on this action.'[212]

In addition, in the UK the Statutory Instruments Act 1946 offers a unified straitjacket for political control.[213] Sections 4 and 5 of the Act determine how a statutory instrument can be laid before Parliament and which procedures are activated once that occurs. As argued earlier, we can assume that the Act could also be made applicable to rules adopted by autonomous public actors. In addition to the other parliamentary committees that scrutinize delegated legislation,[214] this would in particular trigger a review by the Joint Committee for Statutory Instruments.[215] However, this added scrutiny should not be overstated, as in the first sixty-five years of its existence only 0.01 per cent of statutory instruments were rejected

[209] Hartmut Bauer, 'Artikel 80 GG' in Horst Dreier (ed.), *Grundgesetz Kommentar* (Mohr Siebeck 2004) 1847.

[210] BVerfGE 33, 125 (158) *Facharzt*; Thomas Clemens, 'Die Verweisung von einer Rechtsnorm auf andere Vorschriften' [1986] *AöR* 102; also Antje von Münch, *Das Spannungsverhältnis zwischen funktionaler Privatisierung und demokratischer Legitimation* (Nomos 2014) 156.

[211] BVerfGE 33, 125 (157) *Facharzt*.

[212] BVerfGE 107, 59 § 172; Georg Hermes, 'Legitimationsprobleme Unabhängiger Behörden' in Hartmut Bauer, Peter Huber, and Karl-Peter Sommermann (eds), *Demokratie in Europa* (Mohr Siebeck 2005) 478; Florian Becker, *Kooperative und konsensuale Strukturen in der Normsetzung* (Mohr Siebeck 2005) 446; Werner Heun, *The Constitution of Germany* (Hart 2011) 35.

[213] Anthony Bradley, Keith Ewing, and Christopher Knight, *Constitutional and Administrative Law* (16th edn, Pearson 2014) 590; Paul Craig, *Administrative Law* (Sweet & Maxwell 2016) 433.

[214] See e.g. Anthony Bradley, Keith Ewing, and Christopher Knight, *Constitutional and Administrative Law* (16th edn, Pearson 2014) 589.

[215] Ibid., 591; Paul Craig, *Administrative Law* (Sweet & Maxwell 2016) 442.

by Parliament through the intervention of the Joint Committee for Statutory Instruments.[216]

Separate parent statutes that outsource rulemaking power may also set out mechanisms through which the Legislature or the Executive can scrutinize autonomous public or private actors. Due to their scattered nature, the organization of diligent parliamentary supervision is complicated.[217] There are at least four methods through which parent statutes can organize this control.[218]

First, parent statutes will maintain political control over the general functioning of autonomous public actors. Parliament will remain in charge of financing the autonomous public actor and it always has the 'nuclear option' of discontinuing its existence.[219]

Second, Parliament can apply the affirmative, super-affirmative, and negative scrutiny mechanisms to a specific rule through which it can also accept, condone, or veto outsourced rules.

Third, Parliament could require mechanisms and notifications to ensure knowledge of and control over regulatory activities of the autonomous public or private actor. The latter can account for its actions either to Parliament or a minister. In the first instance, the Legislature may impose a reporting requirement for its own benefit or for one of its committees. The UK Office of Communications (Ofcom), for example, remains 'accountable to Parliament' to which it reports annually.[220] In the second instance, parent statutes can enable a minister to appoint or dismiss members, give guidance or directions on the general functioning of the autonomous public actor, organize agreements between ministerial departments and the autonomous public actor, and monitor them.[221] The British Hallmarking Council, the Human Fertilisation and Embryology Authority, and again Ofcom, for example, provide annual reports of their activities to the competent Secretary of State.[222]

Fourth, one traditional control mechanism that Parliament exercises is inherently more difficult when it concerns autonomous public or private actors; namely, parliamentary hearings and interrogations. Parliamentary hearings in the UK are closely linked to ministerial responsibility. Through 'traditional British pragmatism',[223] the theory of ministerial responsibility has adapted to the growing power

216 Ibid., 462.

217 Julia Black, 'Calling Regulators to Account: Challenges, Capacities and Prospects' in Nicholas Bamforth and Peter Leyland (eds), *Accountability in the Contemporary Constitution* (Oxford University Press 2013) 374–5.

218 J. E. Kersell, *Parliamentary Supervision of Delegated Legislation* (Stevens & Sons 1960) 14

219 Paul Craig, *Administrative Law* (Sweet & Maxwell 2016) 85 and 440–1.

220 See e.g. Ofcom, 'Annual plan 2018/2019' (2018) 1, 1.2.; Ofcom, 'Members' Code of Conduct' (2015) section 3.

221 Paul Craig, *Administrative Law* (Sweet & Maxwell 2016) 85 and 92; Laurence Claus, 'Montesquieu's Mistakes and the True Meaning of Separation' [2005] *OJLS* 438.

222 Section 19 of the Hallmarking Act 1973; section 7 of the Human Fertilisation and Embryology Act 1990; Ofcom, 'Members' Code of Conduct' (2015) section 11.

223 Paul Craig, *Administrative Law* (Sweet & Maxwell 2016) 87.

of civil servants and next-step agencies. This evolution implies that members of executive agencies can now be personally held to account for operational or day-to-day decisions.[224] However, ministers remain responsible for the general policy decision in their departments. Given that the relationship between ministers and arm's length bodies is strained even more than that between ministers and civil servants or executive agencies in a growing administration, it must also be deemed possible for Parliament to call on members of an arm's length body to appear before parliamentary hearings. In this sense, the heads of non-ministerial departments have a direct duty to explain their actions to Parliament.[225] Parliament will likewise directly hear a chief executive officer on matters of operational and day-to-day concern.[226]

Such controlling mechanisms positively force the Legislature or the Executive to review outsourced rules.

4.3.3.2 Referral

Political control also needs to be guaranteed when traditional rulemakers refer to standards through the *referral technique*. In France, the Ministry of Economics advises that the referring rulemaker and the referred-to standardization organization must keep each other informed about changes in the referring rule or referred-to standard.[227] The French Council of State also derived from the French statute on standardization that regulatory provisions which refer to all or part of a standard, in terms which impose compliance with it, are illegal unless they have been signed by the Minister of Industry, therefore ensuring bundled oversight by the Minister of Industry.[228] In Germany, traditional rulemakers can only refer to standards if they have previously defined the structural statutory framework, which ensures the Legislature's *ex ante* political influence. Moreover, § 161 of the Stock Corporation Act (*Aktiengesetz*) dictates that corporate governance codes—a type of standard to which the Legislature or the Executive tends to refer—should be published in the Federal Gazette so that the Ministry of Justice can control the evolution of such codes.[229] To a similar extent, the Belgian Council of State Legislative Section allowed for a referral by the Executive to a corporate governance code because in this case the Executive could still 'inspect and supervise the evolutions in corporate

[224] John McEldowney, *Public Law* (Sweet and Maxwell 2016) 429; Margaret L. Liu, 'Ministerial Responsibility and Constitutional Law' [2002] *Coventry LJ* 34.

[225] John Alder, *Constitutional & Administrative Law* (Palgrave 2015) 349.

[226] Paul Craig, *Administrative Law* (Sweet & Maxwell 2016) 93.

[227] Ministère de l'économie, de l'industrie et de l'emploi, *Guide relatif a la bonne utilisation des normes dans la reglementation* (direction générale de la compétitivité, de l'industrie et des services 2009) 14.

[228] French Council of State no. 354752 of 20 November 2013.

[229] Gregor Bachmann, 'Rechtsnatur und Legitimation des Kodex' in Thomas Kremer, Gregor Bachmann, Marcus Lutter, and Axel von Werder (eds), *Kommentar Deutscher Corporate Governance Kodex* (Beck 2016) 43.

governance'.[230] In the US, agencies first have to request permission from the Office of Federal Regulations in order to refer to and incorporate private standards.[231] The defining comparative criterion thus appears to be that politically accountable actors must remain able to control (*ex ante* or *ex post*) any referral to standards made by private and hybrid actors.

Added to this, I reiterate the controlling factor—of the judicial power to alter dynamic referrals to static referrals—coined by the FCC.[232] The referred-to standard would then merely be a fixed rule established by the Legislature at a certain point in time. As mentioned, such a static referral arguably always survives constitutional review. This re-qualification happened, for example, in the *Notargebühren* case on notary fees.[233] I have already indicated that the FCC deemed the referral in para. 144 III of the German Act on costs in matters of voluntary jurisdiction (*Gesetz über die Kosten in Angelegenheiten der freiwilligen Gerichtsbarkeit*) not to be in conformity with the Basic Law. However, in its ensuing considerations the court did not declare the paragraph unconstitutional: 'This referral can also be construed as a constitutionally unobjectionable static referral.'[234] Outside the central countries researched, for example in the Netherlands, legal scholars also support a judicial power to amend dynamic to static referrals in order to maintain democratic control over the referral technique.[235] Static referrals inherently suggest some political control since the referring Legislature or Executive knows exactly what the referred-to standard is and what it will be in the future after the referral.

4.3.3.3 Reception

Political control similarly functions as an essential limit to professional organizations drafting rules in accordance with the *reception technique*. In Belgium and France, this ulterior political control ordinarily occurs through *ex post* ratification of the professional agreement by the Legislature or the Executive, as is the case for extended CLAs and the codes of most professional 'orders'.

On the one hand, ratification appears to be a necessary condition to guarantee political control in this technique. According to the Belgian Council of State Legislative Section, 'no one denies that the statute on collective labour agreements is met with criticism with regard to ... the Belgian Constitution and that its

[230] Belgian Council of State Legislative Section, Advisory opinion (Parliamentary Documents Chamber of Representatives 2336/001, 2009–10) 104, fn. 8.

[231] Emily S. Bremer, 'Incorporation by Reference in an Open-Government Age' (2013) 36 *Harv. J. L. & Pub. Pol'y* 143.

[232] Thomas Clemens, 'Die Verweisung von einer Rechtsnorm auf andere Vorschriften' [1986] *AöR* 81, 118.

[233] BVerfGE 47, 285.

[234] Ibid. (317); Thomas Clemens, 'Die Verweisung von einer Rechtsnorm auf andere Vorschriften' [1986] *AöR* 118.

[235] Richard Neerhof, *Alternatief bestuursrecht: normalisatie en conformiteitsbeoordeling in het publieke belang* (Boom Juridische uitgevers 2016) 285 and 302.

constitutionality is contested by an important part of legal scholarship'.[236] However, the statute's constitutionality still stands.[237] A primary prerequisite for this is the ratification of received private agreements by the Legislature or the Executive.[238] In the same vein, a governmental ratification requirement ordinarily exists for the deontology codes of professional organizations.[239] The Belgian Court of Cassation even decided that if a member of a free profession had been sanctioned on the sole basis of a disciplinary rule that was not (duly) affirmed by the Executive, that sanction could not be enforced if a legislative statute requires such affirmation.[240] Only the deontology codes of veterinarians and attorneys do not have to be affirmed by an act of a politically accountable actor. The literature ascribes the first exception for veterinarians to an inadvertent omission by the Legislature.[241] Nevertheless, the Court of Cassation has accepted the binding force of the veterinarians' deontology code.[242] The second exception, for attorneys, appears to be intentional. It is inspired by the unique function of attorneys in Belgian society and the inherent need for their autonomy from government.[243]

On the other hand, ratification is also not a panacea which in and of itself provides sufficient political control. The Belgian Council of State Administrative Litigation Section annulled article 12 of the organization for real estate agents' deontological code because it imposed exclusive use of the chosen real estate agent which naturally limited the contractual freedom of their clients (third parties).[244] The ensuing ratification by the Executive of that code could not make up for the infraction because the rulemaking act itself (the deontology code) 'has the direct effect of creating duties that are imposed on third parties to the profession'.[245]

[236] Pierre Nihoul, Marc Joassart, and Vinciane Franck, 'Le Conseil d'Etat: chronique de jurisprudence 2004' [2005] *Revue belge du droit constitutionnel* 309.

[237] Belgian Council of State Legislative Section, Advisory opinion (Parliamentary Document Senate 1966–7, no. 148) 93.

[238] Articles 28–34 of the Belgian Statute on Collective Labour Agreements.

[239] Belgian Council of State Legislative Section, Advisory opinion no. 24.600-24.601/AG/AV/2 of 10 October 1995 and 6 October 1995, 67; Jan Velaers, *De Grondwet en de Raad van State Afdeling Wetgeving* (Maklu 1999) 386–7; Patricia Popelier and Jeroen Van Nieuwenhove, 'Decentralisering en privatisering van wetgeving' in Jef De Mot (ed.), *Vrank en vrij: liber amicorum Boudewijn Bouckaert* (Die Keure 2012) 273.

[240] Belgian Court of Cassation *Van Damme v. Orde der architecten*, 23 June 1970, *Arr. Cass.*, 1007 with the advisory opinion of Advocate-General Dumon.

[241] Patricia Popelier and Jeroen Van Nieuwenhove, 'Decentralisering en privatisering van wetgeving' in Jef De Mot (ed.), *Vrank en vrij: liber amicorum Boudewijn Bouckaert* (Die Keure 2012) 270.

[242] Belgian Court of Cassation 11 April 1991 [1990–1] *Arr. Cass.*, 827.

[243] Belgian Council of State Legislative Section, Advisory opinion no. 22.537/2 of 23 June 1993, 106–7; Belgian Council of State Legislative Section, Advisory opinion 6 March 1995 (Parliamentary Document Senate 1994–5 no. 1352/1) 244; Belgian Constitutional Court no. 16/2003, 28 January 2003, B.7.2. See also Belgian Constitutional Court no. 23/97, 30 April 1997, B.4–B.5.

[244] Belgian Council of State Administrative Litigation Section, no. 105 673, 19 April 2002, *Malou et al.*, 8; Belgian Council of State Administrative Litigation Section, no. 144.181, 4 May 2005, *Taft et al.*, 8.

[245] Walter Van Gerven and Steven Lierman, *Beginselen van Belgisch privaatrecht I Algemeen deel—40 jaar later* (Kluwer 2010) 300.

Furthermore, the French Legislature and the Executive need to control a professional organization that performs a task of public service in the exercise of that function.[246] This requirement is inspired by a drive towards democratic legitimacy and is often performed by a positive action of a member of the Executive, such as the extension of a CLA or ministerial confirmation of a rule made by a professional organization.

Article 20, 2 of the German Basic Law is adamant: '*All state authority* is derived from the people.'[247] Rulemaking powers imply the exercise of state authority; also, in essence, 'legal supervision' (*Rechtsaufsicht*) of the exercise of rulemaking powers by private actors is required.[248] More specifically, this boundary is set on having clearly (*bestimmt*) fixed the manner and extent (*Art und Umfang*) of the outsourced competence.[249] In fact, the reception technique quite easily complies with limits that derive from the democracy principle. Stakeholders are receiving more rulemaking input—as opposed to the ordinary rulemaking processes—through this type of functional self-regulation. The entire concept of functional self-regulation has always been strongly intertwined with the democracy principle.[250] Other means for guaranteeing democratic control by functional self-regulation are by establishing a legislative supervisory committee[251] or by auditing the decision-making process of the autonomous public or private actor: in the aforementioned German case on the water corporation for the Lippe river, specific emphasis was placed on governmental control by inviting a government official to the association's meeting.[252]

Finally, in the UK the somewhat different protrusion of the reception technique does not impede the fact that professional organizations in sports or legal services fall under the umbrella of public actors that may exercise, albeit limited, control of them. For example, UK Sport (UKSP) is an executive non-departmental public body sponsored by the Department for Digital, Culture, Media and Sport. Its mission is to work in partnership with private UK sports organizations to improve results in Olympic and Paralympic sports. Moreover, the Bar Standards Board (BSB) and the Solicitors Regulation Authority (SRA) function under the umbrella of the

[246] Aurélie Virot-Landais, 'Les activités de contrôle exercées par les personnes privées chargées d'un service public' [2013] *RDP* 613, I.1.A.

[247] Emphasis added.

[248] Britta Beate Wiegand, *Die Beleihung mit Normsetzungskompetenzen. Das Gesundheitswesen als Exempel* (Duncker & Humblot 2007) 268.

[249] Thomas Holzner, *Konsens im Allgemeinen Verwaltungsrecht und in der Demokratietheorie* (Mohr Siebeck 2016) 491; Britta Beate Wiegand, *Die Beleihung mit Normsetzungskompetenzen. Das Gesundheitswesen als Exempel* (Duncker & Humblot 2007) 222.

[250] Reinhard Hendler, 'Das Prinzip Selbstverwaltung' in Josef Isensee and Paul Kirchhof (eds), *Handbuch des Staatsrechts der Bundesrepublik Deutschland*, vol. IV (Beck 2005) 1125.

[251] Thomas Züll, *Regulierung Im Politischen Gemeinwesen* (Mohr Siebeck 2014) 83.

[252] BVerfGE 107, 59, 2 BVL 5/98 and 6/98 § 182.

Legal Services Board.[253] Sports organizations and the organizations of barristers and solicitors are therefore supervised by public actors.

4.4 Conclusion

In summary, in the light of the democracy principle, the Legislature and the Executive must manage to maintain a degree of political control over autonomous public or private actors to whom they outsource rulemaking powers. Furthermore, this principle dictates that the transfer of powers must be precise and must only concern non policy-oriented matters, which means that they must either be technical or accessory. The democracy principle has therefore been indicated as the main limit on outsourcing rulemaking powers and ultimate 'line of defense'.

The democracy principle has been contrasted with the legality principle as the first line of defense. Both the specific and general legality principle reserve a core of rulemaking powers to the Legislature. The principle of the separation of powers adds a hidden limit on outsourcing rulemaking powers. From an institutional viewpoint, this is done to preserve the powers of the Executive and the Judiciary. From a functional view, the accumulation of powers within one autonomous public, private or hybrid actor may not be exaggerated.

Combined with the democracy principle, the legality principle and the separation of powers principle—as constitutional principles—compensate for the lack of constitutional provisions that regulate the burgeoning practice of outsourcing rulemaking powers.

[253] Ministry of Justice, 'Framework Document Agreement between the Ministry of Justice and the Legal Services Board' (December 2017) 5, 15.

5
Comparative National Outsourcing Safeguards

After having established the limits and the tests—set by constitutional provisions and principles—on outsourcing rulemaking powers, Chapter 5 focuses on the second research hypothesis: there are safeguards with which *all* rules need to comply in order to count as qualitative rules.

Chapter 5 first derives five principles of good rulemaking from the EU Commission's principles of good governance: transparency, a place in the hierarchy of rules, judicial review, representativeness, and efficiency/effectiveness. These constitutional safeguards have especially, but not exclusively, evolved out of the rule of law. Subsequently, I determine the constitutional, legislative, or judicial basis of these five principles of good rulemaking for all types of rulemaking in the countries researched, including statutes and executive rules. Finally, I study how rules made by autonomous public, private, and hybrid actors that are generally more recently developed, more sporadic, and less structured, comply with these safeguards. In relation to these rules, it is especially useful to consider good practice in other countries. In other words, there are standards that rules made by autonomous public, private, or hybrid actors need to meet. There are other means besides political scrutiny and democratic control that can legitimize their rules.[1] Moreover, where statutory clauses impose an obligation on the Executive to comply with certain safeguards when making use of rulemaking powers,[2] similar

[1] Paul Craig, *Administrative Law* (Sweet & Maxwell 2016) 88.

[2] Such as consulting the interested parties, publishing the rules, and making them available to judicial review, etc: *R (On application of Bancoult) v. Foreign Secretary* [2008] UKHL 61; Mark Elliott and Jason N. E. Varuhas, *Administrative Law: Text and Materials* (Oxford University Press 2017) 692; Anthony Bradley, Keith Ewing, and Christopher Knight, *Constitutional and Administrative Law* (16th edn, Pearson 2014) 588.

Outsourcing Rulemaking Powers. Cedric Jenart, Oxford University Press. © Cedric Jenart 2022.
DOI: 10.1093/oso/9780192897831.003.0005

obligations can rest on autonomous public, private, and hybrid actors. Regardless of the status of the rulemaker, rules should have a distinct legislative quality.[3]

5.1 Introduction: five principles of good rulemaking

First, I will briefly revisit the relevance of the second research hypothesis, namely the notion that all rules must meet certain safeguards.

Autonomous public, private, and hybrid actors may actually increase overall respect for rulemaking quality if they receive powers with the specific purpose of paying particular attention to human rights and efficiency.[4] However, they may likewise endanger the quality of rulemaking because they focus more on technical or sector-specific aspects of the law and do not enjoy a similar historical tradition in drafting rules as does the Legislature or the Executive.[5] Outsourcing rulemaking powers seems to rob the citizen of principles of good rulemaking that are institutionally safeguarded by governmental actors. When neither the Legislature nor the Executive create the rules, an autonomous public, private, or hybrid actor must itself uphold the quality of the rules. Therefore, recipients of rulemaking power should also comply with principles of good rulemaking.[6]

Second, I aim to establish the specific safeguards with which these rules must comply. Often inspired by Fuller's eight principles of the internal morality of the law,[7] various commendable lists of principles of good rulemaking have been drafted over recent decades.[8] Popelier, for example, derived the following principles of good rulemaking from the principle of legal certainty: effective publication, clarity of content, compliance with (higher) rules, precision in the application of timing, respect for legitimate expectations, and feasibility.[9]

It was imperative to select from these lists of principles of good rulemaking those that appear particularly problematic when autonomous public, private, or

[3] Nick Barber, 'The Rechtsstaat and the Rule of Law' [2014] *U. Toronto LJ* 452. The Executive and trade unions, respectively; Tímea Drinóczi, 'Concept of Quality in Legislation—Revisited: Matter of Perspective and a General Overview' [2015] *Statute L. Rev.* 219.

[4] Jacques Chevalier, 'Autorités administratives indépendantes et État de droit' [2016] *Civitas Europa* 146; Pascale Deumier, 'Quand le droit souple rencontre le juge dur' [2016] *RTD Civ.* 571.

[5] Jacques Chevalier, 'Autorités administratives indépendantes et État de droit' [2016] *Civitas Europa* 149.

[6] cf. Patricia Popelier *Democratisch regelgeven* (Intersentia 2001) 138; Walter Van Gerven and Steven Lierman, *Beginselen van Belgisch privaatrecht I Algemeen deel—40 jaar later* (Kluwer 2010) 273.

[7] Generality, accessibility, non-retroactiveness, clarity, consistency, feasibility, durability, and compliance with other rules. Lon Fuller, *The Morality of Law* (Yale University Press 1979) 39. Cass Sunstein and Adrian Vermeule, 'The Morality of Administrative Law' (2018) 131 *Harv. L. Rev.* 1926.

[8] Henri Coremans, Marnix Van Damme, Jean Dujardin, Bruno Seutin, and Gerit Vermeylen, *Beginselen van wetgevingstechniek en behoorlijke regelgeving* (die Keure 2016) 120–247; Inge van der Vlies, *Handboek Wetgeving* (Tjeenk Willink 1991) 150–80.

[9] Patricia Popelier, 'Legal Certainty and Principles of Proper Law Making' [2000] 2 *Eur. J. L. Reform* 321; Patricia Popelier, *Rechtszekerheid als beginsel van behoorlijke regelgeving* (Intersentia 1997) 610.

hybrid actors create rules. As mentioned in the introduction to this monograph, the EU Commission adopted five well-known principles of good governance in its White Paper: (1) openness; (2) coherence; (3) accountability; (4) participation; and (5) effectiveness.[10] It did so to counter the criticism that *supranational* EU institutions were insufficiently politically accountable or democratically legitimized. Similar concerns surface with the *intranational* rulemaking actors studied here. It is thus possible to adapt the EU Commission's five principles of good governance to five principles of good rulemaking. When applied to rulemaking actors, legal scholarship in the countries researched has indeed emphasized that a rule needs to: (1) be transparent; (2) have an established position within the hierarchy of rules; and (3) be subject to judicial review.[11] Furthermore, it also confirms the other two principles of good rulemaking: (4) 'representativeness' and (5) 'effectiveness' or efficiency.[12] Facets of this scholarly approach can also be detected in the case law of the countries researched. The Belgian Council of State Legislative Section, for example, laments at least three questionable guarantees in rules made by autonomous public, private, or hybrid actors: (1) 'publication'; (2) 'the position in the hierarchy of rules'; and the lack of (3) 'preventive control of the Council of State' itself.[13] It is imperative to keep emphasizing these principles of good rulemaking because rulemakers may tend to favour pure expediency in rulemaking over such standards.[14]

Third, I will discuss which overarching constitutional principles have inspired these five principles of good rulemaking. The rule of law, with its focus on legal certainty and accountability, can be said to underlie aspects of transparency, the hierarchy of rules, and judicial review.[15]

From a global perspective, over one hundred constitutions recognize the rule of law as a restraint on tyranny.[16]

[10] European Commission, 'European governance–A white paper', Communication of 25 July 2001, COM(2001) 428, C 287.

[11] Manfred Löwisch and Volker Rieble, 'TVG § 1 Inhalt und Form des Tarifvertrages' in Manfred Löwisch and VolkerRieble, *Tarifvertragsgesetz* (Beck 2017) § 988. See also Thorsten Anderl, *Gesetzgebung und kooperatives Regierungshandeln* (Berliner Wissenschafts-Verlag 2006) 256.

[12] Anne Röthel, 'Lex mercatoria, lex sportiva, lex technica—Private Rechtsetzung jenseits des Nationalstaates?'[2007] *JZ* 761; Britta Beate Wiegand, *Die Beleihung mit Normsetzungskompetenzen. Das Gesundheitswesen als Exempel* (Duncker & Humblot 2007) 170; Horst Dreier, 'Artikel 20 GG' in Horst Dreier (ed.), *Grundgesetz Kommentar* (Mohr Siebeck 2004) 88.

[13] Belgian Council of State Legislative Section, Advisory opinion no. 56.941/321 of January 2015, § 14; Belgian Council of State Legislative Section, Advisory opinion no. 39.272/3 of 29 November 2005, § 5.

[14] Donald L. Revell, 'Enhancing the Legislative Process: The Value of the Legislative Drafter' [2011] *Statute L. Rev.* 152; Alec Samuels, 'Ensuring Standards in the Quality of Legislation' [2013] *Statute L. Rev.* 297; Daniel Greenberg, 'Dangerous Trends in Modern Legislation' [2015] *Public Law* 96.

[15] Other aspects of transparency, representativeness, and efficiency/effectiveness fit less neatly within the rule of law. At most, they are part of a substantive (or broad) reading of the rule of law, added to the formal reading of the rule of law (with the emphasis on process). However, they can also serve as emanations of the separation of powers and especially the democracy principle. The history and extent of these principles were thoroughly explained in Chapter 4 of this monograph.

[16] Sumit Bibarya and Elliot Bulmer, 'Rule of Law, Democracy and Human Rights: The Paramountcy of Moderation' in Maurice Adams, Anne Meuwese, and Ernst Hirsch Ballin (eds), *Constitutionalism*

The German rule of law (or *Rechtsstaat*) is explicitly enshrined in article 28 of the Basic Law: 'The constitutional order in the Länder must conform to the principles of a republican, democratic and social state governed by the rule of law, within the meaning of this Basic Law.' Nevertheless, the principle is considered by German case law and scholarship to be broader than this provision in the Basic Law.[17] The rule of law principle has been given many meanings over the past centuries and decades. Historically, the notion of *Rechtsstaat* was a thin concept, which merely provided an alternative to the tyrannical police state (*Polizeistaat*).[18] Over time, some definitions of the rule of law have become real umbrella terms, containing all of the constitutional principles, including the principle of democracy and respect for human rights. In this research, a more focused designation is continuously applied. Two definitions of the German concept of *Rechtsstaat* most resemble this research's definition of the rule of law. First, *Rechtsstaat* is the legal inhibition of public authorities for the purpose of limiting state powers and enhancing individual guarantees of freedom.[19] To a large degree, this inhibition entails certainty of law for the citizens.[20] Second, the *Rechtsstaat* principle implies that: (1) statehood is constituted in law; (2) laws, not people, rule; and (3) statutory rules must be proportionally implemented.[21]

The rule of law principle in France (*état de droit*) has been defined as the principle limiting the exercise of powers and guaranteeing individual freedoms based on the values of legal dogma.[22] Theories of German legal philosophers on *Rechtsstaat* heavily influenced the French interpretation of the rule of law.[23] Carré de Malberg contrasted *état de droit* with *état légal*, which merely entailed an obligation by the administration to comply with statutory law.[24] *Etat de droit* must

and the Rule of Law: Bridging Idealism and Realism (Cambridge University Press 2017) 123; Brian Z. Tamanaha, *On the Rule of Law* (Cambridge University Press 2012) 115.

[17] Kaarlo Tuori, 'L'état de droit' in Michel Troper and Dominique Chagnollaud (eds), *Traité international de droit constitutionnel—Tome 1* (Paris 2012) 654.

[18] Martin Loughlin, *Foundations of Public Law* (Oxford University Press 2017) 318–20; Dietmar von der Pfordten, 'On the Foundations of the Rule of Law and the Principle of the Legal State/Rechtsstaat' in James Silkenat, James Hickey Jr, and Peter Barenboim (eds), *The Legal Doctrines of the Rule of Law and the Legal State (Rechtsstaat)* (Springer 2014) 24.

[19] Florian Becker, *Kooperative und konsensuale Strukturen in der Normsetzung* (Mohr Siebeck 2005) 546.

[20] Christoph Degenhart, *Staatsorganisationsrecht* (Müller 2013) 370.

[21] Katharina Sobota, *Das Prinzip Rechtsstaat* (Mohr Siebeck 1997) 424.

[22] Jacques Chevalier, 'Autorités administratives indépendantes et État de droit' [2016] *Civitas Europa* 145. See for another definition: Daniel Mockle, 'Rule of Law' in Michel Troper and Dominique Chagnollaud (eds), *Traité international de droit constitutionnel—Tome 1* (Dalloz 2012) 661.

[23] Christian Tomuschat, 'Democracy and the Rule of Law' in Dinah Shelton, *The Oxford Handbook of International Human Rights Law* (Oxford University Press 2013) 476; Kaarlo Tuori, 'L'état de droit' in Michel Troper and Dominique Chagnollaud (eds), *Traité international de droit constitutionnel—Tome 1* (Dalloz 2012) 644; Alain Laquièze, 'Etat de droit and national sovereignty in France' in history' in Pietro Costa and Danilo Zolo (eds), *The Rule of Law* (Springer 2007) 261.

[24] Martin Loughlin, *Foundations of Public Law* (Oxford University Press 2017) 322–3; Geranne Lautenbach, *The Concept of the Rule of Law and the European Court of Human Rights* (Oxford University Press 2013) 33.

thus be interpreted as a broader constitutional principle. In other French-speaking legal systems, the rule of law principle has been translated as the *primauté du droit* (Canada) and the *prééminence du droit* (Council of Europe).[25] However, these translations are closer to the legality principle than to the rule of law. Therefore, despite its pitfalls, I consider *état de droit* as the primary French translation of 'rule of law' in France.[26]

In the UK, the rule of law is widely recognized as a constitutional principle.[27] Furthermore, it is often considered the second most important UK constitutional principle after the sovereignty of Parliament.[28] The UK perspective on the rule of law has been portrayed as democratic-constitutional as opposed to the German liberal-constitutional approach.[29] Its meaning is thus inherently broader than safeguards that protect legal certainty.

Although the concepts of *Rechtsstaat*, *état de droit*, and rule of law thus have different histories and focus, they share a concern to avoid tyranny and the infringement of legal certainty. The transfer of rulemaking powers to autonomous public, private, and hybrid actors also needs to comply with such rule of law expectations.[30] Ordinarily, private actors do not have to abide by the rule of law since it only targets state actors.[31] However, when rulemaking powers are outsourced to such actors, they indirectly become part of the state apparatus and thus must also comply with this constitutional principle. The rule of law sets standards that *all* rules must meet in order to be viewed as legitimate.

This comparative exercise on principles of good rulemaking can form the blueprint of a 'law of rules' that should be adopted to ensure uniformity of outsourced rulemaking powers.[32] In fact, the UK has a pioneering role in developing such a framework through its Regulators' Compliance Code 2007 (today known as the Regulators' Code), which provides guidance to a considerable number of autonomous public actors on how to meet quality requirements when exercising their rulemaking powers.[33]

[25] Duncan Fairgrieve, 'Etat de droit and Rule of Law: Comparing Concepts—A Tribute to Roger Errera' [2015] *Public Law* 42.

[26] Ibid., 42–3.

[27] Albert Venn Dicey, *The Law of the Constitution* (Macmillan 1965) 184–95; Geranne Lautenbach, *The Concept of the Rule of Law and the European Court of Human Rights* (Oxford University Press 2013) 75; Mark Elliott and Robert Thomas, *Public Law* (Oxford University Press 2017) 71; Duncan Fairgrieve, 'Etat de droit and Rule of Law: Comparing Concepts—A Tribute to Roger Errera' [2015] *Public Law* 43–4.

[28] Jeffrey Jowell, 'Parliamentary Sovereignty under the New Constitutional Hypothesis' [2006] *Public Law* 562; Tom Bingham, *The Rule of Law* (Penguin 2011) 160.

[29] Gustavo Gozzi, 'Rechtsstaat and Individual Rights in German Constitutional History' in Pietro Costa and Danilo Zolo (eds), *The Rule of Law* (Springer 2007) 239.

[30] Klaus Weisel, *Das Verhältnis von Privatisierung und Beleihung* (Nomos 2003) 171; Nils Christian Ipsen, *Private Normenordnungen als transnationales Recht* (Duncker & Humblot 2009) 238.

[31] Karin Bieback, *Zertifizierung und Akkreditierung* (Nomos 2008) 363.

[32] Lord Steyn, 'Democracy Through Law' [2002] *EHRLR* 727; Cedric Jenart and Stéphanie De Somer, 'Non-Statutory Rulemaking and the Rule of Law' [2017] *Sui Generis* 159–72.

[33] UK Department for Business Enterprise & Regulatory Reform, 'Regulators' Compliance Code', Statutory Code of Practice for Regulators (17 December 2007).

The five principles of good rulemaking permeate the three techniques identified to outsource rulemaking powers in all of the countries studied,[34] and face specific challenges when autonomous public, private, and hybrid actors become the rulemakers.

5.2 Transparency

Transparency is the first safeguard that the rule of law and democracy require from outsourced rules.[35] It is an emanation of the principle of the rule of law and legal certainty, in the sense that there is no legal certainty without transparency of the rules.[36] Transparency has been defined as 'the decision to make visible, or provide access to, the resources on which an exercise of public or private power may be based'.[37] Some legal scholars maintain that transparency is a false and overrated panacea,[38] yet an overwhelming majority of them are adamant that transparency is an essential aspect of the rule of law principle.[39] The French iconic legal thinker, Portalis, stated that 'there needs to be a type of communication between the law and the people for whom the law is made; because it is necessary that the people know or can know that the law exists and that it exists as law'.[40] If the law does not meet these criteria, arbitrariness is never far away.

According to legend, Dionysius the Tyrant, who ruled Syracuse in the fourth century BC, hung his laws so high that the citizens could not read them. The German philosopher Georg Wilhelm Friedrich Hegel remarked that such an act was wrong but that burying rules in a 'cumbrous apparatus' of books or collections, or in a foreign tongue unreadable by anyone but the specialist, would simply repeat that wrong in another form.[41]

[34] Although examples of the reception technique in the US are limited since negotiated rulemaking in the sense of 5 USC § 563 does not fall within the research-specific definition of the reception technique because of the steering role of agencies.

[35] Ingrid Opdebeek and Stéphanie De Somer, *Algemeen bestuursrecht. Grondslagen en beginselen* (Intersentia 2017) 359; Julian Krüper, 'Lawfirm—*legibus solutus*?' [2010] *JZ* 661; Patricia Popelier, *Democratisch regelgeven* (Intersentia 2001) 290.

[36] Véronique Champeil-Desplats, 'Le principe de normativité' in Pierre Albertini (ed.), *La qualité de la loi* (Mare & Martin 2016) 241; Pierre Albertini, 'Pour une revalorisation de la loi' in ibid., 277; Daniel Mockle, 'Rule of Law' in Michel Troper and Dominique Chagnollaud (eds), *Traité international de droit constitutionnel—Tome 1* (Dalloz 2012) 683.

[37] Elizabeth Fisher, 'Transparency and Administrative Law: A Critical Evaluation' [2010] *Current Legal Problems* 274–75.

[38] Neil Duxbury, *Elements of Legislation* (Cambridge University Press 2012) 65–6; Elizabeth Fisher, 'Transparency and Administrative Law: A Critical Evaluation' [2010] *Current Legal Problems* 314.

[39] Mark Elliott and Robert Thomas, *Public Law* (Oxford University Press 2017) 68 and 148–9; Robert Baldwin, Martin Cave, and Martin Lodge (eds), *The Oxford Handbook of Regulation* (Oxford University Press 2010) 108–9; Tímea Drinóczi, 'Concept of Quality in Legislation— Revisited: Matter of Perspective and a General Overview' [2015] *Statute L. Rev.* 216; Tom Bingham, *The Rule of Law* (Penguin 2011) 17.

[40] Richard Desgorces, 'Les modes de publication des lois' in Xavier Linant de Bellefonds (ed.), *Droit et technique. Etudes à la mémoire de Xavier Linant de Bellefonds* (LexisNexis 2007) 161–2.

[41] G. W. F. Hegel (trans. S. W. Dyde), *Philosophy of Right* (Dover Publications 2012 original 1821) 114.

Indeed, in 1999, the French Constitutional Council recognized accessibility and intelligibility as constitutional principles.[42] Accessibility and intelligibility of the rule are referred to as 'transparency' (*transparence*).[43] The Constitutional Council derived these constitutional principles from articles 4 and 5 (on liberty), 6 (on equality), and 16 (on the separation of powers) of the *Déclaration des droits de l'homme et du citoyen*.[44] The first principle of good rulemaking thus draws on transparency as the combination of accessibility and intelligibility.[45]

5.2.1 Accessibility

The first aspect of transparency is accessibility. In order to safeguard the principle of transparency, a diligent delegate should make accessible rules. This accessibility can be guaranteed passively by providing access to a document when it is requested. However, the most relevant type of accessibility for rulemaking is active accessibility, for example publication without restriction and as widely as possible.[46] The English legal philosopher Jeremy Bentham considered publicity 'the very soul of justice'.[47]

With regard to active accessibility, a general constitutional principle to publicize rules has been derived in Belgium from article 190 of the Constitution, which declares that 'no law or decision, or regulation of general, provincial or municipal administration is binding until it has been published in the manner described by the law'.[48] Today, the Belgian Constitutional Court considers article 190 of the Constitution only a partial manifestation of a constitutional publication principle

[42] French Constitutional Council no. 99-421 of 16 December 1999, § 13; Patricia Rrapi, *L'accessibilité et l'intelligibilité de la loi en droit constitutionnel* (Dalloz 2014) 50–1 and 78–9; Pierre Bon, 'L'objectif constitutionnel d'accessibilité et d'intelligibilité de la loi' in Robert Andersen (ed.), *En hommage à Francis Delpérée. Itinéraires d'un constitutionnaliste* (Bruylant 2007) 178; Lucie Cluzel-Métayer, *Le service public et l'exigence de qualité* (Dalloz 2006) 248; Pierre de Montalivet, 'La "juridicisation" de la légistique. A propos de l'objectif de valeur constitutionnelle d'accessibilité et d'intelligibilité de la loi' in Roland Drago *et al.* (eds), *La confection de la loi* (Presses Universitaires de France 2005) 101.

[43] French Constitutional Council, 'Le Conseil constitutionnel et la transparence juridique', French Constitutional Council, online <http://www.conseil-constitutionnel.fr/conseil-constitutionnel/root/bank_mm/pdf/Conseil/transpjuridique.pdf> (last accessed September 2021). In a recent opinion of 15 July 2021 in case C-160/20 EU Advocate General Saugmandsgaard Øe surprisingly did not seem to recognize the accessibility aspect of transparency, § 69, ECLI:EU:C:2021:618.

[44] Laurence Calandri, *Récherche sur la notion de régulation en droit administrative française* (LGDJ 2009) 494–5; Pierre de Montalivet, 'La "juridicisation" de la légistique. A propos de l'objectif de valeur constitutionnelle d'accessibilité et d'intelligibilité de la loi' in Roland Drago *et al.* (eds), *La confection de la loi* (Presses Universitaires de France 2005) 103.

[45] Thomas Züll, *Regulierung Im Politischen Gemeinwesen* (Mohr Siebeck 2014) 75.

[46] Marc Joassart, Laurent Jans, Claudine Mertes, and Marc Oswald, 'Le Conseil d'Etat—Chronique de légisprudence 2013' [2015] *Revue belge de droit constitutionnel* 70.

[47] This statement was made with regard to judicial decisions but could equally apply to rules as well. Jeremy Bentham, *The Works of Jeremy Bentham*, vol. IV (Simpkin, Marshall & Co. 1843) 316.

[48] Frederik Vandendriessche, 'Verzelfstandigde diensten van de federale en deelstatelijke overheid' in Luc Wintgens (ed.), *De verplichting tot bekendmaking van de norm* (die Keure 2003) 145.

'inherent to the rule of law'.[49] In particular, the Belgian Council of State Legislative Section aims to affirm the constitutional publication principle.[50] Rules need to be public in order to become enforceable. In performing this test, a judge will not only verify whether there was a form of publication but also whether the rule was in fact sufficiently accessible.[51] In France, active accessibility does not necessarily imply publication either. Parallel to the case law of the European Court of Human Rights, the French Constitutional Council takes into account information that was already (de facto) available to the constituency to determine the accessibility of a rule.[52] Nevertheless, the publication of a rule remains the go-to measure to prove accessibility. Article 82, 1 of the German Basic Law provides that 'statutes … shall be … promulgated in the Federal Law Gazette'. There is a general principle of transparency that was derived from article 82, 1 of the Basic Law.[53] In the UK, the Hansard Society buttressed the importance of publishing statutes and making them accessible in general in its 1993 report, 'Making the Law'.[54] Even the US Supreme Court suggested that regulations that were not published 'did not exist'.[55]

The sanction for insufficiently published rules may be stringent. 'A fundamental principle … requires that a measure adopted by the public authorities shall not be applicable to those concerned before they have the opportunity to make themselves acquainted with it.'[56] In Belgium, these rules cannot be enforced against a member of the constituency.[57] Equally, in France, publication is required for the rule to become obligatory.[58] In the UK, even if an autonomous public, private, or hybrid actor has not published its rules sufficiently, that does not imply that the rule will automatically become invalid or inapplicable. As long as rulemakers take reasonable steps to distribute the rule in the relevant manner, UK courts will accept its validity. This precept was set out in *R v. Sheer Metalcraft Ltd*.[59] Such an outcome is unsatisfactory in the light of the rule of law, certainly when some decentralized

[49] Belgian Constitutional Court 16 June 2004, no. 106/2004, B.3.1; Jan Velaers, *De Grondwet, een artikelsgewijze commentaar* (die Keure 2019) article 190, § 31; Jan Velaers, 'Artikel 190 van de Grondwet: De bekendmaking in de vorm bij wet bepaald als voorwaarde voor de verbindendheid van wetten, besluiten en verordeningen van algemeen, provincial of gemeentelijk bestuur' in Luc Wintgens (ed.), *De verplichting tot bekendmaking van de norm* (die Keure 2003) 34.

[50] J. E. Kersell, *Parliamentary Supervision of Delegated Legislation* (Stevens & Sons 1960) 6.

[51] Jan Velaers, 'Artikel 190 van de Grondwet: De bekendmaking in de vorm bij wet bepaald als voorwaarde voor de verbindendheid van wetten, besluiten en verordeningen van algemeen, provincial of gemeentelijk bestuur' in Luc Wintgens (ed.), *De verplichting tot bekendmaking van de norm* (die Keure 2003) 52–3.

[52] Patricia Rrapi, *L'accessibilité et l'intelligibilité de la loi en droit constitutionnel* (Dalloz 2014) 34–5.

[53] Thomas Clemens, 'Die Verweisung von einer Rechtsnorm auf andere Vorschriften' [1986] *AöR* 89.

[54] Geoffrey Rippon, *Making the Law: The Report of the Hansard Society Commission on the Legislative Process* (Hansard Society 1992) 108.

[55] *Panama Ref. Co. v. Ryan*, 293 US 388, 412 (1935).

[56] The milestone European Court of Justice Case 98/78 *Racke* ECLI:EU:C:1979:14, § 15.

[57] Frederik Vandendriessche, 'Verzelfstandigde diensten van de federale en deelstatelijke overheid' in Luc Wintgens (ed.), *De verplichting tot bekendmaking van de norm* (die Keure 2003) 171.

[58] Francis Hamon and Michel Troper, *Droit constitutionnel* (LGDJ 2015–16) 707.

[59] *R v. Sheer Metalcraft Ltd* [1954] 1 QB 586, 590; *Halsbury's Laws of England* (5th edn, LexisNexis 2010) 'Executive functions', § 10, fn. 7.

rulemakers 'may charge a reasonable fee for providing a person with a copy of a rule-making instrument'.[60] Fortunately, lack of publication can constitute a proper defence against an alleged criminal offence.[61]

Although the principle of accessibility is thus strongly engrained in the countries researched, it is not as clearly present when autonomous public, private, and hybrid actors make rules through delegation, referral, or reception techniques.

5.2.1.1 Delegation

In principle, when autonomous public actors, often regulators, exercise rulemaking powers after delegation, it is still important that they ensure that their rules are accessible.[62]

To begin with, I analyse whether there is an overarching framework which structures how all delegated rules should be published. In the UK, if the Statutory Instruments Act 1946 is declared applicable to a delegation of rulemaking powers to an autonomous public actor, the standard publication requirements of the Act are likewise triggered.[63] For UK delegated legislation not made under the Statutory Instruments Act, there is no uniform method of publication.[64] Often the Statutory Instruments Act will not be deemed applicable to rules that autonomous public actors develop under their general grant of powers. This would apply to rules made by them without an express reference to the Statutory Instruments Act in the parent statute or—to the extent permissible—rules that were made as a result of sub-delegation by the Executive.[65] There is likewise no overarching Belgian statute which regulates the publication of delegated rules made by autonomous public actors. In France and Germany as well, there is no overarching framework for the publication of binding rules, let alone a time period within which this should be done.[66] Furthermore, no predefined medium has been identified in which these rules should generally be published. This is different in the US where the rules of independent agencies are published in the Federal Register in accordance with the Administrative Procedure Act.

The Legislature or the Executive in the countries without a publication framework can insert a publication requirement in the 'parent statute' that outsources the rulemaking powers. For example, the rules (regulations) of the Belgian federal

[60] Section 138G(5) of the Financial Services and Markets Act 2000.

[61] Section 3(2) of the Statutory Instruments Act 1946. Aileen McHarg, 'Administrative Discretion, Administrative Rule-Making, and Judicial Review' [2017] *Current Legal Problems* 284; Mark Elliott and Robert Thomas, *Public Law* (Oxford University Press 2017) 147.

[62] Laurence Calandri, *Récherche sur la notion de régulation en droit administrative française* (LGDJ 2009) 491.

[63] Paul Craig, *Administrative Law* (Sweet & Maxwell 2016) 433.

[64] Aileen McHarg, 'Administrative Discretion, Administrative Rule-Making, and Judicial Review' [2017] *Current Legal Problems* 286.

[65] Paul Craig, *Administrative Law* (Sweet & Maxwell 2016) 439.

[66] Laurence Calandri, *Récherche sur la notion de régulation en droit administrative française* (LGDJ 2009) 367–9.

Financial Services and Market Authority (FSMA) only enter into force after their approval by the King and their publication in the *Moniteur belge/Belgisch Staatsblad* (Belgian Official Gazette).[67] Articles 3.1.b).3.h), 3.3, 30.8, 34.5 of the Royal Decree of 20 July 2001, on the dangers of ionising radiation, contains a similar safeguard to uphold transparency. The Belgian Federal Agency for Nuclear Inspections stipulates detailed rules as a result of the outsourcing of rulemaking powers. These criteria, procedures and specifications will be published in the Belgian Official Journal. Also, in France individual parent statutes regularly contain such an obligation for autonomous agencies to publish their rules. For example, all decisions of the Commission National du Débat Public (CNDP) (jurisdictional or administrative) are published in a specific category of the Official Journal and on their website, according to article R. 121-6 of the Environmental Code.[68] Other French autonomous agencies, such as the AMF, CSA, and CNIL, already publish their rules, advisory opinions with general applicability, or advisory opinions for state rules through their website, the Official Journal, or their annual report.[69] Article 22 of the 2017-55 Statute on the status of autonomous agencies even establishes that advisory opinions on draft statutes produced by the listed autonomous public bodies must be published. The rules of German autonomous public bodies will usually be published in one of the official state registers (*Amtsblätter*).[70] Parent statutes or other legislation in the UK frequently impose publication of the delegated rules.[71] This occurred for the Financial Conduct Authority, whose rules must be in writing and published in accordance with section 138G of the Financial Services and Markets Act 2000: 'A rule-making instrument must be published by the regulator making the rule in the way appearing to that regulator to be best calculated to bring it to the attention of the public.'[72] The Ofcom Board even publishes its agenda, notes, and minutes.[73] Additionally, the British Hallmarking Council has an obligation to make its directions and regulations in writing but not to publish them.[74]

[67] Article 64 of Belgian Statute of 2 August 2002 on the supervision of the financial sector and on financial services.

[68] Michel Verpeaux 'Une autorité administrative indépendante originale: la CNDP' in Pierre Bon (ed.), *Long cours. Mélanges en l'honneur de Pierre Bon* (Dalloz 2014) 610.

[69] Article L621-6 *Code monétaire et financier*; articles 6 and 27 of Statute 86-1067 of 30 September 1986 *relative à la liberté de communication (Loi Léotard)*; article 71 of Statute 78-17 of 6 January 1978 *relative à l'informatique, aux fichiers et aux libertés*; Laurence Calandri, *Récherche sur la notion de régulation en droit administrative française* (LGDJ 2009) 365 and 395.

[70] Wolf-Rüdiger Schenke, 'Die verfassungsrechtliche Problematik dynamischer Verweisungen' [1980] *NJW* 744.

[71] *Halsbury's Laws of England* (5th edn, LexisNexis 2010) 'Executive functions', § 10, fn. 7.

[72] Section 138G(4) of the Financial Services and Markets Act 2000; Department for Work and Pensions & HM Treasury, 'Supplementary Memorandum from the Department for Work and Pensions & HM Treasury to the Delegated Powers and Regulatory Reform Committee' (26 January 2018) 3, 7.

[73] Ofcom, 'About Ofcom. How Ofcom is run', <https://www.ofcom.org.uk/about-ofcom/how-ofcom-is-run/ofcom-board> (last accessed August 2018).

[74] Section 13(4) of the British Hallmarking Act 1973.

However, rules of traditional rulemakers that delegate rulemaking powers regularly forget or omit how those rules should be published. To the regret of the Belgian Council of State Legislative Section,[75] there is not always a publication framework in Belgium. The Superior Council of Audio-visuals (CSA) of the French-speaking community is not subject to any such publication prerequisite in the Belgian Official Journal.[76]

Even where there is no clear statutory obligation, the general expectation is that rules drafted by such actors will be published.[77] When there is no parent statute that explains the publication method, two possibilities remain.

First, the executive decree ratifying the rule of the autonomous public body counts as valid publication. In France, for instance, publication might occur through or after governmental approval of the delegated rule.[78] However, this would leave a period of uncertainty between the enactment of the delegated rule and publication of the executive decree. Moreover, as already encountered, the Legislature and the Executive do not ratify all outsourced rules. Finally, indirect publication through an executive decree would only make the delegated rule enforceable if it were attached in full to that executive decree.[79] However, such exhaustive reproductions will not often be annexed.[80]

Second, autonomous public, private, and hybrid actors can themselves publicize rules through their own devised method. This will often be the case for rules made by autonomous public bodies within the delegation technique when they publish such rules on their own websites.[81]

5.2.1.2 Referral

The Legislature and the Executive occasionally refer to the standards of—often 'private'—standardization organizations, such as the ISO (international), NBN (Belgium), AFNOR (France), DIN (Germany), BSI (UK), or ANSI (US).

[75] Jan Velaers, *De Grondwet en de Raad van State Afdeling Wetgeving* (Maklu 1999) 380.

[76] David De Roy, 'Le pouvoir réglementaire des autorités administratives indépendantes en droit belge' in *Rapports belges au Congrès de l'Académie de droit comparé à Utrecht* (Bruylant 2006) § 33.

[77] Anne Danis-Fatôme, 'Contrat versus textes règlementaires: un conflit nié?' [2007] *Revue des contrats* 1455, last paragraph.

[78] Laurence Calandri, Récherche sur la notion de régulation en droit administrative française (LGDJ 2009) 368.

[79] David De Roy, 'Le pouvoir réglementaire des autorités administratives indépendantes en droit belge' in *Rapports belges au Congrès de l'Académie de droit comparé à Utrecht* (Bruylant 2006) § 33.

[80] Irène Mathy, 'Etre ou ne pas être une personne juridique distincte de l'Etat, la Communauté ou la Région? L'autonomie avec ou sans personnalité juridique' in Pierre Jadoul, Bruno Lombaert, and François Tulkens (eds), *Le paraétatisme. Nouveaux regards sur la décentralisation fonctionelle en Belgique et dans les institutions européens* (la Charte 2010) 83.

[81] Article 190 of the Belgian Constitution states that rules have to be published in the manner 'described by the law', thus reserving the competence to decide on publication to the Legislature. Following a strict reading of this provision, self-developed publication methods are therefore still not constitutional in Belgium. Rusen Ergec, 'Le principe de légalité à l'épreuve des principes de bonne administration' [1998] *RCJB* 20.

Such standards in and of themselves are often unsatisfactorily published.[82] Admittedly, though, standardization organizations make an effort to ensure that their rules are more accessible.[83] The Institute of Chartered Accountants in England and Wales, for example, initially published its recommendations on accounting principles in *The Accountant* journal. Gee & Co. first published a collected edition of these recommendations in 1944.[84] Before the introduction and popularization of the internet, it remained genuinely difficult to gain access to such standards[85] although today that problem has largely disappeared. For example, most recommendations on accounting principles are freely accessible on the UK Financial Reporting Council's website.[86] In addition, the British Standards Institution (BSI) safeguards transparency (article 4.4), including aspects of accessibility (article 6.1) and intelligibility (article 9.3), in its Standard for Standards.[87]

The publication of standards when state rules refer directly to them is a particularly thorny issue.[88] The question arises as to how the referred-to standard that was adopted by the standard-setting body should be made accessible. The already flawed publication of standards becomes most problematic when traditional rulemakers refer directly to them. Judges and scholars agree that the accessibility requirement for referrals constitutes at least the duty to publish referred-to standards in some form.[89] In a first step, this obligation in Belgium and Germany derives directly from article 190 of the Belgian Constitution and article 82, 1 of the Basic Law. These constitutional provisions do not state that the *text* of the statute shall be promulgated, but the statute itself. This could imply that when a statute refers to an external rule, the entire *content* of the statute, including the private standard, should be published in the Official Journal.[90] In a second step, publication of the referred-to standard can also be derived from the general principle of accessibility which has been established to exist in the countries researched.

[82] Isabelle Desbarats, 'De la normalisation en matière sociale' [15/07/2003] *Issu de Petites affiches*, 4, II.A.

[83] Paul Craig, 'Global Networks and Shared Administration' in Sabino Cassese (ed.), *Global Administrative Law* (Edward Elgar 2016) 164–5.

[84] The Institute of Chartered Accountants in England and Wales, 'Knowledge guide to UK accounting standards', <https://www.icaew.com/library/subject-gateways/accounting-standards/knowledge-guide-to-uk-accounting-standards> (last accessed May 2021).

[85] Richard Král, 'On the Choice of Methods of Transposition of EU Directives' [2016] *E. L. Rev.* 226–7.

[86] The Institute of Chartered Accountants in England and Wales, 'Knowledge guide to UK accounting standards' <https://www.icaew.com/library/subject-gateways/accounting-standards/knowledge-guide-to-uk-accounting-standards> (last accessed May 2021).

[87] BSI Group, 'A standard for standards—Principles of standardization. Standard 0' (BSI Standards Publication 2016) 10, 15, 16, and 29.

[88] BVerwG 5 C 9.14, 26 March 2015. See also Gregor Bachmann, 'Ziele, Prinzipien und Auslegung des Kodex' in Thomas Kremer, Gregor Bachmann, Marcus Lutter, and Axel von Werder (eds), *Kommentar Deutscher Corporate Governance Kodex* (Beck 2016) 32; Helmuth Schulze-Fielitz, 'Artikel 20' in Horst Dreier (ed.), *Grundgesetz Kommentar* (Mohr Siebeck 2004) 242–4.

[89] BVerfGE 26, 338, § 110; Eberhard Baden, 'Dynamische Verweisungen und Verweisungen auf Nichtnormen' [1979] *NJW* 623; Thomas Clemens, 'Die Verweisung von einer Rechtsnorm auf andere Vorschriften' [1986] *AöR* 124.

[90] Ibid., 86.

Most explicitly, the Belgian Council of State Legislative Section stated that it appears incompatible with article 190 of the Belgian Constitution if a technical standard referred to had not been: (1) published; (2) in French, Dutch, and (if possible) in German; and (3) for free (or at least for a reasonable price) to all citizens.[91] Later, I discuss these three shared concerns from a comparative perspective.

5.2.1.2.1 Publication in an Official Journal

First, questionable publication of standards is a recurring concern when the Legislature and the Executive directly refer to such standards.[92] It is ultimately the task of the ordinary courts to establish whether a rule is sufficiently accessible.[93] A mere reference to an undisclosed referred-to document will not suffice.[94] For example, in the Belgian case of *NV Heli Service Belgium*, hundreds of pages originating from an addendum to the Chicago Convention on International Aviation were under scrutiny. In this case, NV Heli Service Belgium was criminally charged with operating a helicopter pad without an airport permit. The definition of what constituted an 'airport' derived, via a referral in the rule, from the addenda of the Chicago Convention which was linked to a referral by a traditional rulemaker to a privately made standard. As the Council of State noted, the volume of such addenda was sufficient to fill two cupboards: 'The attachments can hardly be found and did not even make it into the administrative file before the Council.'[95] The Council of State decided that such a referral was inaccessible rulemaking which could not survive legal scrutiny.[96] Previously, the Belgian Court of Cassation had already ruled that even technical treaties were not properly published if they were merely 'available' at the relevant ministry.[97] In Germany, for similar reasons, a

[91] Belgian Council of State Legislative Section, Advisory opinion no. 36.309/1 of 16 December 2003, 4; Belgian Council of State Legislative Section, Advisory opinion no. 42.307/4 of 7 March 2007, 4; Belgian Council of State Legislative Section, Advisory opinion no. 42.474/4 of 2 April 2007, 3; Belgian Council of State Legislative Section, Advisory opinion no. 44.188/4, 19 March 2008, 4; Belgian Council of State Legislative Section, Advisory opinion no. 53.929/1/V of 18 September 2013, 8–9.

[92] Belgian Council of State Legislative Section, Advisory opinion no. 59.291/3 of 19 May 2016, § 5.

[93] Frederik Vandendriessche, 'Verzelfstandigde diensten van de federale en deelstatelijke overheid' in Luc Wintgens (ed.), *De verplichting tot bekendmaking van de norm* (die Keure 2003) 172.

[94] Jan Velaers, 'Artikel 190 van de Grondwet: De bekendmaking in de vorm bij wet bepaald als voorwaarde voor de verbindendheid van wetten, besluiten en verordeningen van algemeen, provincial of gemeentelijk bestuur' in Luc Wintgens (ed.), *De verplichting tot bekendmaking van de norm* (die Keure 2003) 63.

[95] Belgian Council of State Administrative Litigation Section, no. 145.819, 10 June 2005, *NV Heli Service Belgium*, 4.1.2.2.

[96] Belgian Council of State Administrative Litigation Section, no. 145.819, 10 June 2005, *NV Heli Service Belgium*, 4.1.2.3; Dries van Eeckhoutte and Tim Corthaut, 'Doorwerking internationaal recht in de Europese rechtsorde: verplichting en uitdaging voor de Belgische rechter. Het Air Transport Association of America-arrest van het Hof van Justitie' [2012–13] *RW* 411.

[97] Belgian Court of Cassation, 19 March 1981, *Pacific Employers Insurance Company t./Regie der Posterijen* [1980–1] *Arr.Cass.*, 811–12; Henri Culot and Dries Van Eeckhoutte, 'La normalisation et ses écueils potentiels en droit privé et en droit public' in Jérémie van Meerbeeck, *Droit public/droit privé* (Anthemis 2019) § 25.

referred-to standard that is 'available in a bookstore' would not be adequate as a general mechanism.[98]

Ideally, the referring rule should require the technical standard to be published in a national Official Journal. The Belgian Council of State Legislative Section supported this requirement, for example in its advisory opinion on the referral to private corporate governance codes.[99] The Legislative Section suggests that article 190 of the Belgian Constitution and article 55 of the Special Majority Act Pertaining to the Reform of State Institutions (SMARSI) oblige an integral publication of rules, including referred-to standards, in the Official Journal.[100] Publication of the referred-to standard in the Federal Gazette would likewise fulfil the German publication requirement.[101] Publication of the referred-to document is then preferably done with the (attachment of the) outsourcing rule of the Legislature or the Executive. This is not a stringent obligation. In Germany, for example, case law and scholarship have allowed for later publication of the referred-to standard, such that it is not simultaneously published with the referring rule.[102] Furthermore, there is no German constitutional provision or principle requiring the referred-to standard to be published in the same medium as the referring rule.[103] It is already well-established German case law that an executive regulation, as a rule referred to by a statute, may be published in the Federal Gazette (*Bundesanzeiger*) and not together with the statute in the higher ranked Federal Law Gazette (*Bundesgesetzblatt*). If the referred-to standard is not simultaneously published with the referring rule, it should at least be published in accordance with the procedure as set out in the referring rule.[104]

Unfortunately, publication of the referred-to standard does not always occur in an Official Journal at all. In Germany, Becker has argued that only publication

[98] Wolf-Rüdiger Schenke, 'Die verfassungsrechtliche Problematik dynamischer Verweisungen' [1980] *NJW* 744.

[99] Belgian Council of State Legislative Section, Advisory opinion (Parliamentary Documents Chamber of Representatives 2336/001, 2009–10) 104, fn. 9; see later: Marc Joassart, Laurent Jans, Claudine Mertes, and Marc Oswald, 'Le Conseil d'Etat—Chronique de légisprudence 2014' [2016] *Revue belge de droit constitutionnel* 281.

[100] Unless a specific statute provides otherwise for the federal level. Belgian Council of State Legislative Section, Advisory opinion no. 60.834/VR of 23 February 2017, § 5. Tim Corthaut, Jonas Riemslagh, Dries Van Eeckhoutte, Frédéric Vanneste, and Jeroen Van Nieuwenhove, 'Behoorlijke wetgeving in de adviespraktijk van de afdeling Wetgeving van de Raad van State (2015 en 2016)' [2017] *Tijdschrift voor Wetgeving* 315.

[101] Florian Becker, *Kooperative und konsensuale Strukturen in der Normsetzung* (Mohr Siebeck 2005) 345.

[102] Thomas Clemens, 'Die Verweisung von einer Rechtsnorm auf andere Vorschriften' [1986] *AöR* 87–8.

[103] Ibid., 84; Florian Becker, *Kooperative und konsensuale Strukturen in der Normsetzung* (Mohr Siebeck 2005) 543.

[104] This could be derived from the Belgian Court of Cassation's case law on provincial tax regulations. The province had illegally only published a referral to the changed provisions of a previous year despite the statutory requirement to publish the entire provincial tax regulation: Belgian Court of Cassation 26 April 1990 [1989–90] *Arr. Cass.* 1115 and Patricia Popelier, *De wet juridisch bekeken* (die Keure 2004) 271.

organized by the state can provide for the specific protection of general accessibility, integrity, identity, and reliability of the referred-to standards.[105] In the same vein, the Belgian Council of State Legislative Section demands at the very least publication on the government website.[106]

In fact, one could even argue that the accessibility of executive rules increases if they are available on official websites, as opposed to in a hard copy Official Journal where the rules may be buried within thousands of pages. The internet has some undeniable benefits in relation to making rules generally known and to making them easily accessible. Sole publication on the internet is in line with the approach of the French Council of State and could be reconciled with the position of the Belgian Constitutional Court, given the exponential spread of the internet over the last decade.[107]

Nevertheless, several standard-setting bodies, such as the Accounting Standards Committee of Germany, have opted to publish their standards on their own private websites.[108] In addition, the German Corporate Governance Code is made public on the website of the Codex Commission.[109] In § 161 of the Stock Corporation Act (*Aktiengesetz*), which refers to a Corporate Governance Code, publication on the internet is even prescribed. Sole publication of a standard made by a standardization organization on a private website poses additional difficulties when it is referred to by the Legislature or the Executive. With regard to the identification and registration of livestock, the Belgian federal Legislature left it to private farmers' organizations to adopt procedures and instructions, albeit under the supervision of the Federal Agency for Safety of the Food Chain.[110] In that regard, the Belgian Council of State Legislative Section raised the issue that those rules were only published on the websites of farmers' associations.[111] In the early days of the internet, concerns were expressed about the durability of rules published on the internet.[112]

[105] Florian Becker, *Kooperative und konsensuale Strukturen in der Normsetzung* (Mohr Siebeck 2005) 557.

[106] Belgian Council of State Legislative Section, Advisory opinion (Documents Flemish Parliament 2014–15 no. 161/1), 170.

[107] Belgian Constitutional Court 16 June 2004, no. 106/2004, B.15–22; Belgian Constitutional Court 17 January 2007, no. 10/2007, B.14.1.

[108] <https://www.drsc.de/verlautbarungen/>. Lothar Michael, 'Private Standardsetter und demokratisch legitimierte Rechtsetzung' in Hartmut Bauer, Peter Huber, and Karl-Peter Sommermann (eds), *Demokratie in Europa* (Mohr Siebeck 2005) 453.

[109] Gregor Bachmann, 'Rechtsnatur und Legitimation des Kodex' in Thomas Kremer, Gregor Bachmann, Marcus Lutter, and Axel von Werder (eds), *Kommentar Deutscher Corporate Governance Kodex* (Beck 2016) 42.

[110] Article 5 of the Royal Decree of 1 July 2014 *tot vaststelling van een identificatie- en registratieregeling voor varkens en tot vaststelling van de toelatingsvoorwaarden voor varkensbedrijven*; article 5 of the Royal Decree of 23 March 2011 *tot vaststelling van een identificatie- en registratieregeling voor runderen.*

[111] It also raised the question whether this delegation of powers transgressed basic constitutional principles. Belgian Council of State Legislative Section, Advisory opinion no. 48.671/3 of 28 September 2010, § 12.

[112] Melanie Carly, 'De elektronische bekendmaking van de norm' in Luc Wintgens (ed.), *De verplichting tot bekendmaking van de norm* (die Keure 2003) 288–9; Jan Velaers, 'Artikel 190 van de Grondwet: De bekendmaking in de vorm bij wet bepaald als voorwaarde voor de verbindendheid van

The internet was subject to crashing, and a hard copy could not easily be tampered with. Today, global and recurring hacking scandals have reinvigorated these concerns. Thus, while it is beneficial for rules to be easily accessible with several clicks on the internet, if ill-meaning individuals alter or can alter those rules, that added legal certainty crumbles. A state institution responsible for monitoring, controlling, and verifying the publication of referred-to standards on the internet would then be a viable last resort for guaranteeing the integrity of its content.[113]

In the US, in accordance with the Freedom of Information Act, federal rules are normally published in the Federal Register Code of Federal Regulations in accordance with 5 USC § 552(a)(1). However, if all referred-to standards had to be published it would increase the total length of the Code six- or seven-fold.[114] Accordingly, incorporated referred-to standards are already considered sufficiently published if they are 'reasonably available to the class of persons affected' and the Director of the Office of Federal Regulations has consented to the referral.[115] At the very least, the referring agency and the Office of Federal Regulations keep a hard copy of the referred-to standards for inspection by the public.[116] It can be questioned whether two hard copies which are available in Washington DC make a rule sufficiently accessible.[117]

An overarching test should determine whether an alternative publication method for referred-to standards of standard-setting bodies passes muster, which will usually lead to government publication, albeit not necessarily in an Official Journal.

Clemens developed an interesting publication test for referred-to standards, which I have attempted to finetune in the light of the findings set out earlier.[118] It can be represented mathematically with the following formula: the publication channel of the referred-to standard equals the publication channel of the referring rule, minus one level in the 'hierarchy' of publication channels (if there are multiple publication channels of varying importance). If the referring rule is a statute, then the referred-to standard must be published in a printed governmental publication

wetten, besluiten en verordeningen van algemeen, provincial of gemeentelijk bestuur' in Luc Wintgens (ed.), *De verplichting tot bekendmaking van de norm* (die Keure 2003) 59.

[113] See § 7, 2 *Bundes-Immissionsschutzgesetz*; Wolf-Rüdiger Schenke, 'Die verfassungsrechtliche Problematik dynamischer Verweisungen' [1980] *NJW* 744. See, for a Canadian example: Conseil canadien des normes, *Principaux points à considérer dans l'élaboration et l'utilisation des normes dans les instruments législatifs*, (September 2006) 10, article 6.

[114] Emily S. Bremer, 'Incorporation by Reference in an Open-Government Age' (2013) 36 *Harv. J. L. & Pub. Pol'y* 135.

[115] Emily S. Bremer, 'American and European Perspectives on Private Standards in Public Law' (2016) 91 *Tul. L. Rev.* 325, 346–7.

[116] Emily S. Bremer, 'Incorporation by Reference in an Open-Government Age' (2013) 36 *Harv. J. L. & Pub. Pol'y* 143.

[117] Ibid., 153.

[118] Thomas Clemens, 'Die Verweisung von einer Rechtsnorm auf andere Vorschriften' [1986] *AöR* 100.

medium (but not necessarily the Official Journal, as is the case for the statute itself). If the referring rule is an executive regulation, then the referred-to standard can be published on a website. In that category, I would still recommend publishing all referred-to standards at the very least on a government website with the presumed added security safeguards, although government websites may bury the rule deeper than private websites because of their immense content. The publication medium needs to be safe and able to withstand attempts at falsification. If, ultimately, the referring rule were made by an autonomous public or private actor itself, then the referred-to standard could be considered to be sufficiently published if available in a generally accessible bookstore or if the interested parties know of it. The referred-to standard should then be published so that regulated persons have a realistic chance of accessing it.[119]

This cascading system ties into the perspectives described on the rule of law and legality, since the higher the rules are in the hierarchy, the more essential, general, and policy-driven they are. Such rules need to be published more rigorously. Lower down the hierarchy, rules are more executive, aimed at a specific target group, and technical. From a normative and a comparative perspective, this is a clear and exhaustive test that no longer requires additional appreciation by the rulemaking actor. I would therefore endorse the test as a concrete template for rulemakers who wish to refer directly to standards of standard-setting bodies without flooding their main publication media with referred-to standards.

5.2.1.2.2 Publication in an official language

Second, even if the rule itself were published in an adequate medium, standard-setting bodies could jeopardize the accessibility of the publication due to language issues, since their legal nature often transgresses national borders. For example, in the case of international standards, the constituency of the state in which the referral is made might not understand the language of the referred-to document. Given the prominence of the English language, this issue does not so much arise in the UK or the US, but more in countries with lesser known languages or several official languages.

In Belgium, a country with several official languages, the following question arose: will the referred-to standard be available in an official language (Dutch, French, and German) or only in the original language of the standard (often English or French)?[120]

Article 56 of the 1966 Belgian Statute on Administrative Language Use renders an authentic status to Dutch and French versions of executive and ministerial

[119] Florian Becker, *Kooperative und konsensuale Strukturen in der Normsetzung* (Mohr Siebeck 2005) 344.

[120] Belgian federal Department of Economy, ‚Verwijzen naar normen in technische regelgeving' (March 2017) 14.

regulations. A referral to an English standard that provides no translation in Dutch, French, or German could very well be deemed unenforceable. Even in France, when the referred-to standard has a foreign or international origin, its language might not be French. In 1992, the French Constitution was amended so that article 2, 2 proclaims, 'French is the language of the Republic'. The French language thus received constitutional status. As a result, a statute cannot implicitly diverge from the provision by referring to a referred-to standard in another language.[121] German scholarship has also addressed the issue of referring to external standards that may not be available in the German language. This is deemed unconstitutional. In order for such a referral to pass, at the very least an official translation needs to be made available in the appropriate state publication medium.[122]

In principle, even if the standard is translated, it would often not be the 'official version'. If English is the authentic and binding language, in relation to prior legislative approval of treaties, the Belgian Council of State Legislative Section has already remarked that the official English version should at least be published.[123] Equally, in France, even if a French translation is later adopted or published, this still leaves issues with the binding version of the referred-to standard which French case law has not, as yet, clarified. Likewise, in Germany, when such an official translation is made, a similar problem to that with regard to treaties arises. Each translation is subject to interpretation by the translators and not all legal terminology can be implemented in the German system. So, which language applies to German citizens if there is even the slightest discordance between the two language versions? In parallel with the German scholarship on treaties, I can point to the German dualist tradition. The original text may be declared binding on the German state through the treaty but only the German implementation—and thus the German text version—has direct effect for citizens.[124] The German state's responsibility can then be called into question in the event of an imperfect implementation of the original text. A similar reasoning can be made here. The official, national *translation* is the one that should be directly applicable to citizens in order to comply with the safeguards of the rule of law. Any other interpretation would lead to the contradictory result that the citizen is not deemed to have knowledge of the standard in a foreign language (such as Chinese), but is ultimately bound by the original version of the standard in that other language.

[121] This is implicit in Jean-Marie Pontier, *Droit de la langue française* (Dalloz 1996) 33 and 38.

[122] Florian Becker, *Kooperative und konsensuale Strukturen in der Normsetzung* (Mohr Siebeck 2005) 571; see also Meinhard Hilf, *Die Auslegung mehrsprachiger Verträge* (Springer 1973) 198.

[123] Belgian Council of State Legislative Section, Advisory opinion no. 50.621/3 of 13 December 2011, § 5; Belgian Council of State Legislative Section, Advisory opinion no. 42.222/4 of 11 April 2007, § 4; admittedly, in a different context, the Belgian Constitutional Court considered that the failure to publish in German does not deprive the rule of its binding force within that Belgian language area. Belgian Constitutional Court no. 54/94, 14 July 1994.

[124] Meinhard Hilf, *Die Auslegung mehrsprachiger Verträge* (Springer 1973) 210–11.

Basing itself on the advisory opinions of the Belgian Council of State Legislative Section, the Belgian High Council for Standardization has developed recommendations for the Legislature and the Executive on how to incorporate standards. In this regard, it recommended that the Belgian Bureau for Standardization (NBN) should hastily translate the referred-to rules into Dutch and French, if that had not already occurred.[125]

Nevertheless, it would be exceedingly costly to translate every single standard into the national language and it would often completely miss the target audience. The Belgian Council of State Legislative Section developed a general and pragmatic test to deal with the 'invasion' of foreign languages into public services, despite the 'official languages'. It created this test in the light of various rules that obliged the use of English as non-official language in the exercise of governmental tasks. For example, it recently repeated the test with regard to the Brussels International Business Court. According to the Council: 'public services should in principle use the official languages. However, where such use proves impossible due to the nature of the matter or the needs of the service or if the general interest requires the use of other languages, exceptions to that rule may be allowed'.[126] The logic of this consideration could arguably also be applied to the use of English in the referred-to rule itself. In the same vein, translations of referred-to standards do not always appear to be necessary: if it would be impossible due to the enormous number of texts and intricate layout or in the light of general interest, or if the rule and standards only serve a very particular expert group.[127]

In summary, the approach defending publication in official languages can be endorsed for all of the countries researched. Similarly, the translated standard should be the one that generally binds citizens. However, a constitutional or statutory resolution of this issue could allow for an exception if this obligation would prove impossible due to the nature of the case or the general interest.

5.2.1.2.3 *Publication that is freely accessible*

Third, standardization organizations will normally own the intellectual property or at least a distribution licence for their technical standards and may oppose free and open publication of their research and development. Interested parties normally have to pay a fee in order to access private standards.[128] The British Standards

125 Belgian High Council for Standardization, *Advies over de kenbaarheid en de tegenstelbaarheid aan derden van de Belgische normen waarnaar in de reglementering verwezen wordt*, 21 November 2014, Doc. 15-0631, 6.

126 Belgian Council of State Legislative Section, Advisory opinion no. 62.411/2/AV of 2 March 2018, 59–62 and citations there.

127 See, however, the reservations expressed in Jan Velaers and Cedric Jenart, 'Taalvereisten inzake de bekendmaking van wetten' in Aube Wirtgen (ed.), *Liber amicorum Marnix Van Damme* (die Keure 2021) 575–90.

128 ISO and IEC, *Le recours et la référence aux normes ISO et IEC dans les politiques publiques* (ISO and IEC 2015) 34 and 35.

Institute, for instance, sells it standards through distributors or puts them behind a pay-wall, as do other national standardization organizations. The actual legal question is whether the public interest in knowing the rule, trumps the organization's right to its intellectual property.

Germany has most notably faced this balancing exercise between accessibility and the right to intellectual property when traditional rulemakers directly refer to standards developed by standardization organizations. For example, DIN standards will be sold (and thus published) by the private Beuth publisher with only a notice in the Federal Gazette (*Bundesanzeiger*) in accordance with DIN standard 820.[129] In 1998, the German Federal Constitutional Court (FCC) decided that when the Legislature or the Executive relied on DIN standards, those standards should be ascribed to governmental actors and thus made accessible.[130] In the aftermath of that decision, a compromise was eventually struck by the German federal Legislature in § 5 of the Copyright Act (*Gesetz über Urheberrecht und verwandte Schutzrechte*). Only when the Legislature or the Executive copies the entire text of the standard does the copyright expire. As long as the Legislature or the Executive merely refers to the standard, the intellectual property of the standardization organization remains principally unscathed.[131] However, in that event, § 5, 3 of the Copyright Act obliges the standardization organization or copyright owner to make the referred-to standard available under 'appropriate conditions' (*angemessen Bedingungen*) to the actors bound by the rule. This is seen as a compulsory licence (*Zwangslizenz*) to use the referred-to standards.[132] In its judgment on the case of *City Crash*, the Dutch Council of State Administrative Section also ruled that referred-to standards should be available to affected companies against 'reasonable payment' and to ordinary citizens freely at the offices of the standardization organization.[133] The Belgian Council of State Legislative Section emphasizes that the referred-to standard should comply in any case with 'the demands of knowability', and an obligation to pay for the standard may not 'in a disproportionate manner impede the access to the rule'.[134]

In Germany, the Netherlands, and Belgium, the standardization organization can thus request reasonable compensation for opening their referred-to standards to the general public.

[129] Peter Marburger, *Die Regeln der Technik im Recht* (Heymann 1979) 200–1.

[130] BVerfG, 29 July 1998, Az. 1 BvR 1143/90, § 15.

[131] R. A. J. Van Gestel, 'In de schaduw van het bestuursrecht' in S. E. Zijlstra, R. A. J. Van Gestel, and A. A. Freriks, *Preadvies Privaat Bestuur* (Boom Juridisch 2008) 129.

[132] Christian Bock, 'Der Umgang des Staates mit 'technischen' Normen', Working Paper Researchgate (October 2013) 24; High Council of the Netherlands no. 11/01017, 22 June 2012, *Knooble*, 4.20.

[133] Dutch Council of State Administrative Section, no. 201002804/1/H1, 2 February 2011, 2.4.6, *City Crash*. Richard Neerhof, *Alternatief bestuursrecht: normalisatie en conformiteitsbeoordeling in het publieke belang* (Boom Juridische uitgevers 2016) 241–2 and 288.

[134] Belgian Council of State Legislative Section, Advisory Opinion no. 63.071/3 of 4 April 2018, 7; Belgian Council of State Legislative Section, Advisory no. 64.118/VR of 25 September 2018, 17.

Even if standard-setting bodies keep their IP rights and regulated persons would normally have to pay to gain knowledge of the standards that rule them, traditional rulemakers should improve the accessibility of these rules. They can do so by compensating the intellectual property holder for freely publishing standards or by setting up a fund to partly or fully reimburse companies and, especially, citizens who require access to the standards to comprehend the rules that bind them.[135]

Following the milestone *City Crash* case, the Dutch government listed all national rules of the Dutch standardization body (NEN) to which Dutch legislation referred and made sure that they were all publicly accessible freely on NEN's website starting from 1 January 2016.[136] Such a solution is not possible for international standards set by the ISO, for example, because national states do not have the legal competence or the financial means to broker agreements with these international standard-setting bodies.[137] As early as 1991, the Austrian government decided to publish all directly binding references in the Austrian Gazette and made an agreement with the standardization bodies with regard to IP rights.[138] Moreover, French private standards are sometimes freely accessible on the internet.[139] This is predominantly the case when a French state rule directly refers in a binding manner to the standard.[140]

If Belgian traditional rulemakers directly refer to standards, they principally have a constitutional obligation to make publicly accessible the referred-to standards for which the Belgian Standardization Body (NBN) holds the IP rights.[141] The Legislature should then compensate the NBN for any costs incurred. Nevertheless, Belgium has not yet adopted similar framework rules to that effect as some of its neighbouring countries have done. If the Belgian Legislatures or Executives refer directly to standards, the Belgian High Council for Standardization merely proposes that the Legislature should draft a framework statute, which determines that

[135] R. A. J. Van Gestel, 'Kenbaarheid van NEN-normen waarnaar in wetten wordt verwezen' [2009] *Nederlands Juristenblad* 373. See also R. J. B. Schutgens, 'NEN-normen zijn geen algemeen verbindende voorschriften' [2013] *Ars Aequi* 765.

[136] Cabinet response to the advisory opinions regarding knowability of standards and standardization, *Kamerstukken* II, 2010/11, 27406, no. 193; Dutch government, *Lijst met nationale NEN normen die per 1 januari 2016 kosteloos inzichtelijk zijn via de website van NEN* (3 May 2016).

[137] Conclusion of Advocate-General Langemeijer Dutch High Council, no. 11/01017, 30 March 2012, 23.

[138] § 9 Austrian *Bundesgesetz über das Normenwesen*; Harm Schepel, *Legal aspects of standardisation in the Member States of the EC and EFTA* (EC Commission 2000) 164; Conclusion of Advocate-General Langemeijer Dutch High Council, no. 11/01017, 30 March 2012, 27.

[139] Isabelle Cadet, L''ISO 26000 washing', un risque lié au statut de la norme ISO 26000' [2015] *Revue de l'organisation responsable* 25.

[140] Article 17 *Décret* no. 2009-697 of 16 June 2009 concerning standardisation; France Normalisation, 'Les normes d'application obligatoire', electronic source <http://www.francenormalisation.fr/les-acteurs-de-la-normalisation/normes-obligatoires/> (last accessed January 2019); Conclusion of Advocate-General Langemeijer Dutch High Council, no. 11/01017, 30 March 2012, 27–8.

[141] Belgian High Council for Standardization, *Advies over de kenbaarheid en de tegenstelbaarheid aan derden van de Belgische normen waarnaar in de reglementering verwezen wordt*, 21 November 2014, Doc. 15-0631, 6.

referred-to standards would never be fully published in the Official Journal.[142] They should only contain the number, title, and edition number of the standard. This recommendation does not enhance the accessibility of the standards themselves; it only safeguards the IP rights of the standard setters.

In the UK, explanatory notes of rules that refer to BSI standards, such as the Water Supply Regulations 2018, occasionally refer to where and how these standards can be purchased as digital or hard copies. Moreover, sometimes 'copies of the British and ISO standards referred to in these Regulations are available for inspection free of charge during normal office hours at the offices' of the department that enacted the rule.[143] In the case of the Water Supply Regulations 2018, this is the Department for Environment, Food and Rural Affairs. Added to this, the BSI has an agreement with university and national libraries, through which researchers or interested parties can access standards. This is one way to combine the transparency of rules with IP rights.[144] The BSI also goes to considerable lengths to make navigation through its standards intelligible by offering free workshops and tutorials.

Finally, in the US the question of how to reconcile the publication of referred-to standards with IP rights has been posed. In principle, when a rule refers to a standard that standard enters the public domain and is not subject to the copyright holder's exclusive prerogatives.[145] Bremer calls some of the European solutions, such as requiring an IP waiver or buying out the standardization organizations, aggressive and costly.[146] Instead, she prefers to use technological advances to public advantage by primarily focusing on 'read-only' online tools for the constituency to note the referred-to standards. In my opinion, more extensive means than 'read-only' online tools are necessary to adequately balance IP rights and access to rules. Even if referred-to standards cannot be printed and divulged further via read-only tools, the IP right-holder's entitlements are severely limited by the mere decision of state actors to refer to its standards. For some specific standards containing complicated formulas, 'read-only' could be a sufficient impediment for others to adequately copy the referred-to standard for their personal use, but in most circumstances the intellectual labour that inventors or developers have invested in those standards should be compensated.

[142] Belgian High Council for Standardization, *Advies over de kenbaarheid en de tegenstelbaarheid aan derden van de Belgische normen waarnaar in de reglementering verwezen wordt*, 21 November 2014, Doc. 15-0631, 6.

[143] This is, however, not always free of charge: cf. Explanatory Note to the Building Regulations (Northern Ireland) 2000.

[144] In Belgium, the NBN took a similar approach via the 'NBN Eduportaal'. Other solutions can be found through technological progress, such as read-only access. See Emily S. Bremer, 'Incorporation by Reference in an Open-Government Age' (2013) 36 *Harv. J. L. & Pub. Pol'y* 136–7.

[145] *Veeck*, 293 F.3d at 793.

[146] Emily S. Bremer, 'Incorporation by Reference in an Open-Government Age' (2013) 36 *Harv. J. L. & Pub. Pol'y* 155–6; Emily S. Bremer, 'On the Cost of Private Standards in Public Law' (2015) 63 *U. Kan. L. Rev.* 279, 332–3.

In summary, there are three satisfactory solutions to appease accessibility and the IP rights of standard setters when the Legislature and the Executive refer to their rules. First, the state can buy the intellectual rights such that all directly referred-to standards can be published. Second, the state can provide restricted access to the rules. Third, traditional rulemakers can change the law or adapt their own behaviour, such as copy and pasting more rather than referring to standards, which could also avoid IP problems.

The nuances that this research has brought to an absolute and rigid obligation to publish referred-to standards in an Official Journal freely (and in official languages) within domestic law has been mirrored in EU law by Advocate-General Saugmandsgaard Øe—albeit with noticeably less reservations—in a 2021 opinion on referral to standards: 'I am of the view that the principle of freedom of access to the law does not require that direct access be guaranteed, free of charge, to the ISO standards [...], nor that those standards be published in the Official Journal. The conditions for access to those standards do not constitute a disproportionate obstacle to the possibility for the public to become acquainted with them and reflect an appropriate balance between the requirements of that principle and the various interests at stake.'[147]

The most important outcome is that a rulemaking framework is created for the publication of referred-to standards in order to comply with the principle of transparency. Even if this framework allows for exceptions for free publication of the standard in the national languages in specific contexts, it would still provide better protection for the constituency than the opacity found today in many countries.

5.2.1.3 Reception

Received or ratified private documents created on the basis of the third outsourcing technique also need to be sufficiently published. In Belgium, for example, notification of each extended collective labour agreement (CLA) is published in the *Moniteur belge/Belgisch Staatsblad*. The rulemaking parts of extended CLAs are even integrally published therein.[148] This occurs both in Dutch and French, regardless of the original drafting language. The same publication requirements apply for covenants regarding commercials for the marketing of alcoholic beverages in order to promote the reasonable use of alcohol[149] and for consumer agreements.[150] Article 497 of the Civil Procedure Code also dictates the publication of the rules of the orders of attorneys in the *Moniteur belge/Belgisch Staatsblad*. However, there is

[147] *Case C-160/20, Stichting Rookpreventie Jeugd e.a. v Staatssecretaris van Volksgezondheid, Welzijn en Sport in tegenwoordigheid van: Vereniging Nederlandse Sigaretten- en Kerftabakfabrikanten (VSK)*, ECLI:EU:C:2021:618, Opinion of Advocate- General Saugmandsgaard Øe of 15 July 2021, § 91.

[148] Articles 25 and 30 of Belgian Statute on Collective Labour Agreements. Chris Engels, 'De collectieve arbeidsovereenkomst bijna vijftig jaar na de totstandkoming van de Wet van 5 december 1968—(Eerste deel)' [2017] *Journal des Tribunaux du Travail* fnn. 153–4.

[149] Article 7*bis* of the 24 January 1977 statute concerning the Protection of the Consumer's Health.

[150] Article VI.121 of the Code Economic Law.

no regular explicit provision determining the publication of the deontology codes of other professional organizations, which the Council of State Legislative Section deems to be problematic.[151]

In France, again, a general and overarching publication framework is lacking. This has certainly been lamented in relation to professional orders.[152] Each example of the reception technique will thus have a different way—if any—of explaining and publishing negotiated agreements that have been made into a rule. These rules should also be reasonably accessible. The Minister of Labour publishes any extension decisions of CLAs in the Official Journal;[153] the extended CLA itself is not so widely disclosed but is published in the Bulletin of the Minister of Labour involved in the extension.[154]

In Germany, the rules created through the reception technique must also be accessible. Article 82 of the Basic Law is itself not directly applicable to private rules that have been made binding for third parties through reception and extension, but they are also bound by the publication principle.[155] Ordinarily, a specific statute will stipulate the accessibility of rules adopted by statutory corporations (*Satzungen*) or of CLAs that have been declared generally binding. In fact, government declarations of general applicability are published in the Federal Gazette (*Bundesanzeiger*). CLAs themselves are not published anywhere, but only registered with the Minister of Labour and Social Affairs in accordance with § 6 of the Collective Agreement Act (*Tarifvertraggesetz*). Nevertheless, CLAs are accessible to employees at the office of an employer which is a party to the agreement. Genuine third parties can receive a transcript of a CLA against compensation for their expenses. Some have argued that the lack of publication of the CLA itself renders the whole declaration of general applicability unconstitutional.[156] The FCC, however, has confirmed that the entire rule apparatus of CLAs is adequately accessible.[157]

Publication of other agreements made by private actors may deviate from ordinary publication channels.[158] For the reception of rules made by private actors in particular, the FCC's case law, with its focus on procedural rationality, has inspired the courts in recent years. Transparency is considered an essential aspect of

[151] Belgian Council of State Legislative Section, Advisory opinion no. 22.537/2 of 21 November 1994, 107. Patricia Popelier and Jeroen Van Nieuwenhove, 'Decentralisering en privatisering van wetgeving' in Jef De Mot (ed.), *Vrank en vrij: liber amicorum Boudewijn Bouckaert* (Die Keure 2012) 269.

[152] Sylvain Merenne, 'La portée du règlement intérieur d'un ordre professionnel' [2015] *RDSS* 1042.

[153] French Council of State no. 280606, 26 February 2007; Gérard Vachet, *Négociation. Convention et accord collectif* (JurisClasseur Travail Traité, 5 July 2017) § 122. Example: Executive decree of 25 June 1991 *portant extension d'avenants aux conventions collectives (employés et cadres) des commerces de la quincaillerie et des métaux des régions Bretagne-Pays de la Loire-Centre Ouest.*

[154] Gérard Vachet, *Négociation. Convention et accord collectif* (JurisClasseur Travail Traité, 5 July 2017) § 122.

[155] BVerfG 44, 322, § 79.

[156] Thomas Clemens, 'Die Verweisung von einer Rechtsnorm auf andere Vorschriften' [1986] *AöR* 95.

[157] BVerfG 44, 322, § 80.

[158] Britta Beate Wiegand, *Die Beleihung mit Normsetzungskompetenzen. Das Gesundheitswesen als Exempel* (Duncker & Humblot 2007) 250–1.

the German rulemaking process in order to fulfil this review dutifully.[159] The State Social Court of Berlin-Brandenburg analysed § 92 of the German Social Code V and subjected this provision's joint self-government of insurance and hospital organizations in establishing health policy guidelines to a specific transparency review.[160]

In the UK, the organizations analysed, whose rules traditional rulemakers receive, are aware of the public impact that their rules can have and publicize them clearly on their websites on their own initiative. CLAs cannot be declared generally applicable in the UK or the US,[161] which explains why they are not published at the national level. The handbooks of rules of the UK Solicitors Regulation Authority and of the Bar Standards Board are easily accessible on their respective websites.[162] Likewise, sports governing bodies and organizations, such as United Kingdom Athletics (UKA), make their rules of competition clearly available on their website.[163]

5.2.2 Intelligibility

A second aspect of transparency consists of intelligibility of the rule.[164] Comparative scholarship sends mixed signals on the danger of outsourcing rulemaking powers using the three techniques discussed: delegation, referral, and reception.

There is general criticism of the lack of clarity or the 'opacity' of delegated legislation, especially when autonomous public bodies make delegated rules.[165] However, open and frequent communication of these autonomous public bodies (through their websites) goes a long way towards making their rules more predictable and understandable.

159 Susan Rose-Ackerman, 'Democratic Legitimacy and Executive Rulemaking: Positive Political Theory in Comparative Public Law' in Joana Mendes and Ingo Venzke (eds), *Allocating Authority. Who Should Do What in European and International Law* (Hart 2018) 43–6; Susan Rose-Ackerman, Stefanie Egidy, and James Fowkes, *Due Process of Lawmaking* (Cambridge University Press 2014) 164.

160 e.g. State Social Court of Berlin-Brandenburg, 22 June 2012, no. L 1 KR 296/09 KL, section 2.1; Susan Rose-Ackerman, Stefanie Egidy, and James Fowkes, *Due Process of Lawmaking* (Cambridge University Press 2014) 190.

161 Cornell legal information institute, Collective bargaining.

162 Solicitors Regulation Authority, *SRA Handbook* (2017) <https://sra.org.uk/solicitors/handbook/welcome.page> (last accessed January 2019); Bar Standards Boards, *BSB Handbook* (2018) <https://www.barstandardsboard.org.uk/regulatory-requirements/bsb-handbook/> (last accessed August 2018).

163 United Kingdom Athletics (UKA), *Rules of Competition* (2018–20) <https://www.uka.org.uk/competitions/rules/> (last accessed January 2019).

164 Daniel Greenberg, 'Dangerous Trends in Modern Legislation' [2015] *Public Law* 99: 'the restaurant owner ... ought to be able both to access [the rule] and to understand it, if they are to be expected to have a respect for the rule of law and the wish to comply with it'.

165 Mark Elliott and Robert Thomas, *Public Law* (Oxford University Press 2017) 147; Julia Black, 'Calling Regulators to Account: Challenges, Capacities and Prospects' in Nicholas Bamforth and Peter Leyland (eds), *Accountability in the Contemporary Constitution* (Oxford University Press 2013) 362–4.

The referral technique can both decrease and increase the intelligibility of a rule.[166] On the one hand, many referrals within a rule leave the citizen with many pieces of a puzzle that can only be reconstructed by identifying all the referred-to standards. An exaggeration of referrals could result in a kaleidoscope of rules, utterly confusing the entire constituency.[167] On the other hand, a referral to a specific standard is always more understandable than an open norm. The static referral technique has the additional benefit of allowing the easy attachment of the referred-to standard as an annex to the referring rule.[168] Dynamic referrals often increase the readability and predictability of the rule because they allow the Legislature or the Executive to write its most important aspects in the referring rules, while referencing the referred-to standard. Without the referral, these most important aspects would often be buried in pages of often technical details.[169] Extra-parliamentary rules can thus be made more intelligible than the statutes themselves.[170]

Received and negotiated agreements as a basis for rules, such as extended CLAs, would appear to be generally more readable than the more technical rules that flow from delegation or referral techniques. Moreover, in France, the advisory opinion on the extension of the CLA by the National Commission of Collective Negotiation is published in the Official Journal.[171] This advisory opinion can help the constituency to understand the rule.

If it is accepted that outsourced rules can theoretically comply—and sometimes even strengthen—intelligibility, autonomous public, private, and hybrid actors still have at least four important working points when attempting to create more comprehensible rules.

First, this result might be accomplished when other autonomous public, private, and hybrid actors or the general public are consulted. Examples of consultation are mushrooming, such as occurs with the UK Financial Conduct Authority which must consult the UK Prudential Regulation Authority and vice versa, while providing an explanation for the purpose of the proposed rules for all to read.[172]

[166] Ministère de l'économie, de l'industrie et de l'emploi, *Guide relatif a la bonne utilisation des normes dans la reglementation*, direction générale de la compétitivité, de l'industrie et des services (2009) 10; Pierre de Montalivet, 'La "juridicisation" de la légistique. A propos de l'objectif de valeur constitutionnelle d'accessibilité et d'intelligibilité de la loi' in Roland Drago *et al.* (eds), *La confection de la loi* (Presses Universitaires de France 2005) 132.

[167] Georg Wegge, 'Zur verfassungsrechtlichen Abgrenzung unbestimmter Rechtsbegriffe von unzulässigen dynamischen Verweisungen am Beispiel der "betriebswirtschaftlichen Grundsätze" nach § 6 Abs. 2 Satz 1 KAG NW, DVB1 1997, 648 ff.' [1997] *DVBl.* 648; Alfred G. Debus, *Verweisungen in Deutschen Rechtsnormen* (Duncker & Humblot 2008) 141.

[168] Pierre Brunet, 'Les normes législatives et administratives' in Pascale Gonod, Fabrice Melleray, and Philippe Yolka (eds), *Traité de Droit Administratif* (Dalloz 2011) 502.

[169] Alfred G. Debus, *Verweisungen in Deutschen Rechtsnormen* (Duncker & Humblot 2008) 103.

[170] Matthias Herdegen, 'Informalisierung und Entparlamentarisierung politischer Entscheidungen als Gefährdungen der Verfassung' [2003] *VVDStRL* 18.

[171] Gérard Vachet, *Négociation. Convention et accord collectif* (JurisClasseur Travail Traité, 5 July 2017) § 122.

[172] Sections 138I and 138J of the Financial Services and Markets Act 2000.

Correspondingly, under the heading of 'transparency of standards', article 4 of the Regulation on European Standardisation 1025/2012, obliges European and national standardization organizations to send draft standards to the other standardization organizations. An obligation to give notice of proposed rulemaking is also present in the US Administrative Procedure Act.[173] Given the fact that consultation can also lead to wider representation, this step in the rulemaking process is further discussed under the heading of 'representativeness' later in the chapter.

Second, internal debates by a rulemaker may elucidate the extent of the rules. Autonomous public, private, and hybrid actors show reticence to share their thinking process before determining their rules. For example, autonomous public bodies in Belgium or France do not traditionally publish their internal debates—as opposed to Parliament—since they do not wish to endanger their collegiate decision-making.[174] Within the Executive, there is a secret of deliberation. Although autonomous public, private, and hybrid actors are independent of the Executive, their collegiate decision-making without publishing internal debates can still be considered as an application of the secrecy of deliberation when exercising executive powers in France.[175] Likewise, in Germany, the meetings of autonomous public, private, and hybrid actors are not necessarily public. It is not uncommon for an actor, such as the Accounting Standards Committee of Germany (Deutsche Rechnungslegungs Standards Committee or DSRC), to keep minutes of these meetings but only to publish a summary on its website.[176]

Third, although an express motivation for the eventual rule mainly reinforces legal protection against the actions of the government, it also clarifies the content of the rules.[177] German law does not generally require that reasons must be given when drafting sub-statutory rules.[178] According to some scholars, there is an unwritten constitutional principle that sound legislation should give reasons (*Begründungspflicht*), but this is not judicially enforceable.[179] During the parliamentary preparation of the Belgian federal statute of 29 July 1991 regarding the explicit motivation of individual[180] administrative acts, it was suggested that general

[173] 5 USC § 553(b).

[174] Clémence Dumont, 'Le Conseil supérieur de l'audiovisuel, une autorité de régulation indépendante' [2010] *CRISP* 29 and 78.

[175] Anne Debet, Lois sur les autorités administratives indépendantes: quels changements pour la CNIL? [2017] *Communication Commerce électronique*, comm. 56, 5.

[176] § 12, 2 Satzung DSRC; Lothar Michael, 'Private Standardsetter und demokratisch legitimierte Rechtsetzung' in Hartmut Bauer, Peter Huber, and Karl-Peter Sommermann (eds), *Demokratie in Europa* (Mohr Siebeck 2005) 453.

[177] See for the various functions of a duty to give reasons, e.g. Opdebeek Ingrid and Stéphanie De Somer, 'The Duty to Give Reasons in the European Legal Area. A Mechanism for Transparent and Accountable Administrative Decision-Making? A Comparison of Belgian, Dutch, French and EU Administrative Law' [2016] *Public Administration Yearbook (Rocznik Administracji Publicznej)* 103.

[178] Hermann Pünder, 'Democratic Legitimation of Delegated Legislation—A Comparative View on the American, British and German Law' [2009] *ICLQ* 371.

[179] Anna Jasiak, *Constitutional Constraint on Ad Hoc Legislation* (Intersentia 2011) 261.

[180] Article 1 of the Belgian Statute of 29 July 1991 regarding the explicit motivation of administrative acts.

(non-individual) rules should be subject to a formal motivation requirement.[181] This idea was eventually discarded, mainly because general and abstract rules come to light through 'procedures that already provide more safeguards for material and formal motivation'.[182] However, when autonomous public, private, and hybrid actors effectively create the rules, as they exceedingly do, there are fewer pre-existing mechanisms to ensure the publication of motives. Preferably, these actors should also formulate their rules with explanatory sections. In the same vein, the UK Statutory Instruments Committee suggested that explanatory notes to delegated rules should be provided.[183] While it may prove challenging to find the explanation and motivations for these rules, autonomous public bodies increasingly do so, simultaneously with their duty to give reasons for administrative acts.[184] Ultimately, according to the US Administrative Procedure Act, after consideration of the relevant matter presented, the (autonomous) agency incorporates a concise general statement of the basis and purpose of the rules adopted.[185]

A fourth means to provide more intelligibility within a rulemaking process is for the drafter of the rule to create clear and structured rules.[186] For more traditional rulemaking types, such as statutes and executive regulations, these guarantees have steadily developed over the years. For example, the French author Stendhal stated that to ensure that his grim and naturalist novels acquired the right tone, he read several pages from the Code Civil daily.[187] The clarity of the Code thus still had to undergo important evolutions at that time. When rulemaking power is delegated to autonomous public, private, and hybrid actors, they need to ensure that their rules are clear in order for the constituency to understand what the finalized rules will accomplish. In the UK, the Statutory Instruments Committee proposed that verbosity be avoided and short and clear titles used.[188] Lengthy delegation chains made the exact binding rule itself increasingly less clear. However, rules should also not become too infantile and simple. If the rules do not meet the intricacy of the regulated matter, this increases the factual power of the courts, which will

[181] Ingrid Opdebeek and Ann Coolsaet, 'Toepassingsgebied ratione materiae van de Wet Motivering Bestuurshandelingen' in Ingrid Opdebeek and Ann Coolsaet (eds), *Formele motivering van bestuurshandelingen* (die Keure 2013) 69–70.

[182] Belgian Senate Commission of Behaviour (Parliamentary document Senate *BZ* 1988, 215/3) 15.

[183] K. C. Wheare, 'Controlling Delegated Legislation: A British Experiment [1949] *J. Politics* 759–60.

[184] Ingrid Opdebeek and Stéphanie De Somer, 'The Duty to Give Reasons in the European Legal Area: A Mechanism for Transparent and Accountable Administrative Decision-Making?' [2016] *Public Administration Yearbook* 97 and 107; Cedric Jenart and Stéphanie De Somer, 'Non-Statutory Rulemaking and the Rule of Law: Towards a "Law of Rules"?'[2017] *Sui-Generis* 24.

[185] 5 USC § 553(c).

[186] Laurence Boisson de Chazournes, 'Changing Roles of International Organizations' [2009] *International Organizations L. Rev.* 659; Danielle Hanna Rached, 'Doomed Aspiration of Pure Instrumentality: Global Administrative Law and Accountability' [2014] *Global Constitutionalism* 361.

[187] Stendhal to Honoré de Balzac on 20 October 1840 in Paul Arbelet, 'La véritable lettre de Stendhal à Balzac' (1917) 24 *Revue d'Histoire littéraire de la France* 537, 552 as cited in Neil Duxbury, *Elements of Legislation* (Cambridge University Press 2012) 59.

[188] K. C. Wheare, 'Controlling Delegated Legislation: A British Experiment [1949] *J. Politics* 759–60.

ultimately have to apply the rules to complicated constellations of facts. Where applicable, autonomous public, private, and hybrid actors should thus also not fear the use of highly technical and applied language in their rules.

5.3 Hierarchy of rules

In order to comply with a second principle of good rulemaking, outsourced rules need to be clearly within the hierarchy of rules after a traditional rulemaker has transferred rulemaking powers. The hierarchy of rules is specifically recognized as deriving from the rule of law principle in France.[189] In Germany, this principle is enshrined in article 20, 3 of the Basic Law, according to which the Legislature is bound by the constitutional order and the Executive and the Judiciary are bound by statute.[190] The hierarchy of rules is generally not recognized as an aspect of the UK rule of law[191] where there is not as strong a focus on the hierarchy of rules as there is in the continental European countries researched or in the US. Arguably, this omission is due to the absence of a written constitution and of hierarchically structured categories of rules in legal scholarship. Still, there is an implicit hierarchy of rules in the UK which largely satisfies itself with the difference between primary legislation (made by the Legislature) and secondary legislation (made by the Executive and all other actors but the Legislature).

Comparing the countries researched, the hierarchy of rules created by the Legislature and the Executive is usually rather straightforward—at least to a certain extent—following the legitimacy chain.[192] The first link in the chain (Constitution) will trump the second link (statutes), which in turn trumps the third link (executive decrees), etc. However, autonomous public, private, and hybrid actors are not directly part of the constitutionally devised legitimacy chain. In an increasingly diverse and complex society, the rise of new rulemaking methods does not necessarily undermine the existing hierarchy of rules; they just need to fit into that hierarchy.[193] It is the responsibility of the Legislature or the Executive to design a clear

[189] Jacques Chevalier, 'Autorités administratives indépendantes et État de droit' [2016] *Civitas Europa* 149.

[190] It is also enshrined in article 31 of the Basic Law, according to which federal law is supreme over law of the federated entities; however, that dynamic falls out of the scope of this research.

[191] See, as an exception e.g. Paul Craig, 'Accountability and Judicial Review in the UK and EU: Central Precepts' in Nicholas Bamforth and Peter Leyland (eds), *Accountability in the Contemporary Constitution* (Oxford University Press 2013) 192–5.

[192] Danielle Hanna Rached, 'Doomed Aspiration of Pure Instrumentality: Global Administrative Law and Accountability' [2014] *Global Constitutionalism* 344; Martino Maggetti, 'Legitimacy and Accountability of Independent Regulatory Agencies: A Critical Review' [2010] *Living Reviews in Democracy* 4.

[193] Lothar Michael, 'Private Standardsetter und demokratisch legitimierte Rechtsetzung' in Hartmut Bauer, Peter Huber, and Karl-Peter Sommermann (eds), *Demokratie in Europa* (Mohr Siebeck 2005) 395; Katrin Schwärzel, 'Die kooperierende rechtserzeugende Gewalt in der kompetenzrechtlichen, legitimatorischen und instrumentellen Krise?' [4/2007] *HFR* 6, § 15.

framework in which autonomous public, private, or hybrid actors can operate and thus develop their rules. The Belgian Council of State Legislative Section, for one, takes offence at the transfer of power to autonomous public, private, and hybrid actors where the hierarchy of rules is unclear.[194] It is crucial to the hierarchy of rules that the position of each rule—made pursuant to legislative delegation—is known. Traditional rulemakers should at least clarify this legal order in their rulemaking preparation and possibly in the outsourcing rule itself. Regardless of any clear indication in primary legislation, autonomous public, private, and hybrid actors have a duty to comply with and explicitly confirm that hierarchy in order to safeguard the rights and the legal certainty of those subject to their rules. The principle of a hierarchy of rules has not been formulated so strongly in the German Basic Law as to imply that any rules falling outside the hierarchy will be unconstitutional.

One necessary preliminary step is that outsourced rules consistently remain in the same hierarchical position. For example, section 14 of the UK Interpretation Act 1978 determines that the entity that enacts a rule, a regulation, or a bylaw can also itself amend, review, or dispense with that rule.[195] Specific parent statutes could enshrine a similar possibility for an autonomous public, private, and hybrid actor to change self-made rules and thus to maintain the same hierarchical status. This occurred in section 21(3) of the 1973 UK Hallmarking Act: 'any power conferred by this Act to make an order shall include a power to vary or revoke the order by a subsequent order'.[196]

The hierarchy of rules within the countries researched affects all three techniques used to outsource rulemaking powers: delegation, referral, and reception.

5.3.1 Delegation

It is difficult to put delegated rules made by autonomous public, private, and hybrid actors into traditional rulemaking categories. Especially in Germany, this is not for want of trying. The rules that result from a delegation to a public autonomous actor could arguably be represented as a *Verwaltungsvorschrift* or as a guideline.[197] However, neither of these categories is truly appropriate because—contrary to *Verwaltungsvorschriften*—rules of autonomous public bodies are not made within the administration and will bind people outside the administration. Contrary to guidelines, they bind people in an abstract manner. These rules thus do not appear

[194] Belgian Council of State Legislative Section, Advisory opinion no. 39.272/3 of 29 November 2005, § 5; David De Roy, 'Le pouvoir réglementaire des autorités administratives indépendantes en droit belge' in *Rapports belges au Congrès de l'Académie de droit comparé à Utrecht* (Bruylant 2006) § 30.

[195] William Wade and Christopher Forsyth, *Administrative Law* (Oxford University Press 2014) 736.

[196] Section 21(3) of the Hallmarking Act 1973.

[197] Hans-Heinrich Trute, Wolfgang Spoerr, and Wolfgang Bosch, *Telekommunikationsgesetz mit FTEG: Kommentar* (De Gruyter 2001) 84.

to fall under any recognized legal source (*Rechtsquelle*).[198] Parent statutes must thus determine the hierarchical status of these delegated rules.

Autonomous public bodies in Belgium, such as the FSMA or the National Bank of Belgium, have been delegated various degrees of rulemaking powers. The Belgian Council of State Legislative Section particularly regretted the questionable position of their rules within the general hierarchy of rules.[199] This is one of the reasons why the Council, to this day, principally objects to delegating rulemaking powers beyond the *Trias Politica*. One can assume that rules of autonomous public, private, and hybrid actors are inferior to the Constitution, special majority statutes, statutes, statutory decrees or ordinances, and executive decrees but, in the lower rulemaking echelons and among each other, the hierarchical position of these rules is unknown.[200] If the outsourced rule is ratified by an executive decree, a case could be made that they receive the same hierarchical status as the decree.[201] However, that would only offer a solution to the restricted number of outsourced rules that the Legislature or the Executive ratifies.

The status of rules drafted by French *autorités administratives indépendantes* (AAIs) after a delegation of rulemaking authority has also not been definitively distinguished.[202] Admittedly, in many instances their rules are construed in order to supplement or support other existing rules.[203] Consequently, rulemaking conflicts seldom occur and the case law does not have many opportunities to weigh outsourced rules against traditional rules. However, conflicts may still occur. As a matter of principle, the hierarchical ladder of rules corresponds to the hierarchical ladder of rulemaking actors in France.[204] However, it is not even certain whether AAIs have obtained a linear position on that hierarchical ladder of rulemaking actors because there is no ministerial responsibility for them.[205] Controlling measures, such as a government commissioner,[206] barely manage to create a linear

[198] Britta Beate Wiegand, *Die Beleihung mit Normsetzungskompetenzen. Das Gesundheitswesen als Exempel* (Duncker & Humblot 2007) 75.

[199] Jan Velaers, *De Grondwet en de Raad van State Afdeling Wetgeving* (Maklu 1999) 381 and references.

[200] Yves Lejeune, *Droit constitutionnel belge* (Larcier 2014) 130.

[201] Irène Mathy, 'Etre ou ne pas être une personne juridique distincte de l'Etat, la Communauté ou la Région? L'autonomie avec ou sans personnalité juridique' in Pierre Jadoul, Bruno Lombaert, and François Tulkens (eds), *Le paraétatisme. Nouveaux regards sur la décentralisation fonctionelle en Belgique et dans les institutions européens* (la Charte 2010) 83.

[202] András Sajó, 'Les autorités indépendantes' in Michel Troper and Dominique Chagnollaud (eds), *Traité international de droit constitutionnel—Tome 2* (Dalloz 2012) 345.

[203] Stéphanie Dubiton, *La protection des libertés publiques par les autorités administratives indépendantes, une solution démocratique?* (LGDJ 2016) 94.

[204] Denys de Béchillon, *Hiérarchie des normes et hiérarchie des fonctions normatives de l'état* (Economica 1996) 7; Véronique Champeil-Desplats, 'Hiérarchie des normes. Principe justificatif de la suprématie de la constitution' in Michel Troper and Dominique Chagnollaud (eds), *Traité international de droit constitutionnel—Tome 1* (Dalloz 2012) 734.

[205] Clément Chauvet, 'La personnalité contentieuse des autorités administratives indépendantes' [2007] *Issu de Revue de droit public* 379, II.A.

[206] Jean-Marc Sauvé, 'Les autorités administratives indépendantes' for *Transcription d'intervention Comité d'évaluation et de contrôle des politiques publiques (CEC) sur les autorités administratives indépendantes* (Conseil d'État 2010) § 2.

connection between the Executive and the AAI. The autonomous public body can still only position itself with certainty under the Legislature and the Executive as a rulemaking actor. Therefore, the rules of an AAI are of lower value than statutes or executive regulations.[207] The French Court of Cassation has even suggested that the rules created by the Committee on Banking Regulation (Comité de la réglementation bancaire), an AAI, cannot supersede contractual agreements of private parties.[208] French scholarship, however, correctly counters that rules made by AAIs are still binding and therefore apply forcefully to private contracting parties.[209] Ordinarily, the exercise of their rulemaking powers will be of a public order (*ordre public*), in which case it is illegal under French contract law to depart from them. The French Council of State Legislative Section summarizes: 'in the unlikely event of a conflict between the provisions of a *recommendation* of the Conseil supérieur de l'audiovisuel and those laid down in the contractual specifications of a broadcasting company, the latter take precedence, in principle, over the former, in accordance with the hierarchy of norms. However, the situation is different if it is clear from the legislative provisions in question that the legislator intended to entrust the Conseil supérieur de l'audiovisuel alone, as an *independent public authority, with the task of laying down*, by way of derogation from the Prime Minister's regulatory power, *all the conditions for the application of the field in question.*'[210]

With regard to the UK, there is a Regulator's Compliance Code that codifies some rule of law safeguards that autonomous public bodies must uphold. This code is hierarchically inferior to diverging statutory regulations. The Code does not free autonomous public bodies from the requirement to comply with statutory obligations.[211] Those obligations can be derived from the Statutory Instruments Act 1946 or another parent statute. However, apart from the inferior hierarchical status in relation to Acts of Parliament, it remains unclear how outsourced rules relate to secondary rules from the Executive or other autonomous public, private, and hybrid actors. Finally, there is no clear ranking of the legal value of Orders, Rules, and Regulations; in short, of secondary legislation.[212] A similar conclusion applies to the US although it is generally accepted that the waterfall of Constitution, statute, executive order, and agency regulation applies.

207 Tanneguy Larzul and Pierre de Montalivet, *Droit constitutionnel de l'administration* (JurisClasseur Administratif 2017) § 21; Yoan Vilain, 'Demokratische Legitimität und Verfassungsmäßigkeit unabhängiger Regulierungsbehörden. Von den ursprünglichen Bedenken bis zur richterlichen Eingliederung in das französische Verwaltungssystem' in Johannes Masing and Gérard Marco (eds), *Unabhängige Regulierungsbehörden* (Mohr Siebeck 2010) 24.

208 French Court of Cassation of 3 June 2003 (9–13 November 2003) *Gaz. Pal.* 3763.

209 Anne Danis-Fatôme, 'Contrat versus textes règlementaires: un conflit nié?' [2007] *Revue des contrats* 1455, II.

210 Frech Council of State Legislative Section of 17 October 2017, N° 393566, § 12. (Emphasis added).

211 UK Department for Business Enterprise & Regulatory Reform, 'Regulator's Compliance Code', Statutory Code of Practice for Regulators (2007) 7, 1.4.

212 Anthony Bradley, Keith Ewing, and Christopher Knight, *Constitutional and Administrative Law* (16th edn, Pearson 2014) 587–8.

5.3.2 Referral

Standards of private standardization bodies in and of themselves do not have a hierarchical position in the hierarchy of rules. Such a hierarchy must be developed in the public sphere, and unincorporated private standards remain outside the public sphere. The Belgian Council of State Legislative Section succinctly supported the position that a technical standard does not in itself have the status of a rule.[213] Nevertheless, external standards must comply with state rules.[214] In the same vein, article 9.2 of the British Standard for Standards states that 'standards are always subordinate to the law'.[215]

The legal status of external referred-to standards after a referral is more intricate. As a rulemaking technique, (dynamic) referral to documents of standardization organizations should comply with the constitutional safeguard of a clear hierarchy of rules.

In France, this debate has been primarily approached in the scholarship from the angle of annexes attached to statutes. Brunet distinguished a number of ways in which to treat these annexes hierarchically, two of which are relevant to this research.[216] First, the (annexed) external standards may be perceived as merely documents providing additional information on the traditional rule. In this sense, the referred-to standard has no internal legal value whatsoever. This position is also defended with regard to the external documents to which the French Constitution refers, such as the EU Treaties in article 88-1. The argument is that these external documents do not automatically have the same hierarchical status as the Constitution.[217] However, as already discussed, the Constitutional Council interprets the Declaration of the Rights of Man and of the Citizen as being of constitutional value due to a reference to it in the preamble to the current French Constitution. A second approach, therefore, defends the position that the referred-to standard is a necessary addition and thus receives the same hierarchical position as the referring rule.

The first approach was taken in the Netherlands. In the Building Regulation 2003, the Dutch Executive referred directly to NEN standards 6069 and 8700 to

[213] Belgian Council of State Legislative Section, Advisory opinion no. 56.941/3 of 21 January 2015, 3.4 and 3.8.2. See, e.g., also Belgian Council of State, Advisory opinion on the Ministerial Executive Decree *tot uitvoerings van het Vergunningsbesluit van 22 november 2013*, 2. 'A CEN-standard is not binding in and of itself. The creation of the rule happens through the Ministerial Executive Decree.'

[214] Ministère de l'économie, de l'industrie et de l'emploi, *Guide relatif a la bonne utilisation des normes dans la reglementation*, direction générale de la compétitivité, de l'industrie et des services (2009) 8–9, § 2.5; Denys de Béchillon, *Hiérarchie des normes et hiérarchie des fonctions normatives de l'état* (Economica 1996) 12.

[215] BSI Group, 'A standard for standards—Principles of standardization. Standard 0' (2016) article 9.2.

[216] Pierre Brunet, 'Les normes législatives et administratives' in Pascale Gonod, Fabrice Melleray, and Philippe Yolka (eds), *Traité de Droit Administratif* (Dalloz 2011) 502.

[217] Agnès Roblot-Troizier, *Contrôle de constitutionnalité et normes visées par la Constitution française* (Dalloz 2007 24.

determine the necessary fire resistance for building construction. Knooble BV, as an organization that represents the interests of companies and service providers in the building sector, argued that these referred-to standards had become generally binding regulations (*algemeen verbindende voorschriften* or AVVs) because of the direct referral. Categorizing these standards as AVVs would give them a determined position in the hierarchy of rules and would, for example, lead to a constitutional and statutory obligation to publish referred-to standards.[218] The Hague Court of First Instance had initially agreed with Knooble BV that the referred-to standards were AVVs because they were generally binding on third parties.[219] This was judicial recognition of the second approach. However, the Court of Appeals of The Hague and ultimately the High Council of the Netherlands disagreed with Knooble BV because the actual rulemaking actors did not establish the referred-to standards, they merely referred to them.[220] This meant Dutch judicial recognition of the first approach.

The second approach is apparently taken in Germany, where a referred-to standard would receive the hierarchical status of the referring standard due to the incorporation of its context.[221] This case law was initially developed with regard to federal statutes that refer to 'sub-state' statutes of federated entities. The content of these sub-state statutes could be reviewed as if they were federal statutes.[222] Parallel reasoning has been made for referred-to standards of standardization organizations, such that their content could be reviewed as if they were statutes. In the opposite direction, the content of federal statutes cannot be reviewed as if they were lower ranked rules, in the case of these lower ranked rules (*in casu* collective labour agreements) referring to them.[223]

The hierarchical position of referred-to standards has not yet been clearly identified in Belgium, France, the UK, or the US. In evaluation, the second approach, which is taken in Germany, appears most in line with the principle of positioning each rule against the other existing rules. The first approach, as maintained by the Dutch High Council, is a pragmatic way of avoiding all the obligations of ordinary rules in relation to referred-to standards. However, ultimately, the referred-to

[218] See earlier on accessibility in relation to the referral technique. See also the Dutch Publication Statute of 4 February 1988 read together with article 89 of the Dutch Constitution.

[219] Dutch Court of First Instance of the Hague no. 274010/HA ZA 06-3308, 31 December 2008, *Knooble*, § 5.

[220] Dutch Court of Appeals of the Hague nos 200.029.693/01 and 200.031.136/01, 16 November 2010, *Knooble*, §§ 8–9; High Council of the Netherlands no. 11/01017, 22 June 2012, *Knooble*, §§ 4.8–4.9.

[221] Florian Becker, *Kooperative und konsensuale Strukturen in der Normsetzung* (Mohr Siebeck 2005) 543; Helmuth Schulze-Fielitz 'Artikel 20 Rechtsstaat' in Horst Dreier (ed.), *Grundgesetz Kommentar* (Mohr Siebeck 2004) 244.

[222] BVwG 32, 249; Thomas Clemens, 'Die Verweisung von einer Rechtsnorm auf andere Vorschriften' [1986] *AöR* 65–6.

[223] BVerfGE 39, 260 (270); Alfred G. Debus, *Verweisungen in Deutschen Rechtsnormen* (Duncker & Humblot 2008) 92. Otherwise lower ranked rulemakers could indirectly develop a new recourse to fight federal statutes in court.

standards are incorporated into the referring rule and thus factually form part of it. It should thus be the responsibility of the national constitution or statutory rules to determine the referred-to standards' hierarchy of rules and the obligations that entails.

5.3.3 Reception

The hierarchy of 'received' private agreements should also be determinable.

First, the question arises as to whether the 'received' rules can be subsumed into a traditional category of rules. In Germany, the typical rule that is created within the reception technique through functional self-government is the *Satzung*. The FCC defined a *Satzung* as a rule 'adopted by a *statutory corporation* [*Körperschaften des öffentlichen Rechts*], with a view to its legally conferred autonomy, affecting the persons belonging to and subject to it'.[224] The rules of professional orders, which constitute the backbone of this technique, fall perfectly within the above-mentioned definition of the FCC. Such professional orders are statutory corporations that adopt rules with effect for persons belonging to and subject to them.

However, not every type of received rule can be easily placed within the traditional hierarchy of rules. As a result, if traditional rulemakers receive and extend a professionally made agreement, after which the agreement can bind third parties, an overarching constitutional or statutory provision could establish how the rule relates to statutes or executive decrees in all of the countries researched.

An exemplary hierarchical framework is in place for collective labour agreements in Belgium. Article 51 of the Belgian Statute on Collective Labour Agreements gave substance to the principle of the hierarchy of rules by conscientiously listing the hierarchical worth of all labour-related contracts and obligations:[225] (1) compulsory statutory provisions; (2) collective labour agreements concluded within the National Labour Council and declared generally binding by the Executive (hereinafter: extended); (3) extended CLAs concluded within a joint committee; (4) extended CLAs concluded within a joint subcommittee; (5) *non*-extended CLAs concluded within the National Labour Council; (6) *non*-extended CLAs concluded within a joint committee; (7) *non*-extended CLAs concluded within a joint subcommittee; (8) CLAs concluded outside a joint body; (9) written individual labour contracts; and (10) *non*-extended CLAs concluded within a joint body in the economic sphere in which an employer resides—even though the employer has not signed the agreement.

[224] BVerfG 10, 20, § 116 (emphasis added).

[225] Article 51 of the Belgian Statute on Collective Labour Agreements. See also Patrick Humblet and Marc Rigaux, *Belgian Industrial Relations Law* (Intersentia 2005) 99 etc.

The Belgian Council of State Legislative Section had initially advised that article 51 of the CLA statute be removed, among other reasons, because it was superfluous as a statutory provision. It argued that the overview itself was declarative and did not provide a new binding rule;[226] the provision simply confirmed and made clear what could be derived from other provisions (of the CLA statute or other statutes). However, the Council conceded that the article was of great use 'from a doctrinal point of view and for legal practice'.[227] The Belgian Legislature still maintained the provision, with its overview of the hierarchy of rules. Subsequently, the Belgian Court of Cassation welcomed this clearly drafted hierarchy of rules by the Legislature.[228]

This explicit framework is not extended to other categories of 'received' agreements. In this respect, the hierarchical value of deontological codes made by Belgian professional orders is unclear.[229] The Belgian Council of State Legislative Section likewise demands that statutes on consumer agreements regarding terms and conditions, information, and advertisements between sellers and consumers clarify the legal value of such agreements.[230] The Council of State made the same demand for hierarchical clarity for the statute that introduced covenants for commercials for the marketing of alcoholic beverages.[231]

If there is no traditional category of rules that applies to outsourced rules, or if there is no statutory or executive indication of their hierarchical status, the legal system relies on the hierarchy principle to determine the value of those outsourced rules. The declaration of general applicability of a CLA in Germany has been rubberstamped as a *sui generis* rule.[232] It is neither a statute nor an executive regulation and ranks below both of those legal sources. When French traditional rulemakers receive professional agreements, the received rules need to comply with established state rules.[233] The French National Bar Council's rules have to comply with hierarchically higher rules, which include statutes, executive regulations, and EU law.[234] The French hierarchy of rules poses problems that are

[226] Belgian Council of State Legislative Section (Parliamentary Documents Senate 1966–7, no. 148) 127.

[227] Ibid.

[228] Belgian Court of Cassation, no. S.98.0014.F, 5 June 2000, *Laboratoires d'analyses médicales P. R. c/ H. D. et C.N.E* [2002] *Soc. Kr.* 8.

[229] Patricia Popelier and Jeroen Van Nieuwenhove, 'Decentralisering en privatisering van wetgeving' in Jef De Mot (ed.), *Vrank en vrij: liber amicorum Boudewijn Bouckaert* (Die Keure 2012) 269.

[230] Pierre Nihoul, Marc Joassart, and Vinciane Franck, 'Le Conseil d'Etat. Chronique de Jurisprudence—2006' [2007] *Revue belge de droit constitutionnel* 322.

[231] Belgian Council of State Legislative Section, Advisory opinion no. 39.272/3 of 29 November 2005, § 5.

[232] Thomas Clemens, 'Die Verweisung von einer Rechtsnorm auf andere Vorschriften' [1986] *AöR* 100.

[233] Denys de Béchillon, *Hiérarchie des normes et hiérarchie des fonctions normatives de l'état* (Economica 1996) 512.

[234] Jean-Michel Braunschweig, 'Le pouvoir normatif du Conseil national des Barreaux une querelle enfin tranchée' [8 July 2004] *Issu de Gazette du Palais* 10.

more challenging when two rules that were created subject to the reception technique clash. The French Council of State aimed to anticipate this conundrum by requiring the minister who can extend a CLA to first verify 'whether the professional scope ... for which the extension is envisaged is not already included in the scope of another ... collective agreement extended by executive decree'.[235]

5.4 Judicial review

Third, the necessity of judicial control and protection can be derived from the existing constitutional safeguards and the rule of law.[236] As set out in Chapter 1 of this monograph, I did not consider judicial control to be an independent limit to the outsourcing of rulemaking powers, but rather a universal guarantee against the illegal exercise of rulemaking competences which equally applies to autonomous public, private, and hybrid actors. In France, access to judicial review to contest rules is accepted as a guarantee that flows from the French perspective of the rule of law.[237] The Constitutional Council explicitly recognized judicial review as a constitutional principle in 1986.[238] In Germany, judicial review (*Gerichtliche Nachprüfbarkeit*) also serves as a guarantee derived from the rule of law[239] to which all rules should be subject.[240] This principle of good rulemaking also finds its foundations in the German Basic Law: article 19, 4, first sentence proclaims that if a public authority violates any person's rights, he or she may have recourse to the courts. A denial of judicial review would result in parliamentary absolutism and would infringe the liberty of citizens.[241] In the same vein, access to the courts and judicial review is a recognized element of the UK rule of law.[242]

[235] French Council of State no. 270174 of 15 May 2006; Dominique Chelle and Xavier Prétot, 'Quid du concours des conventions collectives au regard de la procédure d'extension?' [2001] *Recueil Dalloz* 1915.

[236] *Klass v. Germany* no. 5029/71 (ECtHR, 6 September 1978) § 55 and Case C-231/15 *Prezes urzędu komunikacji elektronicznej, Petrotel sp. Z o.o. W płocku v. Polkomtel sp. Z o.o.* ECLI:EU:C:2016:440, Conclusion of Opinion of Advocate-General M. Campos Sánchez-Bordona, §§ 60–3; Geranne Lautenbach, *The Concept of the Rule of Law and the European Court of Human Rights* (Oxford University Press 2013) 101.

[237] Kaarlo Tuori, 'L'état de droit' in Michel Troper and Dominique Chagnollaud (eds), *Traité international de droit constitutionnel—Tome 1* (Dalloz 2012) 651 and 661; Laurence Calandri, *Récherche sur la notion de régulation en droit administrative française* (LGDJ 2009) 562.

[238] French Constitutional Council no. 86-207 of 26 June 1986, § 23 : 'les autres garanties résultant des principes et règles de valeur constitutionnelle et en particulier celles relatives au contrôle juridictionnel'. Catherine Teitgen-Colly, 'Les instances de régulation et la Constitution' [1990] *RDP* 229.

[239] Werner Heun, *The Constitution of Germany* (Hart 2011) 43; Karin Bieback, *Zertifizierung und Akkreditierung* (Nomos 2008) 363.

[240] Roland Geitmann, *Bundesverfassungsgericht und 'offene Normen'* (Duncker & Humblot 1971) 103.

[241] Heinrich Triepel, 'Der Weg der Gesetzgebung nach der neuen Reichsverfassung' [1920] *AöR* 456, 537.

[242] Mark Elliott and Robert Thomas, *Public Law* (Oxford University Press 2017) 391; Mark Elliott, 'The Ultra Vires Doctrine in a Constitutional Setting: Still the Central Principle of Administrative Law' (1999) 58 *Cambridge LJ* 157; Neil Parpworth, *Constitutional and Administrative Law* (Oxford University Press 2016) 44.

Below, I first compare the manner in which judicial review takes place in the countries researched. I will then juxtapose the standards of review that national courts set on outsourced rules.

5.4.1 Completion of review

As will be explained in the subsections on judicial review in relation to each of the three outsourcing techniques, administrative courts are the main reviewing bodies for rules made by autonomous public, private, and hybrid actors in Belgium and France. In addition, German administrative courts can review sub-statutory rules against higher rules or against the Basic Law through either an abstract or a concrete review mechanism.[243] Moreover, the Belgian, German, and French Constitutional Courts and Council have determined the possibility and extent of the transfer of rulemaking powers to autonomous public, private, and hybrid actors.

In the US, federal courts are competent to rule on outsourced federal rules with the US Supreme Court having rendered a number of key judgments on outsourcing rulemaking powers. UK ordinary courts equally apply a crucial controlling function to the exercise of rulemaking powers.[244] Contrary to the continental European countries studied, all judicial review in the UK occurs through a monist Judiciary in a strict sense. The courts being a foundational branch of the *Trias Politica*, their review of any rulemaking powers does not bode well for some commentators.[245] Nevertheless, there are no other actors at present to fulfil this task. There is no constitutional court and UK administrative tribunals do not have similar competences to the Belgian, French, or German administrative courts. Tribunals are gaining in importance in the UK but they can certainly not be equated to courts.[246]

Below, I further examine the possibility of review for outsourced rules in relation to the three outsourcing techniques recognized.

5.4.1.1 Delegation

Above all under domestic law, the rules made by autonomous public, private, and hybrid actors should not escape judicial scrutiny. When rulemaking powers are

[243] Susan Rose-Ackerman, Stefanie Egidy, and James Fowkes, *Due Process of Lawmaking* (Cambridge University Press 2014) 207.

[244] Paul Craig, *Administrative Law* (Sweet & Maxwell 2016) 433; Robert Thomas, 'Agency Rulemaking, Rule-Type, and Immigration Administration' [2013] *Public Law* 153.

[245] See for Ireland: Eoin Carolan, 'Democratic Accountability and the Non-Delegation Doctrine' [2011] *Dublin U. LJ* 220–52, (ii) Substantive Problems of a Partial Non-Delegation Doctrine.

[246] Alex Carroll, *Constitutional and Administrative Law* (Pearson 2015) 635–6; Mark Elliott, 'Ombudsmen, Tribunals, Inquiries: Ref-Fashioning Accountability Beyond the Courts' in Nicholas Bamforth and Peter Leyland (eds), *Accountability in the Contemporary Constitution* (Oxford University Press 2013) 236–7. Although see Edward Jacobs, *Tribunal Practice and Procedure* (Legal Action Group 2016) 7.

delegated, the constitutional guarantees of *legal recourse* face additional threats. Such judicial protection could potentially take two forms: *ex ante* and *ex post*. Admittedly, *ex ante* judicial advisory opinions do not attest to jurisdiction and judicial review in the traditional sense of the concept. Nevertheless, they emanate from independent bodies that exercise judicial control. Both types of scrutiny help to better combat the agency problems of adverse selection and moral hazard.[247] Adverse selection exists when the delegator and the delegatee do not share the same information and therefore experience opportunity costs. Moral hazard is another agency problem in which the delegatee may pursue different goals to the delegator or take more risks because the delegatee is not ultimately responsible. By giving *ex ante* judicial protection, for example through preliminary advisory opinions, the rule-drafter will receive more information on the legality of the rule (to fight adverse selection). *Ex post* judicial protection, by contrast, fights illegalities and the possible abuse of power (to counter the moral hazard).

Ex ante judicial protection in Belgium is undertaken by the Council of State Legislative Section, which advises on draft executive rules and on draft statutes for which an advisory opinion is requested. These advisory opinions are not binding but have proven to be highly influential for all types of rules. For the Executive, neglecting to request this advice will even result in the non-application of the rule by the ordinary courts and the administrative courts (article 159 of the Belgian Constitution) or the invalidation of the rule by the Council of State Administrative Litigation Section (article 14 of the Statute on the Council of State). Importantly, the most technical rules made by the Executive are also subject to the review of the Council of State Legislative Section.[248] The accessory and technical nature of outsourced rulemaking powers would thus not remove the need for *ex ante* judicial protection. However, autonomous public, private, and hybrid actors do not even have the possibility to receive any such prior counsel while drafting their rules. Therefore, these rules run the risk of violating other rules, of being drafted carelessly, or of ending up with contradictions between the Dutch and the French versions.[249]

The French Council of State principally also has the competence to subject draft rules to its advisory scrutiny. Plantey points to the fact that this *ex ante* function actually lies close to how Napoleon Bonaparte envisaged the body of the Council of State,[250] as its idea is derived from the Council of the King, which exercised a

[247] Kaare Strøm, Wolfgang C Müller, and Torbjörn Bergman, 'The Moral Hazards of Parliamentary Democracy' in Dietmar Braun and Fabrizio Gilardi (eds), *Delegation in Contemporary Democracies* (Routledge 2006) 39.

[248] Jan Velaers, *Preadvies. De wetgevingsadvisering door de Raad van State in België* (Tjeenk Willink 2000) 15.

[249] David De Roy, 'Le pouvoir réglementaire des autorités administratives indépendantes en droit belge' in *Rapports belges au Congrès de l'Académie de droit comparé à Utrecht* (Bruylant 2006) § 30.

[250] Alain Plantey, 'Le rôle du Conseil d'Etat dans la confection de la loi' in Roland Drago *et al.* (eds), *La confection de la loi* (Presses Universitaires de France 2005) 55.

legislative role under the French monarchy. Article 52 of the French Constitution of 17 December 1799 conceived of the French Council of State as a body to revise draft executive rules. Historically, the *ex ante* advisory practice of the French Council of State thus focused on the statutes proposed or executive decrees drafted by the Executive. It was only in 2008 that the French Council of State also received the power to advise on draft statutes proposed by Members of Parliament.[251] There are two main categories of executive decrees in France: 'ordinary executive decrees' and 'executive decrees before the Council of State'. The first category of executive decrees allows for the advice of the Council of State but does not force that advice upon the Executive. The second category consists of executive decrees for which the French Constitution, a legislative text, or even an executive text obliges the advisory opinion of the Council of State. If the obligation to consult the Council of State is ignored, this is cause for illegality and invalidation of the executive decree, which can be invoked by the Council of State on its own initiative in its *ex post* review.[252]

In France, much like in Belgium, no obligation, or even possibility, rests on autonomous public, private, and hybrid actors putting their draft rules *ex ante* before the Council of State. As a result, a contradictory situation was created in which traditional rulemakers face heavier *ex ante* judicial review than autonomous public, private, and hybrid actors. Certainly, when these rules touch on a fundamental right, the question arises whether a lack of 'the essential guarantee' of an advisory opinion from the Council of State is not too substantial a loss for autonomous public, private, and hybrid actors as rulemaking actors. This is all the more regrettable since the European Court of Human Rights has made clear in the past that it considers the opportunity to receive an advisory opinion of the Council of State Legislative Section to be within the procedural rationality of its balancing test.[253]

There is no Council of State in Germany, the UK, or the US that can exercise *ex ante* review. This preventive review is instead included in the preventive scrutiny to which parliamentary committees subject legislative proposals.[254]

Ex post judicial protection remains the most consequential type of review for rules in the countries researched, also when they have been outsourced.

[251] Article 39 of the constitutional statute no. 2008-724; Mariette Todorova, 'Le Conseil d'État, conseiller du Parlement: premier bilan' [2013] *Revue française de droit constitutionnel* 126.

[252] French Council of State no. 80819 of 28 May 1971, *Association des directeurs d'instituts et de centres universitaires*; Pierre Brunet, 'Les normes législatives et administratives' in Pascale, Fabrice Melleray Gonod, and Philippe Yolka (eds), *Traité de Droit Administratif* (Dalloz 2011) 521; Prime Minister and Council of State, *Guide de légistique—third edition* (La documentation française 2017) 60. However, the advisory opinion does not need to be complied with.

[253] *Garib v. Netherlands* no. 43494/09 (ECtHR, 6 November 2017) § 150. The ECtHR also takes into account the scrutiny by the national constitutional court for its procedural rationality review: *Dakir v. Belgium* no. 4619/12 (ECtHR, 11 July 2017) § 57.

[254] Mark Elliott and Jason N. E. Varuhas, *Administrative Law: Text and Materials* (Oxford University Press 2017) 681–2.

The Belgian Constitutional Court is primarily competent to review statutory rules against selected provisions of the Constitution, including human rights and the federal division of competences. At first sight, it would appear that the Constitutional Court could have difficulty evaluating the justiciability of constitutional principles inhibiting autonomous public, private, and hybrid actors when a statute outsources rulemaking powers. First, the court does not have a clear mandate to scrutinize constitutional principles, which—as seen earlier—genuinely constitute the limits on outsourcing rulemaking powers. The Constitutional Court cannot examine constitutional principles without a parallel constitutional provision.[255] Second, even if a constitutional principle benefited from a parallel provision, the court is highly deferential to the relationship between the *Trias Politica*. 'Neither … the Constitution nor … the Special Majority Act on the Constitutional Court grants the court authority to determine a violation of article 33 of the Constitution [stating that all powers derive from the nation]'.[256] Nevertheless, the Constitutional Court has found a resourceful way of including constitutional principles in its review. It does so by establishing discrimination through the previously mentioned articles 33, 105, 108, etc. of the Constitution if someone is wrongly deprived of a rule by a democratically elected deliberative assembly.[257] Rather than evaluating constitutional principles or provisions directly,[258] the Constitutional Court applies the anti-discrimination test of articles 10 and 11 of the Constitution to observe rulemaking delegation.[259]

The Belgian Council of State Administrative Litigation Section will often have the power to review rules of autonomous public, private, and hybrid actors because its competence covers unilateral administrative acts of public rulemakers under article 14 of the Statute on the Council of State.[260] However, for decisions made by certain regulators, such as the rules on tariffs by the Flemish Energy Regulator

[255] Belgian Constitutional Court no. 64/2008, 17 April 2008, B.10; Belgian Constitutional Court no. 73/2004, 5 May 2004, B.8.

[256] Belgian Constitutional Court no. 33/2014, 27 February 2014, B.10; Belgian Constitutional Court no. 6/2013 14 February 2013, B.21.2.

[257] e.g. Belgian Constitutional Court no. 86/2015, 11 June 2015, B.8-22.2–22.3; Belgian Constitutional Court no. 99/2011, 31 May 2011, B.4.2; Belgian Constitutional Court no. 94/2003, 2 July 2003, B.20.1; Belgian Constitutional Court no. 82/2007, 7 June 2007, holding 2; Belgian Constitutional Court no. 122/2008, 1 September 2008, B.4.6; Belgian Constitutional Court no. 41/2011, 15 March 2011, B.12; Belgian Constitutional Court no. 117/2013, 7 August 2013, B.36.1; Belgian Constitutional Court no. 76/2014, 8 May 2014, B.11; Belgian Constitutional Court no. 33/97, 29 May 1997, B.32.3.

[258] Belgian Constitutional Court no. 114/2007, 19 September 2007; Jan Theunis, 'Behoorlijke wetgeving in de rechtspraak van het Grondwettelijk Hof 2009–2010' [2011] *Tijdschrift voor Wetgeving* §§ 45–7.

[259] It deems itself incompetent to do so: Belgian Constitutional Court no. 114/2007, 19 September 2007, B.30.1 and Belgian Constitutional Court no. 154/2007, 19 December 2007: Jan Theunis, 'Behoorlijke wetgeving in de rechtspraak van het Grondwettelijk Hof 2009–2010' [2011] *Tijdschrift voor Wetgeving* § 42.

[260] e.g. for the CSA: Clémence Dumont, 'Le Conseil supérieur de l'audiovisuel, une autorité de régulation indépendante' [2010] *Courrier hebdomadaire du CRISP* 72–3.

VREG, the competence to annul has been assigned to the Court of Appeals of Brussels.[261]

French autonomous agencies remain subject to judicial control of their excess of powers.[262] The overarching philosophy behind this requirement is that traditional rulemakers should not be allowed to shield some of their decisions from judicial review by offloading them to autonomous public, private, and hybrid actors.[263] Initially, it was debated whether AAIs were even administrative authorities whose acts could be subject to *ex post* judicial review; however, in the *Retail* case, the Council of State put beyond any doubt that the Médiateur de la République, as an AAI, was an administrative authority.[264] The French Constitutional Council established judicial control on rulemaking acts as an additional requirement for the delegation of rulemaking powers to autonomous agencies in its previously mentioned 1986 *CNCL* judgment and 1989 *CSA* judgment.[265] The outsourced rules need to be 'subjected to a legality *control*'.

In France, administrative courts perform the annulation review of any decision made while exercising the prerogatives of public power. This applies regardless of whether the rulemaking powers were transferred by a legislative delegation.[266] There is an exception to this rule, namely when the traditional division between the administrative and ordinary courts would result in the fragmentation of a competence which the Legislature wants to keep unified and consistent (*bloc de compétence*). Often the parent statute establishing the AAI will also decide on the competent judicial body to review its decisions.[267] For example, the French Legislature entrusted the ordinary courts with competence of adjudication of all decisions of the French Competition Council, although the standard public power test would have made the administrative courts competent. The Constitutional

[261] Article 4.1.34 of the Flemish Energy Statute of 8 May 2009. Also, the federal CREG and the Brussels Brugel: Paul Bondeel, 'Over twee decennia groei en ontstane bloei: bijzondere bevoegdheden in het hof van beroep te Brussel' [2016] *TBH* 727–9; Laura De Deyne, *Markttoezicht in de energiesector* (Intersentia 2017) 107.

[262] Bertrand Marais, 'Convergence entre télécommunications et audiovisuel en France' [9 August 2008] *Gazette du Palais* 5, I.1.2.

[263] Sébastien Martin, 'Les autorités publiques indépendantes: réflexions autour d'une nouvelle personne publique' [2013] *Revue de droit public* 53, II.A.1.

[264] French Council of State no. 05130 of 10 July 1981, *Retail*, § 1; Jean-Louis Autin and Emmanuel Breen, *Autorités Administratives Indépendantes* (JurisClasseur Administratif 75, 4 April 2017) § 144; Jean-Marc Sauvé, 'Les autorités administratives indépendantes' for *Transcription d'intervention Comité d'évaluation et de contrôle des politiques publiques (CEC) sur les autorités administratives indépendantes* (Conseil d'État 2010) B.1.

[265] French Constitutional Council no. 86-217 of 18 September 1986, § 23; Bertrand Marais, 'Convergence entre télécommunications et audiovisuel en France' [9 August 2008] *Gazette du Palais* 5, I.1.2; Jean-Louis Autin and Emmanuel Breen, *Autorités Administratives Indépendantes* (JurisClasseur Administratif 75, 4 April 2017) § 144.

[266] French Council of State, 6 December 1907, nos 04244, 04245, 04246, 04247, 04248, 04249; Denis Baranger, 'Executive Power in France' in Paul Craig and Adam Tomkins (eds), *The Executive and Public Law* (Oxford University Press 2010) 224–5.

[267] Jean-Louis Autin and Emmanuel Breen, *Autorités Administratives Indépendantes* (JurisClasseur Administratif 75, 4 April 2017) § 154.

Council condoned the unification of this 'competence unit'.[268] Sometimes courts will interpret their competences broadly and establish such a competence unit. The Paris Court of Appeals, for instance, on the basis of a broadly formulated parent statute (article 2134-2 of the Code of Transports), accepted that the competence to evaluate an AAI's dispute resolution decisions could equally entail the power to review an AAI's abstract and generally binding rules, as expressed in such dispute resolution decisions.[269] Accordingly, the ordinary court claimed competence to review outsourced rules based on its competence to review an AAI's dispute resolutions.[270]

The most important French administrative court to exercise *ex post* judicial review on sub-statutory rules is the French Council of State.[271] It was not until article 9 of the statute of 24 May 1872 that the Council of State received this adjudicative power.[272] The primary role of the Council of State also applies to instances when rulemaking powers have been delegated to AAIs, because article 311-1, 4 of the Administrative Justice Code broadly states that the Council of State is competent for recourse against administrative decisions made by collegial organs with nationwide competence.[273]

The French Executive and all interested persons must have the possibility of bringing an action against a binding rule drafted by an AAI.[274] Outsourced rules that have been annulled or found to be invalid by the administrative courts have included clear-cut rules, such as the rule made by the High Authority of Health detailing the individual evaluation criteria for physicians, but without a sufficiently clear delegation.[275] Nevertheless, terminological notes with a rulemaking function have also been scrutinized.[276] Ultimately, apparent soft law—to the degree that it is imperative and determines one of the essential parameters of the regulated matter—must be regarded as adversely affecting the applicant and thus as a reviewable act.[277] As a result, even advisory opinions, circular letters, or recommendation

[268] French Constitutional Council no. 86-224 of 23 January 1987, § 15. Jean-Louis Autin and Emmanuel Breen, *Autorités Administratives Indépendantes* (JurisClasseur Administratif 75, 4 April 2017) § 154.

[269] Court of Appeals Paris nos 2014/17660, 2014/17680, 2014/17688, 2014/17695 of 17 December 2015, *SNCF Réseau*, Thomas Pez, 'Le règlement des différends et la fonction de régulation' [2017] *RFDA* 643, §§ 28 and 31.

[270] Ibid., § 28.

[271] Ferdinand Mélin-Soucramanien and Pierre Pactet, *Droit constitutionnel* (Sirey 2017) 631.

[272] Mariette Todorova, 'Le Conseil d'État, conseiller du Parlement: premier bilan' [2013] *Revue française de droit constitutionnel* 125.

[273] Jean-Louis Autin and Emmanuel Breen, *Autorités Administratives Indépendantes* (JurisClasseur Administratif 75, 4 April 2017) § 152.

[274] Clément Chauvet, 'La personnalité contentieuse des autorités administratives indépendantes' [2007] *Issu de Revue de droit public* 379, II.A.

[275] French Council of State no. 320827 of 17 November 2010, *Société Arthus Consulting*.

[276] Michel Degoffe, 'Constitution et compétences normatives économiques des "autorités de régulation"' [22 January 2009] *Issu de Petites affiches* 18, I.B.

[277] French Council of State no. 331858 of 3 May 2011; Jean-Bernard Auby, 'Autorités administratives indépendantes—Les AAI encore et toujours' [2014] *Droit Administratif* § 5; Florence Chaltiel, 'La

that produce a notable effect on a policy matter can become reviewable.[278] Administrative courts have declared themselves competent to annul these advisory opinions if they have a notable effect on the relationship between market players.[279] The time period within which a procedure needs to be initiated starts to lapse at the moment that the advisory opinion is published (on the internet).[280] French scholarship criticizes the criteria to review soft law, the application of which is often difficult to fathom.[281]

In Germany, after the delegation of rulemaking powers to an autonomous public body, the delegatee becomes a 'public authority' in accordance with paragraph 1, 4 of the Administrative Procedure Act (*Verwaltungsverfahrensgesetz* (VwVG)). However, this German administrative procedure act does not apply to the exercise of rulemaking powers (§ 9 VwVG). Nevertheless, autonomous public bodies need to respect constitutional fundamental rights; they can be subjected to state responsibility via specific parent statutes; and their rules can thus come under review by the German courts (§ 47 of the Administrative Court Code, *Verwaltungsgerichtsordnung*, VwGO).

In the UK, courts are not competent to invalidate primary legislation.[282] Secondary legislation—that can flow from legislative delegation or prerogative powers—falls within the remit of powers of judicial review.[283] Only rarely will courts strike down delegated legislation.[284] They can also declare delegated legislation partially invalid.[285] The role of UK courts within this *ex post* review is vital as access to courts is a fundamental constitutional right in the UK. Often this right will be honoured by allowing courts to review the individual decision-making powers of an autonomous public body. However, as Craig correctly stated with respect to delegation of rulemaking powers away from the traditional Executive,

recevabilité des recours contre des actes de droit souple (À propos des décisions du Conseil d'État du 21 mars 2016)' [16 September 2016] *Issu de Petites affiches* 11, introduction.

[278] Jean-Louis Autin and Emmanuel Breen, *Autorités Administratives Indépendantes* (JurisClasseur Administratif 75, 4 April 2017) § 93; Florence Chaltiel, 'La recevabilité des recours contre des actes de droit souple (À propos des décisions du Conseil d'État du 21 mars 2016)' [16 September 2016] *Issu de Petites affiches* 11, introduction.

[279] Jean-Louis Autin and Emmanuel Breen, *Autorités Administratives Indépendantes* (JurisClasseur Administratif 75, 4 April 2017) § 93.

[280] French Council of State no. 388150 of 13 July 2016, *société GDF Suez*, § 6; Pascale Deumier, 'Quand le droit souple rencontre le juge dur' [2016] *RTD Civ.* 571.

[281] Florence Chaltiel, 'La recevabilité des recours contre des actes de droit souple (À propos des décisions du Conseil d'État du 21 mars 2016)' [16 September 2016] *Issu de Petites affiches* 11, II.B.

[282] *Halsbury's Laws of England* (5th edn, LexisNexis 2010) 'Executive functions', § 10.

[283] Anthony Bradley, Keith Ewing, and Christopher Knight, *Constitutional and Administrative Law* (16th edn, Pearson 2014) 593; William Wade and Christopher Forsyth, *Administrative Law* (Oxford University Press 2014) 737, etc.

[284] Mark Elliott and Robert Thomas, *Public Law* (Oxford University Press 2017) 155.

[285] *Agricultural, Horticultural and Forestry Industry Training Board v. Aylesbury Mushrooms* [1972] 1 WLR 190; William Wade and Christopher Forsyth, *Administrative Law* (Oxford University Press 2014) 748.

'agency choices should not be immune from ... oversight merely because they assume the form of a rule'.[286] Courts, therefore, also exercise judicial review of delegated legislation. Furthermore, statutes that delegate rulemaking powers cannot be interpreted as if containing full-fledged 'ouster clauses', excluding any kind of judicial review of the delegated legislation.[287]

The House of Lords has restrictively read delegations by the Legislature to the Executive that would limit judicial review. The renowned *Anisminic* case, for example, dealt with a disputed tribunal decision on the redistribution of indemnities paid by Egypt after nationalizations of UK companies during the Suez Crisis.[288] The question arose as to whether the UK courts were competent despite the exclusion of their authority under section 4(4) of the Foreign Compensation Act 1950. The House of Lords eventually allowed judicial review even though it contravened the literal reading of the Act. The House of Lords arguably reached this flexible interpretation of a clear statutory provision by reading the statute in conformity with a right to judicial review derived from the rule of law.

5.4.1.2 Referral

Because of the differing or unclear legal value and hierarchical position of referred-to standards in the national jurisdictions, procedural questions could arise as to whether these referred-to standards are subject to judicial review.

If the first interpretation is followed, in which referred-to standards have no hierarchical value whatsoever, they themselves cannot be found illegal. They would merely be an instrument to interpret the binding law. If the second interpretation is followed, in which the referred-to standards receive the same hierarchical status as the referring rule, the standards should be subject to the same review as the referring rule.

In this latter sense, the French Constitutional Council has already scrutinized an agreement that was annexed to a statute and established a medical monitoring visit for absence from work due to illness or accident.[289] The lack of French case law and scholarship on the (dynamic) referral technique and its constitutionality still epitomizes the difficulty of portraying the nature of the judicial review that courts exercise on referred-to standards in France. The German FCC will review

[286] Recently *R (On the application of Privacy International) v. Investigatory Powers Tribunal* [2017] EWHC 114 (Admin). See in general Paul Craig, *Administrative Law* (Sweet & Maxwell 2016) 469 as also cited in Aileen McHarg, 'Administrative Discretion, Administrative Rule-Making, and Judicial Review' [2017] *Current Legal Problems* 284.

[287] *Anisminic Ltd v. Foreign Compensation Commission* [1968] UKHL 6. Mark Elliott and Robert Thomas, *Public Law* (Oxford University Press 2017) 74; William Wade and Christopher Forsyth, *Administrative Law* (Oxford University Press 2014) 751.

[288] *Anisminic Ltd v. Foreign Compensation Commission* [1968] UKHL 6. Mark Elliott and Robert Thomas, *Public Law* (Oxford University Press 2017) 74. The UK Supreme Court has not yet diverged from this case law, but has distinguished a case regarding security and intelligence: *R (On the application of A) v. Director of Establishments of the Security Service* [2009] UKSC 12.

[289] French Constitutional Council, no. 77-92 DC, 18 January 1978, § 4.

referred-to standards if a federal statute refers to them.[290] Likewise, for different types of sub-statutory rules, the referring rules will dictate the competent judge for the entire (dynamic) referral. Michael considered whether a court could annul the standard in isolation if there is nothing wrong with the referring rule itself.[291] In my opinion, it would be difficult to maintain that the referring rule is constitutional within a referral, if the *incorporated* referred-to standard is unconstitutional. Using a hyperbolic comparison, this could be equated to a patient not being dead because it was 'only' his/her donor heart that stopped beating.

The judicial review of the technique of referring to technical standards is not clearly known in the US, Belgium, or the UK. In the US, if a party has violated the underlying referring rule via a breach of the referred-to standard that party can be sanctioned by the courts.[292] However, when an agency does not receive the green light of the Office of the Federal Register to refer dynamically to a standard, but does so anyway, the courts will not accept the binding effect of that referral.[293] The Belgian Council of State Legislative Section scolded the federal Legislature for lack of *ex post* judicial protection; n a draft statute that referred to a corporate governance code in order to establish the several liability of corporate directors, no mechanism existed 'to scrutinize the content of the referred-to standard'.[294] In the UK, direct judicial review of a standard made by a private standardizing organization is not permitted.[295] It is unclear to what degree courts can evaluate private standards when a traditional rulemaker—usually the Executive—refers to that private standard in a rule.

Regardless of whether a court can directly review referred-to standards, the question arises as to whether judicial review can influence the type of referral itself, namely whether it is dynamic or static. As already encountered, the FCC addressed this issue in the *Notargebühren* case. It can avoid invalidating a referring rule that contains a dynamic referral by interpreting it as a static referral. In fact, this is just a type of teleological statutory interpretation in which the Legislature or the Executive is no longer presumed to have aimed for the (dynamic) change in the referred-to standard. Indirect support for this approach can be found in the case law of the Belgian Constitutional Court with regard to the federal division of competences:

290 Thomas Clemens, 'Die Verweisung von einer Rechtsnorm auf andere Vorschriften' [1986] *AöR* 68.

291 Lothar Michael, 'Private Standardsetter und demokratisch legitimierte Rechtsetzung' in Hartmut Bauer, Peter Huber, and Karl-Peter Sommermann (eds), *Demokratie in Europa* (Mohr Siebeck 2005) 454–5.

292 *A contrario*: Emily S. Bremer, 'Incorporation by Reference in an Open-Government Age' (2013) 36 *Harv. J. L. & Pub. Pol'y* 190–1. *Veeck*, 293 F.3d at 803–4.

293 Emily S. Bremer, 'Incorporation by Reference in an Open-Government Age' (2013) 36 *Harv. J. L. & Pub. Pol'y* 138.

294 Belgian Council of State Legislative Section, Advisory opinion no. 40.492/2 of 12 June 2006, 6.

295 Robert Baldwin, Martin Cave and Martin Lodge (eds), *The Oxford Handbook of Regulation* (Oxford University Press 2010) 115–16.

After the second Belgian state reform, health care was partly transferred to the federated entities, but the central government maintained the competence of existing 'systematic legislation' (*organieke wetgeving*'). Although this referral was not precisely directed to one statutory rule, the parliamentary preparation of the second state reform made clear that it concerned one specific piece of legislation: the 1963 Hospital Statute.[296] When asked about the extent of this concept, the Belgian Constitutional Court declared that 'systematic legislation' was not limited to the exact legislation at the moment of the second state reform.[297] This competence can change depending on the evolution of health-care management. Van Nieuwenhove correctly considers this example to be a 'dynamic referral'.[298] However, the court also meaningfully nuanced this, stating that the federal government could not 'retrieve competences that had been assigned to the federated entities' by simply amending the 'systematic legislation'.[299] The Constitutional Court thus seemingly allows for dynamic referrals but warns that it will monitor them for any abuse or transgressive use of the transferred power. It may make the original referral static if a future amendment amounts to a type of federal disloyalty. This limit set by the Constitutional Court on dynamic referrals in the federal division of competences can similarly apply in the horizontal division of rulemaking powers. Dynamic referrals would then be acceptable, but the competent court can always ascertain whether the rulemaking powers have been exercised in compliance with the intent of the transferring actor through a teleological interpretation.[300] No specific mechanisms would then have to be built in to assess the legal value of the referred-to standard. Throughout their interpretation of referring rules, judges could automatically review the acceptability of dynamic referrals.

Finally, a parallel lesson can be drawn from the UK private law referral technique in labour law. When private labour agreements refer to collective labour agreements, UK courts have assumed the competence to refuse to apply vague referrals and incorporations.[301] This nuancing practice could also give UK courts a reviewing authority when the Executive refers to privately made standards. UK

[296] Belgian parliamentary preparation Special Majority Act pertaining to the Reform of State Institutions (Parliamentary Documents Senate 1979–80 no. 434/2) 122.

[297] Belgian Constitutional Court no. 108/2000, 31 October 2000, B.1.4.1.

[298] Jeroen Van Nieuwenhoven, 'Het gezondheidsbeleid' in Bruno Seutin and Geert van Haegendoren (eds), *De bevoegdheden van de gemeenschappen* (die Keure 2017) 215–16. See, for another example of a dynamic referral in the Belgian federal division of competences in article 5, §1, II, 2nd, b of the Special Majority Act pertaining to the Reform of State Institutions: Tim Opgenhaffen, 'Het beleid inzake maatschappelijk welzijn' in Bruno Seutin and Geert van Haegendoren (eds), *De bevoegdheden van de gemeenschappen* (die Keure 2017) 341.

[299] Belgian Constitutional Court no. 108/2000, 31 October 2000, B.1.4.1.

[300] In a specifically Belgian context, it could equally be based on article 159 of the Belgian Constitution, which states that 'courts only apply general, provincial or local decisions and regulations provided that they are in accordance with the law'.

[301] *Malone v. BA* [2011] ICR 125 distinguished in *British Airline Pilots Association v. Jet2.com Ltd* [2017] EWCA Civ 20; John Bowers, *A Practical Approach to Employment Law* (Oxford University Press 2017) 31.

executive rulemakers are even sufficiently aware of the possible problematic nature of referrals in the sense that they introduce provisions on how to interpret these referrals. For example, section A4(5)(b) of the UK Building Regulations 1976 states that 'any reference to a British Standard or British Standard Code of Practice shall be construed as a reference to a British Standard or a British Standard Code of Practice published by the British Standards Institution'. The interpretation of BSI standards via the referral technique is explained in section 2 or 3 of rules such as the Plugs and Sockets (Safety) Regulations 1994, the Motor Vehicle Tyres (Safety) Regulations 1994, the Pedal Bicycles (Safety) Regulations 2003, and the Renewables Obligation Order 2015.

5.4.1.3 Reception

Ultimately, in relation to the reception of professional agreements, legal protection also deserves attention.

Ex ante, the Belgian Council of State Legislative Section does not directly review received external documents. Similar safeguards, such as those in place when traditional rulemakers create rules, can only occur using instruments through which traditional rulemakers receive or extend professional agreements. For example, the competent minister can request the advice of the Belgian Council of State Legislative Section before extending a CLA.[302] However, not every extending rule of a Legislature or Executive provokes *ex ante* review. The Belgian Royal Decree that ratifies deontology codes is not even considered to be a rulemaking instrument, which is why the Council of State Legislative Section does not assess it.[303] In France, the decision to extend a CLA by the competent minister cannot be put before the French Council of State for advice. This outcome thus differs from the Belgian situation.

Ex post, the Belgian Council of State Administrative Litigation Section may be competent to review received documents. The concerned decentralized rulemaker might pass the: (1) organic criterion; and the (2) functional criterion of being an administrative authority in the light of article 14 of the Coordinated Statutes on the Council of State.[304]

(1) If the autonomous rulemaker is public, all of its unilateral administrative acts are subject to judicial review by the administrative courts. This is the case for the rulemaking powers exercised by public professional corporations. However, as an exception. Following article 611 of the Belgian Judiciary Code, the Court of Cassation has jurisdiction to annul rules of the

[302] Article 5 of the Belgian Coordinated Statutes on the Council of State.

[303] Belgian Council of State Administrative Litigation Section, no. 105 673, 19 April 2002, *Malou et. al.*, 7; Belgian Court of Cassation 20 November 2003, no. D020028N. Juan Castiaux and Julie Alardin, *Le droit disciplinaire dans la jurisprudence* (Larcier 2014) 82.

[304] Ingrid Opdebeek and Stéphanie De Somer, *Algemeen bestuursrecht* (Intersentia 2017) 308–18.

Flemish and French/German-speaking order of attorneys for procedural irregularities, illegality, and *ultra vires* actions.[305] The Constitutional Court explicitly accepted this alternative recourse as being sufficient for judicial review.[306]

(2) If the autonomous rulemaker is private, only unilateral regulatory acts that bind third parties are reviewable by the administrative courts.[307] For example, in one case the Council of State Administrative Litigation Section determined that the Belgian health-care fee system (consisting of agreements between health providers and health insurers) is not a 'contract' but a rule. Moreover, it is a rule that falls within its review competence since it bound third parties. It could thus be invalidated whenever it violated formal or material rulemaking requirements.[308] In other cases, 'received' professional agreements can be conceived as contractual documents. Article 26 of the previously mentioned Statute on Collective Labour Agreements states that CLAs concluded by joint committees are not considered unilateral executive acts themselves, which is why the Belgian Council of State Administrative Litigation Section cannot annul them.[309] The Constitutional Court confirmed that this limitation was constitutional because the constituents maintain sufficient legal recourse due to the competence of the labour courts to review CLAs.[310]

In France, there is also reasonable clarity on judicial review against rules that have been categorized under the reception technique.

(1) The existence of AFNOR in France influences the manner in which courts can evaluate technical standards. Technical standards that have been registered but not homologated fall within the competence of the ordinary French courts. However, the decision by AFNOR to grant approval to such a private standard is administrative in nature, and interested parties can thus challenge the decision before the administrative courts.[311] Indirectly, the

[305] Article 501, 611 of the Belgian Civil Procedure Code. In accordance with article 502 of the Belgian Civil Procedure Code, a specifically described arbitration court could also receive actions against the order's rules. Frédéric Georges and Barbara Sias, 'L'élaboration de la norme déontologique de l'avocat et son contrôle' in Yves Kevers (ed.), *La déontologie contre le droit* (Larcier 2018) 39–41.

[306] Belgian Constitutional Court no. 16/2003, 28 January 2003, B.6.3.

[307] Ingrid Opdebeek and Stéphanie De Somer, *Algemeen bestuursrecht* (Intersentia 2017) 318.

[308] Belgian Council of State Administrative Litigation Section, no. 205.919, 28 June 2010, 33.

[309] See also: Jean-François Gerard, 'À propos des conventions collectives et du Conseil d'Etat' [1991] *Journal des Tribunaux du Travail* 321–3.

[310] Belgian Constitutional Court 37/93, 19 May 1993; Kristof Salomez, 'Artikel 578' in Paul Dauw, Dirk Scheers, and Bart Wylleman (eds), *Wet en duiding burgerlijk procesrecht* (Larcier 2011) artikel 578, 3rd.

[311] Jacky Richard and Laurent Cytermann, 'Le droit souple' in Christian Vigouroux *et al.* (eds), *Les rapports du Conseil d'État* (Conseil d'État 2013) 75; Lucie Cluzel-Métayer, *Le service public et l'exigence de qualité* (Dalloz 2006) 34.

administrative courts can therefore influence the legal effect of the private standard. It is highly controversial whether the private standard itself would become an administrative act after AFNOR's decision to homologate and could then equally be challenged before the administrative courts. A 1999 French Council of State decision appears to point in the direction of administrative justiciability of the homologated standard. In this judgment, the Council considered a standard that had not been granted approval as non-reviewable because it had 'no "vocation" to apply' to any other entities than those who subscribed to the standard, and thus it did not exercise 'public power'.[312] An *a contrario* interpretation of this decision would suggest that homologated standards have the 'vocation' to be generally binding and thus invoke public power. However, Cluzel-Métayer considered that such *a contrario* reasoning would go too far, based on the myriad of possible motives for homologating a standard and based on the essence of a standard which continues to be grounded in voluntary compliance.[313] The dominant scholarly interpretation in France thus maintains that the administrative court can only review the ministerial homologation decision and not the standard itself, regardless of whether the standard has been homologated.

(2) The extension of CLAs by the competent minister can be subject to a procedure for excess of powers.[314] The Council of State has even annulled ministerial extension decrees because they conflicted with free competition.[315] The refusal by a minister to extend a clause of a CLA is fully administrative and thus solely comes under the competence of an administrative judge. Parallel to the homologated standards, recourse to the administrative courts is taken against the ministerial decree that extends the CLA and not against the CLA itself, which remains a private law contract.[316] Principally, if the administrative court has a question regarding the interpretation of the CLA, the administrative court should consult the ordinary courts through a preliminary question procedure.[317] The Council of State has accepted that an administrative judge can involve manifestly clear interpretations of the

[312] French Council of State no. 189478 of 24 March 1999.

[313] Lucie Cluzel-Métayer, *Le service public et l'exigence de qualité* (Dalloz 2006) 35.

[314] Gérard Vachet, *Négociation. Convention et accord collectif* (JurisClasseur Travail Traité, 5 July 2017) § 123.

[315] French Council of State no. 230804 of 30 April 2003, *Synd. prof. des exploitants indépendants des réseaux d'eau et d'assainissement* as discussed in Michel Bazex and Sophie Blazy, 'Droit de la concurrence et extension des conventions collectives' [June 2003] *Droit Administratif*, comm. 123.

[316] Folke Schmidt and Alan C. Neal, 'Collective Labour Agreements' in Otto Kahn-Freund and BobHepple (eds), *International Encyclopaedia of Comparative Law—Labour Law* (Mohr Siebeck 1978) 69.

[317] Arnauld Noury, 'Note conventions et accords collectifs—Extension et appréciation des conventions collectives: contrôle par la juridiction administrative ou renvoi préjudiciel devant le juge judiciaire? '[29 April 2008] *La Semaine Juridique Social* § 1; Gérard Vachet, *Négociation. Convention et accord collectif* (JurisClasseur Travail Traité, 5 July 2017) § 124.

CLA in the evaluation of the extension act as an application of the principle of good *judicial* administration.[318]

(3) The French Council of State's case law that introduced judicial review of administrative acts of professional orders dates back to two milestone judgments during the Vichy regime in the Second World War: the cases of *Monpeurt*[319] and *Bouguen*.[320] The *Bouguen* case branded the competences of professional orders, through which they participated in the execution of a public service, as administrative acts.[321] That case itself dealt with a demand by the Superior Council of the Order of Physicians for a physician to close his second practice due to an order-imposed prohibition on having more than one practice. The Council of State recognized its competence to review this decision and concurred with Mr Bouguen that the Order of Physicians had acted in excess of its powers. The Conflict Tribunal (*Tribunal des Conflits*) later affirmed in the *Barbier* case (and others), the principle that even private entities could adopt administrative acts and be subjected to the competence of administrative courts when executing a public service.[322] In this case, the Board of Air France had attempted to enforce the rule that air hostesses would have their employment terminated as soon as they married. Whenever professional orders receive rulemaking powers, administrative judges will check whether the adopted rules are legal; that is, they do not counter a higher rule such as articles 34 and 37 of the French Constitution or general principles of individual freedom.[323] Just as occurs with the delegation technique, recommendations of good practice can amount to genuine 'rules' if they have a generally binding and imperative influence.[324] Rules that establish professional deontology have particularly been subject to review for excess of powers.[325]

[318] French Council of State no. 331805 of 23 March 2012; Cécile Hablot, 'De quelques observations sur l'extension des conventions collectives' [2016] *Les Cahiers Sociaux* 164.

[319] French Council of State of 31 July 1942, *Montpeurt*.

[320] French Council of State of 2 April 1943, *Bouguen*; Michel Lascombe, 'Les ordres professionnels', Doctoral thesis, University of Strasbourg (1987) 353.

[321] Disciplinary decisions, though, do not fall within this category: Benoît Delaunay, 'L'ordre professionnel, septuagénaire vaillant mais surveillé' [2013] *AJDA* 1361; Martine Lombard and Gilles Dumont, *Droit administratif* (Dalloz 2003) 91.

[322] Jean François Lachaume, *Droit administratif* (Thémis 2002) 153–5.

[323] Michel Lascombe, 'Les ordres professionnels', Doctoral thesis, University of Strasbourg (1987) 215–16; Sylvain Merenne, 'La portée du règlement intérieur d'un ordre professionnel' [2015] *RDSS* fn. 6; Marceau Long, Prosper Weil, Guy Braibant, Pierre Delvolvé, and Bruno Genevois, *Les grands arrêts de la jurisprudence administrative* (Dalloz 2013) 340.

[324] Laurence Calandri, *Récherche sur la notion de régulation en droit administrative française* (LGDJ 2009) 565.

[325] Marceau Long, Prosper Weil, Guy Braibant, Pierre Delvolvé, and Bruno Genevois, *Les grands arrêts de la jurisprudence administrative* (Dalloz 2013) 341; see, for other examples, Sylvain Merenne, 'La portée du règlement intérieur d'un ordre professionnel' [2015] *RDSS* 1042.

In Germany, private actors can also fall within the ambit of para. 1, 4 of the Administrative Procedure Statute (*Verwaltungsverfahrensgesetz*).[326] For rules drafted as a result of the reception technique, § 47 (1) of the Administrative Procedure Regulation (*Verwaltungsgerichtsordnung*, VwGO) declares that bylaws related to the Construction Regulation (*Baugesetzbuch*) can be directly reviewed by the federal Administrative Appeals Court (*Oberverwaltungsgericht*). In addition, § 47, (1), 2 VwGO continues, stating that other bylaws of the Länder are also subject to the jurisdiction of the Administrative Appeals Court if the Land's legislature provides for this. There is an incidental competence of the labour courts for CLAs. The administrative path used to be permitted for questioning the legality of declarations of general applicability.[327] However, since 2015, both direct and incidental review are reserved for the labour courts.[328]

Judicial review of privately made agreements that the British state receives is a widely discussed topic in UK constitutional law. The answer to the question of whether there is judicial review of rules of private organizations is principally negative. There is no public law remedy for contracting out public functions.[329] Moreover, the relationship between regulator and regulated, as analysed in the reception technique, is usually contractual.[330] For breaches of contract, contractual remedies are available, not judicial review.[331] Judicial review remains a public law remedy. For example, with regard to rules made by Lloyd's of London, courts have been reticent to allow for judicial review of—what they consider to be—non-public bodies.[332]

Traditionally, in relation to cases concerning sports governing bodies, UK courts have refused public law remedies precisely because of the existing consensual relationship between the sports governing body and the athlete. Most famously, the *Aga Khan* case decided on whether judicial review could annul decisions made by

[326] Because of this, the private actor will be required to respect fundamental rights and it will itself lose a considerable part of its private autonomy: Britta Beate Wiegand, *Die Beleihung mit Normsetzungskompetenzen. Das Gesundheitswesen als Exempel* (Duncker & Humblot 2007) 145; Antje von Münch, *Das Spannungsverhältnis zwischen funktionaler Privatisierung und demokratischer Legitimation* (Nomos 2014) 31.

[327] BVerwG 8 B 30.14, II, § 3.

[328] § 2a, (2) 5 and § 98 *Arbeitsgerichtsgesetz*; BAG 21 September 2016, 10 ABR 48/15 § 41; Legislative Proposal from the Government, *Entwurf eines Gesetzes zur Stärkung der Tarifautonomie (Tarifautonom iestärkungsgesetz)*, BT-Drs. 18/1558, 45.

[329] *R (On the application of Oxford Study Centre Ltd) v. British Council* [2001] EWHC Admin 207; *R v. Servite Houses, ex p. Goldsmith* (2001) 33 HLR 35; Paul Craig, *Administrative Law* (Sweet & Maxwell 2016) 840; Tony Prosser, 'The Powers and Accountability of Agencies and Regulators' in David Feldman (ed.), *Oxford Principles of English Law: English Public Law* (2nd edn, Oxford University Press 2009) 252.

[330] Clive Lewis, *Judicial Remedies in Public Law* (5th edn, Sweet & Maxwell 2014) 2-068. Although no express contract is needed.

[331] Rosmarijn Van Kleef, 'Reviewing Disciplinary Sanctions in Sports' [2015] *Cambridge J. Int'l & Comp. L.* 6–7; Clive Lewis, *Judicial Remedies in Public Law* (5th edn, Sweet & Maxwell 2014) 2-062.

[332] *R v. Lloyd's of London, ex p. Briggs* [1993] 1 Lloyd's Rep 176, DC as approved by *R (On the application of West) v. Lloyd's of London* [2004] EWCA Civ 506 and followed in *R (On the application of West) v. Society of Lloyds* [2003] EWHC 1189. Paul Craig, *Administrative Law* (Sweet & Maxwell 2016) 846.

a sports governing body.[333] Aliysa, the Aga Khan's horse, was found to have a prohibited substance in her urine after having won The Oaks. As a result, the Jockey Club disqualified the horse and rider. The Aga Khan wished to fight this decision through judicial review before the UK courts but, ultimately, the Court of Appeal ruled that the Aga Khan had no recourse to judicial review against the decision of the Jockey Club. Sports governing bodies are often established as private corporate bodies.[334] Even though a Royal Charter had founded the Jockey Club and the Privy Council had to approve its rules, the Jockey Club was not sufficiently embedded in the governmental structure to warrant a public remedy.[335] In contrast, Denning LJ urged, in a dissenting opinion in *Russel v. Duke of Norfolk*, that sports governing bodies should act in accordance 'with the rules of natural justice' when they decided on a person's livelihood, and thus triggered *ultra vires* review by courts.[336] However, this remains a minority view.[337]

One important argument speaks in favour of maintaining the refusal in *Aga Khan* to review the rules of sports governing bodies. The contractual resolution of conflicts between private regulators and the regulated (i.e. between sports governing bodies and athletes) can actually be comparable to judicial review with public remedies. Admittedly, public law remedies tend to come into effect more rapidly and are procedurally easier to invoke.[338] Nevertheless, substantively, contractual remedies are said today to ensure equivalent standards to public remedies, since any type of public law review would not supersede the mild rationality review of a decision of a sports governing body.[339]

However, the absence of judicial review has been criticized for at least five reasons. First, contractual remedies often take too long or achieve no real satisfaction given the specific nature of an athlete's career.[340] This makes it even more bizarre or even 'perverse' that contractual private law remedies are being stretched to situations in which no actual contracts have been concluded.[341] Second, transnational arbitration has become central to resolving sports conflicts. Arbitrators

[333] *R. v. Disciplinary Committee of the Jockey Club, ex p. the Aga Khan* [1993] 1 WLR 909. David Pannick, 'Judicial Review of Sports Bodies' (1997) 2 *Jud. Rev.* 152; Peter Leyland and Gordon Anthony, *Textbook on Administrative Law* (Oxford University Press 2016) 223.

[334] Simon Boyes, 'Sport In Court: Assessing Judicial Scrutiny of Sports Governing Bodies' [2017] *Public Law* 374–5.

[335] Clive Lewis, *Judicial Remedies in Public Law* (5th edn, Sweet & Maxwell 2014) 2-064.

[336] *Russel v. Duke of Norfolk* [1949] 1 All ER 109. Simon Boyes, 'Sport in Court: Assessing Judicial Scrutiny of Sports Governing Bodies' [2017] *Public Law* 364.

[337] *R (On the application of Mullins) v. Jockey Club Appeal Board (No. 1)* [2005] EWHC 2197 (Admin).

[338] Michael J. Beloff, 'Watching Out for the Googly: Judicial Review in the World of Sport' (2009) 14 *Jud Rev*. 141.

[339] Mark Elliott and Robert Thomas, *Public Law* (Oxford University Press 2017) 566; Rosmarijn Van Kleef, 'Reviewing Disciplinary Sanctions in Sports' [2015] *Cambridge J. Int'l & Comp. L.* 8.

[340] Gerdy Jurgens and Frank Van Ommeren, 'The Public–Private Divide in English and Dutch Law: A Multifunction and Context-Dependant Divide' [2012] *Cambridge LJ* 189.

[341] David Pannick, 'Judicial Review of Sports Bodies' (1997) 2 *Jud. Rev.* 153.

look to the courts for guidance wherever possible.[342] If the UK courts decline the interpretation of any public law principles with regard to sports rules, the arbitrators will primarily blindly take the wheel or follow foreign case law. The status quo, therefore, tarnishes the influence of UK legal principles in a major transnational legal field such as sports law. Third, there are plenty of examples of common law countries, such as Australia and New Zealand, with a similar legal tradition and structure that have allowed for public law challenges of decisions made by sports organizations.[343] Fourth, even the UK courts have already made an exception for some types of cases, namely when the sports organization restricts trade through its acts.[344] Fifth, the refusal to judicially review the rules and decisions of sports governing bodies does not fit well with the *Datafin* case law.[345] In this case, the claimant Datafin and another company competed to take over a third company. Datafin reproached its competitor for not having complied with the code of conduct of the Panel on Takeovers and Mergers. However, the Panel dismissed the claim, which prompted Datafin to seek judicial review. The High Court explicitly recognized its reviewing powers for decisions of private actors, such as the Panel on Takeovers and Mergers, which do not accord with the rules that they have made.[346] Companies voluntarily choose to affiliate with the Panel on Takeovers and Mergers and to abide by its rules, just as athletes choose to adhere to the rules of sports governing bodies.[347] Moreover, the functions exercised by the Jockey Club in *Aga Khan* do not appear to be less 'public' than those of the Panel on Takeovers and Mergers.[348] Sports governing bodies are thus considered a type of public–private hybrid and should trigger judicial review in that capacity.[349]

For these five reasons, it would be useful to extend judicial review to situations falling under the reception technique. In fact, the ruling precedent of *Aga Khan* would not even have to be overturned to reach that result. It may simply be distinguished from this research's main focus. The previously cited case law that

[342] Simon Boyes, 'Sport in Court: Assessing Judicial Scrutiny of Sports Governing Bodies' [2017] *Public Law* 377–8. Michael J. Beloff, 'Pitch, Pool, Rink, ... Court? Judicial Review in the Sporting World' [1989] *Public Law* 110.

[343] Michael J. Beloff, 'Watching Out for the Googly: Judicial Review in the World of Sport' (2009) 14 *Jud. Rev.* 140.

[344] Simon Boyes, 'Sport in Court: Assessing Judicial Scrutiny of Sports Governing Bodies' [2017] *Public Law* 365 and 372.

[345] *R v. Panel on Takeovers and Mergers, ex p. Datafin Plc* [1987] QB 815. More recently applied in *Panel on Takeovers and Mergers v. King* [2017] CSOH 156. Robert Baldwin, 'The Next Steps: Ministerial Responsibility and Government by Agency' [1988] *Modern L. Rev.* 627; Tom Lowe, 'Public Law and Self-Regulation' [1987] *Company Lawyer* 562–80; Tony Prosser, 'The Powers and Accountability of Agencies and Regulators' in David Feldman (ed.), *Oxford Principles of English Law. English Public Law* (Oxford University Press 2009, 2nd edition) 250.

[346] William Wade and Christopher Forsyth, *Administrative Law* (Oxford University Press 2014) 733.

[347] David Pannick, 'Judicial Review of Sports Bodies' (1997) 2 *Jud. Rev.* 152.

[348] Michael J. Beloff, 'Watching Out for the Googly: Judicial Review in the World of Sport' (2009) 14 *Jud. Rev.* 137.

[349] Simon Boyes, 'Sport in Court: Assessing Judicial Scrutiny of Sports Governing Bodies' [2017] *Public Law* 370.

refused judicial review of decisions made by sports organizations, for example, did not concern rulemaking powers. *Aga Khan*'s majority opinion rigorously studied whether the exact functions exercised were public or private. UK legal scholarship has developed a variety of possible tests to determine what constitutes public functions.[350] Whereas the disciplinary decision for doping use eventually did not pass muster as a public function, the pure exercise of rulemaking powers would be more likely to qualify as a public function.[351] Arguably, the creation of rules that bind athletes through a sports governing body's factual monopoly could be considered to be public functions and allow for judicial review. Rulemaking powers within private bodies could thus trigger public law remedies.

5.4.2 Standard of review

The standard of judicial review can be influenced when rulemaking powers are outsourced. The countries researched have different methods of ensuring judicial protection of outsourced rules.

Is it possible to distinguish a common standard of review that their courts set on autonomous public, private, and hybrid actors?

On the one hand, decreased political accountability would suggest stricter judicial scrutiny in the light of the democracy principle. The delegation of rulemaking powers to autonomous agencies by the Belgian Constitutional Court appears stricter than delegation from the Legislature to the classical Executive.[352] The Belgian Constitutional Court appears more willing to review the delegation of rulemaking powers to autonomous agencies than to the 'traditional Executive'. Some German scholarship also defends the position that the margin of appreciation should decrease for an actor that creates rules if that actor is not sufficiently democratically legitimized.[353] UK authors perceive that the intensity of the review for outsourced rules is higher than the scrutiny for rules or regulations made by a ministerial department (i.e. the Executive).[354] An increase in judicial accountability would then counterbalance the decrease of political accountability within autonomous public, private, and hybrid actors.

[350] Gerdy Jurgens and Frank Van Ommeren, 'The Public–Private Divide in English and Dutch Law: A Multifunction and Context-Dependant Divide' [2012] *Cambridge LJ* 187. Colin D. Campbell, 'The Nature of Power as Public in English Judicial Review' [2009] *Cambridge LJ* 92–6; Peter Leyland and Gordon Anthony, *Textbook on Administrative Law* (Oxford University Press 2016) 223.

[351] Clive Lewis, *Judicial Remedies in Public Law* (5th edn, Sweet & Maxwell 2014) 2-069.

[352] Daan Bijnens, Peter Schollen, and Jan Theunis, 'Behoorlijke wetgeving in de rechtspraak van het Grondwettelijk Hof 2013–2014' [2015] *Tijdschrift voor Wetgeving* 97.

[353] Lothar Michael, 'Private Standardsetter und demokratisch legitimierte Rechtsetzung' in Hartmut Bauer, Peter Huber, and Karl-Peter Sommermann (eds), *Demokratie in Europa* (Mohr Siebeck 2005) 455.

[354] Anthony Bradley, Keith Ewing, and Christopher Knight, *Constitutional and Administrative Law* (16th edn, Pearson 2014) 869.

On the other hand, through its initiative to delegate rulemaking powers to an autonomous public, private, or hybrid actor, traditional rulemakers mark these matters as often being technical or detailed, which would theoretically require lighter judicial review. Moreover, in the light of the institutional separation of powers principle, a dispersal of rulemaking powers (legislative and executive) would also demand that judicial influence is, at least, not further increased.[355] In France, an administrative judge needs to grant a large margin of appreciation to the minister and their extension of a CLA.[356] In the UK, if the outsourced rules apply as statutory instruments, they can be subjected to a two-pronged direct review: procedural *ultra vires* review and substantive *ultra vires* review.[357] If they are not statutory instruments, common law public remedies apply. There is no determined answer as to whether courts should subject these rules to a type of reasonableness or proportionality review. However, there appears to be a preference for the reasonableness test out of deference to the public body's discretion.[358]

In the US, the *Chevron* doctrine aims to clarify this matter if Congress intended to delegate (rulemaking) power to agencies.[359] First, one should verify whether Congress has spoken directly to the precise question and, if the intent of Congress is clear, give effect to the unambiguously expressed intent of Congress. Second, if the statute is silent or ambiguous on the issue, the court leniently looks for a permissible construction of the statute.[360] Especially, if no policymaking power but only interpretative rules have been outsourced, the courts should verify the 'thoroughness evident in its consideration, the validity of its reasoning, its consistency with earlier and later pronouncements, and all those factors which give it power to persuade, if lacking power to control'.[361]

Given these opposing forces, the type of the rule that is adopted seems more influential in determining the standard of review than the type of rulemaker. The more technical the area of competence, the lower the standard of review by courts generally.[362] For example, the French Council of State has limited the ambit of its scrutiny concerning technical matters,[363] such as will often be the case when autonomous public, private, and hybrid actors are concerned. At the same time,

355 Rob Van Gestel, 'Kaderwetgeving en de verstrooiing van de wetgevende macht.' [2012] *RegelMaat* 163.

356 French Council of State no. 157399 of 5 June 1996.

357 Paul Craig, *Administrative Law* (Sweet & Maxwell 2016) 454–5 and 458; Mark Elliott and Jason N. E. Varuhas, *Administrative Law: Text and Materials* (Oxford University Press 2017) 686–7; Alex Carroll, *Constitutional and Administrative Law* (Pearson 2015) 174–5.

358 Paul Craig, *Administrative Law* (Sweet & Maxwell 2016) 469; Alex Carroll, *Constitutional and Administrative Law* (Pearson 2015) 174–5.

359 *Chevron USA, Inc. v. Natural Resources Defense Council, Inc.*, 467 US 837 (1984). Cass R. Sunstein, 'Chevron Step Zero' (2006) 92 *Virg. L. Rev.* 247.

360 *Chevron USA, Inc. v. Natural Resources Defense Council, Inc.*, 467 US 842–3 (1984).

361 *Skidmore v. Swift & Co.*, 323 US 140 (1944).

362 Case C-493/17 *Heinrich Weiss and Others* ECLI:EU:C:2018:815, Opinion of Advocate-General Wathelet, §§ 115–17.

363 French Council of State no. 84878 of 16 April 1986, *Cie Luxembourgeoise de télédiffusion*.

the standard of review for rules made by autonomous public, private, and hybrid actors is stricter for compulsory competences and more flexible for discretionary competences.[364] This notion is also supported by the *Chevron* deference in the US when policymaking powers are transferred by Congress.

5.5 Representativeness

As a fourth matter, adequate 'representation' is a principle of good rulemaking to which all rulemaking actors should aspire.[365] Representativeness—albeit a difficult notion to define—has at least the potential to increase democratic legitimacy of an autonomous public, private, or hybrid actor.[366] Representativeness implies that the people making the rule act on behalf of a wider group that will be affected or bound by that rule. It is a corollary of the rule of law in a broad sense as well as the democracy principle. UK courts, for their part, protect 'as constitutional, the right of participation in the democratic process'.[367] This process can lead to the creation of rules.

Legislators and civil servants can pursue self-centred goals but, by being part of the public apparatus, they are expected to be more altruistic than private and independent lawmakers.[368] Public participation especially becomes an issue when autonomous public, private, or hybrid actors have authority to create rules.[369] Various scholars have criticized their perceived lack of representativeness.[370] By guaranteeing representativeness within the rulemaker, one defends a constitutional safeguard that is inherent to traditional rulemaking.

Direct elections, for example, can achieve representativeness. At the level of the Legislature, the election of Parliament embodies the required level of representation. The Executive also derives its representativeness either from the people (US and France) or from Parliament (UK, Germany, and Belgium). A second supportive element of representativeness is increasingly found within the

[364] Jean-Louis Autin and Emmanuel Breen, *Autorités Administratives Indépendantes* (JurisClasseur Administratif 75, 1 April 2017) § 165.

[365] Hermann Pünder, 'More Government With the People: The Crisis of Representative Democracy and Options for Reform in Germany' [2015] *German LJ* 715; Patricia Popelier, *Democratisch regelgeven* (Intersentia 2001) 290.

[366] Pierre Brunet, 'La représentation' in Michel Troper and Dominique Chagnollaud (eds), *Traité international de droit constitutionnel—Tome 1* (Dalloz 2012) 608; Clémence Dumont, 'Le Conseil supérieur de l'audiovisuel, une autorité de régulation indépendante' [2010] *CRISP* 28

[367] Lord Steyn, 'Democracy Through Law' [2002] *EHRLR* 731.

[368] Catherine Donnelly, *Delegation of Governmental Power to Private Parties: A Comparative Perspective* (Oxford University Press 2007) 93–4 and references.

[369] Susan Rose-Ackerman, Stefanie Egidy, and James Fowkes, *Due Process of Lawmaking* (Cambridge University Press 2014) 199.

[370] Clémence Dumont, 'Le Conseil supérieur de l'audiovisuel, une autorité de régulation indépendante' [2010] *CRISP* 28. For think tanks: Marc Patard, *La démocratie entre expertise et influence. Le cas des 'think tanks' français* (Dalloz 2014) 429.

Executive: this concerns the consultation of citizens or stakeholders. At the level of the Executive, in relation to delegated legislation, statutes can oblige the rulemaker to consult stakeholders. Consultation means that 'the person or body consulted should be given a reasonably ample and sufficient opportunity to state [its] views before the mind of the [rulemaker] becomes unduly fixed'.[371] If the rulemaker does not consult all relevant stakeholders, there is a risk that only experts or wealthy stakeholders have encouraged the rulemaker. Evidently, the question arises as to which part of the community needs to be consulted to the detriment of others and whether they are willing to respond.[372] Public consultation has flourished in France since the 1970s.[373] It is a crucial method for involving citizens in a decision-making process that will bind them. This also applies in Germany; however, there is no overarching statutory or other rule that requires consultation or representativeness in sub-statutory law.[374] Consultation is also an essential control mechanism for UK rulemaking.[375] Recently, in the Consultation Principles 2018, the UK government gave guidance on the centre of gravity of consultation processes.[376]

Sometimes the delegating statute will clearly designate which stakeholders the rulemakers need to consult. If the UK delegated rulemaker does not consult all of the required stakeholders, courts can declare the rule partially invalid; that is, valid for the stakeholders consulted and invalid for the stakeholders that have not been consulted.[377] On other occasions, statutes have imposed an obligation on the Executive to consult but without specifying which actors need to be involved.[378] Section 23(3) of the UK Legislative and Regulatory Reform Act 2006, for example, determines that the relevant minister has to consult 'persons appearing to him to be representative of persons exercising regulatory functions' and 'such other persons as he considers appropriate' in order to adopt a code of practice in relation to the exercise of regulatory functions.[379] This eventually led to the creation of the Regulators' Compliance Code.

[371] William Wade and Christopher Forsyth, *Administrative Law* (Oxford University Press 2014) 756.

[372] Colin Gavaghan, 'Reproductive Technologies and the Search for Regulatory Legitimacy: Fuzzy Lines, Decaying Consensus, and Intractable Normative Problems' in Roger Brownsword, Eloise Scotford and Karen Yeung (eds), *The Oxford Handbook of Law, Regulation, and Technology* (Oxford University Press 2017) 1006–7.

[373] Lucie Cluzel-Métayer, *Le service public et l'exigence de qualité* (Dalloz 2006) 301.

[374] Hermann Pünder, 'Democratic Legitimation of Delegated Legislation—A Comparative View on the American, British and German Law' [2009] *ICLQ* 371.

[375] Paul Craig, *Administrative Law* (Sweet & Maxwell 2016) 433; Alex Carroll, *Constitutional and Administrative Law* (Pearson 2015) 172–1; Neil Duxbury, *Elements of Legislation* (Cambridge University Press 2012) 78–9.

[376] UK Government Cabinet Office, 'Consultation Principles' (2012).

[377] William Wade and Christopher Forsyth, *Administrative Law* (Oxford University Press 2014) 748.

[378] Anthony Bradley, Keith Ewing, and Christopher Knight, *Constitutional and Administrative Law* (16th edn, Pearson 2014) 597.

[379] UK Department for Business Enterprise & Regulatory Reform, 'Regulator's Compliance Code', Statutory Code of Practice for Regulators (2007) 5.

Is there a common law duty for the UK Executive to consult stakeholders even if the UK Legislature has not implemented this in a statutory law? UK scholarship is unanimous in holding that there is no such general common law duty to consult stakeholders.[380] However, UK case law has induced a 'duty to act fairly' from 'natural justice'.[381] In specific and individualized decisions, the duty to act fairly will result in a duty to consult stakeholders. At first sight, this appears to exclude rulemaking powers which are inherently general and abstract. Nevertheless, the case of *Bank Mellat (No. 2)* attested to the fact that the exercise of rulemaking powers can also become sufficiently particularized as to impose on the Executive a duty to consult.[382] In this case, secondary legislation had imposed a general and abstract prohibition on doing business with one particular Iranian bank in the fight against terrorism. That bank needed to be heard or consulted to some degree, and singling it out was determined to be disproportionate and irrational.

Although autonomous public, private, or hybrid actors cannot be held directly accountable through elections, that does not mean that they should not respect the principle of representativeness when they enact general rules. Some of them, such as the French CNDP (Commission National du Débat Public), have even been purposefully founded to improve the public debate and representation of the underrepresented.[383] They will then particularly safeguard their independence and will perform consultations within the three outsourcing techniques of delegation (Section 5.5.1), referral (Section 5.5.2), and reception (Section 5.5.3).

5.5.1 Delegation

With regard to the delegated rulemaking power of autonomous public, private, or hybrid actors, the principle of representativeness consists of two pillars: independence of the rulemaker and its ability to consult stakeholders. First, the independence of an autonomous public, private, or hybrid actor and of its members is necessary to attain impartiality and in order not to let certain interests prevail without just cause.[384] It defends representativeness in a broad sense such that, even

[380] Mark Elliott and Jason N. E. Varuhas, *Administrative Law: Text and Materials* (Oxford University Press 2017) 676; Paul Craig, *Administrative Law* (Sweet & Maxwell 2016) 449; Mark Elliott and Robert Thomas, *Public Law* (Oxford University Press 2017) 147; William Wade and Christopher Forsyth, *Administrative Law* (Oxford University Press 2014) 747.

[381] *Bapio Action Ltd & Another v. Secretary of State for the Home Department & Another* [2007] EWCA Civ 1139, Sedley LJ.

[382] *Bank Mellat v. Her Majesty's Treasury (No. 2)* [2013] UKSC 39, [46]; Mark Elliott and Jason N. E. Varuhas, *Administrative Law: Text and Materials* (Oxford University Press 2017) 677.

[383] Michel Verpeaux, 'Une autorité administrative indépendante originale: la CNDP' in Pierre Bon (ed.), *Long cours. Mélanges en l'honneur de Pierre Bon* (Dalloz 2014) 607.

[384] UK Department for Business Enterprise & Regulatory Reform, 'Regulator's Compliance Code', Statutory Code of Practice for Regulators (2007) 17(9); Dina Mishra, 'An Executive-Power Non-Delegation Doctrine for the Private Administration of Federal Law' [2015] *Vanderbilt L. Rev.* 1600–1.

if not all voices are heard, a generally supported decision can be reached. Second, autonomous public, private, or hybrid actors must consult stakeholders before drafting their rules. If statutory law often imposes consultation on the Executive in order to enhance democratic influence on the decision-making process, that consideration should play a part *a fortiori* for outsourced rulemaking.[385] It pays to look for compliance with these two fundamental elements of independence and consultation.

According to article 28 of the Belgian Constitution: 'Everyone has the right to address petitions signed by one or more persons to the public authorities. Constituted bodies are alone entitled to address petitions under a collective name.' Constituted bodies are those that have been created by either the Constitution or statutes. This provision was adopted to avoid a situation in which organizations—especially trade unions—could draw up petitions without the consent of their members.[386] If Belgian autonomous public, private, or hybrid actors cannot collectively petition for legislation because the constitutional framers feared under-inclusiveness, their rules should surely be sufficiently representative. Decentralized rulemakers should therefore tread carefully with regard to the influence that they themselves experience from lobbying organizations in order to respect the constitutional safeguard of representativeness. An important means to ascertain representativeness is thus to guarantee the independence of the autonomous public, private, or hybrid actor itself.

In the delegation of rulemaking powers to AAIs in France, the representativeness of an AAI is also closely linked to its independence. Although citizens are not directly represented within an AAI, the latter needs to be independent of politics and industry.[387] As mentioned, Organic Statute 2017-54 and Statute 2017-55 of 20 January 2017 have clarified the entire legal status of French AAIs or APIs.[388]

The independence of AAIs from politics is ambiguous. On the one hand, French politics can still indirectly influence AAI policies. The democracy principle's obligation to maintain a degree of political control over an AAI has arguably inspired this influence. For example, in accordance with article 13 of the French Constitution,

[385] Paul Craig, *Administrative Law* (Sweet & Maxwell 2016) 461.

[386] Karel Rimanque, *De Grondwet gewikt en gewogen* (Intersentia 2003) 90; Jacques Sambon, 'Le droit de pétition et le déclenchement de procédures par le public: de la participation réactive à la participation proactive?' in Benoît Jadot (ed.), *La participation du public au processus de décision en matière d'environnement et d'urbanisme* (CEDRE 2004) 50 etc.

[387] Jean-Louis Autin and Emmanuel Breen, *Autorités Administratives Indépendantes* (JurisClasseur Administratif 75, 4 April 2017) § 21.

[388] Statute no. 2017-55 of 20 January 2017 *portant statut général des autorités administratives indépendantes et des autorités publiques indépendantes*; Pascale Idoux, 'Le nouveau statut général des AAI et API' [2017] *AJDA* 1115; LexisNexis, 'Publication des lois portant statut général des autorités administratives indépendantes (AAI) et des autorités publiques indépendantes (API)' [2017] 4 *La Semaine Juridique Administrations et Collectivités territoriales*, act. 70. Albeit that the various kinds of status of AAIs were already converging to some degree: Stéphanie Dubiton, *La protection des libertés publiques par les autorités administratives indépendantes, une solution démocratique?* (LGDJ 2016) 370.

the Executive appoints the members of an AAI by either a simple executive decree or an executive decree deliberated in the Council of Ministers.[389] On the other hand, French politics cannot directly steer the direction of an AAI. For example, the appointment of AAI members is in principle irrevocable according to established Council of State case law.[390] Moreover, the appointments apply for a fixed term and should, as a matter of EU-inspired[391] principle, not be renewed in order to reduce further temptations of governmental pressure. Article 7 of Statute 2017-55 allows for appointments to AAIs and APIs to be renewed only once. Finally, article 10 of Statute 2017-55 introduces a list of professional incompatibilities, which contains many public functions.[392]

The independence of AAIs from industry appears stricter, to ensure that at least some interests are not 'overrepresented'. For example, article 9 of Statute 2017-55 on the general status of AAIs prohibits any 'conflicts of interest' for the members of the AAI. Moreover, article 10 of Statute 2017-55 further prohibits members of an AAI from taking up leading positions in the companies that it regulates, or any lucrative function if they are full-time employees of the AAI. Finally, the heterogeneous composition of many AAIs, consisting of several categories of public agents, such as magistrates and Members of Parliament, but also typical expert administrators, forms a buffer safeguarding the autonomous public body from diverging from its purpose of improving the common good.[393]

It is also clear in Germany that private interests may not dominate the rulemaking process. For example, para. 342 of the Commercial Code (*Handelsgesetzbuch*) enables the Executive to recognize organizations whose functions include advising the Executive to develop or interpret rules on accounting. One major condition mentioned in the paragraph is that these organizations need to be independent (*unabhängig*). The organization that has ultimately been recognized to support rulemaking action on accounting is the Deutsche Rechnungslegungs Standards Committee (DRSC). It can be disputed whether this committee is an autonomous public body with rulemaking powers,[394] but the debate that has sprung from its so-called 'independence' is relevant to all German decentralized rulemakers.

[389] French Council of State, 'Considérations générales. Les autorités administratives indépendantes' in Renaud Denoix de Saint Marc (ed.), *Reports: French Council of State* (Conseil d'État 2001) 314.

[390] French Council of State, 7 July 1989, no. 56627, *Ordonneau*; Pascale Idoux, 'Le nouveau statut général des AAI et API' [2017] *AJDA* 1115, II A; Stéphanie Dubiton, *La protection des libertés publiques par les autorités administratives indépendantes, une solution démocratique?* (LGDJ 2016) 218.

[391] Anne Debet, 'Lois sur les autorités administratives indépendantes; quels changements pour la CNIL?' [2017] *Communication Commerce electronique*, comm. 56, 3.

[392] Pascale Idoux, 'Le nouveau statut général des AAI et API' [2017] *AJDA* 1115, II A.

[393] Jean-Louis Autin and Emmanuel Breen, *Autorités Administratives Indépendantes* (JurisClasseur Administratif 75, 4 April 2017) § 35.

[394] Definitely after § 292a HGB (which referred as an open rule to the interpretations of the DRSC) was lifted due to the transposition of the Fair Value Directive 2003/38/EG (Parliamentary Preparation Bundestag, *Entwurf Gesetz zur Einführung internationaler Rechnungslegungsstandards und zur Sicherung der Qualität der Abschlussprüfung, Bilanzrechtsreformgesetz—BilReG*, no. 326/04, 49).

Pursuant to *a fortiori* reasoning, autonomous public, private, or hybrid actors that actively participate in rulemaking should definitely be independent from industry interests.[395] As soon as they create rules (whether indirectly or otherwise), their neutrality should be guaranteed and this should be mirrored in the representativeness of the organization.[396] Otherwise, rules risk becoming the result of a private deal not of a political compromise.[397]

The independence of UK autonomous public bodies, as public regulators, was accepted as one of the Hampton Principles, which in their turn resulted in section 9.1 of the Regulators' Compliance Code 2007.[398] The independence of UK autonomous public bodies does not exclude the power of the Legislature to decide on their funding, or of the Executive and ministers to appoint their board or other members.[399] Ministers appoint most of their members on the advice of other ministers or external bodies.[400] The Financial Conduct Authority (FCA), for example, was established as an autonomous public body with delegated rulemaking powers. The Treasury appoints the majority of the members of the FCA's governing body.[401] Non-executive members of the Office of Communications (Ofcom) are appointed by the Secretary of State for Culture, Media and Sport.[402] The Secretary of State can likewise remove those Ofcom members from office in the case of bankruptcy, conflict of interest, misbehaviour, or misconduct, in accordance with para. 2(4) of the Ofcom Act 2002. Through these political appointments, there is a risk that traditional rulemakers will appoint members of an autonomous public, private, or hybrid actor to further their own political interests. In this regard, the Human Fertilisation and Embryology Authority (HFEA) has been criticized because the minister would only appoint members that adhere to its political convictions.[403] Other measures must then guarantee the independence of autonomous public, private, or hybrid actors. Concerning funding, Ofcom is partially protected against

[395] Some claim that the DRSC's independence only exists on paper. It is led by a Standardization Council. The Council consists of seven to nine members: three auditors, two industry representatives, one financial analyst, and one scientist. The members of the Standardization Council are appointed by the Supervisory Board that itself has eighteen members, all of whom are auditors, industry representatives, or scientists. Two crucial groups that are ignored in this equation are the creditors and the middle class. Lothar Michael, 'Private Standardsetter und demokratisch legitimierte Rechtsetzung' in Hartmut Bauer, Peter Huber, Karl-Peter Sommermann (eds), *Demokratie in Europa* (Mohr Siebeck 2005) 450–1.

[396] Stefan Storr, 'Verfassungsrechtliche Direktiven des demokratischen Prinzips für die Nutzung privatrechtlicher Organisations- und Kooperationsformen durch die öffentliche Verwaltung' in ibid., 429.

[397] Katrin Schwärzel, 'Die kooperierende rechtserzeugende Gewalt in der kompetenzrechtlichen, legitimatorischen und instrumentellen Krise?' [4/2007] *HFR* 5, § 11.

[398] UK Department for Business Enterprise & Regulatory Reform, 'Regulators' Compliance Code', Statutory Code of Practice for Regulators (2007) section 9.1, 17.

[399] John Alder, *Constitutional & Administrative Law* (Palgrave 2015) 351.

[400] Ian Harden, 'A Constitution for Quangos?' [1987] *Public Law* 32.

[401] Paragraph 2 of Sched. 1ZA to the Financial Services and Markets Act 2000; William Wade and Christopher Forsyth, *Administrative Law* (Oxford University Press 2014) 121.

[402] Ofcom, 'Members' Code of Conduct' (2015) section 5.

[403] Tony Prosser, 'The Powers and Accountability of Agencies and Regulators' in David Feldman (ed.), *Oxford Principles of English Law: English Public Law* (2nd edn, Oxford University Press 2009) 276.

sole governmental or industry influence because it is funded by industry while also receiving grant-in-aid from the government.[404] A degree of independence is safeguarded within Ofcom by maintaining a register of interests and through the duty of impartiality, as enshrined in its code of conduct.[405] Further obligations of objectivity and independence are overseen in an advisory fashion by a Commissioner for Public Appointment, who has likewise adopted a code of practice.[406]

In the US, independence in relation to delegation of rulemaking powers has been evaluated more stringently because of the Due Process Clause. In the *Amtrak* saga, cited previously, Congress had delegated Amtrak and the Federal Railroad Administration the power to jointly create performance metrics and standards to divide the national railways between freight operators and Amtrak's passenger transport. This was done in section 207 of the Passenger Rail Investment and Improvement Act (PRIIA) of 2008 to ensure the punctuality of trains. As mentioned, the US Supreme Court relinquished the claim that Amtrak was a private entity and would therefore not be able to receive such powers.[407] However, the US Supreme Court referred the other constitutional issues back to the Circuit Court. One year later, the DC Circuit Court struck down Amtrak's power to co-decide on those rules. Regardless of the fact that Amtrak was a governmental entity, it was also still a corporation with private interests which created independent constitutional infringements. Finally, the court concluded, 'as did the Supreme Court in 1936, that the due process of law is violated when a self-interested entity is "entrusted with the power to regulate the business ... of a competitor" '.[408] Both Amtrak and the freight operators compete for the use of scarce railway tracks and the lack of Amtrak's *independence* disrupts the equilibrium of due process.[409] Amtrak went on to decide on national railway performance metrics and standards and the US Supreme Court declined to hear another appeal on the case.[410] However, as US law

[404] Ofcom, 'What is Ofcom?' <https://www.ofcom.org.uk/about-ofcom/what-is-ofcom> (last accessed January 2019).

[405] Section 1 and Schedule to the Office of Communications Act 2002; Ofcom, 'Members' Code of Conduct' (2015) section 1, 17 and 18.

[406] John Alder, *Constitutional & Administrative Law* (Palgrave 2015) 352.

[407] *Department of Transportation v. Association of American Railroads*, 575 US __ (2015). On appeal from US Court of Appeals *Association of American Railroads v. United States Department of Transportation* No. 12-5204, 2 July 2013.

[408] US Court of Appeals *Association of American Railroads v. United States Department of Transportation*, No. 12-5204, 29 April 2016, 20.

[409] Moreover, section 207 PRIIA infringed on the Appointments Clause of article II US Constitution because those metrics and standards are effectively adopted by an arbitrator who is not appointed by the President with the advice and consent of the Senate: '... and [the President] shall nominate, and by and with the Advice and Consent of the Senate, shall appoint Ambassadors, other public Ministers and Consuls, Judges of the supreme Court, and all other Officers of the United States, whose Appointments are not herein otherwise provided for, and which shall be established by Law: but the Congress may by Law vest the Appointment of such inferior Officers, as they think proper, in the President alone, in the Courts of Law, or in the Heads of Departments.'

[410] Joanna Marsh, 'US Supreme Court ruling paves way for performance metrics for rail', Freightwaves online (4 June 2019) <https://www.freightwaves.com/news/u-s-supreme-court-ruling-paves-way-for-performance-metrics-for-rail> (last accessed May 2021).

now stands, a lack of representativeness could lead to the invalidation of the delegating and/or delegated rule.

In addition, apart from independence, autonomous public bodies should also be concerned with consultation processes. For example, EU Directive 2002/21/EC on electronic communications networks and services establishes that 'it is important that national regulatory authorities consult all interested parties on proposed decisions and take account of their comments before adopting a final decision'.[411] Consultation does not amount to a genuine hearing of the parties concerned.

The US Supreme Court held that when a relatively small number of persons is concerned, who are exceptionally affected, they have a right to a hearing, which is ordinarily not the case for the transfer of rulemaking powers.[412] In any event, section 553 of the Administrative Procedure Act (APA) imposes (broadly defined) federal agencies to provide general notice and an opportunity to participate on any proposed rule through submission of written data, views, or arguments with or without the opportunity for oral presentation.

Belgian autonomous public bodies increasingly consult stakeholders and publish these consultations on their websites. For example, the Flemish Energy Regulator (VREG), 'organizes a public consultation on the design of tariff methodology. During this consultation, all stakeholders will have at least forty-five calendar days to submit their comments to VREG. At the end of that period, VREG will publish a reasoned consultation report on this within forty-five calendar days.'[413] In its turn, the federal energy regulator (CREG) has an obligation to consult with 'market players' for the exercise of its rulemaking powers.[414]

The UK Regulators' Compliance Code 2007 also imposes a duty to consult in order to receive regulatory guidance from stakeholders.[415] Section 5.3 of the Regulators' Compliance Code determines that 'regulators should involve regulated entities in developing both the content and style of regulatory guidance'. Participation and consultation are crucial for an autonomous public, private, or hybrid actor to maintain democratic legitimacy and avoid self-service.[416] Statutory rules tend to impose an obligation on decentralized rulemakers to consult representative bodies, and UK legal scholars urge the Legislature to strengthen these

[411] EU Directive 2002/21/EC of the European Parliament and of the Council of 7 March 2002 on a common regulatory framework for electronic communications networks and services (Framework Directive), recital 15; András Sajó, 'Les autorités indépendantes' in Michel Troper and Dominique Chagnollaud (eds), *Traité international de droit constitutionnel—Tome 2* (Dalloz 2012) 346.

[412] *Bi-Metallic Investment Co. v. State Board of Equalization*, 239 US 441 (1915); *Londoner v. City and County of Denver*, 210 US 373 (1908).

[413] Article 4.1.31, §2 of the Flemish Energy Decree.

[414] Article 19*bis* of the federal Electricity Act.

[415] UK Department for Business Enterprise & Regulatory Reform, 'Regulators' Compliance Code', Statutory Code of Practice for Regulators (2007) section 5.3, 13.

[416] Robert Thomas, 'Agency Rulemaking, Rule-Type, and Immigration Administration' [2013] *Public Law* 153; Paul Craig, *Administrative Law* (Sweet & Maxwell 2016) 468.

efforts by better formalizing useful stakeholder groups.[417] Before its upheaval in 2013, the Financial Services Authority (FSA) always had to publish a draft of proposed rules 'in the way appearing to it to be best calculated to bring them to the attention of the public'.[418] This obligation now also weighs on its successors: the FCA and the PRA.[419] When these draft rules are made known to the public, they must be comprised of a notice that representations about them can be made. If the FCA and PRA eventually adopt the rule, they need to have engaged with those representations and publish an account of it. Ofcom is often also cited for its consideration of consultation processes that are not merely pro forma.[420] Its consultation round of July 2015, for example, effectively resulted in amendments of its rules.[421] Finally, the HFEA goes to considerable lengths to consult interested people in its rulemaking activities. In addition to consultation papers, it has organized online patient panels, annual conferences for stakeholders, deliberative groups, and opinion polls to supplement traditional consultation mechanisms.[422]

5.5.2 Referral

The principle of representativeness has also significantly affected the development of new rulemaking techniques such as technical standardization and referrals.

When the Legislature and the Executive refer to such standards, they make it binding on actors that have probably not been included in the drafting process. Admittedly, referring traditional rulemakers are directly or indirectly representative of the people, but they do not always grasp the full extent of their referrals. Experts from multinational companies are usually strongly represented within the bodies of standardization organizations, whereas it would be more cumbersome to find the necessary expertise among consumers.[423]

In an advisory opinion on the referral to corporate governance codes, the Belgian Council of State thus criticized the questionable representativeness of the drafters of the codes, presumably serving corporate interests above the interests of

[417] Ian Harden, 'A Constitution for Quangos?' [1987] *Public Law* 29; Douglas Wass, 'Checks and Balances in Public Policy Making' [1987] *Public Law* 195.

[418] Former section 155 of the Financial Services and Markets Act 2000; Tony Prosser, 'The Powers and Accountability of Agencies and Regulators' in David Feldman (ed.), *Oxford Principles of English Law: English Public Law* (2nd edn, Oxford University Press 2009,) 269–70.

[419] Sections 138I(1)(b) and 138J(1)(b) of the Financial Services Act 2012. Department for Work and Pensions & HM Treasury, 'Supplementary Memorandum from the Department for Work and Pensions & HM Treasury to the Delegated Powers and Regulatory Reform Committee' (2018) 3, 7.

[420] John McEldowney, *Public Law* (Sweet and Maxwell 2016) 528.

[421] Eleanor Steyn, 'OFCOM's Revised Guidelines on Fines—A New Emphasis on Deterrence' [2016] *Entertainment L. Rev.* 151–2.

[422] Human Fertilisation and Embryology Authority, 'Annual report and accounts 2016/17' (2017) 8; Tony Prosser, 'The Powers and Accountability of Agencies and Regulators' in David Feldman (ed.), *Oxford Principles of English Law: English Public Law* (2nd edn, Oxford University Press 2009) 276–7.

[423] Lucie Cluzel-Métayer, *Le service public et l'exigence de qualité* (Dalloz 2006) 30.

clients and third parties.[424] The referred-to standards should be created through an inclusive and representative process. Also, in Germany, DIN standards have been regularly criticized for a lack of representativeness. In 1987, the Federal Administrative Court held that 'one must not overlook the fact that DIN standards are agreements between interested parties that have the aim of influencing the market mechanism'.[425] UK-based private standard-setting organizations such as the IASB and BSI are also occasionally criticized for only focusing on industry interests to the detriment of consumer interest and participation.[426]

Nevertheless, proponents of technical standards primarily emphasize the inclusive process of creating standards to which traditional rulemakers will refer.[427] This concern for 'stakeholder representation' can already be found in the indirect referrals of the EU standardization process.[428] The same conclusion applies to national direct referrals. In relation to representative organizations adopting referred-to or other standards, French scholarship has defended the position that this will increase the legality and the legitimacy of that technical standard.[429] Therefore, the golden rule according to the French Ministry of Economy is that standardization organizations at least attempt to construe their standards by consensus, taking into account the advisory opinions of interested parties.[430] German DIN standard 820, which describes the procedural aspects of standardization, demonstrates that working groups, which are assumed to be balanced interest committees, prepare the standards.[431] With the aim of influencing the UK rulemakers, it is important for standard-setting bodies to safeguard the representative balance within their regulatory activity. BSI's systematic attention to the participation of all interested parties can counter UK criticism via both pillars of representativeness. Article 4.1.3 of the Standard for Standards summarizes two of the four defining characteristics

[424] Pierre Nihoul, Marc Joassart, and Vinciane Franck, 'Le Conseil d'Etat. Chronique de Jurisprudence—2006' [2007] *Revue belge de droit constitutionnel* 322.

[425] Bundesverwaltungsgericht 22 May 1987 (BverwGE 77, 285, 291).

[426] Walter Mattli, 'Private Transnational Governance' in Jacob Katz Cogan, Ian Hurd, and Ian Johnstone (eds), *The Oxford Handbook of International Organizations* (Oxford University Press 2016) 177–9; Robert Baldwin, Martin Cave, and Martin Lodge (eds), *The Oxford Handbook of Regulation* (Oxford University Press 2010) 114 and 115; Mislav Mataija, *Private Regulation and the Internal Market: Sports, Legal Services, and Standard Setting in EU Economic Law* (Oxford University Press 2016) 248–9.

[427] Delphine Misonne, 'La normalisation technique' in Philippe Gerard, François Ost, Michel Van de Kerchove, Isabelle Hachez, Yves Cartuyvels, and Hugues Dumont (eds), *Les sources du droit revisitées—Tôme I* (Anthemis 2012) 506–7.

[428] Article 5 of Regulation (EU) No. 1025/2012 of the European Parliament and of the Council on European Standardisation.

[429] Franck Gambelli, 'Définitions et typologies des normes techniques' [11 February 1998] *Issu de Petites affiches* 5, 1.1.

[430] Ministère de l'économie, de l'industrie et de l'emploi, *Guide relatif a la bonne utilisation des normes dans la reglementation* (direction générale de la compétitivité, de l'industrie et des services 2009) 7. See also Joan Le Goff and Stéphane Onnée, *Puissance de la norme. Défis juridiques et managétiaux des systèmes normatifs contemporains* (EMS 2017) 119.

[431] Harm Schepel, *The Constitution of Private Governance: Product Standards in the Regulation of Integrating Markets* (Hart 2005) 114.

of British standards: they need to be made by independently balanced and broadly representative standing committees that reach agreement by consensus, and they need to be made subject to unrestricted open consultation.[432] Before adopting a standard, it will ordinarily publish a draft standard that is open for comment from the general public for six to eight weeks.[433]

5.5.3 Reception

With regard to the reception technique, professional agreements will occasionally be required to obtain final approval from a traditional rulemaker.[434] Through this consent, the Legislature or the Executive assumes responsibility for the rule.[435] For example, in Belgium, France, and Germany a member of the Executive must agree to an extended CLA. Approval does not diminish the autonomy of the autonomous public, private, or hybrid actor itself; it merely influences the freedom of the decentralized rulemaker to exercise its autonomy.[436] The German Minister of Labour cannot amend the content or the duration of a CLA. He or she can only decide whether or not to declare the CLA generally binding.[437] In the same vein, the competent Belgian and French ministers cannot cherry-pick the content of an extended CLA.[438] The representativeness of received agreements can thus not be entirely absorbed based on ratifications by traditional rulemakers.

Furthermore, the required level of representation should already be present at the source at which the agreements are being made. Professional orders and sports federations inherently consist of the members to which their rules apply because membership is required in order to exercise the profession or to participate in a sporting event.[439] Given the homogeneous nature of professional groups and

[432] BSI Group, 'A standard for standards—Principles of standardization. Standard 0' (2016) 7. See also 7.1 and article 5.8 for the specific protection of representative balancing and consultation respectively. More in general: Harm Schepel, *The Constitution of private Governance: Product Standards in the Regulation of Integrating Markets* (Hart 2005) 124–6.

[433] Peter Marburger, 'Legal and Organizational Aspects of Technical Standardization at the National and European Level' in K. H. Lindackers (ed.), *Safety Aspects of Technical Standards* (Springer 1992) 202.

[434] Alfred G. Debus, *Verweisungen in Deutschen Rechtsnormen* (Duncker & Humblot 2008) 199.

[435] Hermann Pünder, 'Democratic Legitimation of Delegated Legislation—A Comparative View on the American, British and German Law' [2009] *ICLQ* 353. The consent may also be required within the delegation to private actors: Britta Beate Wiegand, *Die Beleihung mit Normsetzungskompetenzen. Das Gesundheitswesen als Exempel* (Duncker & Humblot 2007) 219.

[436] Gerhard Leibholz and Hans Justus Rinck, *Grundgesetz für die Bundesrepublik Deutschland* (Otto Schmidt 1971) 623.

[437] Florian Becker, *Kooperative und konsensuale Strukturen in der Normsetzung* (Mohr Siebeck 2005) 438.

[438] Arnauld Noury, 'Note conventions et accords collectifs—Extension et appréciation des conventions collectives: contrôle par la juridiction administrative ou renvoi préjudiciel devant le juge judiciaire?' [29 April 2008] *La Semaine Juridique Social* § 1; Articles 28–34 of the Belgian CLA Statute of 5 December 1968.

[439] Michel Lascombe, 'Les ordres professionnels', Doctoral thesis, University of Strasbourg (1987) 144; Denys de Béchillon, *Hiérarchie des normes et hiérarchie des fonctions normatives de l'état* (Economica 1996) 505.

associations that partake in these rulemaking processes, it appears democratically desirable to allow them to decide on their rules themselves.[440] The majority rule of the entire federation in Parliament may then not be best equipped to deal with the particular issues:[441] this can be seen as an application of the subsidiarity principle.[442]

The Belgian Constitutional Court determined that 'whenever a statute invokes the concept of a representative organization of a category of persons, the notion of representativeness means that the positions taken by the organization are deemed to represent those of the represented'.[443] The Belgian Council of State Legislative Section requires private lawmakers—whose documents will receive third-party binding force after ratification or extension by the Executive—to be sufficiently representative of the people who the rule will bind.[444] For example, when two large groups in society with diverging interests bargain over a collective agreement, such as consumers and sellers[445] or employers and employees,[446] this raises 'essential concerns' with the Council with regard to the 'representativeness of the organizations'. This requirement also exists for professional organizations that make rules for their members.[447]

In France, AFNOR consults stakeholders, including consumers, before homologating a technical standard. However, the Director General ultimately decides whether to homologate a private standard, principally accepting majority support.[448] CLAs can only be extended if their drafters were sufficiently representative of the parties that would be bound by the original or extended CLA. Parity commissions have to conclude these CLAs.[449] The origin of these commissions dates back to the Treaty of Versailles of 1918 and the foundation of the International Labour Organization. Article 133-1 of the French Labour Code establishes that

440 Thomas Holzner, *Konsens im Allgemeinen Verwaltungsrecht und in der Demokratietheorie* (Mohr Siebeck 2016) 177; Fritz Ossenbühl, 'Gesetz und Recht—Die Rechtsquellen im demokratischen Rechtsstaat' in Josef Isensee and Paul Kirchhof (eds), *Handbuch des Staatsrechts der Bundesrepublik Deutschland*, vol. V (Beck 2005) 160; see also: Florian Becker, *Kooperative und konsensuale Strukturen in der Normsetzung* (Mohr Siebeck 2005) 380–1.

441 Werner Heun, *Das Mehrheitsprinzip in der Demokratie* (Duncker & Humblot 1983) 214.

442 Gregor Bachmann 'Ziele, Prinzipien und Auslegung des Kodex' in Thomas Kremer, Gregor Bachmann, Marcus Lutter, and Axel von Werder (eds), *Kommentar Deutscher Corporate Governance Kodex* (Beck 2016) 32.

443 Belgian Constitutional Court no. 33/97, 29 May 1997, B.2.5.1.

444 Belgian Council of State Legislative Section, Advisory opinion no. 39.272/3 of 29 November 2005, § 6.

445 Belgian Council of State Legislative Section, Advisory opinion no. 40.116/1 of 20 April 2006, § 2.

446 Belgian Council of State Legislative Section, Advisory opinion 18 November 1966 (Parliamentary Documents Senate 1966–7, no. 148) 93; Patricia Popelier, *Democratisch regelgeven* (Intersentia 2001) 247.

447 Belgian Council of State Legislative Section, Advisory opinion no. 54.536/2/2 of 19 December 2013, § 7.3.

448 Lucie Cluzel-Métayer, *Le service public et l'exigence de qualité* (Dalloz 2006) 30; France Normalisation, *Règles pour la normalisation française* (Electronic Source October 2017) 54.

449 Gérard Vachet, *Négociation. Convention et accord collectif* (JurisClasseur Travail Traité, 5 July 2017) § 91.

representative organizations of employees and representative organizations of employers need to conclude CLAs.[450] Article 133-2 of the Labour Code lists a number of requirements for an organization of employees to be recognized as representative: a considerable number of effective members, independence, membership fees, experience or age, and patriotic attitude.[451]

Legal scholarship has especially criticized the last criterion for being outdated and judges have added other criteria, such as the number of non-member employees affected.[452] Article L 2151-1 of the Labour Code, for its part, enumerates the criteria for an organization of employers to negotiate CLAs. They need to be representative, independent, financially transparent, and have existed for two years within the relevant professional or geographic area. More precisely, the companies that constitute the organization of employers must represent a minimum of 8 per cent of all companies that belong to professional organizations of employers of the relevant professional branch.[453] According to article 2261-19 of the Labour Code, after the valid conclusion of a CLA, it may not be extended if one or more employers—who combined employ 50 per cent of all employees of the employers represented within the relevant professional branch—object.[454]

Another safeguard that increases the representative input for extended CLAs is the mandatory advisory opinion of the National Commission for Collective Negotiation (*Commission nationale de la négociation collective*), which consists of labour unions.[455] The competent minister needs to request this advisory opinion before he or she can extend the CLA even though the content of the advice itself is not binding.[456]

As a German example of the reception technique, Weisel denounces the transfer, within § 112 Social Code V, of rulemaking powers to health insurance organizations and hospital organizations because the resulting rules are applicable to hospitals, *regardless of their membership* of the hospital organization.[457] German scholarship also warns of a blinkered view (*verengtes Staatsdenken*). The

[450] Cécile Hablot, 'De quelques observations sur l'extension des conventions collectives'[2016] *Les Cahiers Sociaux* 164; Gérard Vachet, *Négociation. Convention et accord collectif* (JurisClasseur Travail Traité, 5 July 2017) § 92.

[451] Guillaume Tusseau, 'À propos de la représentativité syndicale' [1 July 2005] *Issu de Revue du droit public* 919, I.A.2.

[452] Ibid., I.B.1.

[453] Gérard Vachet, *Négociation. Convention et accord collectif* (JurisClasseur Travail Traité, 5 July 2017) § 93.

[454] Cécile Hablot, 'De quelques observations sur l'extension des conventions collectives' [2016] *Les Cahiers Sociaux* 164, Gérard Vachet, *Négociation. Convention et accord collectif* (JurisClasseur Travail Traité, 5 July 2017) § 98.

[455] Arnauld Noury, 'Note conventions et accords collectifs—Extension et appréciation des conventions collectives: contrôle par la juridiction administrative ou renvoi préjudiciel devant le juge judiciaire?' [29 April 2008] *La Semaine Juridique Social* 1278; Gérard Vachet, *Négociation. Convention et accord collectif* (JurisClasseur Travail Traité, 5 July 2017) § 110.

[456] French Council of State no. 60311 of 20 February 1987.

[457] Klaus Weisel, *Das Verhältnis von Privatisierung und Beleihung* (Nomos 2003) 173.

professional organizations often lack diversity. The FCC has emphasized the importance of representative membership of the decentralized rulemaker, especially with regard to CLAs.[458] Not all those represented appear to be meaningfully represented in the decision-making process because the application of their rules extends beyond the members of the group at the time of creating the private agreement.[459] In the light of this, it must be reiterated that representative organizations receive more powers within the rulemaking process in Germany because their primary goal is to defend certain fundamental rights, such as the labour right or the freedom of profession. However, even from this perspective, the sword cuts both ways. It is especially relevant that these professional actors are sufficiently representative, because their rules will almost inherently encroach on the fundamental right to labour or the freedom of profession of the non-represented citizens subject to the rule.[460]

With regard to sports governing bodies, it was suggested that the UK should organize sports collective bargaining such as that found in US major league sports. Apart from the argument that it would enhance the power of athletes, this can be seen as an impetus to improve the 'balance of interests' within sports governing bodies by giving athletes a stronger voice.[461]

5.6 Efficiency or effectiveness

As a fifth matter, rulemakers and rules should be efficient and effective when exercising outsourced rulemaking powers. Something is efficient if, considering the available means, the goal is approached in the best way. The principle of efficiency has been described as the maximum result for minimum effort.[462] Efficiency is a concern for the optimization of time and resources, which should motivate the exercise of state powers. Something is effective if it reaches its goal.[463] There

[458] BVerfG 44, 322, § 74; Britta Beate Wiegand, *Die Beleihung mit Normsetzungskompetenzen. Das Gesundheitswesen als Exempel* (Duncker & Humblot 2007) 171.

[459] Reinhard Hendler, 'Das Prinzip Selbstverwaltung' in Josef Isensee and Paul Kirchhof (eds), *Handbuch des Staatsrechts der Bundesrepublik Deutschland*, vol. IV (Beck 2005) 1217; Michael Sachs, 'Artikel 20 GG' in Michael Sachs, *Grundgesetz Kommentar* (Beck 2011) 801; see, for comparable reasoning: Matthias Herdegen, 'Informalisierung und Entparlamentarisierung politischer Entscheidungen als Gefährdungen der Verfassung' [2003] *VVDStRL* 18.

[460] BVerfG 33, 125, § 123; Christoph Degenhart, *Staatsorganisationsrecht* (Müller 2013) 137; Fritz Ossenbühl, 'Satzung' in Josef Isensee and Paul Kirchhof (eds), *Handbuch des Staatsrechts der Bundesrepublik Deutschland*, vol. V (Beck 2005) 366. The freedom of association of the rulemaking actor itself may be limited because of its exercise of state authority (Florian Becker, *Kooperative und konsensuale Strukturen in der Normsetzung* (Mohr Siebeck 2005) 563).

[461] Simon Boyes, 'Sport in Court: Assessing Judicial Scrutiny of Sports Governing Bodies' [2017] *Public Law* 374–5.

[462] Alexandre Flückiger, 'L'évaluation législative ou comment mesurer l'efficacité des lois' [2007] *Revue européenne des sciences sociales* 85.

[463] Karen Yeung, *Securing Compliance—A Principled Approach* (Hart 2004) 30.

is a general sense that to defend the legal system and its exercise of authority, rulemakers or their rules need to be monitored so that they are effective.[464] Actors should primarily be *efficient* and create *effective* rules. However, the scholarly distinction between efficiency and effectiveness is not clearly maintained in the countries studied, which is why I discuss them as one combined principle of good rulemaking.

In France, effectiveness applies as a quality guarantee within the rule of law.[465] Although it has not yet been enshrined in the French Constitution, as is the case in article 170 of the Swiss Constitution, the principle has increasingly been attributed with a legal meaning.[466] The Swiss constitutional provision posits that: 'the Federal Assembly shall ensure that federal measures are evaluated with regard to their effectiveness'. A proposed similar constitutional amendment in France to article 34, 1 of the French Constitution, which would constitutionalize the safeguard of effectiveness, eventually failed.[467] Efficiency is also a recognized constitutional principle in Germany.[468] Its recognition rests on two main pillars. First, the German administration is bound to a diligence principle.[469] Diligence cannot be reached without striving for efficiency. An efficient rulemaker not only focuses on the result, but also on the manner in which that result is reached. After all, tax revenue funds its operations.[470] Second, every time a rule limits human rights, the effectiveness of that rule will come under scrutiny.[471] From a law and economics point of view, the proportionality test—to which many human rights violations will eventually boil down—is actually a balancing of economic efficiency and effectiveness.[472]

Other principles, such as transparency and representativeness, strongly connect to efficiency. It would prove to be inefficient to rule through inaccessible or

[464] Rob van Gestel, 'The Deparliamentarisation of Legislation: Framework Laws and the Primacy of the Legislature' (2013) 9 *Utrecht L. Rev.* 122.

[465] Pierre Albertini, 'Pour une revalorisation de la loi' in Pierre Albertini, *La qualité de la loi* (Mare & Martin 2016) 277; Alexandre Flückiger, 'L'évaluation législative ou comment mesurer l'efficacité des lois' [2007] *Revue européenne des sciences sociales* 88; Jacques Chevalier, 'Autorités administratives indépendantes et État de droit' [2016] *Civitas Europa* 146.

[466] Alexandre Flückiger, L'évaluation législative ou comment mesurer l'efficacité des lois [2007] *Revue européenne des sciences sociales* 86. Article 170 of the Swiss Constitution: 'The Federal Assembly shall ensure that federal measures are evaluated with regard to their effectiveness.'

[467] Alexandre Flückiger, L'évaluation législative ou comment mesurer l'efficacité des lois' [2007] *Revue européenne des sciences sociales* 88.

[468] Thomas Mann, 'Artikel 80 GG' in Michael Sachs (ed.), *Grundgesetz Kommentar* (Beck 2011) 1637.

[469] Chris Backes, Mariolina Eliantonio, and Sander Jansen, 'Conclusions' in Chris Backes, Mariolina Eliantonio, and Sander Jansen (eds), *Quality and Speed in Administrative Decision-Making: Tension or Balance?* (Intersentia 2016) 168.

[470] Jörn Kruse, 'Unabhängige Staatliche Institutionen' in Theresia Theurl (ed.), *Unabhängige staatliche Institutionen in der Demokratie* (Duncker & Humblot 2013) 61.

[471] Chris Backes, Mariolina Eliantonio, and Sander Jansen 'Conclusions' in Chris Backes, Mariolina Eliantonio, and Sander Jansen (eds), *Quality and Speed in Administrative Decision-Making: Tension or Balance?* (Intersentia 2016) 168.

[472] Aurelien Portuese, 'Principle of Proportionality as Principle of Economic Efficiency' [2013] *Eur. LJ* 612.

incomprehensible rules or to let biased entities create the rules.[473] Furthermore, global scholarship has accused autonomous public, private, or hybrid actors of primarily choosing the side of industry over public support, because industry is organized in the most consistent and reliable manner.[474] This mutual disconnect between the rulemaker and those subject to the rule can only last for a limited period before the loss in other principles of good rulemaking, such as representativeness and transparency, outweighs economic gains. Nevertheless, the following overview shows that traditional rulemakers install safeguards to ensure efficiency as an *autonomous principle* when outsourcing rulemaking powers. A perceived lack of efficiency may thus very well be one of the main reasons to outsource any type of powers.[475]

Autonomous public, private, or hybrid actors may influence the efficiency and effectiveness of the rules they make, depending on the specific technique by which they were given: delegation (Section 5.6.1), referral (Section 5.6.2), or reception (Section 5.6.3).

5.6.1 Delegation

The New Public Management movement, which reignited the delegation of rulemaking powers to autonomous public bodies in the UK, centres around three pillars, all starting with the letter 'e': economy of resources, efficiency, and effectiveness.[476] Section 8 of the Public Bodies Act 2011 arguably best identifies the ever-present focus on efficiency and effectiveness when delegating rulemaking powers to autonomous public bodies. Through an executive order, ministers are competent to amend the status of bodies located at arm's length but they can only do so if it improves 'efficiency, effectiveness and economy, . . .'. Prominent UK legal scholars, such as Craig, have rightly elected to dedicate a title of their work on the efficiency and effectiveness of public regulators.[477] Moreover, with regard to the protection of representativeness when delegating rulemaking powers to them, I have

[473] Laurence Calandri, *Récherche sur la notion de régulation en droit administrative française* (LGDJ 2009) 495; Guillaume Dezobry, 'L'indépendance des autorités de régulation économique à l'égard des opérateurs régulés' [2012] *Revue française d'administration publique* 648; Gabriel Eckert, 'L'indépendance des autorités de régulation économique à l'égard du pouvoir politique' [2012] *Revue française d'administration publique* 631.

[474] Marver H. Bernstein, *Regulating Business by Independent Commission* (Princeton University Press 1966) 144.

[475] Bertrand Mathieu, 'La crise de la démocratie représentative: constat et éléments d'explication' [2015] *Constitutions* 317, I; Stéphanie Dubiton, *La protection des libertés publiques par les autorités administratives indépendantes, une solution démocratique?* (LGDJ 2016) 366–967.

[476] Gavin Drewry and Philip Giddings, 'The Origins of the Next Steps Programme' in Philip Giddings (ed.), *Parliamentary Accountability. A Study of Parliament and Executive Agencies* (Palgrave Macmillan 1995) 5; Adam Tomkins, 'The Struggle to Delimit Executive Power in Britain' in Paul Craig and Adam Tomkins (eds), *The Executive and Public Law* (Oxford University Press 2010) 23.

[477] Paul Craig, *Administrative Law* (Sweet & Maxwell 2016) 94–5.

already referred to the Hampton Principles, which were eventually enshrined in the Regulators' Compliance Code 2007. Section 9 of the Code provides that 'regulators should be accountable for the efficiency and effectiveness of their activities'.[478] Subsequently, the Code states that regulators need to consider 'costs [and] effectiveness'.[479] Ultimately, the Code prescribes to the continuous review and improvement of risk methodologies.[480] All safeguards enshrined in the Regulators' Compliance Code are expected to lead eventually to more efficiency and effectiveness within the public regulators.[481]

Criticism of rulemaking powers exercised by autonomous public bodies often departs from a perceived lack of efficiency. Efficiency losses may occur indirectly. A joint memorandum of the UK civil service warned of the damaging influence of hiving off governmental functions on the morale of the civil service or on industrial relations.[482] The decrease in efficiency might also be directly attributed to the suboptimal performance of an autonomous regulator. Not every transfer of rulemaking powers automatically increases rulemaking efficiency if there is insufficient precaution.[483] For example, this criticism was uttered in respect of the UK Civil Aviation Authority.[484] The French Senate even aimed to cancel HADOPI, which was an autonomous public body concerned with the Distribution and Protection of Intellectual Property on the Internet, because 'it had not brought the proof of efficiency of [an adopted mechanism]'.[485]

Since legal scholarship disagrees on the question of whether transferring rulemaking powers to autonomous public, private, or hybrid actors increases rulemaking efficiency, the Legislature and the Executive should structurally check their performance and efficiency. Through diverse methods, regulators could be made to understand the benefits and costs of their actions.[486]

At least three measures could be introduced in order to review the efficiency of the rules made by independent regulators. First, as previously discussed, the Executive can ordinarily appoint the members of the regulator such that the most

[478] UK Department for Business Enterprise & Regulatory Reform, 'Regulators' Compliance Code', Statutory Code of Practice for Regulators (2007) section 9, 17.

[479] Ibid., section 3.1, 11.

[480] Ibid., section 4.5, 13.

[481] Ibid., 5.

[482] Gavin Drewry and Philip Giddings, 'The Origins of the Next Steps Programme' in Philip Giddings (ed.), *Parliamentary Accountability. A Study of Parliament and Executive Agencies* (Palgrave Macmillan 1995) 5.

[483] András Sajó, 'Les autorités indépendantes' in Michel Troper and Dominique Chagnollaud (eds), *Traité international de droit constitutionnel—Tome 2* (Dalloz 2012) 358.

[484] Robert Baldwin, 'The Next Steps: Ministerial Responsibility and Government by Agency' [1988] *Modern L. Rev.* 624.

[485] Xavier Bioy *et al.*, 'Autorités administratives indépendantes et libertés fondamentales (Janvier–juin 2016)' [14 December 2016] *Issu de Petites affiches* 4, I.A.2.

[486] Margherita Pieraccini and Emma Cardwell, 'Impact Assessments for Nature Conservation: Effective and Reflexive?' [2016] *Public Law* 93; Elizabeth Fisher, 'Transparency and Administrative Law: A Critical Evaluation' [2010] *Current Legal Problems* 271–2.

experienced and knowledgeable people are given the decisive power.[487] Second, a more general type of scrutiny of efficiency can be exercised by reviewing the accounts or the annual report of an independent regulator.[488] However, these two measures focus on the efficiency of regulators and only indirectly on the effectiveness of their rules. Therefore, third, the most promising method to keep abreast of the effectiveness of the rules occurs through regulatory impact assessments (RIAs),[489] which bridge the gap between decision-making deliberation and the economic outcomes of the regulation.[490]

Conceptually, RIAs have met with criticism because they imply monitoring and supervising costs and could thus, paradoxically, make general regulatory activities less efficient.[491] Content-wise, multiple shortcomings have been attributed to RIAs, such as the fact that rulemakers consider RIAs as instruments for which they merely have to tick boxes.[492] RIAs generally do not push rulemakers to investigate alternatives to their envisaged plans, despite Cabinet guidelines on the review of public bodies urging them to do so.[493] Consequently, the UK Regulatory Policing Committee was created to advise on the compliance of RIAs with the guidance created in the Treasury's Green Book and the Better Regulation Framework concerning the evidence presented and the quality of analysis.[494] In this context, it is crucial to conclude that an RIA is not an additional justification to explain why a certain rule is adopted, but rather a genuine and neutral analysis of the consequences of said rule.[495]

While these RIAs have existed for some time now, 'techniques such as performance indicators and forms of regulatory impact assessments are relatively new'.[496] In France, article 8 of Organic Statute 2009-403 of 15 April 2009, describes for the Executive the necessity of putting before the Council of State the estimated impact

[487] Jean-Louis Autin and Emmanuel Breen, *Autorités Administratives Indépendantes* (JurisClasseur Administratif 75, 4 April 2017) § 35.

[488] Pierre de Montalivet, 'Constitution et autorités de régulation' [2014] *Revue de droit public* 316, I.B.2.

[489] Anne-Sophie Denolle, 'Les études d'impact: une révision manquée?' [2011] *Revue française de droit constitutionnel* 503.

[490] Margherita Pieraccini and Emma Cardwell, 'Impact Assessments for Nature Conservation: Effective and Reflexive?' [2016] *Public Law* 97.

[491] Catherine Donnelly, *Delegation of Governmental Power to Private Parties: A Comparative Perspective* (Oxford University Press 2007) 82 and 102; Margherita Pieraccini and Emma Cardwell, 'Impact Assessments for Nature Conservation: Effective and Reflexive?' [2016] *Public Law* 110.

[492] Ibid.; Rob van Gestel and Marie-Claire Menting, '*Ex Ante* Evaluation and Alternatives to Legislation: Going Dutch?' [2011] *Statute L. Rev.* 214 and 223. In the Netherlands, they therefore use an alternative method, namely the Integrated Framework for Policy Analysis and Legislation, yet this has also not been deemed to be sufficient by the OECD. Ibid., 209.

[493] Paul Craig, *Administrative Law* (Sweet & Maxwell 2016) 95.

[494] Margherita Pieraccini and Emma Cardwell, 'Impact Assessments for Nature Conservation: Effective and Reflexive?' [2016] *Public Law* 95–6.

[495] Anne-Sophie Denolle, 'Les études d'impact: une révision manquée?' [2011] *Revue française de droit constitutionnel* 511.

[496] Elizabeth Fisher, 'Transparency and Administrative Law: A Critical Evaluation' [2010] *Current Legal Problems* 287.

of the end product of the proposed legislation on the national legal order, as well as the financial, economic, social, environmental, and employment consequences.[497] Equally, for delegations in Germany, relevant RIAs could achieve increased efficiency. These RIAs in Germany are prescribed for statutes, executive regulations, and rules of municipalities.[498] The phenomenon of RIAs, also widespread in Belgian legislatures, ensures that the whims of politics are counterbalanced by economic sanity. On the Belgian federal level, only draft statutes or royal decrees negotiated by the Council of Ministers should be subject to RIAs.[499] On the federated entity level, in Flanders at the end of 2018, the Flemish government unfortunately decided to suspend the system of RIAs for the foreseeable future.[500]

The question arose whether rules made by autonomous public bodies were also subject to the obligation to make RIAs. The French Prime Minister declared that any rule which places additional burdens on companies must be subject to an RIA.[501] Nevertheless, Belgian, French, and German autonomous public, private, or hybrid actors are not under a general obligation to draft RIAs. This is remarkable since autonomous public bodies, such as the Belgian Institute for Post and Telecommunications (BIPT-IBPT), sometimes perform RIAs of legislative or executive rules.[502] In UK legal practice, we can distinguish multiple examples of regulators exercising rulemaking powers that are under a statutory duty to perform a type of RIA. The Financial Services and Markets Act 2000, for example, imposes on the FCA and the PRA that they subject their rules to an efficiency and cost–benefit analysis.[503] Ofcom is likewise known for completing various RIAs.[504] Also in the US, Executive Orders 12866 and 13563 task the Office of Management

[497] The French Constitutional Council declared the initial statutory obligation 'from the beginning of the development of the legislative proposal' unconstitutional because it transgressed the division of powers between the Legislature and the Executive (French Constitutional Council no. 2009-579 of 9 April 2009, §§ 12–13).

[498] Ulrich Karpen, 'Regulatory Impact Assessment: Current Situation and Prospects in the German Parliament' [2015] *Amicus Curiae* 16; Dirk Zeitz, 'Better Regulation in Germany as Quality Assurance System: Recent Development and Current Challenges' [June 2016] *Netherlands Administrative Law Library*, title 3 DOI: 10.5553/NALL/.000025.

[499] Articles 5 and 6 of the Federal Statute of 15 December 2013 *houdende diverse bepalingen inzake administratieve vereenvoudiging* and Royal Decree of 21 December 2013 *houdende uitvoering van titel 2, hoofdstuk 2 van de wet van 15 december 2013 houdende diverse bepalingen inzake administratieve vereenvoudiging*. Koen Poel and Wim Marneffe, 'De federale regel-gevingsimpactanalyse: een stand van zaken na zes maanden' [2014] *Tijdschrift voor Wetgeving* 185–201.

[500] Peter Van Humbeeck, 'De juiste vragen op het juiste moment in de juiste volgorde', *De Standaard* (21 December 2018) 35.

[501] Anne-Sophie Denolle, 'Les études d'impact: une révision manquée?' [2011] *Revue française de droit constitutionnel* 514.

[502] e.g. BIPT-IBPT, 'Regulatory impact assessment on a fourth operator of the mobile network in the Belgian market' (2018).

[503] Sections 138I and 138J of the Financial Services and Markets Act 2000; Tony Prosser, 'The Powers and Accountability of Agencies and Regulators' in David Feldman (ed.), *Oxford Principles of English Law: English Public Law* (2nd edn, Oxford University Press 2009) 269–70.

[504] John McEldowney, *Public Law* (Sweet and Maxwell 2016) 528.

and Budget (OMB) to review certain draft regulations before their proposal and before their enactment.[505]

5.6.2 Referral

Concerning the second technique of referrals, I perceive an accumulation of expertise especially within standardization organizations.

It is presumed that self-regulation—which is the status of standards before state rules refer to them—can attain a high level of efficiency and effectiveness with low monitoring costs and enforcement costs, since the regulated are voluntarily under the control of the regulator.[506] The validity of a technical standard to which no state rule refers, completely depends on its efficiency.[507]

In its annual report, the French Council of State developed a number of criteria on 'flexible law' to evaluate the efficiency of a technical standard, namely the probability that the standard will be complied with, the existence of opposition, the result-oriented formulation, and the difficulty of assuring control of the standard.[508] However, this report also correctly pointed out that as long as the technical standard has not evolved from soft law into a hard law rule, the requirement of efficiency remains non-compelling.[509] Similarly, German industry itself drafts Germany's DIN standards with a high degree of expertise[510] and UK standard-setting bodies already attempt to reach high levels of efficiency through self-regulation. The BSI lists the two remaining characteristics of British standards—apart from balanced representation and consultation—as those developed by experts and subject to systematic and periodic review by the BSI.[511] More specifically, the BSI thus aims to maintain its efficiency and effectiveness by revising (and possibly updating) its standards every five years.[512]

505 Lauren Moxley, 'E-Rulemaking and Democratic' [2016] *Administrative L. Rev.* 671.

506 Robert Baldwin, Martin Cave, and Martin Lodge, *Understanding Regulation: Theory, Strategy, and Practice* (Oxford University Press 2011) 140.

507 Isabelle Vacarie and Alain Supiot, 'Santé, sécurité et libre circulation des marchandises (règles juridiques et normes techniques)' [1993] *Droit social* 18, II; ISO and IEC, 'Le recours et la référence aux normes ISO et IEC dans les politiques publiques' (2015) 5.

508 Jacky Richard and Laurent Cytermann, 'Le droit souple' in Christian Vigouroux *et al.* (eds), *Les rapports du Conseil d'État* (Conseil d'État 2013) 137.

509 Ibid., 11.

510 Harm Schepel, *The Constitution of Private Governance: Product Standards in the Regulation of Integrating Markets* (Hart 2005) 114 and 122.

511 BSI Group, 'A standard for standards—Principles of standardization. Standard 0' (2016) 7.

512 Article 6.2.1, Standard for Standards; Peter Marburger, 'Legal and Organizational Aspects of Technical Standardization at the National and European Level' in K. H. Lindackers (ed.), *Safety Aspects of Technical Standards* (Springer 1992) 202.

5.6.3 Reception

The presumption that interested parties will more readily detect the exact problem is also of benefit with respect to the efficiency of private or hybrid actors and the effectiveness of their received agreements within the reception technique. Efficiency and effectiveness are assumed because of the professional groups' close connection to interest groups. The compulsory membership of professional organizations[513] and their internally selected leadership in the countries researched suggest that the enactment or amendment of any rule will respond to a need of the regulated and will lead to compliance.

In France, especially when CLAs are extended, the *ex ante* report made by 'a group of experts'—which can be requested by the competent minister, a professional organization of employers, or a professional organization of employees in accordance with article L.2261-27-1 of the Labour Code—expounds on the economic and social effects and thus the efficiency of the proposed extendable CLA.[514]

However, the presumed presence of efficiency and effectiveness within the reception technique is certainly not guaranteed. Moreover, the UK and the US teach us that some typical examples of the reception technique in the other countries researched do not necessarily further the overall effectiveness of rules. This has particularly been studied in relation to CLAs, which can be extended and attain general applicability in Belgium, France, and Germany but not in the UK or the US, as common law countries. To add to this, UK CLAs can only lead to limited remedies for the parties that enter into them. We may assume that the primary goal of CLAs is to improve the working conditions of employees without impairing the employment rate for the regulated. While it is apparent that CLAs and their extensions have improved the working conditions of employees in the other countries studied, the employment rate is considerably higher in the UK than in some of these other countries.[515] This trend also occurs in other countries that do not allow the extension of CLAs.[516] Oesingmann's empirical study suggested that CLAs, as an example of the reception technique, and which contribute to workers' rights, also threaten the overall effectiveness of the rules by producing lower employment rates.

[513] Robert Baldwin, Martin Cave, and Martin Lodge, *Understanding Regulation: Theory, Strategy, and Practice* (Oxford University Press 2011) 141.

[514] Article 1, IV of ordinance 22 September 2017 *portant diverses mesures relatives au cadre de la négociation collective*.

[515] Katrin Oesingmann, 'The Extension of Collective Labour Agreements in Europe' [2016] *CESifo DICE Report* 63–4.

[516] Ibid.

5.7 Conclusion

Chapter 5 has tested the second research hypothesis by scrutinizing the rule of law hallmarks with which outsourced rules should comply. This conclusion summarizes the findings. At least five select principles of good rulemaking must be guaranteed within outsourced rules: (1) transparency; (2) respect for the hierarchy of rules; (3) judicial protection; (4) representativeness; and (5) efficiency and effectiveness.

These safeguards are inspired by the five principles of good governance of the EU Commission. They are reflected for example by the legisprudence of the Belgian Council of State Legislative Section. Often these requirements also flow from constitutional principles, as recognized by the French Constitutional Council or in Germany, the UK, and the US. However, hardly any overarching statutes or executive decrees structure these requirements, which means that it is only possible to draw a picture of the protection of these five safeguards in a piecemeal and casuistic manner, based on instances of rulemaking powers that have been outsourced.

The standard of transparency, in particular, may shed an unfavourable light on the current state of rulemaking by autonomous public, private, and hybrid actors. With regard to intelligibility, these actors that receive outsourced powers have made some progressive steps. They could still create more intelligible rules in relation to how they consult the general public, share their internal debates, divulge their motives, and phrase or structure their rules clearly. Accessibility and, more specifically, the requirement of publication is a recurring concern for the judicial bodies of the countries researched. Despite the seemingly limited purview of article 190 of the Belgian Constitution and article 82 of the Basic Law and the transparency principles in France, the UK, or the US, the requirement to make rules accessible applies to all types of outsourcing of rulemaking powers. However, no overarching statute regulates the publication of all rules made by autonomous public, private, and hybrid actors.

Often, the accessibility (publication channels) of *delegated rules* is determined by an ad hoc enabling statute or is up to the discretion of the autonomous public body. The lingering concern is the current constitutional status of the common practice of publishing delegated rules electronically on a website. The technique of *referrals* raises lesser known, yet fundamental, questions. The Belgian Council of State Legislative Section, for example, emphasizes that the 'essential elements of accessibility and intelligibility' need to be safeguarded within these referrals.[517] However, it must be asked what this entails when a traditional rulemakers refers to: (1) an unpublished standard made by a standardization body, with (2) only English and/or French as the operative language and (3) that body holds the IP rights of a certain

[517] e.g. Belgian Council of State Legislative Section, Advisory opinion no. 53.929/1/V of 18 September 2013, 9.

rule and thus cannot freely distribute it. Chapter 5 systematically discussed these three problematic aspects and concluded that: (1) referred-to standards must genuinely be knowable and securely accessible. Moreover, (2) I urged the direct translation of referred-to standards, with that translation becoming the binding version for the constituency. However, sometimes such translation may prove impossible due to the nature of the topic or if the needs of the service or of the general interest do not allow for translation. Consider, for example, very specific and expert-level aviation rules that no one would read aside from the technical staff in expert companies. Finally, (3) referred-to standards should principally be freely accessible through compulsory licences or statutory exceptions. A statutory or constitutional regulation of this matter is urgently called for. The enabling statutes or executive rules within the *reception technique* sometimes establish a publication scheme but these schemes can be very diverse. For example, extended CLAs are published less widely in Germany and France than in Belgium. Moreover, such enabling rules are not always necessary within the reception technique. Even if they are, they often do not describe how received agreements should be publicized. Professional or sports organizations, especially, make their own 'rules' widely accessible via personal media, such as their private websites.

In general, outsourced rules also do not enjoy a clearly established position in the hierarchy of rules. Despite the importance of this principle in Belgium, France, Germany, and the US, the hierarchy of rules only plays a fringe role in the UK. This also applies when rulemaking powers are outsourced. UK constitutional law rarely references the hierarchy of rules which is such a vital structuring principle in the other countries researched. However, this does not imply that outsourced rules do not have any position in the UK hierarchy of rules. There are two main foundational ideas: primary legislation trumps secondary legislation (among which are included outsourced rules) and any autonomous public, private, and hybrid actor can amend or revoke its rules.

Even in the other countries researched, most of the outsourced rules do not fit within the ordinary theory of legal sources. Often they will merely be considered *sui generis* and rank below traditional legal sources. In practice, this has not yet resulted in many clashes or conflicts; however, the Belgian Council of State Legislative Section has openly lamented this state of affairs on various occasions.

Again, a surprisingly vital topic in contemporary comparative public law is the hierarchical status of referred-to standards. One stance sees referred-to standards as external documents without a position in the hierarchy of rules. This approach is taken in the Netherlands. In another stance, the referred-to standard has the same hierarchical position as the referring rule which can equally trigger other template principles of good rulemaking such as a fixed publication method. This approach is apparently followed in Germany and initially by a lower Dutch court. The Belgian, French, UK, and US positions have not yet been clearly established. In the light of granting referred-to standards the clearest position possible, I have called for statutory or constitutional regulation of this matter. Likewise, the hierarchical position of received agreements is often unknown. Sometimes statutes or executive rules will expand on the definition and legal position of extended CLAs or professional agreements, but usually it is up to the autonomous public, private, and hybrid actors themselves—and, in fact, citizens—to estimate how these 'rules' rank among state rules and among other outsourced 'rules'.

Judicial review is possibly the most important element in the rule of law principle as applied to outsourced rules. The Belgian and French Council of State exercise no *ex ante* legality review on them. However, delegated rules can be reviewed *ex post* through various legal procedures in the countries researched. In the UK, courts may not be competent to review primary legislation but they can scrutinize secondary legislation. In doing so, they concretize the above-mentioned constitutional principles and the manner in which they limit the rulemaking powers of autonomous public, private, and hybrid actors. Referred-to standards can only be directly reviewed insofar as they are considered to receive the same hierarchical status as referring rules. However, even if referred-to standards cannot be directly reviewed, they can still influence the validity of the referring rule. Furthermore, courts should have the competence to turn seemingly dynamic referrals into static referrals in order to safeguard the constitutional principles of good rulemaking. For the reception technique, the European continental countries studied here have assigned their administrative or ordinary courts the task of reviewing the received agreements or the ratification act by which usually the Executive receives the agreement. However, with the characteristic case of sports governing bodies, UK law especially is in disaccord over the question of whether public law remedies can structure the rulemaking powers within mandatory monopoly organizations. The ruling *Aga Khan* case law suggests that only private law and contractual remedies can affect the decisions made by such sports governing bodies.[518] UK legal scholarship, however, is increasingly calling for the interpretation of common law public law principles by courts to be extended to these private actors that de facto exercise public functions. This call may actually comply with existing case law because the precedents discussed did not concern rulemaking powers, as analysed in this research.

Surprisingly perhaps, the standard of review has not been raised—as a matter of principle—for outsourced rules. To the contrary, outsourced rules often receive a certain margin of appreciation. This is in line with the institutional separation of powers. For the Legislature and the Executive, decreased rulemaking powers for autonomous public, private, and hybrid actors would then lead to decreased reviewing powers by the courts. Ultimately, the technical nature of rules determines the standard of review more profoundly than the type of rulemaking actor.

[518] Unless the Human Rights Act 1998 is applicable.

The final two safeguards that autonomous public, private, and hybrid actors need to comply with when making rules are representativeness and an efficient search for effective rules. Here also, this research established that—in the absence of a framework regulation—decentralized rulemakers should increase their attention to involving stakeholders and ensure that their rules are genuinely at least as effective as those made by traditional rulemakers. In relation to representativeness, this goal can be achieved by providing safeguards ensuring the independence of rulemakers and their systematic consultation of citizens and stakeholders. In order for autonomous public, private, and hybrid actors to remain efficient and their rules effective, the Legislature and the Executive should scrutinize their leading officials or annual reports. Moreover, they should impose qualitative RIAs on outsourced rules. Autonomous public, private, and hybrid actors themselves might also opt to perform RIAs, even if a governmental obligation to do so remains absent.

To conclude, the countries researched tend to find pragmatic solutions to the problems that the outsourcing of rulemaking powers may pose. Nevertheless, despite the fact that Germany and France rely on a more expansive constitutional framework with regard to outsourcing than Belgium, the UK, or the US, the phenomenon of outsourcing rulemaking powers is handled in an equally or even more haphazard manner. The 2017 Organic Statute and the Statute on the status of AAIs was a step in the right direction, by solidifying the independence of French AAIs, for example. In the UK, autonomous public bodies especially need to abide by more and clearer provisions and principles that safeguard transparency, judicial review, representativeness, and efficiency/effectiveness than in the other countries researched. The UK Regulators' Compliance Code and the US Administrative Procedure Act are the clearest examples of such an overarching enactment of the safeguards expected of autonomous public bodies and their rules. These statutory and executive provisions or judge-made principles serve as an example for the other countries, demonstrating that—despite few constitutional limits to the outsourcing of rulemaking powers—their rules can maintain quality and legitimacy by faithfully complying with good rulemaking safeguards.

It will ultimately be up to the autonomous public, private, and hybrid actors themselves or to the courts to answer the question of whether an outsourced rule complies with the principles of good rulemaking or the rule of law. I have, therefore, reiterated the appeal that I previously made, along with Stéphanie De Somer, of creating an overarching framework statute for autonomous public, private, or hybrid actors: a 'law of rules' in order for those decentralized rulemakers to better comply with these principles of good rulemaking and the 'rule of law'.[519]

[519] Cedric Jenart and Stéphanie De Somer, 'Non-Statutory Rulemaking and the Rule of Law' [2017] *Sui Generis* 159–72.;

6
World Anti-Doping Agency Case Study

This chapter contains a case study on the fight against doping, focusing on anti-doping rulemakers. It will elucidate the role of the three techniques of outsourcing of rulemaking powers within the countries researched, as well as the relevant limits or safeguards under which they operate.

The World Anti-Doping Agency (WADA) is generally seen as a success story in transnational lawmaking in the literature.[1] It rapidly professionalized and streamlined the fight against doping in sports across borders. However, several recent WADA decisions have led scrutiny to turn from the hunted towards the hunter. Some of these decisions concerned WADA as an executive body, such as the suspension of Russian athletes from the 2016 Olympic Games in Rio de Janeiro (Brazil). Other decisions concerned WADA as a rulemaking actor. The latter type of decision is of most concern to this research.

6.1 Introduction

Chapter 6 examines whether and how the countries researched implement WADA-made rules by outsourcing some of their own rulemaking powers. Occasionally, I will discuss other anti-doping actors in the countries investigated, although the focal point remains WADA.

The two general research hypotheses resonate throughout this case study on WADA via the following questions. First, how do constitutional principles limit the possibility of outsourcing rulemaking powers to WADA? This issue is tackled

[1] Kathryn Henne, 'WADA, the Promises of Law and the Landscapes of Antidoping Regulation' [2010] *Political and Legal Anthropology Rev.* 306; Richard Pound, 'The World Anti Doping Agency: An Experiment in International Law' [2002] *International Sports Law Rev.* 59.

Outsourcing Rulemaking Powers. Cedric Jenart, Oxford University Press. © Cedric Jenart 2022.
DOI: 10.1093/oso/9780192897831.003.0006

nation by nation. Second, how does WADA safeguard the rulemaking guarantees that national legislatures and executives normally uphold? This concept will be structured functionally, according to the five principles of good rulemaking (transparency, established position within the hierarchy of rules, subject to judicial review, representativeness, and efficiency/effectiveness).

6.1.1 Evolution of transnational anti-doping policy

Contrary to what its global relevance might suggest, WADA is not a body established by an international treaty. Combined with the revolution of the tertiary sector and the advent of peace in the Western world after the Second World War, competitive sports became a focal point of wealth and societal development from the second half of the twentieth century. Within a decade, suspicious deaths and athletes' performances led policymakers to consider the idea of banning certain stimulants. The English word 'dope' or 'doping'—at that time not yet exclusively linked to sports performance—was originally derived from the Dutch word '*doop*', a liquorice sauce with stimulating effects that the Dutch colonists were given by indigenous peoples.[2] Soon the definition of doping transformed from a functional one to a more formal one. For the legal certainty of athletes, there needed to be precise lists that distinguished doping from other substances and methods. Doping was combatted along two lines with diverging policy goals: one by private sports federations united through the Olympic Movement and one by public actors that aimed to ban doping in sports both internationally and domestically.

The first line of combat has been maintained by sports governing bodies (SGBs). The organization of competitive sports has a pyramidal structure. Competitive swimmers, for example, normally have one main objective: to perform at the Olympic Games. Individual athletes join a local sports clubs (e.g. Swimming Club Brabo Antwerp) which is part of a national sports organization (The Royal Belgian Swimming Federation) which is itself dependent on one international sports federation (the International Swimming Federation) which ultimately answers to the International Olympic Committee (IOC). These SGBs relish their autonomy concerning the rules of the game and it would be erroneous to assume that the private international sports community was not concerned with doping in the second half of the twentieth century. Originally, SGBs saw doping as an infringement of the rules of the game. More precisely, the use of performance-enhancing substances was considered to contravene fair play and the spirit of sport.[3] Small steps were continuously taken and milestones often coincided with global scandals. For

[2] Van Dale, *Dictionary Dutch Language* (Van Dale uitgevers, 2016) reference word: doping.

[3] Barrie Houlihan, *La victoire à quel prix? Le dopage dans le sport et l'élaboration de politiques contre le dopage* (Council of Europe 2003) 148.

example, the deaths of cyclists Knud Enemark Jensen and Tom Simpson were both highly mediatized, the former at the 1960 Rome Olympics and the latter in the 1967 Tour de France. As early as 1963, the IOC ordered the drafting of a prohibited list of methods and substances,[4] the first of which was drafted in 1967 to combat doping as an unfair competitive method.[5] International sports federations would usually follow suit and adopt their own prohibited list. Ordinarily, these would integrate the IOC's prohibited list, but that was not always the case; for example, the cycling federation (UCI) did not do so. This discordance led to much uncertainty for both athletes and controlling officials.[6]

The second line of combat was maintained by state actors, independently from the actions of SGBs.

From a domestic perspective, several nations acknowledged the importance of professional sports for societal, economic, and health purposes. The use of doping, however, especially endangered the health of the athletes and the population that saw themselves reflected in their sporting heroes. These states also tended to establish a list of prohibited substances although such lists were not exhaustive. Other substances or products that were used to 'artificially enhance the performance of athletes who participate in or prepare for a competition'—and which could harm their physical or mental health—were considered doping.[7]

From an international law perspective, the Council of Europe adopted a recommendation in 1967 to condemn, dissuade, and penalize users of doping. The Council of Europe defined doping as 'agents foreign to the organism, or of physiological substances in excessive quantities or introduced by an abnormal channel, with the sole purpose of affecting artificially and by unfair means the performance of such a person when taking part in a competition'.[8] In 1988, the positive doping test of sprinter Ben Johnson during the Seoul Olympics provoked worldwide condemnation. Not long after, a second leap was made towards doping-free sports: the Council of Europe's 1989 Anti-Doping Convention. The Convention resembles more an obligation of means than an obligation of result. The first two paragraphs of article 4 of the Anti-Doping Convention indeed create binding obligations on State Parties to restrict the availability of doping and to incentivize private anti-doping schemes, but only 'where appropriate'. Under article 4.3 of the Convention, the Parties merely had to 'assist', 'take appropriate steps', and 'encourage'. The Convention notably introduced the 'complementary responsibilities' of public authorities and voluntary sports organizations to combat doping. It also

[4] Leigh Anderson, 'Drugs banned in Sport', *Drugs.com* (2014) <http://www.drugs.com/wada/> (last accessed January 2019).

[5] Technische Universität München, 'Prohibited List', <http://www.doping-prevention.sp.tum.de/doping-in-general/prohibited-list.html> (last accessed January 2019).

[6] BOIC, *Sport zonder doping* (Janssen Pharmaceutica 1986) 12.

[7] e.g. Article 1 of the Belgian Statute prohibiting doping in sports competitions of 2 April 1965.

[8] Preamble to the Resolution on the Doping of Athletes, Recommendation adopted by the Ministers' Deputies of 29 June 1967.

emphasized the importance of fair play and the health of athletes, which would become the cornerstone of subsequent anti-doping measures.

Most importantly, the 1989 Council of Europe's Anti-Doping Convention introduced a prohibited list to nation-states. In fact, the Convention set up a monitoring group that could establish a list of pharmacological classes of doping agents and doping methods banned by international sports organizations.[9] When it was established, the monitoring group decided to embrace the Prohibited List developed under the auspices of the IOC. As soon as WADA created the unified Prohibited List (see later), the monitoring group incorporated it as its own.[10] Today, the Convention has entered into force in the 47 Contracting States of the Council of Europe, as well as Morocco, Tunisia, Belarus, Canada, and Australia.

It would take until the 1998 Chinese growth hormone scandal and the 1998 Festina affair in the Tour de France before the global sports community institutionally collaborated with state actors in the First World Conference on Doping in Sport in 1999. The Festina affair involved a Belgian physiotherapist, working for the Festina cycling team, who was caught at the French border with amphetamines, EPO, testosterone, growth hormones, and syringes. The First World Conference led to the Lausanne Declaration on Doping in Sport and laid the foundations for WADA. The Declaration itself remained hesitant in its reference to an 'International Anti-Doping Agency' which would 'have as its mandate, notably, to coordinate the various programmes necessary to realize the objectives that shall be defined jointly by all the parties concerned'. WADA was founded in 1999 as a private foundation, subject to article 80 of the Swiss Civil Code. The primary objective of WADA has been to coordinate and promote the fight against doping at a transnational level.[11] In its pursuit of this objective, WADA has drafted a World Anti-Doping Code and eight International Standards, of which the List of Prohibited Methods and Substances is the most important.

During the 2003 Second World Conference on Doping in Sport, WADA took over custody of the Prohibited List from the IOC and presented its own World Anti-Doping Code.[12] The Second World Conference also led to the 2003 Copenhagen Declaration on Anti-Doping in Sport. The Copenhagen Declaration paved the way for WADA standards to be implemented by nation-states. However, an international convention was needed to place binding obligations on governments; something that a mere declaration could not do.[13] All these international

[9] Article 11.1.be of the Council of Europe 1989 Anti-Doping Convention.

[10] Alain Dufaut, 'Rapport fait au nom de la commission des Affaires culturelles (1) sur le project de loi, adopté par l'Assemblée Nationale, relatif à la lutte contre le dopage et à la protection de la santé des sportifs 2005–2006 no. 12' (12 October 2005) 12.

[11] Article 4 of the revised statutes of the World Anti-Doping Agency 2014.

[12] Irene Mazzoni, Osquel Barroso, and Olivier Rabin, 'The List of Prohibited Substances and Methods in Sport: Structure and Review Process by the World Anti-Doping Agency' [2011] *J. Analytical Toxicology* 609.

[13] Paul Marriott-Lloyd, 'International Convention against Doping in Sport', UNESCO SHS/2010/PI/H/2, 3.

agreements would therefore eventually lead to the 2005 UNESCO International Convention Against Doping in Sport.

The 2005 Convention Against Doping in Sport entered into force on 1 February 2007. By 2020, 190 countries had either acceded to or ratified the Convention. This is significantly more than the Parties to the 1989 Council of Europe Anti-Doping Convention. Even by UNESCO's standards, the Convention was an unmitigated success. No other UNESCO Convention was construed and entered into force so rapidly. The Convention was seen as 'a living document'.[14] It incorporated the main standards of WADA, either as an annex or as an appendix. The Prohibited List and the Standards for Granting Therapeutic Use Exemptions are annexes to the UNESCO Convention. The World Anti-Doping Code, the International Standard for Laboratories, and the International Standard for Testing are appendices. This distinction between annex and appendix is more than just semantic. Articles 4.2 and 4.3 of the Convention proclaim that the annexes are an integral part of the Convention, while the appendices, on the other hand, place no binding obligation on the signatory states. Moreover, article 4.1 of the UNESCO Convention, determines that State Parties merely commit themselves to the *principles* of the Code;[15] the World Anti-Doping Code in its entirety is thus not binding on nation-states as a result of international law.[16] The WADA Code, as a product of a private foundation, cannot receive binding legal force akin to that of a national statute.[17] At most, some French literature compares the value of the WADA Code to a non-binding international treaty.[18]

The Prohibited List, however, stands as a rule that binds nation-states. Only its direct effect and enforceability is questionable. For dualist countries, which consider national law and international law to be two irreconcilable legal spheres, binding force never automatically results in direct effect and enforceability. For monist countries, however, binding international obligations could reverberate in the national sphere with direct application to citizens. However, the precise reach and interpretation of the Prohibited List remains opaque, rendering it unlikely that any citizen or a Party to the UNESCO Convention will resort to the List without explicit national implementation.[19]

[14] Idid., 4.

[15] Article 4.1 of the UNESCO International Convention Against Doping in Sport.

[16] French Council of State, 23 October 2009, no. 321554; French Council of State, 28 October 2009, no. 327306. See, for the ways in which states and their athletes can be bound by WADA-made rules: Cedric Jenart, 'The Binding Nature and Enforceability of Hybrid Global Administrative Bodies' Norms Within the National Legal Order: The Case Study of WADA' [2018] *European Public L.* 411–32.

[17] Alain Dufaut, 'Rapport fait au nom de la commission des Affaires culturelles (1) sur le project de loi, adopté par l'Assemblée Nationale, relatif à la lutte contre le dopage et à la protection de la santé des sportifs 2005–2006 no. 12' (12 October 2005) 12.

[18] Gerald Simon, 'Le point de vue du professeur' in Luc Silance (ed.), *Le dopage, Qui réglemente? Qui sanctionne?* (Anthemis 2012) 101.

[19] Judith Schmidt, *Internationale Dopingbekämpfung* (Boorberg 2009) 137.

6.1.2 Autonomous public or private actors

Two protagonists in the fight against doping in sport, the national anti-doping organizations (NADOs) and WADA, have all the features of autonomous public or private actors.

6.1.2.1 National Anti-Doping Organizations (NADOs)

According to the WADA Code 2021, NADOs are the entities designated 'by each country as possessing the primary authority and responsibility to adopt and implement anti-doping rules, direct the collection of Samples, manage test results and conduct Results Management at the national level'. If this designation has not been made by the competent public authority(ies), the entity 'shall be the country's National Olympic Committee or its designee'.[20] Contrary to states but similarly to SGBs, NADOs subscribe directly to the WADA Code. The discretion of NADOs is thus not only limited indirectly through the state that opted to incorporate the WADA documents but *also* directly through the WADA Code itself.

Belgium has a unique NADO structure. Although Belgium is only one of more than 25 federated states in the world, it is the only country in the world with more than one NADO. Each of Belgium's federated entities (Flanders, the French Community, the German-speaking Community, and Brussels) has its own NADO. Arguably, the reason for this is Belgium's unique system of *in foro interno, in foro externo*, which gives the federated entities treaty powers for their domestic competences.[21] Another reason could be Belgium's strong voice on doping matters thanks to Prince Alexandre de Mérode, who was head of the drug testing policy of the IOC for a staggering term of 35 years (from 1967 to 2002). The legal relevance of Belgium's four NADOs seems to reside in the federated entities' shared preference for public NADOs that are still subject to some type of control. This inclination arguably historically derives from the Belgian Anti-Doping Commission that was founded in 1967 when sports and health were still unified federal competences. The Commission existed under the aegis of the Belgian Minister of Health and Family.[22] Nevertheless, even in 2016, the Executive's control on the Flemish NADO, for example, led to an outcry by a top civil servant that 'the Flemish fight against doping is terminally ill'.[23]

The German NADO is called Die Stiftung Nationale Anti-Doping Agentur Deutschland (NADA). Germany chose a truly private body, a foundation, to

[20] WADA, *World Anti-Doping Code 2021*, 171.

[21] This competence became world news in 2016 because of the initial decline of Wallonia to agree to CETA—the Comprehensive Economic and Trade Agreement between Canada and the European Union.

[22] Article 3 of the Belgian Statute prohibiting doping in sports competitions of 2 April 1965.

[23] Dominique Minten and Marc Mercy, 'Vlaamse dopingstrijd doodziek', *De Standaard* (5 July 2016); NADO Flanders, 'Persmededeling: Reactie op het artikel in De Standaard van Yves Defoort van dinsdag 5 juli 2016: de Vlaamse dopingbestrijding is doodziek', NADO Flanders (5 July 2016).

regulate the national fight against doping;[24] it was created in 2002 and serves, according to its bylaws, to coordinate the national fight against doping through tests within and outside competition. This does not mean that the NADO is completely isolated from the state. First, the majority of financing originates from public actors, with 84 per cent of its funding coming from the federal government.[25] The rest of the funding is derived from the *Länder*, the city of Bonn, private sports federations, and private sponsors. Second, the German Anti-Doping Statute 2015 expands on the exchange of personal data between the government and the German NADO in order to further parallel their goals: namely prosecution by the state and disciplinary action by the NADO or the private sports organizations.[26]

The French Legislature cited article 15.1 of the WADA Code 2003 to justify the establishment of its NADO, the Agence Française de la Lutte contre le Dopage (AFLD). According to this provision, only one organization should be responsible for directing testing during a sports event. The AFLD has the powers to adopt and implement anti-doping rules but it also conducts disciplinary hearings. The French Legislature created 'une autorité publique indépendante', a quasi-autonomous non-governmental organization with legal competence. The predecessors of AFLD were the Laboratoire national de dépistage du dopage (LNDD) and primarilythe Conseil de prevention et de lutte contre le dopage (CPLD). Both were *établissements publics*, which are associations of public law that need to promote a goal of general interest. These types of associations had still been under the hierarchical supervision of the Executive and could receive instructions from it.[27] The parliamentary preparation of the 2006 Statute clearly testifies to the intent of the French Legislature to free the French NADO from any 'limiting' ties with the Executive.[28] The independence of the AFLD was further assured by its collegial composition, with members from high courts and tribunals, the irrevocable nature of the members' mandate, the fixed and long duration of those mandates, and the absence of preliminary financial control.[29]

UK Anti-Doping (UKAD) is the competent NADO in the UK. Its mission statement references the 'right of an athlete to compete in a doping free sport'.[30] UKAD thus regulates the implementation and management of the UK's anti-doping rules. The agency was conceived in 2007 by the UK Department for Culture, Media and

24 Deutscher Bundestag, Gesetzentwurf der Bundesregierung eines Gesetzes zur Bekämpfung von Doping im Sport 18/4898, 13 May 2015, 2.

25 Ibid., 34.

26 Sections 8, 9, and 10 of the German Statute on the Fight Against Doping of 10 December 2015.

27 Roland Drago, 'Pour ou contre les autorités administratives indépendantes' in Robert Andersen (ed.), *En hommage à Francis Delpérée. Itinéraires d'un constitutionnaliste* (Bruylant 2007) 468.

28 Alain Dufaut, 'Rapport fait au nom de la commission des Affaires culturelles (1) sur le project de loi, adopté par l'Assemblée Nationale, relatif à la lutte contre le dopage et à la protection de la santé des sportifs 2005–2006 no. 12' (12 October 2005) 46.

29 Ibid., 47.

30 UKAD, Funding Agreement between the Department for Culture, Media and Sport and UK Anti-Doping for 1 April 2010–31 March 2011 (24 June 2010), 1.

Sport on the recommendation of UK Sport and serves as an independent, autonomous governmental body.[31] It was founded as a non-departmental public body with the structure of a company limited by guarantee.

The United States Anti-Doping Agency (USADA) is a private (non-profit, non-governmental) organization. The Congress of the United States has recognized USADA as the official antidoping agency for Olympic, Pan American, and Paralympic sport in the United States.[32] It is partly funded by the United States Olympic Committee (USOC) and the Office of National Drug Control Policy (ONDCP), yet is not subject to government supervision in that capacity.[33]

These NADOs thus differ in legal status; nonetheless, they were all created to comply with article 22.8 of the WADA Code 2021, which explicitly requires NADOs to be sheltered from political influence: 'Each government should respect the autonomy of a National Anti-Doping Organization in its country ... and not interfere in their operational decisions and activities'. The Belgian Council of State stressed this requirement in 2021 with regard to the Brussels NADO.[34] The NADOs discussed here combine two common features. On the one hand, they have all been founded or at least funded by their national governments. On the other hand, their operational work has been made as independent from government intervention as possible. It is, thus, indeed possible to consider these NADOs as autonomous public or private actors.

6.1.2.2 WADA as an autonomous public or private actor

The question whether WADA is an autonomous public or private actor must also be directly addressed. WADA represents a unique interplay between private and public actors. Many of its features were created in order to safeguard an optimal 'equal partnership' between those private and public actors.

First, the history that eventually led to the establishment of WADA shows the interdependence between public and private actors in battling the use of doping. Second, to maintain its internal balance, WADA's revised statutes dictate that the Olympic Movement and public authorities must equally fund the Agency.[35] The Olympic Movement is a consortium of private actors consisting of the IOC, various international sports federations, national Olympic Committees, and each organizing committee for the Olympic Games. Public authorities are usually nation-states represented by continent. Third, WADA's Foundation Board has thirty-six members, half of whom must be nominated by the Olympic Movement.

[31] Jack Anderson, *Modern Sport Law: A Textbook* (Hart 2010) fn. 101.

[32] US Public Law 107-67, § 644.

[33] USADA Annual Report 2019, pp. 33 and 32 <https://www.usada.org/wp-content/uploads/2019-USADA-Annual-Report.pdf> (last accessed May 2021).

[34] Belgian Council of State Legislative Section, Advisory opinion no. 70.010/1/V of 21 September 2021, § 13.

[35] Article 6.6 revised statutes WADA 2016.

Public authorities appoint the other half of the Foundation Board members.[36] The Foundation Board is WADA's highest decision-making body. Fourth, the position of WADA's Foundation Board chairman also alternates between public authorities and the Olympic Movement after every second three-year term.[37] Finally, the vice-chairman must be nominated by the public authorities if the chairman is nominated by the Olympic Movement, and vice versa.[38] Academics have defined WADA as a private actor with public features and, usually, as a hybrid actor.[39]

WADA is subject to little or no input from citizens through democratic elections. Both a formal and a functional argument attest to this assertion. Formally, WADA is not an organization based on public international law but a private foundation subject to Swiss law. Treaties are usually ordained with internal mechanisms through which state representatives can amend their chosen direction. Citizens can hold these state representatives accountable. This accountability system obviously does not apply in the same way to private foundations. Functionally, of the thirty-six members of WADA's Foundation Boards, eighteen are representatives of the Olympic Movement, consisting of private actors without political accountability. Moreover, none of the eighteen representatives of the public authorities genuinely represents a state; instead, all of them represent a continent. For the European continent, the seats are divided between the European Union and the Council of Europe. Ultimately, the decisions of the Foundation Board are taken by an absolute majority of votes, meaning that private actors can always block the representatives of public actors. WADA thus has questionable political accountability.

6.1.3 Rulemaking powers

A subsequent key question is whether these NADOs or WADA exercise rulemaking powers.

Although NADOs 'have the power to adopt anti-doping rules', they mainly exercise executive powers in the sense that they generally manage and implement the rules made by WADA in a national context. Therefore, NADOs are only of minor relevance for the development of the argument in this chapter.

The rulemaking powers of WADA are broader and thus more relevant, as WADA adopts highly influential documents, such as the Prohibited List and the

[36] Article 6.1-6.2 revised statutes WADA 2016.

[37] Article 7.2 revised statutes WADA 2016.

[38] Article 7.3 revised statutes WADA 2016.

[39] Kathryn Henne, 'Reforming Global Sport: Hybridity and the Challenges of Pursuing Transparency' [2015] *Law & Pol'y* 338; Ken Foster, 'Global Administrative Law: The Next Step For Global Sports Law', University of Westminster School of Law Research Paper no. 12-10 (2012) 7; Lorenzo Casini, 'Down The Rabbit Hole: The Projection of the Public/Private Distinction Beyond the State' Jean Monnet Working Paper 08/13 (2013) 7. See in general: Tony Porter and Karsten Ronit, 'Self-Regulation as Policy Process: The Multiple and Criss-Crossing Stages of Private Rule-Making' [2006] *Policy Sciences* 54.

World Anti-Doping Code. These documents can function as binding rules from two perspectives.

On the one hand, having established that states have an obligation to implement at least the principles of WADA's documents, they might thus outsource an aspect of their rulemaking powers to WADA. WADA's Prohibited List and the World Anti-Doping Code contain various provisions that enact, accept, or establish abstract, general, and obligatory norms that have the purpose and effect of altering an individual's legal rights, duties, and relations.

On the other hand, there is the duty of athletes and sports organizations to subscribe to and incorporate the Prohibited List and the World Anti-Doping Code.[40] In this case, the legal persons become part of a contractual relationship. Both the regulator and the regulated are parties to that agreement. Nevertheless, athletes associated with a sports organization that has incorporated WADA documents might experience these documents to be rules rather than contractual clauses. The consent that athletes—often implicitly—give to these documents is far removed from the actual contract between an athlete and their sports club. The validity of this consent through the private sports federation has therefore been questioned in both scholarly and judicial arguments.[41] These WADA documents still show the hallmarks of a rule. They are essential, general, and abstract, and the subjected legal person (athlete) has no de facto influence on them.

The techniques that the countries researched developed to implement WADA rules within their jurisdictions will thus prove crucial to effective compliance with these rules.

6.2 Comparative limits on outsourcing rulemaking powers to WADA

In order to test the first research hypothesis about the limits to the outsourcing of rulemaking powers, the techniques for implementing WADA rules in the countries researched need to be analysed. These techniques are often explained by the legislative tradition that the country has in the fight against doping. The following sections explain the techniques used to outsource rulemaking power to WADA and the limits each impose on these techniques, assisted by the shared constitutional principles established for the countries researched.

National Legislatures or Executives have utilized or attempted to utilize the three techniques to outsource rulemaking powers to WADA: delegation of rulemaking powers, referral (dynamic) to standards, and reception of agreements.

[40] Comment to Introduction World Anti-Doping Code 2021, 16.

[41] Antoine Duval, 'The Pechstein Ruling of the Oberlandesgericht München—Time for a New Reform of CAS?', Asser International Sports Law Blog (19 January 2015).

6.2.1 Delegation

The first method used to outsource rulemaking powers boils down to the genuine delegation of rulemaking powers. In Germany (NADA) and the US (USADA), the NADOs are private organizations that did not receive genuine rulemaking powers.

The French Code of Sports invites French traditional rulemakers to delegate some of their powers to the French NADO, which is an autonomous public actor: namely the AFLD. Article L232-15 designates the AFLD to make an annual list of athletes who must report their whereabouts for one fixed hour per day so that doping controls can be carried out. Article 19 of Annex II-2 to article R232-86 of the Code of Sports determines that the AFLD can draft a deliberation in which it sets out the conditions to comply with the whereabouts regulations ('*conditions déterminées par une délibération*'). These conditions were developed in AFLD Deliberation no. 54 of 18 October 2007 concerning the transmission and management of location information from athletes subject to individual checks and concerning penalties for failure to comply. Deliberation no. 54 was correctly recognized as an exercise of executive rulemaking powers by the European Court of Human Rights (ECtHR) in the *FNASS* case.[42] In the context of anti-doping regulation, France thus has no difficulties in delegating rulemaking powers that are limited in their field of application and content to an autonomous public body.

The Belgian Council of State Administrative Litigation Section was asked in the *Sporta* case whether the rulemaking power to adopt the WADA Code and the International Standard could be delegated to the Secretary General of the Department of Sport.[43] In an *obiter dictum*, the Belgian Council of State Administrative Litigation Section made an important observation about WADA as a recipient of rulemaking powers. According to the Council, WADA is a 'private organization to which no rulemaking power is or may be delegated'.[44] The Council of State Legislative Section later affirmed that constitutional limit.[45] Soon after the *Sporta* judgment, a Belgian federated Legislature was still concerned about the national divergence from WADA's rules and so devised an alternative system to delegate rulemaking powers to WADA. According to draft article 7, para. 3 of the 2012 Flemish Anti-Doping Statute, the World Anti-Doping Code would be binding 'for all athletes, supervisors, team managers, sports association and laboratories'. This was not a direct delegation of rulemaking powers to WADA. While the Flemish Legislature must still act, it refers dynamically to a privately made document.

42 *Fédération Nationale des Associations et des Syndicats Sportifs (FNASS) ea v. France* no. 48151/11 and 77769/13 (ECtHR, 18 January 2018) §§ 160–3. See also later on judicial review of WADA-made rules.

43 Belgian Council of State Section Administration 15 February 2012, no. 218.000, § 3.4.

44 Ibid. § 19; Marinus Vroman, 'Belgium: Belgian Council of State Decision' [2012] *International Sport L. Rev.* 40.

45 Belgian Council of State Legislative Section, Advisory opinion (21 January 2015 no. 56.941/3) § 14.

Despite the fact that the Flemish Legislature steered clear of a fully fledged delegation of powers, the Belgian Council of State Legislative Section still criticized the referral in its *ex ante* advisory opinion on the draft. No Belgian statute can refer bindingly to a private external rule if the future extent of that rule cannot be foreseen. Although wrapped in a dynamic referral, the provision was in fact interpreted as a delegation of powers. If such an all-encompassing referral were allowed, the Legislature could part with its constitutionally granted responsibilities and avoid ordinary lawmaking procedures.[46]

The UK government founded UKAD and recognized WADA's fundamental role in coordinating the fight against doping.[47] UKAD has been delegated some governmental powers which arguably also implicitly entails the transfer of rulemaking powers. This is in effect also what UKAD does through the UK Anti-Doping Rules.[48] The UK Sport Anti-Doping Rules have been adopted by UKAD and mirror the rules (especially the Code) of WADA. Aside from these rules, UKAD especially exercises its control and individual decision-making powers on SGBs and athletes with regard to anti-doping rules.[49]

None of the countries researched explicitly delegated rulemaking powers to WADA. However, if UK legislators had decided to delegate rulemaking powers to WADA, the UK Parliament would experience few theoretical limits to that. The sovereignty of powers doctrine today still grants the UK Parliament a great deal of leeway to outsource rulemaking powers if it so wishes. This applies as long as the UK Parliament does not cede its own sovereignty.

6.2.2 Referral

Sometimes statutes or executive regulations do not delegate rulemaking powers but instead refer to a precise article or provision of the WADA Code. The use of the referral technique in relation to WADA-made rules can, for example, be found in the UK Anti-Doping Rules. A specific provision of these rules would then read: 'Pursuant to / In accordance with / Under / On the basis set out in / As provided in [World Anti-Doping] Code article X ...'.[50] For example, articles 4.2.5 (on therapeutic use exemptions), 10.14.4 (on the status of an athlete during

[46] Belgian Council of State Legislative Section, Advisory opinion (Documents Flemish Parliament 2011 no. 1554/1) 113.

[47] Ivan Waddington and Andy Smith, *An Introduction to Drugs in Sport: Addicted to Winning?* (Routledge 2009) 47.

[48] UKAD, UK Anti-Doping Rules 2015 < https://ukad.org.uk/resources/document/uk-anti-doping-rules> (last accessed May 2021).

[49] UKAD, 'What we do' <https://ukad.org.uk/our-organisation/what-we-do/> (last accessed May 2021).

[50] Article 3.1; 4.2.3; 4.5.1; 5.2.5; 5.3.2; 7.1.3; 7.9.6; 7.9.7; 10.12.1; 13.4.1; 14.1.1; Appendix UK Anti-Doping Rules 2015.

ineligibility), and 14.1 (confidentiality of reporting) of the UK Anti-Doping Rules 2021 contain such references.

The French Council of State does not exclude the possibility of a future direct referral to the Code. It opined that 'in the absence of any referral in the French Sports Code to the World Anti-Doping Code' it cannot be directly invoked in the French legal order.[51] *A contrario*, this consideration seems to imply that a direct referral to the World Anti-Doping Code could lead to the direct invocation of the Code in the French legal order.

The legality principle in Germany has had an important impact on the decision not to indirectly refer to WADA's Prohibited List. The parliamentary preparation for the German Anti-Doping Statute even explicitly defines this limit: criminal law. The German Legislature deemed it necessary to avoid such an indirect dynamic referral 'to the extent that also future changes to the Attachment affect German criminal law'.[52] The Bundesrat also clearly advocated the 'denouement of anti-doping criminal law and WADA's Prohibited List'.[53] Criminal law is generally subject to a specific legality principle (*nulla poena, sine lege*).[54] The case law of the German Bundesverfassungsgericht (FCC) established that '*gewisse Spezifierungen*' (detailed matters) of rulemaking powers may be delegated to the Executive, even when the specific legality principle applies.[55] The Executive can be more closely scrutinized by the Legislature, which is arguably why its rulemaking[56] power in criminal law matters is accepted, while the Legislature felt obliged to avoid a dynamic referral to WADA rules.

Such dynamic referrals to external documents are equally problematic for the Belgian Council of State. In fact, the Council recognizes a dichotomy between dynamic referrals that clarify a simultaneous delegation of powers to the Executive, on the one hand, and dynamic referrals that contain direct legal obligations for citizens, such as athletes, on the other.[57] The latter category, namely dynamic referrals creating binding rules, is deemed problematic. The former category, namely dynamic referrals accompanying delegations to the Executive, is perfectly acceptable because the power of decision still resides with the Executive as a traditional rulemaker that can exercise control. The Legislature has merely provided more guidance to the Executive in executing the statute. As a consequence of the

[51] French Council of State, 18 July 2011, no. 338390.

[52] German Bundestag, Gesetzentwurf der Bundesregierung eines Gesetzes zur Bekämpfung von Doping im Sport 18/4898 (13 May 2015) 24.

[53] *Idem*, 51.

[54] Markus D. Dubber, 'The Legality Principle in American and German Criminal Law: An Essay in Comparative Legal History' [2010] *SSRN* 13.

[55] German Bundestag, Gesetzentwurf der Bundesregierung eines Gesetzes zur Bekämpfung von Doping im Sport 18/4898 (13 May 2015) 24.

[56] Ibid., 24.

[57] Belgian Council of State Legislative Section (Documents Flemish Parliament 2014–2015 no 161/1) 169.

Council's legisprudence, Belgian Legislatures will not refer to the WADA Code as a whole, but they do refer to specific provisions of the Code in certain instances.

Article 8 of the 2006 French Statute Against Doping in Sports simplified the transposition of WADA's Prohibited List for the French jurisdiction: 'The list of substances and methods mentioned in this article is the one adopted through the Anti-Doping Convention signed in Strasbourg on 16 November 1989 or any ulterior agreement with the same purpose'. This article *refers* dynamically to the 1989 Anti-Doping Convention and thus indirectly to WADA's Prohibited List.[58] The List has to be published in the Official Journal and publication serves as a declarative act proclaiming the List's validity through a national statute: 'In practice, the applicable list in France is the one adopted by WADA, because the monitoring group of the Ant-Doping Convention, that enacts the prohibited list, has taken the stance to systematically adopt WADA's Prohibited List'.[59]

French scholarship not only cites the wish to conform to this international treaty and the WADA Code as motivation for this technique, but also the desire to remain more in control.[60] Undoubtedly, the French Legislature was also addressing a specific problem of efficiency when it decided to indirectly refer to WADA's Prohibited List. The annual confirmation of the Prohibited List in France as a constitutive action led to an awkward straddling of international responsibility and national applicability.[61] In many cases, there was a time interval between the entry into force of the Prohibited List on the international level and the decree or statute introducing the Prohibited List in the national legal order.

Only a month after the adoption of the 2006 Statute against doping in Sport, the relevant provisions on doping were transferred to the Code of Sports by *ordonnance* 2006-596 of 23 May 2006, in an initiative of the Ministry of Youth Affairs and Sport to bundle together all relevant sports laws. The former article 8 of the 2006 Statute Against Doping in Sport is in essence still present in article L232-9 of the Code of Sports. This provision today no longer refers to the 1989 Anti-Doping Convention, but—via article L230-2 of the Code of Sports—to the 2005 UNESCO International Convention Against Doping in Sports. However, the French technique of dynamic referral has not changed. The current Anti-Doping Statute provides that: 'the list of [prohibited] methods and substances is the one elaborated on in the application of the [2005 Convention,] ... or any ulterior agreement with the same subject that replaces it. [The list] is published in the Official Journal of the

[58] Alain Dufaut, 'Rapport fait au nom de la commission des Affaires culturelles (1) sur le project de loi, adopté par l'Assemblée Nationale, relatif à la lutte contre le dopage et à la protection de la santé des sportifs 2005–2006 no. 12 (12 October 2005) 34.

[59] Ibid., c. La mise en conformité de la législation française avec le code mondial antidopage.

[60] Marc Peltier, 'La transposition du code mondial antidopage dans l'ordre juridique interne' [2016] *Petites Affiches* 16.

[61] Alain Dufaut, 'Rapport fait au nom de la commission des Affaires culturelles (1) sur le project de loi, adopté par l'Assemblée Nationale, relatif à la lutte contre le dopage et à la protection de la santé des sportifs 2005–2006 no. 12 (12 October 2005) 61.

French Republic.'[62] France therefore uses the detour of referring to an international treaty, rather than referring directly to the WADA rules.

In Germany, as well, the *Arzneimittelgesetz*—criminalizing the trade in doping products—referred to a 'prohibited list of substances' that was attached to the 1989 Anti-Doping Convention under the auspices of the Council of Europe. At first sight, attachments to that agreement appear to be made by multilateral public actors, if not for the discussed fact that this attachment copies WADA's Prohibited List.[63] Second, the primary provision of the 2015 Law on the Fight against Doping in Sport (*Gesetz zur Bekämpfung von Doping im Sport*) also refers to an international treaty: 'A doping product, which is a substance of Annex I to the 2005 UNESCO Convention against Doping in Sport, is forbidden.'[64] Moreover, Annex I of the 2005 UNESCO Convention against Doping in Sport is, in fact, WADA's Prohibited List. The German Legislature thus did not refer directly to provisions of the WADA Code. Just like France, it has utilized an intelligent combination of a dynamic referral to an international treaty, which itself incorporated WADA rules. This technique to make the Prohibited List applicable in Germany might be perceived as a type of dynamic referral but with increased national checks. The 2005 International Convention against Doping in Sports has a prohibited list attached, which is as equally binding for signatory states as the list in the 1989 Anti-Doping Convention. This list is also an exact copy of WADA's Prohibited List. Every year, the Prohibited List is adapted by WADA, incorporated by the UNESCO Convention, and then accepted—through an opt-out procedure—by the Parties to the Convention.[65] Unless two-thirds of the signatories object, the changes that WADA makes to the Prohibited List automatically amend the UNESCO Convention. Only those signatories that expressly object to the amendment will not be bound by it. Naturally, signatories will have little choice but to accept WADA's changes if they do not want to face repercussions, such as the ban of their athletes from Olympic competitions. However, *de jure*, the signatories can decide not to accept WADA's revisions.

6.2.3 Reception

The third method used to outsource rulemaking powers to WADA is the reception of their standards. Ratifications of or recognition of WADA's contractual terms and

[62] Article 232-9 of the French Code of Sports.

[63] German Bundestag, Gesetzentwurf der Bundesregierung eines Gesetzes zur Bekämpfung von Doping im Sport 18/4898 (13 May 2015) 24.

[64] Article 1, Sections 2 and 3 of the German Statute on the Fight against doping in Sport.

[65] Dries Van Eeckhoutte and Tom Loose, 'Wijziging zkt. Instemming Het probleem van de parlementaire instemming met vereenvoudigde verdragswijzigingen', KU Leuven Working Paper No. 105 (January 2007) 17-20-22.

conditions can be seen as examples of this category, with a minor degree of control on self-regulation.

First, such reception could occur by means of a treaty, statute, or regulation. Belgian competent Legislatures do not eschew this method for anti-doping legislation. The WADA Code, especially, is usually recognized and implemented through the transposition of provisions of the original WADA Code into national legislation. An important example of this could even be found in the Flemish Legislative Decree on whereabouts requirements, which is clearly based on the 2010 version of the WADA Code.[66] Second, the Belgian Legislatures leave room for SGBs, and especially athletes, to bind themselves 'contractually' to the World Anti-Doping Code and the International Standards.

The transnational exchange on doping in sports has led Germany to receive and extend WADA rules to third parties by transcribing their content. For example, section 1 of the Law on the Fight against Doping in Sport explicitly mentions fairness, equal opportunities, and health as grounds for state intervention. Those notions are derived from the World Anti-Doping Code.[67] Germany also allows its athletes to bind themselves contractually to the World Anti-Doping Code and the International Standards.

Given the previously described preference in the UK for controlled self-regulation, there are many examples of the reception technique in the UK in which the state allows and enables athletes to bind themselves to the stringent WADA anti-doping rules through the athlete's membership of sports federations. This possibility is hardly limited and it is equally debated whether the UK courts could even review such rules with public law remedies in the light of the *Aga Khan* case law discussed in Chapter 5.

6.3 Comparative safeguards that WADA-made rules need to meet

To varying degrees, WADA receives rulemaking powers from (a selection of) the countries researched. This second half of this chapter focuses on the responsibilities that rest on WADA as a recipient of rulemaking powers that allow it to make legitimate rules.

The Belgian Council of State implicitly underlines the importance of WADA's responsibilities to uphold legislative standards. The Council mentions—with regard to the dynamic referral to provisions of the WADA Code that confer binding

[66] Article 20 of the Flemish Legislative Decree of 25 May 2012 regarding the prevention and the fight against doping in sports versus article 14.3 of the World Anti-Doping Code 2010.

[67] World Anti-Doping Agency, *Purpose, scope and organization of the World Anti-Doping Program and the Code 2015*, 11.

obligations on citizens—that this lacks normal safeguards within the lawmaking process (such as the Council's own advisory opinions).[68] However, as will be shown in the discussion of the principle of transparency, traditional rulemakers cannot be expected to guarantee all these safeguards when they outsource rulemaking powers. This argument emphasizes the responsibilities of WADA to offer safeguards of good rulemaking commensurate with those that the Legislature or the Executive grant in order to receive sufficient legitimacy. To the extent that WADA can receive some degree of rulemaking powers, it is also expected to provide such safeguards.

The five previously mentioned principles of good rulemaking (transparency, established position within the hierarchy of rules, subject to judicial review, representativeness, and efficiency/effectiveness) determine the way in which WADA must be structured and how it must create rules in order to comply with the same constitutional standards as traditional rulemakers. WADA's Foundation Board itself proclaimed at one particular meeting that 'everybody at WADA was open to looking at how to make WADA more transparent, efficient, and so on'.[69]

6.3.1 Transparency

The first principle of good rulemaking that WADA needs to uphold is transparency. Especially in the context of sport, transparency implies openness and a readiness to reform.[70]

With regard to *accessibility*, the Legislature and the Executive will often not publish the rules of autonomous public and private actors and thus those of WADA to which they refer. The Belgian federated entities provide for—at most—partial publication of WADA rules, usually amounting to the Prohibited List.[71] The Belgian Council of State Legislative Section also observed that 'aside from the question whether a referral to rules of WADA was in conformity with the rules and principles [of the Constitution] the question *also arises as to the transparency of these rules*'.[72] Moreover, it recently adopted an advisory opinion on a related type of external document: the Codex Alimentarius. This Codex bundles together international food guidelines, codes of practices, and standards with the aim of improving the quality, safety, and fairness of the food trade. Just like the WADA

[68] Belgian Council of State Legislative Section, Advisory opinion (Documents Flemish Parliament 2014–15, no. 161/1), 169.

[69] Foundation Board WADA, 'Minutes of the WADA Foundation Board Meeting', Montreal, Canada (18 May 2017) 4.

[70] Kathryn Henne, 'Reforming Global Sport: Hybridity and the Challenges of Pursuing Transparency' [2015] *Law & Pol'y* 342.

[71] Belgian Council of State Legislative Section, Advisory opinion no. 50.763/3 of 17 January 2012, 4.

[72] Belgian Council of State Legislative Section, Advisory opinion (Documents Flemish Parliament 2014–15, no. 161/1), 169 (emphasis added).

rules, the Codex Alimentarius has been partly created by actors involved in international law; however, the Codex itself only sets non-binding guidelines.[73] If a Belgian rule refers to the Codex Alimentarius, it should do so with sufficient precision to point to the exact guideline in question and—'if the original guideline is insufficiently accessible'—by publishing directly or through an attachment in the *Moniteur belge/Belgisch Staatsblad*.[74]

Given that the publication of outsourced rules at the domestic level is at most regulated in a sporadic manner, WADA itself has an important responsibility for providing for sufficient publication of its rules, and it does not shy away from that responsibility: both WADA's revised statutes and the World Anti-Doping Code prescribe transparency.[75] Nevertheless, WADA itself has had a troubled relationship with granting access to its documents. For that purpose, I highlight here an issue of accessibility through the addition of the product 'meldonium' to WADA's List of Prohibited Substances in January 2016. The tennis player Maria Sharapova was famously caught using the product in March 2016. From a legal perspective, Sharapova's mistake is not so clear-cut. In autumn 2015, it was announced that the substance of meldonium would be added to WADA's Prohibited List for 2016. Allegedly, athletes had been informed on various occasions of this change to the Prohibited List and, in addition, it would be expected that tennis players and their entourage would be cognisant of amendments to the List. Everyone is expected to know the law: *nemo censetur ignorare legem*. Nevertheless, the question arises as to whether this Latin maxim still applies fully when the primary lawmakers are private or hybrid actors such as WADA. When the identity of the regulator shifts, do the standards and safeguards for those regulated remain the same?

On the one hand, WADA's most influential documents—the Code and the Prohibited List—are easily accessible.[76] The Code and the List are clearly highlighted on WADA's homepage. The question then arises as to whether a rule published on the internet meets the same safeguards as a traditionally published rule.[77] Three pragmatic arguments would suggest that it does. First, many states have, in practice, stopped publishing and distributing printed editions of their Official Journal for practical, budgetary, and ecological reasons. Second, in many respects documents on the internet are more accessible today than documents requested

[73] Food and Agriculture Organization of the United Nations, Codex Alimentarius <http://www.fao.org/fao-who-codexalimentarius/about-codex/en/> (last accessed January 2019).

[74] Marc Joassart, Laurent Jans, Claudine Mertes, and Marc Oswald, 'Le Conseil d'Etat. Chronique de légisprudence 2013' [2015] *Revue Belge de droit constitutionnel* 123, § 134.

[75] Article 10.1 of WADA's revised statutes and article 24.1.4 of the World Anti-Doping Code 2021.

[76] Belgian Council of State Legislative Section, Advisory opinion no. 51.790/3 of 18 September 2012 on a draft executive decree of the Flemish government regarding the exercise of the legislative decree of 25 May 2012 regarding the prevention and fight against doping in sport.

[77] Marc Joassart, Laurent Jans, Claudine Mertes, and Marc Oswald, 'Le Conseil d'Etat—Chronique de légisprudence' [2013] *Revue belge de droit constitutionnel* 123.

at the desk of the organization's international seat.[78] An overwhelming majority of athletes who participate in international competitions will have access to the internet. Third, WADA's governance documents can be reached in three mouse clicks from WADA's homepage (resources > governance > document). The three-click rule is an unofficial rule in web design, which means that in order for a document to be accessible three clicks should suffice to reach the surfer's destination.[79]

On the other hand, although the comment to article 4.1 of WADA's Code states that 'for the sake of predictability, a new Prohibited List will be published every year whether or not changes have been made', WADA still has much room for improvement with regard to the intelligibility of its rules. This can be shown with three examples.

First, minutes of the decision-making bodies of WADA are often published months after the event.[80] The minutes of the Foundation Board meeting of 18 November 2015, for example, were only published on 13 May 2016. In addition, sometimes these minutes are published in just one of the official languages (English or French). Second, the decisions of Expert Groups, such as that which establishes the Prohibited List, are completely removed from the public eye. The reasons provided for this are twofold. In the first instance, it is argued that the public does not need to know why a certain product has been included on the Prohibited List because the three requirements that underlie selection by the Expert Group (health, spirit of the sport, and fair play) are 'sufficiently well-known'. In the second instance, the lack of the provision of motives will in any event be addressed by the fact that WADA's Executive Board always needs to ratify any decision and WADA's Foundation Board members have access to the relevant motives and reports. However, these reasons are insufficient to safeguard intelligible rules. First, knowing the standards on which a decision is based is never sufficient to motivate a rulemaking or executive decision. Second, supervision of these internal actors might give some reassurance of the quality of the rule but this still does not make the decision itself more transparent with respect to athletes and the general public. Finally, in its reports on human enhancement technologies in sport, the UK Science and Technology Committee called for '"clear reasoning" given by WADA ... as to why substances and methods are on the prohibited list'.[81] The lack of transparency in the build up to the release of the annual Prohibited List created parliamentary 'disappointment'.[82]

[78] Annemie Schaus (ed.), *Entre ombres et lumières: cinquante ans d'application de la Convention européenne des droits de l'homme en Belgique* (Bruylant 2009) 310.

[79] Jeffery Zeldman, *Taking Your Talent to the Web: Making the Transition from Graphic Design to Web Design* (New Riders 30 May 2001) 92–3.

[80] Although the meetings are publicly accessible on request.

[81] House of Commons Select Committee on Science and Technology, 'Human Enhancement Technologies in Sport', Second Report of Session 2006–07, HC 67 (February 2007).

[82] Ibid., p. 24, 'Prevention and Detection of Doping (WADA Code)'.

6.3.2 Established position within the hierarchy of rules

Some autonomous public and private actors also have a responsibility to respect the hierarchy of rules.

With regard to the delegation technique, the French government confirmed in its argumentation before the ECtHR that the AFLD, which was awarded rulemaking powers on anti-doping in sports, 'has to conform to the inherent requirements of the hierarchy of rules'.[83] Autonomous public actors thus have to submit to rules that are higher in the hierarchy of rules, such as treaties, statutes, and executive regulations.

However, in order for an external document to be ranked in the hierarchy of rules, such as collective labour agreements in Belgium or referred-to standards from standardization organizations in Germany, the external document must be recognized as a rule in the national legal order. This is not the case for either the WADA Code or the Prohibited List in the countries researched. The Belgian Council of State Legislative Section appears to suggest the non-existent legal (and thus hierarchical) status of referred-to standards: '[from dynamic referral] does not flow that the texts would receive the force of law of the statutory rule and that executive decrees could be based on it in itself'.[84] In Germany, a dynamic referral could result in the referred-to standard receiving the hierarchical status of the referring rule. However, the German Legislature does not refer dynamically to the WADA Code or the Prohibited List, but to the treaties that incorporate these rules made by WADA.

Therefore, WADA documents themselves will normally remain private external documents that are not ranked in the national hierarchies of rules. WADA itself thus also need not respect these in order to gain legitimacy. Nevertheless, despite a stuttering start, WADA has been paying an increasing amount of attention to national and international constitutional principles and human rights in its creation and evaluation of anti-doping rules. For example, prior to the 2015 and 2021 versions of the WADA Code, the former president of the ECtHR was asked to analyse the potential human rights violations in the Code.[85]

[83] *Fédération Nationale des Associations et des Syndicats Sportifs (FNASS) ea v. France* nos 48151/11 and 77769/13 (ECtHR, 18 January 2018) 131.

[84] Belgian Council of State Legislative Section, Advisory opinion (21 January 2015 no. 56.941/3) 3.4 and 3.8.2.

[85] Jean-Paul Costa, 'Legal Opinion on the Draft 2015 World Anti-Doping Code', on behalf of WADA (2013); Jean-Paul Costa, 'Legal Opinion on the Draft 2021 World Anti-Doping Code', on behalf of WADA (2019).

6.3.3 Subject to judicial review

Judicial protection is the third principle of good rulemaking that WADA should respect in order to gain legitimacy. Its rules need to be subject to judicial review in order for them to comply with the rule of law.

National courts allow deference to WADA as an actor within the *lex sportiva*. However, if a WADA rule clearly contravenes individual rights, national courts will intervene. With regard to doping use, human rights protection is a particularly complicated matter; this is because athletes may be bound by WADA documents through both domestic law incorporating the rule *and* through their membership of a private sports federation, which often will have indirectly signed the WADA Code.

Especially in Germany, national courts have readily intervened in order to protect fundamental rights.

In Germany, the *Krabbe* cases were instrumental in the current standard sanction of a two-year suspension for inadvertent doping use. Here, the rule of law in a strict sense (*Rechtsstaat*) impacted rulemaking outsourcing to private anti-doping actors. Even before the existence of WADA when prohibited lists were still made by private SGBs, courts scrutinized the effective protection of athletes' rights. The rule of law principle thus influenced the outcome of the *Krabbe III* case.[86] Katrin Krabbe was a two-time world champion track runner who was caught using the product Clenbuterol in an out-of-competition test. However, the product did not yet feature on the doping list accepted by the German Athletics Association (DLV), which is why the DLV only suspended her for one year for unsportsman-like drug use.[87] The International Association of Athletics Federations (IAAF) subsequently added an extra two years to the suspension because of the similarity of Clenbuterol to prohibited anabolic steroids. The combined sanctions of the German Athletics Association and of the IAAF amounted to a suspension of three years. Eventually, the Munich Court of First Instance and Court of Appeals decided that there was no basis for the imposition of doping sanctions by the IAAF for products that resembled prohibited substances within the IAAF's rules.[88] The rules stipulated that only national sports organizations were competent to declare a suspension due to lack of sportsmanship.[89] Autonomous public and private actors thus have to abide by the rules that they themselves have made: *patere legem quem ipse fecisti*.

[86] Peter Charlish, 'Drugs in Sport' [2012] *Legal Information Management* 115.

[87] Klaus Vieweg and Andreas Krause, 'Sports Law Supplement 2013 Germany' for *International Encyclopaedia of Laws* (Kluwer 2013) 196.

[88] The Court of Appeals of Munich (OLG Munich) basically affirmed. OLG Munich, available at *SpuRt* 1996, 133: LG München I, *SpuRt* 2001, 238.

[89] Andrej Lang, 'Global Administrative Law in Domestic Courts. Holding Global Administrative Bodies Accountable', Viterbo Administrative Law Seminar (2008) 22.

More recently, the *Pechstein* cases elucidate the way in which ordinary courts can scrutinize access to a fair trial within the disciplinary procedures of the SGBs. Claudia Pechstein was suspended because of irregularities in her Athlete Biological Passport. According to article 13.2.1 of the 2015 World Anti-Doping Code, in cases arising from participation in an international event or in cases involving international-level athletes, decision may be appealed exclusively to the Court of Arbitration for Sport (CAS). In this case, CAS affirmed Pechstein's suspension.

Subsequently, Pechstein proceeded to fight the competence of CAS in a domestic Bavarian court. According to one of her main arguments, the hearings before CAS did not comply with the rights of the defendant because, for example, the arbitrators were chosen from a closed list selected by a body (Le Conseil International de l'Arbitrage en matière de Sport, CIAS) in which athletes were chronically underrepresented. The German Court of First Instance and the Court of Appeals agreed with Claudia Pechstein and demonstrated national adherence to human rights as a limit on an autonomous public and private actor's rulemaking and adjudicative powers.[90] However, the Bundesgerichtshof, the highest ordinary court, disagreed and affirmed the sanctions against Pechstein. As of 2021, this high-profile case is still pending before the FCC.[91] However, in a parallel fashion, the ECtHR rendered judgment on this question in October 2018.[92] It held article 6(1) ECHR applicable since Pechstein had been forced to agree to the arbitration proceedings and since she 'earned her living' through the exercise of the sport, for which she had to agree to the arbitration clause.[93] The ECtHR did not consider CIAS to be a partial tribunal; however, it did establish a violation of the Convention because there had not been a public hearing by CIAS.[94]

Likewise, in France, athletes can file a complaint before the national courts in the case of an infringement of their basic rights, such as the right to privacy or the right of access to trial.[95] In fact, French cyclist Jeannie Longo has already brought a basic rights case. She appealed a decision of the AFLD to treat her as an international athlete who had to abide by the whereabouts rules. The French Council of State did not find a breach of article 8 ECHR because there was an equal balance between the privacy interest of the athlete and the obligation to protect health and fair play for the state. In January 2018, the ECtHR sided with the French Council of State on precisely the same legal issue: the whereabouts rules—originally created by WADA

[90] See also: District Court (LG) of Frankfurt 7 October 2020 no. 2-06 O 457/19.

[91] Ralf Petzold, 'Olympia-Siegerin Claudia Pechstein: "Ich will Geschichte schreiben"', *Mallorcazeitung* <https://www.mallorcazeitung.es/sport/2021/05/16/olympia-siegerin-claudia-pechstein-will/82310.html> (last accessed May 2021).

[92] *Mutu and Pechstein v. Switzerland* nos 40575/10 and 67474/10 (ECtHR, 2 October 2018).

[93] Ibid., § 113.

[94] Ibid., §§ 159 and 183.

[95] However there is deference from the courts in France: Jean-Marc Duval, 'Les arbitres et le droit du sport' in Fabrice Dosseville and Sylvain Laborde (eds), *Les facettes de l'arbitrage: problématiques et recherches actuelles* (Publibook 2011) 297.

and adopted by the AFLD as the French autonomous public actor—are in line with the right to privacy (article 8 ECHR) and the freedom of movement (article 2, Protocol 4 ECHR).[96] The wide margin of appreciation that the ECtHR granted to France and—implicitly—to WADA can be criticized because, by doing so, no national, transnational, or international entity steps up and defends the interests of the athletes.[97] Active athletes are poorly represented within WADA, cannot negotiate their 'contractual' relationship with WADA, have very little power to increase political pressure on national governments to embrace the WADA rulemaking framework, and are confronted with national judges who generally give wide discretion to WADA and the SGBs. Exceptionally, the subsidiarity principle, which inspired the margin of appreciation doctrine, would actually require the ECtHR to develop a stricter review of legal matters that can only be resolved transnationally, such as doping use in sport and the measures used to fight it. In this case, the margin of appreciation of states should be smaller and the protection of athletes' rights stronger.

Rights-based values are comparatively weaker in the UK where a contractual chain also guarantees that an athlete who joins a sports club submits to arbitration for doping cases: the National Anti-Doping Panel (NAPD) rules on doping-related cases. Based on the WADA guidelines, the UK has accepted the Court of Arbitration for Sports as an appeal chamber. UK courts grant significant deference to these arbitrators. In fact, it has been highly uncertain whether UK courts would accept judicial review of a 'contractual' doping rule subject to the *Aga Khan* case law (see Chapter 5). The ordinary UK courts would at most concentrate on whether the decision was *ultra vires*, whether the procedure was fair, and whether the presiding rules were applied correctly.[98]

Finally, WADA itself needs to ensure that its rules are proportionate and sufficiently individualized in order to enjoy continued judicial deference.[99] Otherwise, this judicial deference would contravene a state's duty to protect and to fulfil human

[96] *Fédération Nationale des Associations et des Syndicats Sportifs (FNASS) ea v. France* nos 48151/11 and 77769/13 (ECtHR, 18 January 2018) § 191.

[97] Cedric Jenart, 'Systeem van whereabouts voor elitesporters blijft overeind' [2018] 363*Juristenkrant* 6, Cedric Jenart, '*Fédération Nationale des Associations et des Syndicats Sportifs (FNASS) ea t. Frankrijk*' [2019] *Rechtskundig Weekblad* 1638–9.

[98] Oskar MacGregor, Richard Griffith, Daniele Ruggiu, and Mike McNamee, 'Anti-doping, Purported Rights to Privacy and WADA's Whereabouts Requirement' [2013] *Fair Play* 23; the Swiss Supreme Court took a similar hands-off approach to the rulings of the Court of Arbitration for Sport (Katia Fach Gomez, 'Enforcing Global Law: International Arbitration' [2015] *J. Legal Pluralism and Unofficial L.* 126). Even the European Court of Justice took a rather modest approach in reviewing sports law and anti-doping law cases. The *Bosman* and *Meca-Medina* judgments show that the EU internal market and EU competition law, respectively, limit the freedom of the private sport federations (Case C-415/93 Union Royale Belge des Sociétés de Football Association ASB *v.* Jean-Marc Bosman ECLI:EU:C:1995:463); Case C-519/04 Meca Medina and Majcen *v.* Commission of the European Communities ECLI:EU:C:2006:492).

[99] Marc Peltier, 'La transposition du code mondial antidopage dans l'ordre juridique interne' [2016] *Petites Affiches* 16.

rights. Former WADA President, Sir Craig Reedie, has explicitly confirmed the link between WADA's proper proportionality test and human rights review by domestic courts. As a comment on the demand for a life-long ban for doping cheats in the aftermath of Jamaican track runner Asafa Powell's positive doping test, the WADA President claimed that 'life bans would be challenged and would not be sustainable in law'.[100]

6.3.4 Representativeness

In order to respect representativeness as a principle of good rulemaking, WADA should be representative of the actors it regulates. Here, four main deficiencies are encountered.

First, as a result of the tumultuous last few years, NADO leaders have called for an overhaul of WADA. They have especially targeted the questionable independence of WADA and its executives from sports organizations.[101]

Second, athletes are not sufficiently represented in WADA's decision-making bodies. Article 6.1 of WADA's revised statutes only reserves four of the thirty-six seats of the Foundation Board to athletes. Moreover, WADA's Athlete Committee is merely an advisory standing committee 'to serve as the voice of clean athletes, encouraging integrity and fairness for sport and athletes'.[102] In 2008, the European Athletes Association addressed the lack of athletes' input on WADA's whereabouts system.[103] Today, many athletes have expressed their exasperation with the current anti-doping approach; they 'are losing faith in the system'.[104] According to the WADA Working Group on Governance Matters in 2017, 'the strongest way of ensuring that WADA lived out that ideal was to have increased representation of athletes across the apparatus, in particular in the Foundation Board'.[105]

Third, claims of partiality through the underrepresentation of some nationalities within WADA's leading ranks are encountered. Russian media accused WADA of having a hidden agenda in adding meldonium to the Prohibited List[106] since WADA would have been perfectly aware of the fact that many athletes took the substance. During the 2015 European Games in Baku, almost 9 per cent of the athletes

[100] BBC, 'Doping life bans "not legal", says WADA president Sir Craig Reedie', BBC Online (15 July 2014).

[101] Dan Roan, 'Anti-Doping leaders demand Wada overhaul with clean sport "at crossroads"', BBC Sport online (30 August 2016).

[102] WADA, 'Athlete Committee terms of reference' (December 2014), 1.

[103] Ivan Waddington, 'The WADA Whereabouts Aystem' in Mike McNamee and Verner Møller (eds), *Doping and Anti-Doping Policy in Sport: Ethical, Legal and Social Perspectives* (Routledge 2011) 189–93.

[104] Jeff Raymond, 'Report on EU Anti-Doping Conference', Amsterdam (15 June 2016), 3.

[105] Foundation Board WADA, 'Minutes of the WADA Foundation Board Meeting', Montreal, Canada (18 May 2017) 13.

[106] BELGA, 'Uitvinder meldonium ziet complot: 'Enkel verboden omdat er Olympische Spelen aankomen', Het Nieuwsblad Online (19 March 2016).

reportedly tested positive for meldonium.[107] Meldonium had only been on the monitored list for one year before it was prohibited.[108] Moreover, given the fact that the substance was primarily available in Russia, the prohibition seemed directed to Russian athletes. In the past, the French Senate has also suspected the Prohibited List of being overly influenced by the 'Anglo-American approach'.[109] From a legal perspective, the evaluation is not straightforward. On the one hand, Russia has been one of WADA's most prevalent sponsors.[110] On the other hand, it has little to show for it. Russia has no representative on WADA's Executive Committee or Foundation Board. More importantly, the representation of nationalities in the Expert Group that drafts the Prohibited List, arguably the most influential expert panel, leans strongly towards the Western world. In 2021, the members by nationality were: one Irish, three American, two German, two Australians, one Italian, one British, one British/Swiss, one British/Ghanaian.

Fourth, one can foresee a problem of partiality through the involvement of private companies in the funding system of WADA. WADA is increasingly attempting to find private sponsors.[111] Pharmaceutical companies may thus pay the guards that supervise their products. Much attention has been paid to Russian athletes, but Grindeks, the Latvian manufacturer of meldonium, was also directly affected by the unilateral decision of WADA to add its product to the Prohibited List when the market for its medicine against coronary artery disease inevitably shrunk. Even in less conspicuously relevant markets, the rulemaking power of WADA may provoke distrust. A hyperbolic question could serve to buttress this idea further: what would happen if WADA put Pepsi-Cola on the Prohibited List because of its performance-enhancing functions but not Coca-Cola?[112] There is no legal recourse to appeal such additions to the Prohibited List. WADA's determination is 'final and shall not be subject to challenge by an Athlete or other Person based on an argument that the substance or method was not a masking agent or did not have the potential to enhance performance, represent a health risk or violate the spirit of sport'.[113]

[107] Ben Rumsby, 'Meldonium was used by almost 500 athletes at European Games', The Telegraph Online (9 March 2016).

[108] Carolyn Beans, 'What Does It Take To Get a Drug Banned for Enhancing Athletes' Performance?', NPR Online (14 June 2016).

[109] Alain Dufaut, 'Rapport fait au nom de la commission des Affaires culturelles (1) sur le project de loi, adopté par l'Assemblée Nationale, relatif à la lutte contre le dopage et à la protection de la santé des sportifs 2005–2006 no. 12' (12 October 2005) 61.

[110] Foundation Board WADA, 'Minutes of the WADA Foundation Board Meeting', Montreal, Canada (13 May 2015) 16.

[111] BBC, 'Wada president calls for funding help for doping fight', BBC Online (15 March 2016).

[112] Caffeine has in fact been on the monitored list for over a decade: Carolyn Beans, 'What Does It Take To Get A Drug Banned for Enhancing Athletes' Performance?', NPR Online (14 June 2016).

[113] Article 4.3.3 of the WADA Code 2015.

6.3.5 Efficiency or effectiveness

The ultimate standard that WADA needs to uphold is its efficiency and effectiveness deriving from its expertise. The UK Science and Technology Committee report implicitly questioned WADA's expertise and output legitimacy by stating that more attention should be paid to exact sciences in drafting the Prohibited List.[114] Nevertheless, most stakeholders acknowledge the unique accumulation of expertise within WADA.

Even so, influential voices in the sports world have questioned the use of an expensive anti-doping policy when athletes continue to dope unseen.[115] This argument adds to the already existing questions hovering over the fight against doping in sports. Some athletes will always have genetic or cognitive advantages over other athletes.[116] The question therefore arises as to whether the decision to combat doping in sports is effective in the first place. Although there are sufficient reasons of health, equality, and fair play to defend the conceptual effectiveness of anti-doping rules,[117] it is crucial that WADA does not underestimate its own powers.[118] It should increasingly search for a rulemaking system that leaves as little leeway as possible to doping cheats, particularly because many successes against doping in sports have been made by national, general anti-drugs laws and not so much because of WADA's anti-doping rules.[119] Without success stories, WADA's own output legitimacy[120] risks crumbling accordingly.

According to the Working Group on WADA Governance Matters, the ideal locus to embody efficiency and expertise would be WADA's Executive Committee: 'If the Foundation Board became the primary locus for representation of all of WADA's constituencies, the Executive Committee should become the primary engine for management oversight and strategy'.[121]

[114] House of Commons Select Committee on Science and Technology, 'Human Enhancement Technologies in Sport', Second Report of Session 2006–07, HC 67 (February 2007).

[115] Terry Engelberg, Stephen Moston, and James Skinner, 'The Final Frontier of Anti-Doping: A Study of Athletes Who Have Committed Doping Violations' [2015] *Sport Management Rev.* 277.

[116] Jack Anderson, 'Doping, Sport and the Law: Time for Repeal of Prohibition?' [2013] *Int' J. L. in Context* 151; Stijn Cools, 'Geen geslachtsoperatie meer nodig voor Olympische transgenders', *De Standaard* (26 January 2016) 22–3.

[117] Roberta Furst Wolf, 'Conflicting Anti-Doping Laws in Professional Sports: Collective Bargaining Agreements v. State Law' [2010–11] *Seattle U. L. Rev.* 1636; Cedric Jenart, 'Zelfregulering en de bescherming van grondrechten: de casus van doping in de elitesport' [2016] *TBP* 296.

[118] Rebecca R. Ruiz, Juliet Macur, and Ian Austen, 'Even With Confession of Cheating, World's Doping Watchdog Did Nothing', New York Times Online (15 June 2016).

[119] Dag Vidar Hanstad, Andy Smith, and Ivan Waddington, 'The Establishment of the World Anti-Doping Agency' [2008] *Int'l Rev. for the Sociology of Sport* 247. Cf. the arrest and trial of Doctor Fuentes in Spain.

[120] Vivien A. Schmidt, 'Democracy and Legitimacy in the European Union Revisited: Input, Output and 'Throughput' [2013] *Political Studies* 11.

[121] Foundation Board WADA, 'Minutes of the WADA Foundation Board Meeting', Montreal, Canada (18 May 2017) 12.

6.4 Conclusion

Chapter 6 began by offering an overview of how private and public actors approached one another in the battle against doping by creating hybrid actors. WADA offers an insightful example of how outsourced rules can be directly or indirectly implemented in the countries researched and on how their constitutional systems have limited the possibility of outsourcing rulemaking powers to WADA. In fact, NADOs can also been seen as autonomous public or private actors. Moreover, with regard to the first research hypothesis, they receive some degree of rulemaking powers through the three outsourcing techniques in most of the countries studied.

First, none of the countries researched delegates rulemaking powers to WADA itself. However, France, and arguably the UK, transferred rulemaking powers to their respective NADOs. Second, its four federated entities make Belgium the only country studied that utilizes the direct referral technique with respect to WADA-made rules. France and Germany both refer dynamically, but indirectly, by referring to the 2005 UNESCO Treaty, which itself has incorporated a number of WADA-made rules. Third, the countries researched allow for and control the self-regulation of SGBs that tie their athletes contractually to WADA-made rules. As argued earlier, the complete lack of bargaining power for active athletes if they want to exercise their profession can make this an example of the *reception* of rulemaking powers.

Various constitutional principles limit the extent to which a government can outsource powers which it would otherwise exercise itself. The separation of powers (because WADA or NADOs have not been enshrined in the national constitutions to exercise rulemaking powers), the legality principle (especially with regard to criminal law), and the democracy principle (because of WADA's or the NADOs' limited democratic accountability) all limit the possibility of outsourcing rulemaking powers in the case of anti-doping regulations. Below, I consider these limits in relation to the three outsourcing techniques.

First, national Legislatures cannot *delegate* rulemaking powers to WADA. A direct transfer of competences would be deemed unconstitutional in most countries, including Belgium, France, Germany, and the US. In the UK, a combination of the doctrine of the sovereignty of Parliament, judicial deference, and a reverence for the autonomy of the *lex sportiva* could allow for more leeway in outsourcing rulemaking power to WADA. Delegations of rulemaking powers to NADOs, however, seem unproblematic if they comply with the limits as set out Chapter 4, especially the democracy principle.

The second technique used to outsource rulemaking powers is *referral*. Doping has proven to be a rapidly changing policy area, for which national Legislatures and Executives want to find flexible implementation techniques that do not infringe on constitutional principles. In Belgium, dynamic referral to WADA documents is only considered unproblematic when the rulemaking power cannot bind athletes.

The Flemish Legislature ultimately does refer dynamically to articles of the WADA Code but solely when it simultaneously delegates power to the Flemish Executive; it is avoided in provisions that bind citizens. In Germany and France, direct dynamic referral also contradicts the separation of powers and the democracy principle. As mentioned, France and Germany, therefore, do not dynamically refer to WADA's Prohibited List directly but to treaties that dynamically refer to WADA's Prohibited List.

Third, the ratification or *reception* of existing rules is the method of controlled self-regulation that creates least problems for the shared constitutional principles that limit anti-doping rulemaking in the countries researched. The French Executive, for example, explicitly ratified the annual Prohibited List until its 2006 statute against doping in sport, which started to refer dynamically to the 1989 Anti-Doping Convention and the 2005 Convention against Doping in Sport, respectively. Unfortunately, recognizing the value of a previously determined standard does not match the idiosyncrasies of the ever-changing and highly technical anti-doping rules. Moreover, by recognizing these WADA-made rules, the countries researched also implicitly recognize the validity of the 'contractual' chain that links the athlete via SGBs to WADA. As a result, the reception technique on outsourcing rulemaking powers experiences few limits.

Nevertheless, this does not imply that there are not safeguards with which WADA needs to comply in order to draft 'good rules'. As seen with regard to the second research hypothesis, WADA-made rules especially need to be sufficiently transparent and be subject to judicial review in order for WADA to remain a legitimate rulemaker on doping in sports and in order for it to comply with the rule of law and principles of democracy. With regard to transparency, WADA still has to cover some distance in order to make up for its lack of input legitimacy. Its rules are already reasonably accessible, such that even without additional state publication methods, a case could be made for its compliance with this principle of good rulemaking. With regard to their intelligibility, however, WADA is still largely backtracking. In addition, judicial review of WADA-made rules appears to be sufficient in the countries researched—especially when human rights violations are threatened. The representativeness and effectiveness of WADA's decision-making body and its respect for human rights will further influence how the public perceives this hybrid actor.

Finally, it was only the established position of WADA-made rules within the hierarchy of rules that was largely bereft of importance in this anti-doping case study. This was because the outsourcing techniques used in the countries researched do not grant national legal status to WADA-made rules. Nevertheless, it can be concluded that WADA needs to invest in safeguarding the other principles of good rulemaking if it wants to have a real future as a legitimate drafter of rules in the fight against doping.

7
General Conclusions

The seventh and final chapter of this monograph discusses the general insights (Section 7.1), conclusions (Section 7.2), and recommendations (Section 7.3) that can be drawn from the preceding chapters.

(1) First, I combine the most important *insights* of this comparative monograph on outsourcing rulemaking powers to autonomous public or private actors. The overarching idea framing these insights and arising from this book as a whole is 'convergence from divergence'. Despite a wide variety of ways of outsourcing rulemaking powers and to legally frame such possibilities (divergence), there is a remarkable impetus towards similar motives, techniques, and practices (convergence).

(2) Second, I highlight the primary *conclusions* that can be derived from this research's analysis on both research hypotheses: (a) under certain conditions rulemaking powers can be outsourced to autonomous public and private actors; and (b) there are safeguards that autonomous public and private actors need to heed when they create outsourced rules. I selected Belgium, France, Germany, the UK, and the US as the base for this research.

(3) Third, I make three *recommendations* that should help the legal and practical approach to the outsourcing of rulemaking powers to autonomous public or private actors. More specifically, I recommend that lawmakers and courts in all of the researched countries treat autonomous public, private, and hybrid actors as one constitutional, residuary, category. Moreover, countries should consider adopting a constitutional or statutory provision which actualizes the findings presented here in relation to both research hypotheses. Finally, I suggest good practice concerning which technique of outsourcing can be best used, based on the motive for outsourcing.

Outsourcing Rulemaking Powers. Cedric Jenart, Oxford University Press. © Cedric Jenart 2022.
DOI: 10.1093/oso/9780192897831.003.0007

7.1 Insights: convergence from divergence in motives and techniques

The main theme of the insights of this research, namely that convergences can be found in divergences in the outsourcing of rulemaking powers, is apparent in: the motives that are used in practice to outsource rulemaking powers (Section 7.1.1); the three selected outsourcing techniques (Section 7.1.2); and the fact that these shared evolutions take place despite substantial constitutional differences between the investigated countries (Section 7.1.3).

7.1.1 Three motives to outsource rulemaking powers

Various reasons for outsourcing rulemaking powers have been given,[1] for which I also included a preliminary inventory in Chapter 1 of this research. However, in line with this conclusion on convergence from divergence, I have narrowed these down to three main motives: independence as a buffer from politics (Section 7.1.1.1); expertise and technicality (Section 7.1.1.2); and increased stakeholder input (Section 7.1.1.3). Various legal scholars have designated these three key motives as the reasons why traditional rulemakers outsource rulemaking powers.[2]

7.1.1.1 Independence

Independence, as the first motive, is usually inspired by an aim to overcome the short-term perspectives that usually derive from decisions made by the Legislature or the Executive that are driven by elections.[3] This first goal thus emphasizes the independence of autonomous public or private actors, as opposed to such politically accountable actors.[4] It should not be surprising that the former developed out of a

[1] Neil Parpworth, *Constitutional and Administrative Law* (Oxford University Press 2016) 203; John McEldowney, *Public Law* (Sweet & Maxwell 2016) 232–3; Paul Craig, *Administrative Law* (Sweet & Maxwell 2016) 435; Mark Elliott and Robert Thomas, *Public Law* (Oxford University Press 2017) 138–9

[2] Hugues Dumont, 'La Constitution et le contrôle parlementaire des délégations de pouvoirs aux autorités administratives. Pour un renouveau du régimes parlementaire belge à l'heure de la gouvernance' in André Alen, Arnold Rainer, and Marc Bossuyt (eds), *De Grondwet: verleden, heden en toekomst* (Bruylant 2006) 64–5 and 67–9; John Huber and Charles Shipan, *Deliberate Discretion: The Institutional Foundations of Bureaucratic Autonomy* (Cambridge University Press 2002) 11; David Epstein and Sharyn O'Halloran, *Delegating Powers: A Transactions Cost Politics Approach to Policy Making under Separate Powers* (Cambridge University Press 1999) 7–9; Kathleen Bawn, 'Political Control versus Expertise: Congressional Choices about Administrative Procedures' (1995) 89(1) *Am. Pol. Science Rev.* 62.

[3] Catherine Durose, Jonathan Justice, and Chris Skelcher, 'Governing at Arm's Length: Eroding or Enhancing Democracy?' [2015] *Pol'y & Politics* 140.

[4] EU Directive 2009/72/CE of the European Parliament and of the Council of 13 July 2009 concerning common rules for the internal market in electricity and repealing Directive 2003/54/EC, recital 33; Stéphane Hoynck, 'Indépéndant de qui? Les trois âges de l'indépendance des régulateurs des télécommunications en Europe' [2012] *Revue française d'administration publique* 799; Stéphanie Dubiton, *La protection des libertés publiques par les autorités administratives indépendantes, une solution démocratique?* (LGDJ 2016) 3.

need for more neutrality and independence. The most prominent example of this motive can be found in the Europeanization of domestic law in the Member States of the EU.[5] The EU strives for a number of shared objectives that cannot deviate from their course according to the whims of temporary politics. Another corroboration of independence as a motive is the aim of searching for external funds or avoiding competition between Executive departments.[6]

7.1.1.2 Expertise

The second motive is arguably most often cited to defend the transfer of rulemaking powers to autonomous public or private actors, especially in the US; namely, their increased cost-efficiency and expertise.[7] Indeed, some regulatory matters are so technical and difficult that we may not expect politicians to grasp them fully.[8] Moreover, it is argued that without outsourcing rulemaking powers, the Legislature or the Executive could be mired in details to the detriment of essential responsibilities, such as exercising political control.[9] As such, the rulemaking task would become so complex and time-consuming that traditional politically accountable rulemakers could not focus on more fundamental policy areas.[10] In Chapter 5, I engaged with these preconceptions and concluded that autonomous public or private actors may have some presumption of efficiency over the Executive and the Legislature. However, this is not always self-evident, and traditional politically accountable rulemakers will and should implement measures such as performance review and regulatory impact analyses to safeguard that efficiency and expertise.

7.1.1.3 Stakeholder input

The third motive, increased stakeholder input with the aim of gaining support, represents a means of embracing self-regulation and agreements that were previously made by those who were confronted with potential issues on a daily basis. This type of rulemaking can answer social and professional needs where ordinary legislation falls short.[11] From a more cynical perspective, this motive may be inspired by a

[5] Rob Van Gestel, 'The Deparliamentarisation of Legislation: Framework Laws and the Primacy of the Legislature' [2013] *Utrecht L. Rev.* 111.

[6] John McEldowney, *Public Law* (Sweet & Maxwell 2016) 242.

[7] 2.a. Circular A-119 US Office of Management and Budget for standards; Eoin Carolan, 'Democratic Accountability and the Non-Delegation Doctrine' [2011] *Dublin U. LJ* III, Delegation as a Necessary Feature of Modern Government; Paul Craig, *Administrative Law* (Sweet & Maxwell 2016) 433; Walter Mattli, 'Private Transnational Governance' in Jacob Katz Cogan, Ian Hurd, and Ian Johnstone (eds), *The Oxford Handbook of International Organizations* (Oxford University Press 2016) 173.

[8] See, with regard to the Commission for Banking, Finances and Insurances: Belgian Chamber of Representatives (Parliamentary Documents Chamber of Representatives no. 348/1, 1995–6) 4.

[9] Wolf-Rüdiger Schenke, 'Die verfassungsrechtliche Problematik dynamischer Verweisungen' [1980] *NJW* 743.

[10] Eberhard Baden, 'Dynamische Verweisungen und Verweisungen auf Nichtnormen' [1979] *NJW* 625; Florian Becker, *Kooperative und konsensuale Strukturen in der Normsetzung* (Mohr Siebeck 2005) 538.

[11] Stéphanie Dubiton, *La protection des libertés publiques par les autorités administratives indépendantes, une solution démocratique?* (LGDJ 2016) 2.

desire to pass on a hot potato and avoid responsibility. In summary, this third motive entails that a select representation of civil society should make such decisions (and bear the perceived responsibility for them).[12]

These three reasons—independence through a buffer, expertise, and stakeholder input—also emerge within the reviewing criteria of the Belgian Council of State Legislative Section.[13] The German case likewise reaffirms the three overarching motivations for outsourcing rulemaking powers: (1) to neutralize the whims of political fluctuations; (2) to increase expertise or flexibility; and (3) to involve stakeholders in order to enhance their compliance with future rules.[14] In fact, international legal scholarship attributed three very similar motives to the outsourcing of rulemaking or other powers to international bodies, namely: (a) to create a political buffer for making dispassionate decisions;[15] (b) to make use of the heightened expertise within an international body;[16] and (c) to shift responsibility to a more distant actor.[17]

7.1.2 Three techniques to outsource rulemaking powers

I distinguished three types of outsourcing of rulemaking powers: delegation, referral, and reception. This distinction is unique to this research but has some similarities to existing scholarly categories, such as the German 'Delegation', 'Inklusion', and 'Akzeptanz'.[18]

7.1.2.1 Delegation

Delegation is the clearest and most committed type of outsourcing. Across the globe, including in Belgium, France, Germany, the UK, and the US, constitutional law is acquainted with the phenomenon of delegated powers. The politically accountable delegator mandates the delegatee to exercise well-defined rulemaking competences in its place. Such delegations primarily occur for the benefit of network industry regulators, such as autonomous public bodies in the fields of finance,

[12] Alfred G. Debus, *Verweisungen in Deutschen Rechtsnormen* (Duncker & Humblot 2008).

[13] Belgian Council of State Legislative Section, Advisory opinion no. 53.459/1 of 1 July 2013, 7.

[14] e.g. Georg Hermes, 'Legitimationsprobleme Unabhängiger Behörden' in Harmut Bauer, Peter Huber, and Karl-Peter Sommermann (eds), *Demokratie in Europa* (Mohr Siebeck 2005) 479; Hans-Ulrich Karpen, *Die Verweisung als Mittel der Gesetzgebungstechnik* (De Gruyter 1970) 11.

[15] Kathleen Bawn, 'Political Control Versus Expertise: Congressional Choices about Administrative Procedures'[1995] *Am. Pol. Science Rev.* 62–3.

[16] Stavros Gadinis, 'Three Pathways to Global Standards: Private, Regulator, and Ministry Networks' [2015] *Am. J. Int'l L.* 9; Maurizia De Bellis, 'Public Law and Private Regulators in the Global Legal Space' [2011] *ICON* 426.

[17] Tim Büthe, 'The Globalization of Health and Safety Standards: Delegation of Regulatory Authority in the SPS Agreement of the 1994 Agreement Establishing the World Trade Organization' [2008] *Law and Contemporary Problems* 249.

[18] Nils Christian Ipsen, *Private Normenordnungen als transnationales Recht* (Duncker & Humblot 2009) 232–5.

energy, and telecommunications.[19] A research-specific description of delegation thus proves necessary.

On the one hand, the notion of delegation is sometimes used too narrowly. I opted not to maintain the artificial distinction between delegation and attribution, which is still reluctantly maintained in Belgian, French, and to some extent even German public law. The definition given to 'delegation' there is too limited to adequately describe the ways in which politically accountable actors effectively transfer power to various other actors. Delegation would then essentially imply the transfer of exactly the same power of the delegator (e.g. the Legislature that mandates the Executive to make statutory laws). The mere enhancement of the powers of the recipient should be called 'attribution' (e.g. the Legislature that mandates the Executive to make executive decrees on wider competences). However, this distinction between delegation and attribution does not exist in other (common law) countries. Moreover, other scientific disciplines, such as the political sciences, also do not distinguish between delegations and attributions, to the benefit of one overarching delegation category.

On the other hand, the notion of delegation is sometimes also utilized too broadly.[20] EU Advocate General Campos Sanchez-Bordona even described the non-binding reference to standards as 'legislative delegation in favour of a private standardisation body'.[21] The Dutch Second Chamber of Parliament equally considered (dynamic) referrals to be de facto delegations at one point.[22] In doing so, the concept of delegation risks losing many of its nuances.

I therefore simultaneously widened and limited the definition of delegation to the genuine transfer of governmental powers to another actor. It proved possible to apply this shared definition over the researched countries.

7.1.2.2 Referral

The Legislature and the Executive regularly directly refer in their own rules to the prescriptive elements of an external document that an autonomous public or private actor has drafted.

Referrals, as researched in this monograph, are carried out by traditional politically accountable actors to private and hybrid standards. This type of referral occurs in Belgium, France, Germany, the UK, and the US.[23] Primarily, lower ranked

[19] e.g. EU Directive 2002/21/EC of the European Parliament and of the Council of 7 March 2002 on a common regulatory framework for electronic communications networks and services (Framework Directive) granting broad 'regulatory' powers to national regulatory authorities (article 3); Eva Krodel, *Öffentlich-rechtliche und privatrechtliche Rundfunkorganisation in Großbritannien im Lichte der Rundfunkfreiheit* (Verlag Dr Kovač 2015) 247–8.

[20] Andreas Kruck, *Private Ratings, Public Regulations* (Palgrave Macmillan 2011) 8; Paul Verbruggen, *Enforcing Transnational Private Regulation* (Edward Elgar 2014) 273.

[21] Opinion of AG Campos Sanchez-Bordona, Case C-613/14 *James Elliott Construction Ltd v. Irish Asphalt Ltd* ECLI:EU:C:2016:63, § 55.

[22] Dutch Council of State, Advisory opinion on *regels betreffende zelfstandige bestuursorganen. Kaderwet zelfstandige bestuursorganen* (Dutch Parliament Second Chamber 2000–1, no. 27 426) A 4.

[23] Alfred G. Debus, *Verweisungen in Deutschen Rechtsnormen* (Duncker & Humblot 2008) 36–7.

rules refer to standards because those rules are more detailed, flexible, and require more expertise.[24]

The external documents to which the Legislature and the Executive usually refer are technical standards made by 'non-market private international standard setting bodies' and, arguably, their most well-known examples are the International Standardization Organization (ISO), the International Electrotechnical Commission (IEC), and the International Accounting Standards Board (IASB).[25] However, these are not exclusive examples. The World Anti-Doping Agency (WADA), for example, is more than a standard-setting body. Nevertheless, the research has unveiled examples which refer directly to prescriptive WADA-made standards.

This research systematically addressed the difference between static and dynamic referrals. Static referrals only concern external document at the time of referral whereas dynamic referrals also incorporate subsequent changes to that external document. The ISO itself indicates that dynamic referrals to its standards are not possible.[26] This fact shows that standard-setting bodies themselves are not eager to have traditional rulemakers refer directly to them, certainly not dynamically.

However, the ISO's stance has been refuted throughout this monograph. In Germany, France, and Belgium dynamic referrals definitely occur and are—under strict conditions—constitutional. Likewise, in the UK there would be no impediment to the Legislature dynamically referring to standards, if even delegation is broadly allowed. This, albeit hesitant, acceptance of dynamic referrals within some researched countries reflects examples in other researched countries. On a federal US level, *dynamic* referrals are considered to be prohibited.[27] 'Incorporation by reference of a publication is limited to the edition of the publication that is approved. Future amendments or revisions of the publication are not included.' However, at the US state level, they may be allowed, as is the case in Alaska.[28]

[24] Ministère de l'économie, de l'industrie et de l'emploi, *Guide relatif a la bonne utilisation des normes dans la reglementation* (Direction générale de la compétitivité, de l'industrie et des services 2009) 15.

[25] Paul Craig, *UK, EU and Global Administrative Law* (Cambridge University Press 2015) 573; Walter Mattli, 'Private Transnational Governance' in Jacob Katz Cogan, Ian Hurd, and Ian Johnstone (eds), *The Oxford Handbook of International Organizations* (Oxford University Press 2016) 174–5.

[26] ISO and IEC, *Le recours et la référence aux normes ISO et IEC dans les politiques publiques* (ISO and IEC 2015) 26.

[27] 1 US Code of Federal Regulations 51.1.f; Emily S. Bremer, American and European Perspectives on Private Standards in Public Law (2016) 91 *Tul. L. Rev.* 325, 347.

[28] In accordance with Alaska Statute § 44.62.245(a): 'In adopting a regulation that incorporates a document or other material by reference, a state agency may incorporate future amended versions of the document or other material if the adopted regulation identifies or refers to the document or other material followed by the phrase "as may be amended", the phrase "as amended from time to time", or a similar provision.'

7.1.2.3 Reception

With regard to 'reception' as a third outsourcing technique, the Legislature and the Executive recognize or receive the rules made by professional organizations. Various terms have been used to describe similar phenomena, for example 'recuperation'.[29]

This research noted a growing realization that professional agreements could strongly resemble government regulation, and certainly when the state *ex ante* or *ex post* recognizes those agreements as rules.[30] 'Private associations are considered governments when they exhibit, to a significant extent, certain fundamental characteristics ... they exercise power over both members and non-members, often in vital areas of individual and societal concern.'[31]

The most important examples of the reception technique are, on the one hand, the codes of professional organizations or 'orders' and, on the other, collective labour agreements. Under the impetus of the International Labour Organization, the extension of collective labour agreements has been widespread worldwide.[32] This was noticeable in three of the researched countries—Belgium, France, and Germany—but not in the UK or the US. Finally, in the UK the conditions that sports organizations set for athletes could be seen as an example of the reception technique. In this light, the reception technique has been approached as a bottom-up type of rulemaking.

7.1.3 Similarities despite differences between the researched countries

Despite seemingly significant constitutional differences, a similar impetus for the outsourcing of rulemaking powers can be found in the researched countries. Here I show this insight with regard to the status of each national constitution (Section 7.1.3.1), domestic institutional systems (Section 7.1.3.2), and each country's approach to international law (Section 7.1.3.3).

[29] Véronique Ranouil and Pierre-Charles Ranouil, 'Le professeur de droit des nouvelles technologies et le droit mou: bref bavardage entre amis' in Xavier Linant de Bellefonds (ed.), *Droit et technique. Etudes à la mémoire de Xavier Linant de Bellefonds* (LexisNexis 2007) 431.

[30] See, for *ex post* reception or recognition: Paul Verbruggen, *Enforcing Transnational Private Regulation* (Edward Elgar 2014) 274–5.

[31] Catherine Durose, Jonathan Justice, and Chris Skelcher, 'Governing at Arm's Length: Eroding or Enhancing Democracy?' [2015] *Pol'y & Politics* 143 citing Lakoff and Rich, *Private Government: Introductory Readings* (Glenview 1973) 1–6.

[32] International Labour Organization, *Article IV Collective Agreements Recommendation number 91* (Geneva 1951). Thorsten Schulten, 'The Meaning of Extension for the Stability of Collective Bargaining in Europe', ETUI Research Paper, Policy Brief 3/2016 [2016)]. Available at SSRN: <https://ssrn.com/abstract=2792100 or http://dx.doi.org/10.2139/ssrn.2792100>, 2.

7.1.3.1 Status of the constitution

The first difference between the constitutional set-ups of the researched countries is the fact that only four have a written and codified constitution, namely Belgium, France, Germany, and the US. The UK has no codified constitution and is heavily reliant on its doctrine of parliamentary sovereignty. The UK thus takes an outlier position due to the fact that it does not have a written and codified constitution.

Admittedly, this divergence brings to bear an understanding of the variety of outsourcing techniques in relation to the stringency of the limits of the outsourcing of rulemaking powers. These limits are weakest in the UK. The variety of techniques to outsource rulemaking powers in general appears to be influenced by the stringency of the limits placed on outsourcing rulemaking powers. If these limits are extremely strict, as is principally the case in Belgium, France, Germany, and the US, many varieties and examples of rulemaking powers being outsourced to autonomous public or private actors are found. This is done by traditional rulemakers actors looking for alternative methods to comply with strict constitutional demands. However, when there are few express limits to the outsourcing of rulemaking powers—as is the case for the UK Legislature due to the sovereignty of Parliament—the diversity of outsourcing techniques diminishes, leading to a primary reliance on the delegation technique. Why have a more intricate outsourcing technique if a general and broad delegation of powers to autonomous public or private actors appears equally acceptable?[33] Legal strategies are therefore crucial for the understanding of outsourcing techniques.

Despite this divergence, this research established that rulemaking powers are being extensively outsourced in all of the researched countries, regardless of the presence of a written constitution and regardless of the variety of outsourcing techniques.

7.1.3.2 Institutional system of democratic governance

Second, one should not disregard, but also not overstate, the influence of differing domestic democratic systems on the outsourcing of rulemaking powers.

On the one hand, the democratic system can lead to a wide disparity between researched countries. It has been argued that the influence of the doctrine of the separation of powers increases in presidential or semi-presidential systems and decreases in parliamentary systems. The research supports this claim with regard to outsourcing rulemaking powers. France is the only researched country with a semi-presidential system. The French Constitutional Council prides itself on its

[33] This theory is, e.g., buttressed by the fact that the UK Executive uses the referral technique more widely. The status of delegations of governmental powers by the Executive without parliamentary authorization is highly questionable, explaining the Executive's search for alternative outsourcing techniques.

interpretation of the 'French version' of the separation of powers.[34] There have been examples in which the French Constitutional Council has ruled against the transfer of powers to an autonomous public or private actor, both from an institutional and a functional separation of powers point of view. In line with the French outcome, in the US presidential system the US Supreme Court has emphasized the separation of powers since its earliest case law on the outsourcing of rulemaking powers. The exercise of rulemaking powers by private actors—even with the approval of the President—was deemed contrary to the separation of powers principle in the case of *Schechter Poultry*.[35] The separation of powers doctrines in the parliamentary systems of Belgium, Germany, and the UK on this issue were notably less influential.[36]

Furthermore, Rose-Ackerman has defended the notion that presidential systems create a greater incentive to rein in executive rulemaking with statutory provisions than do parliamentary systems.[37] She points, in the first instance, to the US and its 'semi-constitutional' Administrative Procedure Act.[38] For similar reasons, Jensen and McGrath have argued that presidential systems lead to the institution of autonomous or other agencies more than parliamentary systems.[39] Doubtless, there is some truth in both of those assertions.

However, on the other hand, diverging democratic systems still face similar challenges and methods to counter those challenges. First, this monograph has clarified that in parliamentary, semi-presidential, and presidential systems, administrative or other forms of rulemaking are limited by other means than explicit statutes, namely constitutional principles. In addition, the choice of a presidential or semi-presidential system rather than a parliamentary system, as occurred in the US or France, is not necessarily the nail in the coffin for Parliament's powers. On the contrary, in the US the non-delegation doctrine in favour of the Legislature is—at least in theory—essential and in France the de facto rulemaking powers of the French Legislature were judicially enlarged despite the de jure limitation of its powers.[40] In parliamentary systems such as Belgium, Germany, and the UK,

[34] French Constitutional Council no. 86-224 DC of 23 January 1987, § 15-23. Jean-Philippe Feldman, 'La séparation des pouvoirs et le constitutionnalisme. Mythes et réalités d'une doctrine et de ses critiques' [2010] *Revue française de droit constitutionnel* 488.

[35] *A. L. A. Schechter Poultry Corp. v. United States*, 295 US 495 (1935); Kimberly N. Brown, 'We the People, Constitutional Accountability, and Outsourcing Government' (2013) 88 *Ind. LJ* 1347, 1366.

[36] See for Germany: Susan Rose-Ackerman, Stefanie Egidy, and James Fowkes, *Due Process of Lawmaking* (Cambridge University Press 2014) 165.

[37] Susan Rose-Ackerman, 'Democratic Legitimacy and Executive Rulemaking: Positive Political Theory in Comparative Public Law' in Joana Mendes and Ingo Venzke (eds), *Allocating Authority. Who Should Do What in European and International Law* (Hart 2018) 32–6.

[38] Susan Rose-Ackerman, 'Democratic Legitimacy and Executive Rulemaking: Positive Political Theory in Comparative Public Law' in Joana Mendes and Ingo Venzke (eds), *Allocating Authority. Who Should Do What in European and International Law* (Hart 2018) 39.

[39] Christian B. Jensen and Robert J. McGrath, 'Making Rules about Rulemaking: A Comparison of Presidential and Parliamentary Systems' [2011] *Political Research Quarterly* 665.

[40] Louis Favoreu, 'Le pouvoir normatif primaire du Gouvernement en droit français'[1997] *Revue française de droit constitutionnel* 723–5.

Parliament reigns de jure, but it is actually the Executive that is de facto in full control. Moreover, this research has attested to the fact that even in parliamentary systems rulemaking powers have been outsourced to various levels within the Executive *and* to autonomous public or private actors.

7.1.3.3 Approach to international law

This research might not have focused on the transfer of rulemaking powers within international or transnational institutions themselves; however, the increasing importance of international and global administrative law has been ever-present.

A third diverging factor among researched countries is their dissimilar approaches to international law. Two of the researched countries are monist (Belgium and France), two are dualist (Germany and the UK), and one takes a middle position (the US)[41]. Nevertheless, this research revealed—in three distinct ways—the strong converging factors of internationalization and globalization on domestic rulemaking in general, and on outsourcing rulemaking powers, more specifically.

First, the existence of each outsourcing technique is firmly grounded in evolutions that coincide with internationalization. The *delegation* to autonomous public or private actors in the European researched countries was most powerfully influenced by EU law, which imposes the stipulation that rulemaking or other powers regarding network industries should reside with actors that are autonomous from politically accountable actors. Likewise, the *referral* technique is most frequently used to refer to norms of standard-setting bodies that have been transnationally propelled (often by the ISO) in order to resolve problems of standardization that arise in a globalized society. The *reception* technique only requires a limited role by the state. Sometimes, particularly in the UK, not even ratification by a traditional, politically accountable actor is required. It could be asked whether, in that case, contract law allows professional organizations to freely impose any requirements that they wish on their members. The case law of the European Court of Human Rights, as an international body, clarifies that private professional actors (e.g. sports organizations) can invoke the responsibility of the Contracting State, through the latter's duty to *protect* its citizens (e.g. athletes) against human rights violations.[42]

Second, there is a noteworthy convergence between the outsourcing of rulemaking powers and domestic treaty-making in general. Both treaty-making and outsourcing share a preference for the dynamic or static referral technique. Treaties often refer to other treaties, while statutes may also refer to treaties (e.g. the Human Rights Act 1998 in the UK). Moreover, the Belgian, French, and German cases show how constitutional provisions to make treaties or transfer powers to the international level are utilized to justify the outsourcing of rulemaking powers at

[41] *Medellín v. Texas*, 552 US 491 (2008).
[42] Chapter 2, Section 2.4.2.1 of this monograph.

the national level. Finally, especially in Germany, the issue of the binding version of translated treaties also appeared in this research in relation to the binding language version of referred-to standards. The outcome of this is that the translated version should generally be binding on the constituency.

Third, the entire case study of the World Anti-Doping Agency proved crucial for understanding how the researched countries found different ways of reaching similar outcomes, namely to conform to a transnational anti-doping framework through the outsourcing of rulemaking powers. The Legislature and the Executive within the researched countries are subject to political pressures to apply the international framework because otherwise athletes risk being banned from major sports events. In order to meet these pressures in a flexible way, they resort to outsourcing rulemaking powers. The way in which France and Germany referred to an international UNESCO Treaty rather than directly to the World Anti-Doping Code was an astute detour to avoid domestic constitutional issues. Equally, Belgium, the UK, and—to some extent—the US applied outsourcing techniques to comply with transnational anti-doping regulations. Similarly, the research hinted at other possible case studies, such as ICANN, regarding the US attribution of internet domain names. In addition, the Code of Conduct for Responsible Fisheries and the Codex Alimentarius are produced by international hybrid bodies and are often incorporated into domestic rules.[43] Finally, ISO standards have become so pressing for the researched countries (if not also many others) because the World Trade Organization (WTO) Agreement on Technical Barriers to Trade has created a rebuttable presumption of compliance with trade rules if ISO standards are followed.[44]

Therefore, despite different constitutional attitudes to international law, all of the researched countries face comparable international phenomena and choose similar tactics to tackle them.

In summary, an overarching insight of this monograph is that there are remarkable convergences in motives, techniques, and practices of outsourcing despite seeming (constitutional) divergences. The research has shown that the researched countries are faced with similar pressures to outsource rulemaking powers, regardless of their constitutional, institutional, or international set-ups. It was therefore equally important to scrutinize how constitutional principles have conditioned the outsourcing of rulemaking powers in the researched states.

[43] Ravi Afonso Pereira, 'Why Would International Administrative Activity Be Any Less Legitimate? A Study of the Codex Alimentarius Commission' in Armin Bogdandy, Rüdiger Wolfrum, Jochen Bernstorff, Philipp Dann, and Matthias Goldmann (eds), *The Exercise of Public Authority by International Institutions* (Springer 2009) 547; Paul Craig, *UK, EU and Global Administrative Law* (Cambridge University Press 2015) 576.

[44] Walter Mattli, 'Private Transnational Governance' in Jacob Katz Cogan, Ian Hurd, and Ian Johnstone (eds), *The Oxford Handbook of International Organizations* (Oxford University Press 2016) 175.

7.2 Conclusions with regard to both research hypotheses

In relation to the constitutional limits and safeguards placed on the outsourcing of rulemaking powers, this research has managed to combine domestic provisions, constitutional principles, and principles of good rulemaking.

At the outset, the researched countries are, and have long been, subject to at least one of three influential comprehensive human rights treaties: the International Covenant on Civil and Political Rights (ICCPR), the European Convention on Human Rights (ECHR), and the EU Treaties. As set out in Chapter 2, the Inter-American Convention on Human Rights attaches the clearest limits on outsourcing rulemaking powers but is not applicable to the researched countries. The obligations that derive from the three other treaties have not yet led to a prohibition on outsourcing governmental powers. However, their case law shows some early signs of limits to outsourcing practices. First, article 3, Protocol 1 ECHR could potentially limit the possibility for legislators to outsource all—or most—of their powers. Second, autonomous public or private actors may be seen as state actors that represent a Contracting State in the light of the ECHR if their powers correspond to an international obligation, find their basis in domestic legislation, or have a connection to one of the three branches of government.[45] Generally, the quality of law test for relative human rights is not fazed by the fact that autonomous public or private actors draft rules. Many cases attest to the fact that they can create sufficiently qualitative rules for a human rights limitation to be 'in accordance with the law'. Statutory laws are not necessary. Rules just need to remain sufficiently accessible and foreseeable.

However, this book took a novel approach to the procedural rationality review of especially the ECtHR. This Court consistently takes into account whether the national Parliament, constitutional courts, or councils of state have weighed the interests of all stakeholders in their decision-making processes. This type of balancing of interests by the Legislature, Executive, or Judiciary is often lacking when autonomous public or private actors create rules, certainly *ex ante*. Procedural rationality may thus lead to a heightened threshold for the latter to receive rulemaking powers in a covert fashion. Similarly, for the EU Treaties and the ICCPR, the quality of law test has the most potential to internationally frame the domestic transfer of rulemaking powers to autonomous public or private actors. Nevertheless, overall, these limits and safeguards remain rather vague and indirect.

[45] Chapter 2, Section 2.4.2.1; *Van der Mussele v. Belgium* no. 8919/80 (ECtHR, 23 November 1983); Alexander Williams, 'A Fresh Perspective on Hybrid Public Authorities Under the Human Rights Act 1998: Private Contractors, Rights-Stripping and "Chameleonic" Horizontal Effect' [2011] *Public Law* 151.

For this reason, it proved essential to address the first (Section 7.2.1) and the second (Section 7.2.2) research hypotheses from the national perspectives of each of the researched countries.

7.2.1 Limits to the outsourcing of rulemaking powers (first research hypothesis)

The first research hypothesis that was phrased at the outset of this monograph postulated that—albeit possible—there were shared limits placed on traditional politically accountable actors with respect to outsourcing rulemaking powers.

The first research hypothesis was expanded in a three-pronged way, considering: (1) the traditional limits placed on politically accountable actors when they exchange rulemaking powers among themselves; (2) the constitutional framework for outsourcing rulemaking powers (Chapter 3); and (3) the way in which constitutional principles supplement this constitutional framework in setting limits on the transfer of rulemaking powers to autonomous public or private actors (Chapter 4).

(1) In the first instance, in Belgium, France, Germany, the UK, and the US legal scholars have historically proclaimed a non-delegation doctrine, meaning that rulemaking powers may not be transferred at all. However, the current constitutional texts of Belgium, France, and Germany paint a different picture. Article 105 of the Belgian Constitution, articles 34–8 of the French Constitution, and article 80 of the Basic Law each countenance the transfer of powers from the Legislature to the Executive. In the US, the non-delegation theory has basically been a dead letter since the New Deal. Moreover, in the UK the sovereignty of Parliament empowers it to delegate parts of its powers. Constitutional practice has evolved in a comparable fashion across the researched countries.

The core theoretical locus of all, or the most, essential rulemaking power resides with the Legislature. However, there are few limits barring the delegation of powers to the Executive unless a constitutional provision specifically so provides. The Belgian Constitution, which aimed to restrict the Executive, and the French Constitution, which aimed to strengthen the reserved rulemaking powers of the Executive, have been interpreted similarly and have complied with the practice described earlier. Even the UK, without a written or codified constitution, has evolved in a similar pattern, which makes it easy for the Executive to exercise rulemaking powers. The German Basic Law, which quite precisely enunciates the limits to the delegation of rulemaking powers to the Executive, has evolved into an unpredictable judicial essentialness test. In other words, the impact of constitutional courts on the general delegation doctrine—to the detriment of clear constitutional provisions—has been apparent. Finally, this conceptual outcome has also manifested in other countries, particularly the US.

(2) In the second instance, the constitutions of the researched countries tend not to expand on autonomous public or private actors and certainly not on the possibility of outsourcing rulemaking powers to them. Provisions such as article 87 of the German Basic Law, article 1 of French Organic Statute 2017-54, and article 9 of the Belgian SMARSI only partly contemplate them. However, as discussed, this monograph dug below the surface and found that there are, in fact, various examples of the three outsourcing techniques (delegation, referral and reception) in Belgium, France, Germany, the UK, and the US. As a whole, the researched countries share a current status in which the political reality of outsourcing rulemaking powers far exceeds the degree to which autonomous public or private actors, and their ability to receive governmental powers, have been engrained in the national constitutions.

(3) In the third instance, the genuine key to prove the first research hypothesis must therefore be found in constitutional principles rather than constitutional provisions. Again, it was striking to establish the influence of the highest national courts on this aspect of the delegation doctrine in a broad sense. I structured the case law and legal scholarship on the outsourcing of rulemaking powers in the researched countries around three constitutional principles: the legality principle, the separation of powers, and the democracy principle.

To begin with, I subdivided the legality principle into a 'specific' and 'general' legality principle. A specific legality principle was identified in the Belgian, French, and German constitutions which specifically reserve the core of a competence to the rulemaking power of the Legislature. This phenomenon thus exists in three of the researched countries. The general legality principle safeguards the core of every rulemaking decision for the Legislature. This general legality principle manifests itself in the US, Germany, France, and—until recently—Belgium. In the UK, parliamentary sovereignty can enable the Legislature to transfer even the core of its rulemaking power if Parliament decides to do so. The legality principle is a first substantive limit to the outsourcing of rulemaking powers because the core of the competences that are reserved for the Legislature may not be transferred to any other institution or actor.

Subsequently, I argued that the separation of powers is a potential, yet largely ignored, constitutional principle influencing the outsourcing of rulemaking powers. Only the US Supreme Court, the Belgian Council of State, and the French Constitutional Council have developed the separation of powers as a founding principle to limit the powers of autonomous public or private actors, albeit that the French Constitutional Council has not yet done so with regard to rulemaking powers. If these actors receive rulemaking powers, this may disturb the balance between the Legislature, Executive, and Judiciary (institutional separation of powers). Autonomous public or private actors may diminish the power of the Legislature, the unity of the Executive, or the unique independent status of the Judiciary. I categorized the risk to the institutional separation of powers as most likely to be abstract and academic when autonomous public or private actors receive rulemaking powers. However, if these actors receive rulemaking powers combined with other functions, such as an investigatory or adjudicative function, this is more problematic in the light of the functional separation of powers. Based on comments in legal scholarship and the fledgling case law of the French Constitutional Council, I urged that broader attention should be paid to the functional separation of powers as a practical limit to the outsourcing of rulemaking powers.

Finally, the democracy principle ensures that the people will decide who represents them and thus ultimately on which rules bind them.

The converging test for all outsourcing techniques entails (1) precise transfer of powers (2) for non-policy oriented matters (3) with sufficient political control. The Belgian Constitutional Court has actually adopted these three limits explicitly. The French Constitutional Council has also emphasized all three of these requirements for autonomous public bodies to receive rulemaking powers, namely a determined reach with regard to content and application, in combination with political control. The German FCC especially highlighted the third requirement for private actors, namely sufficient political control. Elements of the three-pronged test surface in the case law of the US Supreme Court. Finally, in the UK, the overarching democratic limit to political control or influence has also been stressed. Elements of these three restrictions are traceable in other legal systems, such as the Netherlands, Austria, and even in the EU's exercise of rulemaking powers through the well-known *Meroni* and *ESMA* case law.

The last requirement to ensure compliance with the democracy principle—sufficient political control—appears especially paradoxical for autonomous public or private actors. Nevertheless, there are means within the three outsourcing techniques for the Legislature and the Executive to exercise a degree of political control on autonomous public or private actors without jeopardizing their autonomy. With regard to the delegation technique, this can be done by adapting the ordinary means of controlling the Executive to autonomous public bodies. Consider, for example, the possibility of hearings of the employees of an autonomous public or private actor on day-to-day business, of receiving annual reports, or even of being notified of new rules. For the referral technique, there should at least be a statutory framework and the possibility for politically accountable actors to follow up on amended referred-to standards. For the reception technique, a politically accountable actor should predetermine the status-defining rules and should ideally ratify the eventual rule *ex post*.

In summary, confirming the first research hypothesis, there are limits to the outsourcing of rulemaking powers in the researched countries that do not derive from constitutional provisions but from constitutional principles. The most common constitutional principles with the greatest impact here are the legality principle, the separation of powers, and the democracy principle. A reasonable balance must be found between political control and the status of an autonomous public or private actor in relation to each of the three outsourcing techniques discussed: delegation, referral, and reception; although, in various ways, all of the researched countries appear to have found such a balance for all outsourcing techniques.

7.2.2 Safeguards for outsourced rules (second research hypothesis)

This monograph also formulated a second research hypothesis: there are guarantees that outsourced rules also need to comply with. In order to test this hypothesis, I first defined five principles of good rulemaking that appear particularly problematic when autonomous public or private actors create rules: transparency, a hierarchy of rules, judicial review, representativeness, and efficiency/effectiveness. These five principles were inspired by the five principles of good governance (openness, coherence, accountability, participation, and effectiveness, respectively) that the EU Commission drafted in its White Paper of 2001. The Commission developed these principles in reply to the criticism that the EU would be insufficiently legitimized because of a lack of political accountability. This criticism greatly resembles the challenges that autonomous public or private actors face on a national level, and thus provides fertile ground for testing this book's second research hypothesis.

Autonomous public or private actors themselves can create good practices, such as the ISO Code of Good Practice for Standardisation.[46] Nevertheless, in order to determine the legal safeguards that must also weigh on outsourced rules, clear and outspoken constitutional or statutory guidance is needed.

(1) Transparency, as a principle of good rulemaking, is protected in Belgium and Germany by constitutional provisions (article 190 of the Belgian Constitution and article 82 of the Basic Law, respectively) and in France, the UK, and the US by a judicially evolved constitutional principle. It consists of both accessibility and intelligibility.

[46] ISO and IEC, 'Code of good practice for standardization', Guide 59 (1994). Matthias Kötter and Gunnar Folke Schuppert, 'Applying the Rule of Law to Contexts Beyond the State' in James Silkenat, James Hickey Jr, and Peter Barenboim (eds), *The Legal Doctrines of the Rule of Law and the Legal State (Rechtsstaat)* (Springer 2014) 86.

With regard to accessibility, the biggest issue is the absence of a framework statute that regulates the publication of outsourced rules for any of the three outsourcing techniques in the researched countries.

Delegated rules made by autonomous public bodies are generally published in the manner described in a parent statute or as the autonomous public body itself deems appropriate. Similarly, for the *referral* technique there is no overarching statute that dictates how referred-to standards should be published. This is all the more concerning because such standards are often: (1) unpublished through an official publication channel; (2) redacted in a language that the constituency may not understand; or (3) available only after paying a substantial fee. Based on the situation in the researched countries, I took the normative stance that such a flawed publication process would only be acceptable: (1) if members of the constituency had a realistic chance of accessing the standard on a government controlled platform; (2) if publication in the country's official language(s), given the nature of the rule, proved impossible or in opposition to the general interest; and (3) if the government generally pre-empted or at least reimbursed the cost of accessing the rule. An important last resort in obtaining a degree of legitimacy for autonomous public or private actors is for them to publish referred-to standards themselves. In addition, for the *reception* technique, publication of extended collective labour agreements or agreements made by a professional organization occurs depending on the statute or executive regulation that 'receives' the professional agreement in the governmental apparatus. Publication rules only exist for particular categories of these received agreements and the extent of that publication varies greatly across the research and other countries.

With regard to intelligibility, outsourced rules are often criticized for being insufficiently clear and understandable. The research proposed four possible ways to further improve the intelligibility of outsourced rules: increased consultation (see point (4) later on representativeness), the publication of internal debates; the publication of the motivation for the rules; and enhanced attention to comprehensible language.

(2) A hierarchy of rules, as a second principle of good rulemaking, is particularly essential to the Belgian, French, German, and US legal systems. This is not the case for the UK legal system where a hierarchy of rules merely determines the dichotomy between primary and secondary rules.

In order to establish the position of outsourced rules within the researched countries' respective hierarchies of rules, I first attempted to position these rules within existing categories of rules, based on national statutes or scholarly theories. Such a partial framework currently exists mainly for rules made using the reception technique. For example, this happens for extended collective labour agreements in Belgium or *Satzungen* as rules made by professional 'orders' in Germany.

Again, however, an overarching statutory framework for delineating the hierarchy of outsourced rules is lacking. This becomes especially problematic when *delegated* rules clash with other rules. One may assume that outsourced rules will be inferior to rules created by traditional, politically accountable, actors, yet there certainly remains legal uncertainty when outsourced rules contradict each other.

With regard to the referral technique, the Dutch High Council did not attribute a hierarchical value to referred-to standards.[47] This was contra to the German position which seems to accept that a standard to which a state rule refers will receive the hierarchical status of that rule. Belgium, France, the US, and the UK are yet to make definitive decisions on this matter. I would support the German approach since it is most candid towards the constituency that becomes bound by the referred-to standard.

(3) Having access to *judicial review*, that is, to a court in order to dispute a rule, is arguably one of the most important principles of good rulemaking. There is no *ex ante* judicial review by, for example, the Belgian or French Councils of State on outsourced rules as such. However, in the researched countries courts can review *ex post* rules made by autonomous public or private actors subject to a delegation. Moreover, amenability to judicial review is an essential requirement of the European Court of Justice for internal EU delegations, as attested to by the *Meroni* and *ESMA* case law.[48]

For the referral technique, this research has established that the hierarchical and legal status of referred-to-standards within the researched countries determines whether the standard is subject to judicial review. This is the case if the referring rule and the referred-to standard are at the same hierarchical level. I support this outcome because of the practical logic according to which referring rules and referred-to standards become inextricably linked. Before a state rule refers to a standard, domestic courts should surely not be able review that standard. Only after a referral to the standard by a state rule could it be incorporated into judicial review. Regardless of whether national courts can directly review the referred-to standard, I examined whether national courts should have or do have the power to influence the type of referral that the referring rule uses. In previous case law, the German FCC reinterpreted a dynamic referral as a static referral in order to comply with constitutional limits and safeguards.[49] This judicial interpretation technique was also adopted in the Netherlands. In the other researched countries, the results of judicial review of the interpretation of referring rules has not yet been clearly established. However, there are also elements in parallel branches of at least Belgian and UK law which would warrant the judicial amendment of a dynamic to a static referral

[47] Irene Scholten-Verheijen, 'National Public Sector and Private Standards. Cases in the Netherlands' in Bernd van der Meulen (ed.), *Private Food Law* (Wageningen Academic 2011) 320–9.

[48] Case C-270/12 *United Kingdom v. European Parliament and the Council of the European Union* ECLI:EU:C:2014:18, § 56.

[49] BVerfGE 47, 285, 1 March 1978.

For the reception technique, Belgian, French, German, and US administrative or ordinary courts can review the received agreements or the ratification act by which a politically accountable actor receives a professional agreement. In the UK, there is an intense debate about the availability of public law remedies for agreements by professional (sports) organizations. By distinguishing rulemaking powers from existing precedent, I argue that they could also be subject to public law remedies.

Finally, the research could not establish a principled heightened or lowered standard of review for outsourced rules. In general, however, outsourced rules should be technical or accessory. The more technical they are, the lower the standard of review becomes, because judges do not have the necessary expertise or discretionary power to substitute the autonomous public or private actor's decision with their own.

(4) Representativeness is a fourth principle of good rulemaking. Politically accountable actors are representative because they have either been directly elected by the people or because they can be held politically accountable by those who have been elected by the people. National constitutions and constitutional principles will guarantee that this acquired representativeness remains by, for example, ensuring the independence of politically accountable actors or—usually in the case of the Executive—imposing requirements of consultation. These two pillars which uphold representativeness, namely independence and consultation, must also be present when autonomous public or private actors create rules.

With regard to the *delegation technique*, EU law often imposes the independence of autonomous public bodies that act as regulators of network industries. Nevertheless, total independence is rarely achieved. For example, a politically accountable actor will remain competent to appoint the officials of the autonomous public body. In all of the researched countries, consulting interest groups may equally comply with the guarantee of representativeness. This research selected a number of examples of autonomous public bodies involving the populace in their decision-making process. The UK and the US, in particular, have widely developed consultation processes for bodies they maintain at arm's length. One improvement to the current systems in the researched countries which focus on consultations would be to construct a matrix with all of the suggestions by civil society on a proposed rule included, as well as a description of how autonomous public or private actors implemented those comments.

At first sight, representativeness does not appear to be the primary concern within the *referral* technique; to the detriment of expertise. However, various commentators have lamented the lack of representativeness within standard-setting bodies, certainly when the Legislature and the Executive refer to their standards. It is crucial that these standard-setting bodies safeguard their independence from industry interests and simultaneously involve non-expert stakeholders in the development of their standards in order for them to become a solid legal basis to which to refer.

With regard to the *reception* technique, representativeness of a rule is—to a certain extent—expected. First, professional organizations that make rules for their members inherently comprise the people who they bind. Second, the Legislature or the Executive often ratifies the outsourced rules, especially in Belgium and France. This ratification bestows some degree of representativeness on the rule. Furthermore, in the researched countries the Legislature or the Executive will not ratify and/or extend these professional agreements unless legal requirements of representativeness have been respected in the original decision-making process.

(5) Efficiency/effectiveness, as a fifth and final principle of good rulemaking, is arguably the most difficult to enforce legally. Theoretically, effectiveness means that the goal is attained; efficiency means that, taking into account the available tools, the goal is approached in the most desirable way.

In respect of the *delegation* of governmental powers, the presumed efficiency within autonomous public bodies has already been praised. In order to further improve the efficiency of autonomous public or private actors, and the effectiveness of their rules, I reiterate the recommendations I made in relation to the provision of sufficient political control in the light of the first research hypothesis; namely, to deferentially appoint and evaluate the staff of autonomous public or private actors and review their annual reports. Furthermore, I argue against a recent tendency in the politics of at least some of the researched countries to reject regulatory impact assessments (RIAs). Rather, I would suggest that the current form of RIAs be strengthened such that they are not merely used as mandatory check boxes, and I would also extend their scope to outsourced rules.

For the *referral* and *reception* techniques, an increased level of efficiency and effectiveness is often presumed because these autonomous public or private actors tend to be better informed on what constitutes the real issue.[50] I have nuanced this presumption in Chapter 5. Nevertheless, because autonomous public or private actors are less strictly regulated, they can more readily and more flexibly choose the right regulatory technique in the right context.[51]

The essential finding of the comparative research on the second research hypothesis with respect to the researched countries is that an overarching framework rule or statute to regulate the transparency, hierarchy, judicial review, representativeness, and effectiveness of outsourced rules is mostly lacking.[52] Hopefully, the overview, as set out in this research, will help to create a common 'law of rules'

[50] *Contra*: Sidney Shapiro, 'Outsourcing Government Regulation' (2003–4) 53 *Duke LJ* 389, 426; Pauline Westerman, 'Who is Regulating the Self? Self-Regulation as Outsourced Rule-Making' [2010] *Legisprudence* 241.

[51] Robert Baldwin, Martin Cave, and Martin Lodge, *Understanding Regulation: Theory, Strategy, and Practice* (Oxford University Press 2011) 147–8; John McEldowney, *Public Law* (Sweet & Maxwell 2016) 242.

[52] With the possible exceptions of the French Statute 2017-55, the UK Regulators' Compliance Code, and the US Administrative Procedure Act.

which will articulate the safeguards of the rule of law, democracy, and the separation of powers.[53]

7.3 Recommendations

Finally, I make three recommendations to lawmakers and courts, which are derived from the insights and conclusions with regard to both research hypotheses: (1) autonomous public, private, and hybrid actors can and should be seen as one constitutionally relevant category; (2) a constitutional provision may help to concretize the principles discussed on the outsourcing of rulemaking powers; and (3) good practice can be suggested to pair primary motives with their most suitable outsourcing technique.

7.3.1 Autonomous public, private, and hybrid actors as one constitutional category

First, I would urge the consideration of autonomous public, private, and hybrid actors as one constitutionally relevant category.

The majority of legal scholarship, or even case law on outsourcing (rulemaking) governmental powers, still distinguishes between autonomous public bodies and private actors.[54] In particular, the accountability of autonomous public bodies and regulators has been subject to both societal and scientific scrutiny. Commentators not only distinguish between public and private actors for didactical purposes, but also to indicate an apparent difference in aptitude to receive governmental powers. Private actors would require 'more legal caution' than public actors.[55]

However, this research can claim to have at least partly rebutted that contention. Rather than emphasizing a manufactured difference between private and public actors, this research used political accountability as its decisive category.

In all of the researched countries, there is a variation on the idea of a political accountability chain, which derives from the people and continues all the way to the Legislature and Executive. A common feature of autonomous public or private actors is that they seemingly do not belong to this accountability chain. I therefore defined them as actors that are not held directly responsible by the citizens through

[53] Cedric Jenart and Stéphanie De Somer, 'Non-Statutory Rulemaking and the Rule of Law: Towards a "Law of Rules"?'[2017] *Sui-Generis* IV.

[54] *A. L. A. Schechter Poultry Corp. v. United States*, 295 US 495 (1935); *Carter v. Carter Coal Co.*, 298 US 238 (1936). See, in general, on traditionally forbidden delegation to private actors in Belgium, among others, Belgian Council of State Administration Section, 15 February 2012, no. 218.000, § 19 and Steven Lierman, *Besturen zonder grenzen. Over grijze zones en blinde vlekken* (Intersentia 2015) 6.

[55] Stefan Griller and Andreas Orator, 'Everything Under control? The "Way Forward" for European Agencies in the Footsteps of the *Meroni* Doctrine' [2010] *E. L. Rev.* 18.

democratic elections. Autonomous public bodies, private actors, and hybrid institutions belong to and constitute this residuary category. Comparative transnational legal scholarship vehemently defends the notion that 'all power-wielders within any regulatory regime should be accountable to those affected, regardless of whether they are to be qualified as public or private'.[56]

In the first instance, political accountability features as a constitutionally relevant category in the advisory opinions of the Legislative Section of the Belgian Council of State.[57] Furthermore, political scientists in particular have considered the actors that exercise governmental powers without such political accountability as one group in the context of the EU and the US.[58] Similar arguments surfaced in the US against delegating rulemaking powers to autonomous public or private actors, which were said to have less electoral accountability, fewer bureaucratic constraints, and less motivation.[59] With regard to the transfer of rulemaking powers to actors outside the *Trias Politica*, the actual decisive criterion is political accountability not the status of public and private actors.

In the second instance, it is important to construe the category of actors that the constitutional texts indicate as being apt to exercise governmental powers.[60] In Belgium, France, Germany, the UK, and the US, no clear proof can be found in constitutional or quasi-constitutional texts of a different status for private actors than for autonomous public bodies. In fact, neither of these categories is explicitly or consequentially named in their constitutional texts. In Belgium, despite the traditional rejection of private lawmakers, legisprudence subjects private actors to the same outsourcing test as autonomous public actors.[61] For a long time this was done implicitly, but since 2021 the Belgian Council of State Legislative Section explicitly adopts the same test on outsourcing rulemaking powers to private actors as to autonomous public actors.[62] A similar conclusion applies tacitly to the US

[56] Deirdre Curtin and Linda Senden, 'Public Accountability of Transnational Private Regulation: Chimera or Reality?' in Colin Scott, Fabrizio Cafaggi, and Linda Senden (eds), *The Challenge of Transnational Private Regulation. The Conceptual and Constitutional Debates* (Wiley-Blackwell 2011) 169–72.

[57] See e.g. Belgian Council of State Legislative Section, Advisory opinion no. 54.536/2/3 of 19 December 2013, § 5, Belgian Council of State Legislative Section, Advisory opinion (Preparatory Documents Chamber of Representatives no. 2491/001) 11 and Belgian Council of State Legislative Section, Advisory opinion no. 24.60024.601/AG AV/2 of 10 October 1995 and 6 November 1995.

[58] Catherine Durose, Jonathan Justice, and Chris Skelcher, 'Governing at Arm's Length: Eroding or Enhancing Democracy?' [2015] *Pol'y & Politics* 139.

[59] Harold J. Krent, 'The Private Performing the Public: Delimiting Delegations to Private Parties' (2011) 65 *U. Miami L. Rev.* 507, 510.

[60] See for support in EU law, the *Romano* case: Case 98/80 *Giuseppe Romano v. Institut national d'assurance maladie-invalidité* ECLI:EU:C:1981:104; Stefan Griller and Andreas Orator, 'Everything Under Control? The "Way Forward" for European Agencies in the Footsteps of the *Meroni* Doctrine' [2010] *E. L. Rev.* 18.

[61] Belgian Council of State Legislative Section, Advisory opinion no. 62.522/3 of 20 December 2017, 7–8; Belgian Council of State Legislative Section, Advisory opinion no. 56.941/3 of 21 January 2015, § 14.

[62] Belgian Council of State Legislative Section, Advisory opinion no. 70.010/3-1/V of 21 September 2021, § 6; Belgian Council of State Legislative Section, Advisory opinion no. 69.455/1 of 25 June 2021, § 5.2.

despite the *Schechter Poultry* US Supreme Court case law. In the UK, parliamentary sovereignty allows the Legislature to outsource rulemaking powers to a private actor as long as Parliament can later reverse that decision. In Germany and France, more counterindications can be found[63] yet compliance with the limits as set out in this monograph could still ensure that the thrust of sovereign functions remains with traditional politically accountable actors.

Finally, the rejection of a distinguishing public–private divide also falls in line with the insights from international and transnational law cited, which suggests that rulemaking actors are increasingly difficult to categorize as either public or private, with actors that receive rulemaking powers increasingly being described as hybrid.[64] A telling example of this is the case study of the World Anti-Doping Agency (WADA) in Chapter 6. WADA can be seen as either a public or a private entity and is therefore primarily considered to be a hybrid entity.[65]

In conclusion, the research's premise that private and autonomous public actors can be considered as one residuary group of possible rulemakers was largely vindicated. Rather than working with complete bans on some categories of actors (private or other), constitutional limits and safeguards should be formulated such that all relevant constitutional principles are constantly complied with. Autonomous public and private power-wielders should be subject to similar strict limits to their exercise of rulemaking powers (first research hypothesis) and the safeguards with which the outsourced rules need to comply (second research hypothesis).

To be clear, this assertion does not imply that, in practice, it would and should always become as easy or as difficult to outsource rulemaking powers to private actors as to autonomous public bodies. Arguably, the democracy test requiring sufficient *political control* will be more difficult to meet for most private actors than for public actors. Moreover, the safeguard of representativeness appears generally more threatened by private actors holding private interests than by public actors. However, this research has shown that an attempt to disentangle private actors and autonomous public actors is artificial and unnecessary. There is, rather, a need for one overarching test that encapsulates all potential power-wielders outside the *Trias Politica*, such that the underlying constitutional principles and the principles of good rulemaking are complied with when rulemaking powers are exercised.

[63] See article 33, 4 of the Basic Law, as discussed, and French Constitutional Council no. 2003-473 of 26 June 2003, § 19.

[64] Walter Mattli, 'Private Transnational Governance' in Jacob Katz Cogan, Ian Hurd, and Ian Johnstone (eds), *The Oxford Handbook of International Organizations* (Oxford University Press 2016) 173–4.

[65] Cedric Jenart, 'On the Legal Status of the World Anti-Doping Agency, NADOs and Disciplinary Bodies' in Niels Appermont and Ulrike Cerelus (eds), *Participatie van de burger in de rechtsorde/Participation du citoyen à l'ordre juridique* (die Keure 2017) 44–56.

7.3.2 Insertion of a constitutional provision

Secondly, I discuss whether it would be useful to adopt a constitutional provision in Belgium, France, Germany, and even the US on limits and safeguards when outsourcing rulemaking powers.[66]

There are possible downsides to explicit constitutional provisions.[67] The most significant downside is that explicit provisions create a determined target for finding loopholes and workarounds.[68] Judicially evolving constitutional principles are more flexible and allow rulemakers and courts to adapt the limits gradually. With regard to the transfer of rulemaking powers to autonomous public or private actors, it would not be realistic to expect that the researched countries would move from a theoretical prohibition—but pragmatic and flexible acceptance of outsourcing rulemaking powers—to strict and unwavering boundaries in explicit constitutional provisions. For example, the Vedel Committee in France declined to insert AAIs (*autorités administratives indépendantes*) and their potential powers into the French Constitution mainly because the French Constitutional Council had already developed a satisfactory framework for this on the basis of constitutional principles. Moreover, of the researched countries, Germany has the clearest general delegation limit in its own Basic Law through article 80.[69] It also has the clearest constitutional entrenchment for autonomous public or private actors of all the researched countries due to article 87 of the Basic Law. Nevertheless, the interpretation by courts of this clear limitation by constitutional provision and the actual development of autonomous public or private actors was dominated by constitutional principles and practices. Certainly, for the first research hypothesis on the limits to the outsourcing of rulemaking powers, constitutional principles have been an adequate surrogate for explicit provisions. In the light of this, one could argue against adopting constitutional provisions on autonomous public or private actors and their powers.

However, if a nation has a written and codified constitution, that constitution should effectively contain the basic principles of the exercise of powers over its people. I thus endorse the enhanced clarity that exists when constitutional provisions set limits on the outsourcing of rulemaking powers.[70] Ultimately, an

[66] For the UK, a recommendation of such a specific constitutional provision would seem far-fetched and fanciful given the absence of any written or codified constitution.

[67] Valérie De Schepper and Emmanuel Slautsky, 'Decentralisering en privatisering van regelgevende bevoegdheid: naar een grondwettelijke verankering?' in *Leuvense Staatsrechtelijke Standpunten* (Die Keure, 2019). Downsides, such as the potential clash between national constitutional and EU law, can be resolved through the national constitutional identity theories discussed, assuming the allocation of rulemaking powers resides within the ambit of core national competences.

[68] Marc Mason, 'Making Way for Change at the Bar: The Practical Implications of the New Bar Standards Board Handbook' [2015] *Professional Negligence* 157.

[69] Other countries worldwide followed Germany's example, such as Peru (article 104 Constitution) and Zimbabwe (article 134 Constitution).

[70] See also Jeffrey Goldsworthy, *Parliamentary Sovereignty. Contemporary Debates* (Cambridge University Press 2010) 111.

overarching guiding constitutional or statutory provision would be helpful from a didactical point of view.

If the idea of adopting a new constitutional provision for autonomous public or private actors is supported, the question then arises as to whether it should contain more than their mere constitutional recognition, such as in article 87 of the Basic Law or Organic Statute 2017-54. Alternatively, we might want the constitutional provision to expand on the powers that can be transferred. Such constitutional provisions to introduce autonomous public or private actors and their rulemaking powers are not unheard of outside the researched countries. Pursuant to article 134, 2 of the Dutch Constitution, rulemaking powers may be granted to autonomous public bodies by or pursuant to a statute. Article 178, 3 of the Swiss Constitution determines that 'administrative tasks' may be delegated by law to public or private organizations, entities, or persons that are not part of the federal administration. The Swiss Bundesgericht has accepted that this provision translates a general principle on the exercise of public power,[71] which is why the broad notion of 'administrative tasks' could encompass rulemaking powers.

When elaborating a more precise constitutional provision, I reiterate the concerns that were raised at the outset of both research hypotheses. The first research hypothesis, regarding the limits to the outsourcing of rulemaking powers, has already been confirmed by the highest courts of the researched countries but deserves confirmation in the most fundamental document(s) of those states. The need for an overarching provision was certainly emphasized in the test on the second research hypotheses which went over the five recognized principles of good rulemaking within outsourced rules. A constitutional provision could refer to a statute in order to avoid too many details in the constitution itself. I noted that the UK framework concerning the exercise of powers by autonomous public or private actors was often clearer than in the other researched countries. Arguably, this has been inspired by the lack of constitutional provisions on the basis of which traditional politically accountable actors and autonomous public or private actors could coordinate their approach to the outsourcing of rulemaking powers. Nevertheless, it appears to be a unique opportunity to insert five fundamental principles of good rulemaking into a constitutional text.

This research has attempted to combine and supersede national tendencies and idiosyncrasies by delving into the core of the outsourcing of rulemaking power. In this sense, a new and universal constitutional provision might be formulated as:[72]

[71] BGE 138 I 196 S. 201; Bernhard Rütsche, 'Was sind öffentliche Aufgaben?' [2013] *Recht* 158.

[72] The suggested provision only concerns rulemaking power since that was the research object of this monograph. However, if such a provision were introduced, it should be considered whether it could be extended to other governmental powers such as individual decision-making and adjudicatory and management powers or tasks.

> *Rulemaking powers can be outsourced to actors that are otherwise not enumerated in this Constitution if this occurs: (a) in a precise manner; (b) for a matter that is not policy-oriented; and (c) under a continuous degree of political control.*
>
> *A specific statute must constitute a framework to ensure that these rules: (1) are transparent; (2) correspond to an established position within the hierarchy of rules; (3) are amenable to ex ante or ex post judicial review; (4) are representative; and (5) are effective.*

This constitutional provision makes the cumulative test of the democracy principle explicit, as the common denominator was encountered in the researched countries.[73] The first limit on the precise transfer of powers avoids the transfer of unrestricted powers. The second limit on the non-policy-oriented nature of the matter formulates a material and an alternative condition (accessory and/or technical). An accessory matter does not concern the core or essential elements of a governmental policy decision. If the transfer goes beyond accessory matters, this is only acceptable if the competence is technical. A technical matter requires a specific educational background or professional experience in order to be completely understood, especially with regard to the applied, medical, and industrial sciences. The third and primary condition is that a politically accountable actor exercises sufficient political control.

Courts have ample experience in determining the precision of, accessorial nature of, and political control exercised on a decision to outsource rulemaking powers. However, it is particularly problematic for a court to establish whether a matter is technical without disposing of the necessary expertise itself. As mentioned, courts must exercise decreased judicial scrutiny (and an increased margin of appreciation) in areas concerning a technical matter. Nevertheless, this does not diminish their capacity to establish whether the outsourced matter *is* or *is not* technical. On the contrary, since courts must establish the technicality of an outsourced matter to determine the degree of their judicial scrutiny, they can simultaneously perform the test that will inform them whether transferred rulemaking powers are technical.

In addition, courts can utilize existing tools to comply with the principles of good rulemaking—such as consultations, the rulemaking motivation, and RIAs—in order to determine whether a rule is technical. Indeed, the second paragraph of the proposed constitutional provision set out earlier also imposes an obligation on the Legislature to develop a framework on the principles of good rulemaking discussed when autonomous public or private actors exercise rulemaking powers.

[73] For the less influential or potential limits that the legality principle and the separation of powers could influence in relation to the outsourcing of rulemaking powers, it suffices that they would still be derived from other constitutional provisions or from those constitutional principles themselves.

Finally, the question arises as to where such a constitutional provision should be introduced. In general, for Belgium, France, Germany, and the US such a proposed constitutional amendment could and should be added to the respective titles on the exercise of governmental powers within their constitutions. Given the unique and residual nature of autonomous public or private actors, it is advisable to create a single and independent provision, section, or chapter which would encapsulate this suggested default provision on the outsourcing of rulemaking powers to such actors.

7.3.3 Good practice correspondence between the three motives and the three techniques for outsourcing

Thirdly, and finally, I propose a good practice solution by linking a preferential outsourcing technique to each primary motive for outsourcing rulemaking powers.

It would be impossible and unwise to advise a normative one-size-fits-all solution that the Legislature and the Executive might choose from the outsourcing techniques. Such choices are always strongly influenced by cultural and political contexts. Domestic divergences could, indeed, be based on a cultural preference and historical evolution within each researched country. For example, as Chapter 4 on the limits on outsourcing made clear, the referral technique is less prominent in the UK than the delegation technique. In addition, preference is usually given in the UK to full self-regulation rather than controlled self-regulation through referrals. Furthermore, even when referrals occur, *dynamic* referrals are more commonplace in Belgium and Germany and rarer in France, the US, and the UK. The French implementation of technical standards adds to these examples. If rulemaking power is outsourced to standard-setting bodies in Belgium, Germany, the US, and even the UK, this usually occurs through the referral technique. However, in France this type of outsourcing usually occurs through the reception technique. The French standardization organization (AFNOR) can homologate standards which a ministerial order may subsequently declare generally binding. This set-up resembles the system of declarations of general applicability for collective labour agreements, which is extremely popular in France.

Nevertheless, given this divergence in outsourcing techniques and motives, it still appears opportune to propose good practice based on identifying the best outsourcing technique for each predominant motive for outsourcing rulemaking powers.

We can summarize this proposal as follows:

Main motive	Independence	Expertise	Stakeholder input
Best technique	Delegation	Referral	Reception

(1) For the first main motive, namely to create *independence* and a buffer from the regulated matter, it would be preferable to use the technique of *delegation*. This is, for example, already the case for autonomous public bodies, as regulators, in—EU developed—network industries. In Germany, autonomous public bodies with delegated rulemaking powers have evolved in areas which need to be isolated from political manoeuvring in order to safeguard consistency and continuity (e.g. the Bundesnetzagentur, the Bundeskartellamt, and the Patent und Markenamt).[74] Moreover, it was not coincidental that the French National Committee on Information and Liberties (CNIL), which needed independence to regulate on information and liberties, was the first French AAI.[75] The referral technique is less useful when the primary goal is independence. When the Legislature and the Executive refer to standards rather than creating an independent decision-maker, the referring actor remains comfortably in the driver's seat, especially when the referrals are static. Even for dynamic referrals, the autonomous public or private actor whose standard is referred to may be a non-permanent actor with determined interests in politics or industry, which works against the goal of independence. In the same vein, the reception technique, which often requires ulterior ratification by a politically accountable actor, does not create sufficient independence.

(2) For the second main motive for outsourcing rulemaking powers, namely the need for more *expertise* and scientific knowledge, dynamic or static *referral* to technical standards would be the best option.[76] Politically accountable actors often apply the referral technique to avoid the cost and effort required to incorporate the referred-to standard. In the case of dynamic referrals, this would also avoid continuously updating the incorporated technical standards.[77] Moreover, the referral technique also helps to customize these standards. The main focus here lies on whether the external document

[74] Thomas Züll, *Regulierung Im Politischen Gemeinwesen* (Mohr Siebeck 2014) 155.

[75] Bettina Süsskind, *Die autorités administratives indépendantes* (Nomos 2010) 41.

[76] ISO and IEC, 'Using and referencing ISO and IEC standards to support public policy' (2015) 9–13, European Commission, 'Methods of referencing standards in legislation with an emphasis on European legislation' (2002 update 2014) 3; Conseil canadien des normes, 'Principaux points à considérer dans l'élaboration et l'utilisation des normes dans les instruments législatifs' (September 2006) A 10; Colin Scott, 'Standard-Setting in Regulatory Regimes' in Robert Baldwin, Martin Cave, and Martin Lodge (eds), *The Oxford Handbook of Regulation* (Oxford University Press 2010) 106 and 113.

[77] Michael C. Dorf, 'Dynamic Incorporation of Foreign Law' (2008) 157 *U. Pa. L. Rev.* 103, 132; this is in general why standards are used in the legal system: Anne Penneau, 'Sécurité des

is actually drafted with increased expertise such that referrals achieve more rulemaking effectiveness than the ordinary legislative process.[78] Legislative or executive acts thus usually refer to external documents of autonomous public or private actors in technical areas such environmental law, sports law, ICT law, and standardization law in general.[79] In contrast to the referral technique, the delegation technique entrusts the rulemaking powers to a specific body. This body can have extensive expertise but, when it reaches its technical limits, so does the delegation technique. The referral technique has the added benefit of flexibility, through which a standard of any group of experts, anywhere in the world, can be incorporated into rules. For its part, the reception technique is less flexible in terms of keeping up with the latest technical state of the art because it requires a predetermined group of professional stakeholders who make agreements on an irregular basis. The initiative here lies with the stakeholders, whereas in the referral technique, the initiative to seek support for complicated and technical matters remains with the Legislature or the Executive.

(3) The *reception* technique is best equipped to ensure that the goal of increasing public support and *involving stakeholders* is attained. This is, for example, the case for collective bargaining. There appear to be societal reasons explaining why the Legislature and the Executive wish to outsource such deliberation processes to these professional bodies.[80] Often the reception evolves due to the existence of pressure groups, the idea of which was engrained during the Middle Ages in guilds and corporations. While these pressure groups were outcast in the aftermath of the French Revolution,[81] they were rehabilitated in the industrial age as trade unions or professional organizations. The reception technique vehemently safeguards the principle of representativeness, partly because the organizations that make professional agreements are inherently closer to their 'constituency'. The flexible and volatile nature of standards and the autonomous public or private actors that produce them using the referral technique would be a disadvantage when the aim is to prove that there is durable and sustainable public support for the rule from all stakeholders. Moreover, the delegation technique does not offer a consensual model necessary to meet the motive

personnes: réglementation ou normalisation? Quelles évolutions, quelles limites?' in Geneviève Viney (ed.), *Liber Amicorum Geneviève Viney* (LGDJ 2008) 773.

[78] Peter Marburger, *Die Regeln der Technik im Recht* (Heymann 1979) 202.

[79] Colin Scott, 'Standard-Setting in Regulatory Regimes' in Robert Baldwin, Martin Cave, and Martin Lodge (eds), *The Oxford Handbook of Regulation* (Oxford University Press 2010) 114–15.

[80] Tanina Rostain, 'Selfregulatory Authority, Markets, and the Ideology of Professionalism' in ibid., 172.

[81] *Décret d'Allarde* of 2 and 17 March 1791 concerning the abolition of guilds.

> of public support, since a genuine delegation of rulemaking powers to professional organizations would arguably give them too much power. This definitely applies when ratification of the delegated rules is not required.

Certainly, there is seldom one sole motive for outsourcing rulemaking powers in a specific context. The delegation of rulemaking powers to autonomous public bodies is not only motived by the need for independence, but also by other reasons, such as greater expertise within those bodies and the technical development of regulations. To the same extent, referrals and receptions may be partly inspired by the pursuit of independence, expertise, and stakeholder involvement.

This proposal is therefore not exclusive or descriptive. It merely recommends good practice based on matching each primary outsourcing motive with the most suitable outsourcing technique. Support for this proposal can be found on three levels.

First, concerning existing practice, EU-inspired independence is usually created using the *delegation* technique. EU legislation that imposes the delegation of powers to autonomous public bodies explicitly quotes the motive of 'independence'. Moreover, the French Statute 2017-55 and the UK Regulators' Compliance Code effectively regulate the 'independence' of autonomous public bodies with delegated powers. This requirement can also be derived from Belgian and German legal practice. In addition, expert technical rules of standard-setting bodies are usually incorporated using the *referral* technique. Debus mentions the fact that the German Standardization Institute (DIN) has 1,000 full-time employees and 34,000 cooperating members.[82] This amount of know-how could not be countered by a typical delegation to one autonomous public body. Finally, professional stakeholders are regularly involved in rulemaking through the *reception* technique. For example, in relation to the extension of collective labour agreements, the motive of offloading responsibility has often been cited.[83]

Second, the proposal can also explain some controversial outsourcing decisions. For example, the deontology codes of free professions in Belgium ordinarily fall within the third outsourcing technique of reception and ratification. Nevertheless, there is one deliberate exception to this rule, namely the deontology code of attorneys which does not require ratification.[84] Although not all examples of the reception technique require ratification, the transfer of powers to the orders of attorneys actually resembles the traditional delegation of rulemaking powers in Belgium.

[82] Alfred G. Debus, *Verweisungen in Deutschen Rechtsnormen* (Duncker & Humblot 2008) 98–100.

[83] Thorsten Schulten, Line Eldring, and Reinhard Naumann, 'The Role of Extension for the Strength and Stability of Collective Bargaining in Europe' in Guy Van Gyes and Thorsten Schulten (eds), *Wage Bargaining under the New European Economic Governance* (ETUI 2015) 366.

[84] Another exception—rules made by the Belgian order of veterinarians—is generally believed to be a legislative oversight.

This result can be partially explained because the Council of State Legislative Section emphasized that in the case of the profession of attorneys the motive of *independence* especially needed to be safeguarded.[85] In the French case, this proposal allows an alternative explanation of why it was the sole researched country to use the reception technique rather than the referral technique to outsource rulemaking powers to standard-setting bodies. Ministerial decrees may declare AFNOR's homologated standards generally binding. Previously, I explained this as a French cultural preference yet, arguably, it also demonstrates the greater emphasis in France on the involvement of stakeholders in the development of technical standards, challenging the primacy of the motive of expertise.

Third, the proposal might contextualize criticism of chosen outsourcing techniques. The example of corporate governance may further attest to the value of the pairings of motives and techniques here. When considering the implementation of corporate governance into state rules, the main reason would seem to be to include autonomous public or private actors within the rule's decision-making process and to create *support from stakeholders* and the broader public for the regulation of corporate excesses.[86] The dominant idea is not so much the *independence* of politically accountable actors, or particular *expertise* on behalf of the rulemaker. The proposal would thus point towards the reception, or extension, by a politically accountable actor of a privately made corporate governance code. Nevertheless, the Belgian federal Legislature opted for the technique of dynamic referral. This decision faced fierce criticism from the Belgian Council of State Legislative Section,[87] mainly because of concerns over the representation of corporate interests versus the interests of clients and third parties.[88] Arguably, the choice of the reception technique, with the possibility of declaring a corporate governance code generally applicable, might have better served those purposes.

In the UK, the intense criticism of the Human Fertilisation and Embryology Authority (HFEA) because of its lack of representativeness, might have been avoided if the reception technique had been utilized rather than the delegation technique. The reception technique inherently entails a bottom-up approach, where the stakeholders (e.g. representatives of patients, doctors, etc.) effectively create the rules, and politically accountable actors at most rubberstamp them. The main motive for outsourcing rulemaking on these ethical issues, indeed, seems to be to involve stakeholders and not, on the whole, to create a buffer from politics.

[85] Belgian Council of State Legislative Section, Advisory opinion of 6 March 1995 (Parliamentary Document Senate 1994–95 no. 1352/1) 244; Jan Velaers, *De Grondwet en de Raad van State Afdeling Wetgeving* (Maklu 1999) 386–7.

[86] Parliamentary Preparation Belgian Chamber of Representatives (Parliamentary Document Chamber of Representatives 22 December 2009, no. 2336/001) 9.

[87] Belgian Council of State Legislative Section, Advisory opinion no. 47.273/2 of 3 November 2009, fn. 8.

[88] Pierre Nihoul, Marc Joassart, and Vinciane Franck, 'Le Conseil d'Etat. Chronique de Jurisprudence—2006' [2007] *Revue belge de droit constitutionnel*, 322.

The extensive use of consultations by the HFEA supports its continued search for inclusiveness.[89]

In relation to this, the late US Supreme Court Justice Scalia also lashed out, in his salient style, against an independent, autonomous 'Medical *Commission*' on which to offload the responsibilities of politically accountable actors:[90]

> I foresee all manner of 'expert' bodies, insulated from the political process, to which Congress will delegate various portions of its lawmaking responsibility. How tempting to create an expert Medical Commission (mostly M.D.'s, with perhaps a few Ph.D.'s in moral philosophy) to dispose of such thorny, no-win political issues as the withholding of life-support systems in federally funded hospitals, or the use of foetal tissue for research.[91]

The potential use of the reception technique in such medical and ethical matters is buttressed by the German example of para. 16 of the Transplantation Act (*Transplantationsgesetz*, TPG) and para. 12a of the Transfusion Act (*Transfusionsgesetz*, TFG) which grant the Federal Chamber of Physicians (*Bundesärztekammer*) the power to determine binding guidelines on issues such as how to use human tissue.

In summary, I have proposed that autonomous public, private, and hybrid actors should be perceived as one, residuary, constitutional category. Moreover, it could be useful to insert a constitutional provision on the outsourcing of rulemaking powers. Lastly, it would be good practice to select one of the three outsourcing techniques (delegation, referral, or reception) depending on the most important motivation for outsourcing rulemaking powers in each case (buffer from politics, increased expertise, or heightened involvement of stakeholders, respectively). If the main motive for outsourcing lies in establishing independence from politics, then politically accountable actors should embrace the delegation technique. If the main motive for outsourcing is expertise, then the technique of referral best addresses that concern. If the main motive for outsourcing is to increase input from the stakeholders, then the reception technique proves paramount.[92]

89 Human Fertilisation and Embryology Authority, *Annual report and accounts 2016/17* (London 2017) 8.

90 *Mistretta v. United States* 488 US 361 (1989) dissenting opinion of Justice Scalia.

91 Ibid. Harold J. Krent, 'The Private Performing the Public: Delimiting Delegations to Private Parties' (2011) 65 *U. Miami L. Rev.* 507, 524.

92 More extensive future empirical research should verify the link between these three main motives and the outsourcing techniques before such practice can be turned into more normative guidelines.

Index

For the benefit of digital users, indexed terms that span two pages (e.g., 52–53) may, on occasion, appear on only one of those pages.